Penguin E...

The Ci...
Proble...

Edited by

D1054112

P...

General Editor

Maurice Vile

Advisory Board

Michael Argyle
Ernest Gellner
K. W. Wedderburn
Alan H. Williams

The City:
Problems of Planning

Selected Readings

Edited by Murray Stewart

Penguin Books

Penguin Books Ltd, Harmondsworth,
Middlesex, England
Penguin Books Inc., 7110 Ambassador Road,
Baltimore, Md 21207, USA
Penguin Books Australia Ltd,
Ringwood, Victoria, Australia

First published 1972
This selection copyright © Murray Stewart, 1972
Introduction and notes copyright © Murray Stewart, 1972
Copyright acknowledgements for items in this volume
will be found on page 482

Made and printed in Great Britain by
Richard Clay (The Chaucer Press) Ltd
Bungay, Suffolk
Set in Monotype Times New Roman

Series Foreword

The Penguin Interdisciplinary Readings represent an attempt to come to grips with one of the most important areas of study in the Social Sciences today. Although each of the disciplines in the social sciences has made great advances during the past twenty years, there is a danger that they will simply continue to pursue, in greater and greater detail, the specialized methods which each of them has evolved. Although this kind of specialized work is necessary, and indeed highly desirable, students of society have become more and more aware of its inherent limitations. The reality of any social situation is that a number of events take place each of which may have economic, political, sociological and other dimensions; each situation has its historical setting and its own psychological components. Individual disciplines abstract from these events, selecting the data which seem relevant to their own assumptions, and elaborating explanations within their own theoretical framework. However, if it is argued that only a partial understanding of the nature of social reality can emerge from such specialized approaches, what are the alternatives?

In the present state of development of the social sciences, there is certainly no integrating theory which can neatly fit together all the pieces to provide a 'complete' picture, if indeed such a complete picture is theoretically possible. Advocates of a holistic social science who reject the fragmented approach of individual disciplines and wish to replace them with a 'global' study of society in all its aspects, simply finish up with a randomly chosen collection of facts. The other alternative is to acknowledge that the study of society must begin by applying the varied techniques of the individual disciplines to 'specific problems' existing in the real world. Such 'problems' may be narrowly conceived or they may be extremely broad in scope. Nevertheless, the existence of a problem to be studied provides the focus for the bringing together of the methods and data of the various disciplines, even if the immediate result is merely to demonstrate how those methods and conclusions conflict, and how each of the disciplines, in pursuing its own particular academic aims, may fail to illuminate the central core of the problem. It is only through such a problem-oriented approach that the beginnings of an integrated social-science might emerge.

The books of Readings grew out of the development at the University of Kent of a number of interdisciplinary courses based upon this view of the present state of the social sciences. Each course will attempt to take a particular area or problem in the social sciences and bring to bear upon it the work which has been done in a number of different disciplines. The first volumes in this series are therefore edited by members of the Faculty of Social Sciences at the University of Kent, based upon the courses which they are preparing, but future volumes in the series will be prepared by a wide range of authors, and it is also intended to produce a series of original texts dealing with specific problems in an interdisciplinary way.

Each volume of Readings, therefore is an attempt by an individual to take a particular problem and to draw from the literature of the subjects concerned those contributions which would seem most likely to illuminate the present state of knowledge in the social sciences relating to that problem, and also to provide the basis for a more integrated understanding of this particular piece of social reality. For each of the editors the selection of the readings must be in one sense a very personal selection, based upon his conception of the nature of the problem, of what is important to the understanding of that problem, and of how the various elements of the different disciplines might eventually be combined to provide such an understanding. Each editor has produced a fairly lengthy introduction which attempts to set his particular choice of materials within the context of the current state of the debate in the disciplines concerned.

If our view of the best way to make progress in the study of the social sciences is correct, this series might provoke the kind of interdisciplinary research, both by groups and by individuals, which may help to make our understanding of the nature of society both more satisfying academically, and more fruitful as a basis for future policy.

M. J. C. Vile

Contents

Introduction

I An interdisciplinary view of urban planning

A glance at the contents lists of the numerous readers on cities which have appeared in the last decade demonstrates both the current extreme concern with urban problems and a general appreciation that, in relation to policy issues, some form of integrated social science is probably required. Indeed the case for an 'interdisciplinary' volume of readings scarcely needs to be made, and the problem is not so much to justify an interdisciplinary approach as to define its scope and delimit its boundaries. The city has been the subject of research and comment from a wide variety of viewpoints. The roles of engineering and architecture as links between the natural sciences and the creative arts are obvious examples of contributions to our understanding of urban questions. In a different sense, literature, from Dickens to Baldwin, and the cinema, Metropolis, or Midnight Cowboy, have made significant observations on urban society. Again the current concern with environmental problems and pollution requires that the technical expertise of the natural sciences be applied in particular social, economic, and political contexts.

The extent of the various interests in urban issues, however, does not excuse the fact that, both in the past and currently, the social sciences, with which this volume is primarily concerned, have largely failed to produce solutions to the 'problems' of modern urban societies. This raises important questions about the nature of social science, its role in the development of policy, the possibility or desirability of a value-free approach and the inherent ideological content of most urban research. Nevertheless leaving aside these general issues of the philosophy and methodology of the social sciences, there are two possible reasons for the failure to cope with urban problems. First, individual disciplines within the social sciences have tended to pursue their own lines of interest rather than accept and investigate the interrelationship of economic, social, political and legal questions. This is a general criticism which can be levelled at the social sciences in relation to various problem areas, the study of the business corporation or development being two obvious examples. More specifically in relation to urban studies, however, social scientists, with the exception of geographers, have historically shown little concern for the spatial implications of their various approaches. This lack of concern stems in part from the nineteenth century emphasis on total societal change, and in part from the absence until the 1930s of any general political concern (either in America or Britain) for intervention to influence the spatial distribution of people and jobs, or to solve the 'problems' of particular geographical areas.

It is arguable, of course, that whilst cities have often been useful vehicles for the study of social or economic theory – Weber's comparative analysis of the city is a prime example – there is no specifically 'urban' theory. It is also clear that what are sometimes defined as 'urban problems' in one society, or by particular disciplines, will be seen in different terms in a different societal context. Nevertheless in the past two decades, or less, there has been widespread and growing concern about the nature of urban life and about the mechanisms and institutions which exist to bring about change in cities. Increasing affluence, paralleled by increasing relative poverty, has produced an awareness of the depth of urban problems. On the one hand affluence has given rise to an increasing demand for space for living, leisure and travel; it has assisted the growth of car ownership, created pressure on scarce environmental resources, and accelerated the development of urban sprawl and suburbia. On the other hand, relative poverty stemming from greater differentials between income groups, has worsened the situations in inner cities. Allied with racial conflict it has in many instances given rise to a decline in standards of housing, health and education and has encouraged the emergence of urban violence. There are numerous other ways in which urban problems manifest themselves, but whatever their characteristics there is widespread agreement both over the essential interdependence of many problems and over the failure of any single discipline to provide adequate tools of analysis. Solutions in effect depend upon our ability to analyse the various processes which give rise to the problems located in cities, and to assess those points to which action can be most appropriately directed. Thus it is the question of intervention, or planning in its widest sense, which has done most to induce social scientists to recognize the co-existence and interrelationship of many urban problems. This has led to the analysis of such issues as the location and use of political power in urban areas, the allocation of scarce public and private resources, and the relative distribution of welfare within and between various groups in the urban community.

This volume focuses on these kinds of issues and is thus predominantly problem- and policy-orientated. In fact the main theme is that of the relationship between the social sciences and urban planning. Such a focus involves the omission of certain areas of urban study which are of undoubted importance. There is little said in this volume about cities in their regional or national context; about whether a national system of cities is needed, or whether there is (or rather, is not) an optimum size for a city. There is only passing treatment of the process of urbanization and of the role of cities in developing countries, and the extensive literature on urban growth is largely omitted. The major justification for omissions of this type is that they raise complex questions relating either to wider economic and social policies, for example, in terms of national development, or to the relationship between national, regional and urban planning. In contrast this volume is deliberately confined to an analysis of the *internal* problems of cities. On the other hand the approach adopted is not that of the identification and analysis of specific problems such as 'the slum','the inner city', 'suburbia', 'transportation' or 'the urban environment'. Here again this is not because such problems are irrelevant or uninteresting but rather because they represent the symptoms rather than the diagnosis of the urban 'disease'. In addition they are so closely interrelated – the problem of the suburb, for example is in many ways the mirror of the problem of the inner city – since an over-view is essential. Thus whilst the context of this volume is the city as a whole, the introduction, and the readings which follow, are based on the view that the central problem is planning itself – how we can manage the process of change in cities in order to achieve the objective of increasing the welfare of those who live there.

Though the philosophy of urban planning has evolved through various stages over the last two centuries, it is not unfair to identify throughout the period an underlying sense of disaffection for urban development together with a conviction that the solutions to urban problems are most easily found by creating new communities in new locations rather than by seeking to improve the existing urban framework. This philosophy of 'anti-urbanism' is compounded from a number of factors, amongst which are a genuine belief that 'urban' life is in some ways less desirable than rural life and, perhaps more importantly, a fear that even if cities are in principle acceptable they have in practice grown far too large. These concerns have often been formulated in terms of the physical environment and one way of looking at the issues is to make the distinction, as Harvey (1970) does, between those who possess 'a geographical imagination' and those who possess 'a sociological imagination'. Architects, engineers, geographers, and planners have traditionally been endowed with the 'geographical imagination' – a tendency to consider urban planning in terms of physical space. Control of land use as a central objective of planning is perhaps the best example of this tendency. Although social scientists for their part have made extensive use, for both theoretical and empirical purposes, of the concepts of physical space and distance; their concern with the city has to a much lesser extent been influenced by these purely physical considerations. Economists have until recently largely ignored spatial problems, with the exception of the major, primarily German, concern with location theory, and even in that area there has been extensive discussion of the distinction between economic and geographical space (Perroux, 1950; Darwent, 1969). In sociology, social structure, and particularly inter-group relations has been analysed in terms of social space, with social distance indicating the extent of various aspects of differential interaction (Bogardus, 1925; Laumann, 1966). Indeed the definition of 'space' and 'distance' provides one of the best examples of a conceptual problem requiring interdisciplinary analysis (Harvey, 1970).

The distinction between the geographical and sociological imaginations or between physical and non-physical space, becomes extremely blurred, however, when one considers that, at both the macro, city-wide scale and at the micro, neighbourhood or dwelling scale, perceptions of physical and social distance vary widely. Lynch (1960), for example, has shown in relation to Boston, that people construct spatial schemas which contain a few main reference points but omit entirely many areas of the city. In Cambridge (England) it was found that 'people perceive, organize, and react to their physical and social environment differently from their neighbors' (Lee, 1968). Others may have a distorted view of physical distance so that they regard certain areas of the city as inaccessible merely because they seldom seek to go there. On the micro scale there is a renewed interest in environmental perception and architectural psychology (Goodey, 1971) typified, for example, by studies of the concept of personal space in relation to environmental design (Sommer, 1969). Whilst the physical environment clearly does not determine social or economic behaviour, it is evident that, at a number of levels there is an important interface between the socio/economic and the physical approaches. Indeed as Harvey (1970) points out, the two approaches are not alternatives.

They should be regarded as complementary. The trouble is that the use of one sometimes conflicts with the use of the other. Any successful strategy must appreciate that spatial form and social process are different ways of thinking about the same thing. We must therefore harmonize our thinking about them both or else create contradictory strategies for dealing with city problems.

Since much of the divergence between strategies derives from 'single discipline' attitudes and professional rigidities on the part of both social scientists and planners, it is clear that any attempt to bridge the gap should adopt an explicitly interdisciplinary viewpoint. The approach taken here involves two elements, the first a broadening of the base from which the relationship of planning and social science stems, the second a more specific integration of the various elements making up that base.

If 'planning' should no longer be primarily concerned with land-use control, it must be redefined as comprehending the management of a wide range of urban services. In this sense planning draws not only from relatively well established areas of applied geography, economics, or sociology, but also from political science, psychology, public and social administration as well as from a number of the newer management sciences. The growth of these specialisms (that is the recognition of the increasingly multi-disciplinary character of planning) makes it even more important, however, for any attempt at integration to be selective. Thus the second element of the approach adopted in this reader involves moving forward from a multi-disciplinary juxtaposition of various disciplines towards the linking together of those concepts and techniques which can best contribute to an overview of the problem of 'planning'. Clearly this is a formidable task involving the development of what Alonso (1971) has christened a 'meta-disciplinary competence', and this reader only provides a brief illustration of what might be possible. The emphasis is on an approach to urban problems which stresses comprehension of the context for problem solving rather than the analysis and prescription of solutions for actual problems. Thus the focus of the remainder of this introduction and the readings which follow is upon a few elements of urban theory – location, spatial and social structure, community and interest, fiscal policy, organization of government and legal constraints – in order to present a (personal) interdisciplinary interpretation of the urban process. This interpretation is designed to highlight those areas where planning, intervention, or management (whichever term is preferred) can most effectively operate.

This focus on planning is followed through a discussion of the historical perspective to planning (section II), and through the presentation of an interdisciplinary model of the urban process involving location and structure (section III) and community and interest (section IV). More specifically the relevance of the social sciences to intervention in the urban system is discussed in section V, with power and legitimacy being covered in the final section. Most of the material relates to Britain and the United States, a limitation determined largely by the constraints of space in this reader, but this is not meant to suggest that planning problems are the same in the two countries. Though there are, of course, marked similarities, in terms of the characteristics of inner areas or suburban development, for example, there are wide differences in the respective roles of central and local government, in legal constraints, and in basic attitudes to urban growth and to planning. It is the purpose of the reader to illustrate these differences as well as the similarities: see Pahl (Reading 3) and Smallwood (Reading 17).

The readings themselves are arranged in five parts which parallel sections II–VI of this introduction. Each part is preceded by a brief explanation of the nature of the various selections, but the readings must be seen in the light of the introduction as well as in their own right. Some are classics, others less well known, but they do not pretend to give a full or representative picture of the literature of urban problems. There are numerous readers already fulfilling this function. Rather the readings seek to illustrate the theme of this introductory essay – the relationship between planning and the social sciences – and are thus of necessity a very personal selection.

II Perspectives

It is easier to assert that there must be an historical perspective to the modern city than to determine the time period over which such a perspective is relevant. Mumford (1961) and Blumenfeld (1967), for example, trace the development of cities from the origins of settlement in caves and early villages, and Sjoberg's review of pre-industrial cities covers over fifty centuries. In this latter study Sjoberg (1960) stresses the similarities between pre-industrial cities (in terms of their class structure, the role of the family, economic organization, the role of political and religious elites) and suggests a theory of urban evolution which identifies technological change as a major factor. An alternative interpretation of pre-industrial urban history is that of Weber (1921) whose analysis of the differences between cities emphasizes both the importance of cities as spatial contexts for social interaction and the central relevance of institutions and their use of power. Again Pirenne's (1925) study of medieval cities is an example of the way in which an understanding of urban history is relevant to the development of theory, in this case location theory.

On the other hand it is possible to argue, as Reissman (1964) does, in rejecting the relevance of pre-industrial cities to the urban processes of the twentieth century, that 'the rise of the industrial city is sufficiently independent as an historical event to allow its separation from the general course of history'. This is an extreme approach, but is one which relates to the view that industrialization is such an important factor and its effects so similar wherever it occurs, that post-industrial societies themselves tend to become similar in terms of their economic and social structures (the convergence thesis). It is possible to accept that there is some continuity in urban history (and thus reject Reissman's view of industrialization), whilst taking the industrial transformation of Europe and the growth of a primarily industrial urban society in the United States in the late eighteenth and early nineteenth centuries, as the starting points for an analysis into the problems of the modern city.

Exactly why the Industrial Revolution occurred where and when it did, is not the concern of this volume. The fact is that with it, and after it, there was associated major urban growth in both Britain and America, arising from shifts in the distribution of population from rural to urban areas, and from international migration in the case of the United States. The proportion of the population of England and Wales living in towns of over 10,000 people increased from 21 per cent in 1800 to 62 per cent in 1900; the proportion in towns of over 100,000 from 10 per cent to 32 per cent. In the United States the proportion in towns of over 2500 people rose from 6 per cent in 1800 to 40 per cent in 1900, and in cities of over 250,000 from 2 per cent to 12 per cent. Urban growth was geographically fairly widely distributed. In Britain, the North West, Northern, West Yorkshire and South East areas become rapidly urbanized, and in the USA, the North East region experienced rapid concentration with a shift from 9 per cent of the population urbanized in 1800 to 61 per cent in 1900.

This demographic cum geographical revolution did not seem of central importance to a number of observers over the period. For example, neither Adam Smith, nor Malthus, nor Mill, nor Marx were primarily concerned with cities but rather with the problems of society as a whole. Marx accepted that urbanization was entirely necessary and welcome within his view of economic and social change. This is not to say that they approved of the conditions in towns at that time – Engels' (1845) description of Manchester is evidence enough that they did not – but rather that they did not regard any specifically urban processes as the ones by which societal change would occur.

However, industrialization and urbanization did provide the impetus for the development of new theories of community which took specific account of the urban growth of the nineteenth century. These 'contrast theories' were generally concerned with the distinction between traditional (rural) communities and modern (urban) communities. Tönnies (1877) contrasted the intimate personal *Gemeinschaft* with a more impersonal, contractual association, *Gesellschaft*; Durkheim (1893) contrasted the 'mechanical solidarity' of societies where there was relatively little specialization arising from the division of labour with the 'organic solidarity' of societies (generally urban) where specialization was extensive. Maine (1884), Cooley (1909) and McIver (1937) made similar types of distinction, but the contrast theory with the most specifically spatial content is the more recent presentation by Redfield (1941) of the theory of the rural/urban continuum. This stemmed from his observations of four communities in Mexico, each representing a point upon a continuum from the city to the peasant village. Many of these contrast theories, particularly Redfield's, are not very satisfactory, either in theory or in the light of the most recent research. Studies of rural communities, for example, have demonstrated that they are not necessarily integrated, intimate or homogeneous (Pahl, 1966; Frankenberg, 1957); nor are urban areas necessarily characterized by the absence of 'community' as the emergence of the urban village demonstrates (Gans, 1962). Finally the idea that particular communities in a market society can be placed at discrete intervals along a continuous scale is clearly misleading given the existence of hierarchies of cities, towns and villages, and the interdependence of communities arising from the relationship between service centres and their hinterlands (Christaller, 1933).

The theories of rural/urban contrast are important, however, for two reasons. First they contain, or at least their urban elements contain, a number of ideas of an 'urban way of life' which have continued to be taken up in studies of urban 'community'. Secondly, and more important in the context of this volume, the idea that urban and rural communities are in a sense 'opposite', and also the implication inherent in several contrasting theories that rural communities are somehow 'better', is a notion which has been and is strongly attractive to some urban planners. The Utopian approach to planning adopted by Geddes (1915), Mumford (1961), and especially Howard (1902) has a central thesis that certain aspects of urban life are unattractive and that removing people from cities is a proper planning objective. This objective is closely tied to a concern about the size of cities as opposed to any of their inherent characteristics, but it is possible to see the 'Green Belt philosophy' and the British and American New Towns of the 1950s and 1960s as expressions of a belief in a rural/urban contrast (even though much of the planning literature of course preceded Redfield).

These points are taken up later but it would be wrong to argue that the only, or even the major, outcome of industrialization and urbanization in the nineteenth century was the development of contrast theories of city growth. There were important developments in urban government both in the UK and the US. In Britain the major cities increased their power and sought to control (or occasionally to avoid having to control) the main urban services in their area (Briggs, 1968). Central government played an increasingly important role but by and large in Britain the form of government remained the same. In the United States in in the early nineteenth century, urban government developed on federal and state lines through a council of two chambers with a complex system of checks and balances. This system proved to be largely a failure given that it provided for account to be taken of a variety of interests and thus encouraged the postponing rather than taking of decisions. Urban conditions worsened, and towards the end of the century there emerged the period of the party boss and machine politics. The 'bosses' fulfilled several social and economic functions as well as their more obvious political roles. They sponsored extensive public investment in a number of cities, albeit for prestige purposes, and controlled large parts of the local labour market as well as influencing the commercial behaviour of local companies. For the poor and unskilled worker the machine offered the opportunity of identifying with success and of gaining large, if temporary, rewards. The boss in effect can be seen as something of a 'benevolent despot' or as an example of the legitimate charismatic authority suggested by Weber (1922). Subsequently there was a movement to reform local government, though some bosses took over mayoral status and continued to operate their machines for many years, Chicago being the obvious example. In other cities, however, more orthodox mayoral authority emerged, and elsewhere government by city manager became the accepted norm.

In Britain there was no one with the charisma of the 'boss' (with the possible exception of Joseph Chamberlain in Birmingham in the 1870s) and the nineteenth century is better characterized by its concern for the provision of minimum standards of housing, sanitation and health, but for economic as much as for social or political reasons. The middle years of the century saw the passing of considerable social legislation – for example the series of Nuisance Removal Acts from 1846–66, the Public Health Act of 1848, and the Housing acts sponsored by Shaftesbury in 1851 and Torrens in 1868. Such reforms were based on a growing awareness of conditions in urban areas, fostered by a host of surveys and reports by various committees, boards, and private individuals. Indeed an outstanding characteristic of the Victorian era, together with the early years of the twentieth century, is the extent to which it catalogued its own social inadequacies. The works of Booth *et al.* (1891), Rowntree (1901), Masterman (1909), Lady Bell (1901) and others formed 'a large pioneering literature of empirical sociology – in many respects still unsurpassed' (Glass, 1955). Not surprisingly these years saw the first planning legislation enacted both in Britain and in America. In Britain the Housing, Town Planning, etc. Act of 1909 gave authorities new powers, albeit generally straightforward extensions of existing ones, over new development but not over existing development. In the United States the New York Zoning Ordinance was upheld by the Supreme Court in 1916 thus providing a firm legal footing for the development of zoning in American cities. This contemporaneous development, however, conceals fairly marked differences in the relative emphasis given in the two countries to 'eminent domain' (the compulsory appropriation of property) on the one hand, and nuisance law and police power techniques on the other (Delafons, 1969). If planning itself became formalized in legislation, and thus grew stronger, the links between the social sciences and planning weakened.

The cause of this was largely the activities of the Utopian planners – Geddes, Howard, and latterly Lewis Mumford, who carried forward the idea of new 'model communities'. These had been created since the end of the eighteenth century – Robert Owen's New Lanark, Titus Salt's Saltaire, Bournville, Port Sunlight and ultimately Letchworth and Welwyn Garden City are examples. They represent attempts to combat urban problems through the formation of entirely new communities, as opposed to the grafting of further growth onto existing towns. The garden city concept relates to a certain extent to the rural/urban contrast theories but in general the sociology of the Utopians has been heavily criticized. Indeed from about 1920 the sociological contribution to the development of planning theory virtually disappeared, and the social content of planning has derived until recently almost entirely from the Geddes heritage of social survey, but as a description rather than explanation of social characteristics and problems.

It is, however, not entirely fair to blame planning for turning its back on the social sciences in Britain in the 1920s and 1930s since there were not at that time in fact many advances of relevance to urban planning. The social surveys of the 1930s – the New Survey of London Life and Labour (LSE, 1930) or Rowntree's second survey of York (1942) for example – were primarily concerned with poverty and unemployment rather than with urban conditions *per se*. The political context had also changed, since in the United Kingdom the first political efforts, in terms of spatial policies, were being made to counter the relative decline of the basic industries which were predominantly located in the northern regions. The pattern of migration in Britain in the first half of the twentieth century was one of extensive net movement towards the West Midlands (with the growth of the motor industry) and to London and the South East. With heavy local unemployment arising from the effects of the inter-war Depression, the 1930s saw the introduction of incentives to alter the distribution of industry and, through the reduction of migration, of population. Despite the Barlow (1940), Abercrombie (1945) and Reith (1946) reports, the designation of the Green Belt and New

Towns in the late 1940s, and the rapid growth of both the first, and the latter, second generation New Towns, it is true to say that Britain has had no consistent urban policy since the beginning of the century. Regional policies, admittedly with urban implications have had political priority and the internal problems of cities in the UK have, until the presentation of and inquiry into the Greater London Development Plan (Greater London Council, 1969), been largely ignored.

This relative absence of urban research and policy in Britain contrasts strongly with the situation in America in the 1920s, where the concern with urban problems was similar in many ways to that of the Victorian reformers in Britain, and where a major emphasis was laid on the development, largely at the University of Chicago, of the theory of human ecology (Burgess and Bogue 1964). In retrospect the Chicago ecologists may have been over-influenced by the facts that confronted them. In the early twentieth century Chicago was receiving massive immigration of a variety of ethnic groups, which tended to cluster and to compete for scarce land, jobs, houses and wealth. In these circumstances the adoption of the Darwinian concepts of invasion, succession, domination and their application to a theory of urban growth was perhaps almost inevitable. The relevance of the work of Park, Burgess, McKenzie and others to urban growth and structure in other American cities and in other countries has since bee widely questioned. Nevertheless their work is of considerable importance within a general urban perspective for two reasons; firstly because of the numerous detailed micro-studies of minority, ethnic, or religious groups, of deviants and of identifiable sub-cultures (e.g. Shaw (1929) on delinquents or Thrasher (1927) on the Gang), and secondly because ecology provided a basis to which many subsequent theories of spatial and social structure can be related. Burgess (1925) applying the ecological principles to urban growth, developed the concentric zone hypotheses suggesting that the city is structured into a number of zones (central business, transitional, lower class housing, higher class housing and commuter) and that growth involves each zone extending its area outwards. Burgess' work is of interdisciplinary significance since it is in relation to location and spatial structure that economics makes its main (indeed probably only) contribution before the 1950s to the development of a specifically urban theory.

The origins of location theory lie in the models relating agricultural land use to urban growth, developed in Germany in the nineteenth century (Hall, 1966). These were given their best early statement in an urban context by Haig (1926), with the elements of location theory reflecting the important role of markets, transport costs and the friction of space. In brief there is a 'trade-off' between the low costs of transport at central locations and the high rents that characterize these locations, and there emerges a gradient of land values, declining from the centre outwards. When various users of urban space compete for land the result is an urban structure where users are allocated to one of a series of concentric zones (as in Burgess' hypothesis).

The fact that simple models of this kind do not conform to reality is not important, since numerous developments of structure theory have explained sectoral growth, suburban centres, the location of specific activities, residential separation etc. What is significant is first that spatial structure, as developed both by the ecologists and by economic location theorists, can be explained by a simple model of competition for scarce land, and second that most variations of spatial structure theory stemmed from, or have given rise to, extensive empirical observation of the process of urban growth and change.

The same empirical base cannot be attributed, however, to the second legacy of the Chicago school – the formulation by Wirth (1938) of his view of 'urbanism as a way of life'. This view has close links with the rural/urban contrast theories, through its stress on the disorganization of urban life, its impersonality, the lack of contact and the heterogeneity of interests. Such a stress fails to acknowledge that many of the empirical Chicago studies (including Wirth (1928) on the Ghetto) demonstrated an inherent regular and organized pattern in certain types of urban behaviour, albeit generally 'problematic' behaviour of gangs, delinquents, etc. Wirth also failed to accept that the 'anomie' that he observed (and which others have since stressed, especially in relation to the suburbs) might well be temporary, and that there could emerge a system of urban values and behaviour leading to a stable, enduring and organized form of urbanism. Thus he gave little weight to the growing volume of studies which were beginning to demonstrate that 'community' – not necessarily a locality-based community – was as important a concept in cities as outside them (Stacey, 1969).

Set against the demographic changes of the nineteenth century and the first half of the twentieth century, the main emphasis of this perspective has been upon the unevenness of the relationship between planning and the social sciences. Given the general disregard of spatial problems by economists, and the lack of any systematic concern with efficient urban administration or management on the part of political scientists, the main contribution to planning theory and practice came through developing sociological ideas on community. Even this contribution is in retrospect ambiguous. While sociological theory clearly did inform planning in the first decades of this century, the misinterpretation of the nature of community had much to do with the development of an anti-urban, physically based planning philosophy. This philosophy saw practical expression in a number of ways such as the frontier mentality of US expansion in the nineteenth century, the model city/garden city movement, and the failure to appreciate the cumulative decline in inner urban areas as the social capital of the nineteenth century became obsolescent.

In contrast, the 1950s and 1960s saw a surge of interest in urban problems. *Post facto* this can be rationalized as a response to 'rising policy issues that were not only of practical significance but were intellectually intriguing' (Perloff and Wingo, 1968), though it is clear in retrospect that in relation to urban economics such issues as the economic growth and stagnation of cities, the local impact of national expenditures, transportation and the role of public services had in fact existed for many years. Similarly, in the political context a radical shift of emphasis occurred. Power rather than function became the central theoretical concept (Wilson, 1968) though here again it is not clear why the emphasis changed towards study of the distribution of political and non-political power or to case studies of particular urban issues. It is interesting to compare the US with Britain, where urban politics is only now beginning to possess connotations other than those relating to public administration.

Urban sociology in turn appears to have found a middle point between a crude spatial environmental determinism (originating from the Utopians again) and the view, expressed for example by Webber (1963) and Gans (1969) that spatial change is only a response to other factors such as technology or social norms. Community studies attract less attention and interest is increasingly focused upon an examination of the spatial and social constraints acting upon individuals or groups in the city. This brings sociology closer to both economics and political science through a more specific concern with the distribution of power in urban areas and with the processes by which resources are allocated

(Pahl, 1969). A final characteristic of the social sciences in the post-war period has been the improvement in methodology (particularly in the use of quantitative techniques) to describe and analyse urban characteristics. This improvement has been seen to some extent in most disciplines but has been concentrated in certain fields, notably urban geography (with an emphasis on urban physical structure and urban systems), urban economics (growth models), transportation modelling, and urban land-use modelling.

Planning itself has also evolved. In Britain the 1947, 1959 and 1968 Acts mark successive advances towards a planning system which takes account of social and economic factors as well as physical land-use aspects. Yet the anti-urban bias remains and even in 1970 the urban social scientist makes only a marginal contribution. It is symptomatic of planning in Britain that a planning study of the Glasgow conurbation should be the last of a series of sub-regional studies covering the whole of Scotland, and that the Greater London Development Plan should be preceded by strategies for virtually every region in England. In America the urban problem is on the surface more fully accepted. Extensive legislation has been passed in attempts to combat poverty, racial tension, poor housing, and inferior health and education facilities in cities; moreover, comprehensive urban planning is widespread in American cities. The Department of Housing and Urban Development was set up in 1965 (albeit with difficulty) (Parris, 1970), and massive financial aid has been given to community development projects (in contrast to the small sums available under the UK urban programme). Finally the anti-urban bias in American philosophy appears to be weakening since while the new towns (like Reston) and the model cities programme have been welcomed, they have also been heavily criticized as non-solutions to American urban problems (Alonso, 1970). There has however been increasing interest in non-metropolitan problems in America representing perhaps a new swing away from the urban emphasis of the past two decades, a reflection possibly, of the very strong hold on American thinking that the anti-urban tradition possesses (White and White, 1964).

Nevertheless there remains on both sides of the Atlantic an increasing concern with the future of the city. This concern has a variety of manifestations, most obvious of which is the increasing volume of urban violence as minority groups (in terms of power) seek a more equitable distribution of urban welfare in its widest sense. Literature, art, cinema and the theatre demonstrate in-

creasing disillusion with the urban environment. The views of
Jacobs (1961) on the prospects for American cities in general, and
of Gottman (1961) on Megalopolis (the urbanized area of the
NE Atlantic seaboard) are well known. It is in the context of such
fears about the future of the modern city in the developed countries that stronger links between the social sciences and urban
planning become necessary. If we are to intervene in the social,
economic and political processes of the city we must better
appreciate both the nature of such processes and the nature of the
intervention process itself.

III The urban process: location and structure

The rationale of planning stems from the belief that if left to
themselves individuals will not make decisions which, when
looked at in aggregate, lead to a maximization of the collective
welfare of the community. Since the placing of constraints upon
individual behaviour is central to planning it is clear that an
understanding of where people wish to live and work is essential.
This section, therefore, looks at two types of question.

1. Where do individuals wish to live and firms wish to establish
factories or offices and how do they reach their location decisions;

2. What overall patterns, expressed as the physical and social
structures of cities, are produced by these location decisions.

The behaviour of individuals or firms in urban space can be
explained in terms of classical location theory. The various urban
location preferences, either those of firms for production purposes, of retail establishments for distribution, or of households
for residential locations, are worked out in terms of competition
for scarce city centre sites. Such locations offer the benefits of
lower transport costs to the centre where revenue is in theory
maximized, greater accessibility to a large labour market, and a
generally wider range of economies of scale. These benefits are,
however, reflected in higher land values so that the firm, or the
household, has to trade off accessibility against rent in order to
pick the optimal location (Alonso, Reading 5). Some of the
ways in which actual location behaviour apparently fails to conform to this theory are easily explicable in terms of adaptations
of the simple model. The most frequently quoted illustration of
this is the apparent inconsistency in the highest value land in
central cities being occupied by the lowest income households,
with the higher-income groups taking lower cost land on the

periphery. This however is acceptable within location theory if accessibility is viewed as an 'inferior' good – like bread – of which less is consumed as incomes rise.

Other aspects of location behaviour are less easy to explain, however, without modifying some of the underlying assumptions of location theory, particularly those concerning the perfection of the urban land market. For instance, residential location decision models, traditionally built up in terms of the trade-off between the costs of the journey to work (accessibility) and the costs of housing (Wingo, 1961) are difficult to explain unless the concept of accessibility is widened to incorporate the various separate accessibilities of the members of the household to work, shops, schools, local services and amenity facilities, and 'housing cost' is defined as including a number of qualitative factors (area and environment) as well as price. For example, social factors such as family ties or links with school or church may strongly influence a household's residential decision (Pahl, 1970a). It has also been pointed out that institutional factors, such as the ability to arrange a mortgage, are likely to be a main determinant of households' location decisions (Richardson, 1971). Finally the 'accessibility to work' thesis requires modification because jobs are no longer concentrated in city centres but are widely distributed throughout metropolitan areas.

The changing locational pattern of employment in cities stems in part from the relatively faster growth of activities already located in outer areas, and also from the relocation of activities from the inner to the outer areas as the constraints of site availability or premises operate upon firms who are seeking growth. It is known that industrialists demonstrate considerable locational inertia and that even when the decision to move is made it is often satisficing rather than optimizing, made in haste, without precedent, and without adequate information (Townroe, 1971). It is also known that decision-takers have widely differing perceptions both of the characteristics of potential new locations and of the relative costs and benefits which such characteristics involve. One example is the extent to which managers consider labour in particular areas to be prone to strike, regardless of the records of industrial disputes in the area (Cameron and Clark, 1966). Nevertheless, the increasing complexity of industrial organization, a growing dependence on specialized markets not necessarily most accessible from central urban locations, changing transport technology, and the relatively greater importance of skilled labour as a scarce factor of production, all reinforce the trend towards job decentralization. If labour problems are central to the firm (as they are increasingly being argued to be), then the ability on re-location to retain existing workers or to recruit new ones is crucial. So if population and jobs are both decentralizing at more or less the same time, then residential and non-residential decisions may in some sense become joint. Thus it is clear that whilst the essence of location theory – the discipline of trading off one factor against another at alternative sites – remains, not only do a variety of social and psychic factors influence individual decisions on residential and industrial location, but also ap-parently independent decisions may in fact be associated with each other.

The preferences of different urban activities for particular loca-tions are reflected in the pattern of urban rents and land values. In general the demand for space produces a land value peak at the centre of the city (though the level of the peak varies from one city to another) with values falling away towards the periphery. The gradient is neither smooth (since there is a relatively steep fall immediately beyond the central area) nor uniform in all directions (since radial accessibility varies from one direction to another). In addition there are local land value peaks where radial and orbital routes intersect, for example, or where a suburban employment or shopping centre has sprung up. Thus the land value surface 'can be likened to a conical hill, the smooth surface of which is distorted by ridges, depressions and minor peaks' (Garner, 1967). The value of land is related to the intensity of use, and city structure can thus also be described in terms of density (of population or employment). Many empirical studies have demonstrated that the population density gradient is a regular negative exponential function of distance from the centre, though densities vary from one city to another according to the density at their centre (determined for example by the age and economic function of the centre over time) and the slope of the gradient, which may be influenced by transport costs, incomes, employ-ment distribution etc. Thus land values and densities provide general indications of the way in which the physical space within urban areas is used, and are central to a wide variety of models of urban spatial structure.

Variations in land values and/or the density of land use reflect both the competition for scarce land with high accessibility and the various preference functions (trade-off or otherwise) of different urban activities. The implication is that these activities will be spatially segregated. Thus many models of structure have sought to explain not merely the pattern of land-uses, but the process of *segregation* of uses. The work of the human ecologists, drawing on the concepts of Darwinian biology, has already been referred to in this respect, and though Burgess' theory of concentric zones is clearly simplistic it remains a classic in terms of urban structural analysis, explicable in terms of economic location theory as well as ecological theory (Burgess, Reading 6). Theoretical models of structure – concentric zones, sectors of growth (Hoyt, 1938) or multiple nuclei of suburban development (Harris and Ullman, 1945) – do not, however, totally explain the patterns of development in modern cities. This is partly because of various topographical and environmental factors which have influenced the historical growth of cities, the observed tendency for higher socio-economic groups to extend their residential areas westwards in the UK, for example (Checkland, 1964). It is also partly because of such factors as the growth of local authority housing, the spread of affluence, and new transport technologies (Hoyt, 1964).

It is beyond the scope of this introduction to discuss the various major advances that have been made in the formulation of models of urban spatial structure, such as those which discuss systems analysis as a technique for structuring the activities and networks of the city (Berry and Horton, 1970). Nor is it necessary to point out that models of structure need to be dynamic in order to explain spatial changes such as the decline of the central area, (Bourne, 1969) or peripheral expansion seen either in terms of wave theory (Blumenfeld, 1954) or as a colonization and consolidation process (Garner, 1967). Again spatial allocation models which simulate the impact upon land use of changes in population, employment, or in the transport network are currently a fashionable tool for planning studies. Spatial structure, therefore, represents a vast field and it is with only part of this – the definition and analysis of sub-areas of the city – that this section is concerned. The following paragraphs therefore outline four ways in which it is possible to look at the characteristics of urban sub-areas.

All four approaches have some roots within the ecological tradition. The first relates to the concept of 'natural areas', small areas of homogeneity segregated from one another by differences of topography, race, occupation, culture, or housing class. There have been numerous studies of such sub-areas of cities as the central business district, the ghetto, the 'zone of transition', the suburb, and above all, the slum.

It has already been pointed out that it is specifically not the intention of this reader to deal with particular urban problems such as the slum. Nevertheless, it is valuable to demonstrate that problems of this type can to a great extent only be looked at within the context of the overall structure of the city. There are no uniformly accepted definitions of slums, though there would be general agreement that they represent clusters of obsolescent and overcrowded housing, lacking in basic facilities, often insanitary, and generally undermaintained. Nor is there a single acceptable theory of slum formation though it is clear that the process involves, either as separate causes or in combination, the cumulative decline of income in (usually central) areas associated with the out-migration of high income groups (Baumol, 1967), the subdivision and undermaintenance of low quality housing stock as it enters the final stages of the filtering process (Grigsby, 1963), and either the unwillingness of property owners to undertake maintenance unilaterally or their inability to organize it multilaterally (Davis and Whinston, 1961). Such reasons are all primarily economic in origin but it is equally possible to see slum formation in social terms as the tendency for immigrants to cities to group together within subcultures where their norms and values can be maintained. It is not self-evident that slums are 'bad'. Indeed Rothenberg (Reading 7) starts from an assumption that cheap, low-quality housing for lower income group households is likely to be an efficient use of resources. There are other arguments (not always convincing) which suggest that the slum has important social and cultural functions to fulfil through the maintenance of a variety of social networks, the provision of anonymity for deviant groups, or the education of newcomers to urban life (Clinard, 1966; Seeley, 1959). Others like Jacobs (1961) have argued that slum clearance on a grand scale can create as many problems as it solves through its effect on the life of the central city.

Of course there are also countless reasons why slums *are* bad as Rothenberg goes on to argue. Living standards in terms of space, sanitation, or safety may be below the minimum acceptable to society, the function of providing low-cost housing may simply not be fulfilled, slums may tend to become racial ghettos or to generate political tension and so breed violence. Nevertheless it is clear that the causes of slums are deep-rooted and complex, that some of their functions may be proper ones, and some of the social implications ambiguous. It is not surprising therefore that there are a number of policy options open. Direct support of low-income families is one solution, incentives for property owners either for rehabilitation or renewal another. Alternatively the public sector can invest directly in a blighted area either through comprehensive redevelopment, or in a partial way in the hope that a 'tipping point' may be reached after which private-sector investment may be encouraged on a scale sufficient to maintain the area. Policy could seek to maintain the social character of an area after the eradication of slums, but here again choices arise. Should the original families be rehoused or should they make way for others in order to allow new forms of community to develop? The problems of slums and renewal are not confined to social and economic issues. Decline in the central city is crucial to any discussion of the tax base of urban governments, and redevelopment of slums (whether or not a residential element is allowed in the redevelopment), is often seen as a source of revenue – and thus of political strength – for inner area governments. Legal issues also arise in relation to questions of compulsory purchase, compensation and planning inquiries (Hart, 1968).

A second approach to the analysis of sub-areas is through empirical investigation on a city-wide scale – on the basis of census tract or enumeration district data, for example. A variety of t echniques exist, one of which, Social Area Analysis, developed in relation to Los Angeles (Shevky *et al.*, 1949; 1955), attempts to reduce a large number of variables down to three basic indices of social rank, urbanization and segregation. This technique has been subject to criticism (Hawley and Duncan, 1957). In addition it has been relatively little applied, with only a few studies being undertaken outside the United States, for example in Rome (McElrath, 1962) and Newcastle-under-Lyme (Herbert, 1967). As Robson (1969) points out, however, the basic objective of social area analysis, the reduction of a very large number of variables down to a few general indicators, is perfectly valid. His use of component analysis in a study of Sunderland involved reducing thirty variables relating to 263 districts down to five main components, each roughly equivalent to a general index of social class or housing condition, etc. Grouping the various component scores in areal terms produced a more meaningful framework than a simple ecological model of housing classes had done. One of

Robson's main points was that within housing areas (particularly local authority areas) there were significant differences which only a multivariate approach would reveal. Such an approach involving the combination of various related variables to form composite indices is becoming increasingly relevant to urban policy formulation and implementation. If resources have to be allocated selectively, as they have, for example, under the Urban Programme in England, the ability to identify small areas of adverse social conditions is clearly necessary. Analyses of urban structure are not of course confined to the social or economic variables. It is possible, indeed, to treat voting behaviour, election turn-out, the physical environment, or illness, in very much the same way in order to obtain a systematic view of the characteristics of urban sub-areas.

A third approach involves the study of separation – or segregation – through analyses of the extent to which the distribution of residences or employment is related to indicators of social class, income, or race. It has been demonstrated, for example, that in the United States negroes are more segregated than other racial or ethnic groups (Lieberson, 1963; Taueber and Taueber, 1965). In terms of occupation, too, it has been suggested that there is relatively greater segregation of the highest and lowest socio-economic groups than of groups not at the extremes of the scale. Duncan and Duncan (1955, Reading 8) describe the development of a number of indices – of segregation, isolation, concentration and centralization – designed to express the degree of residential segregation of occupations.

A fourth and final general approach involves the definition of functional areas of the city, areas which do not necessarily conform to administrative areas. For instance the distribution of retail activities can be looked at in terms of shopping catchment areas, which will vary by type of shop (specialized or everyday), according to the minimum size of the market (the threshold), the frequency of shopping trips, and the patterns of accessibility (Berry, 1967). Accessibility – in terms of journey to work – has also figured prominently in labour market studies (the spatial relationship of job location to residential location), but the spatial aspects of urban labour markets are extremely complex, being influenced by institutional problems, market imperfections – particularly lack of information – and the differing perceptions of firms and workers as to the extent of the market (Goldner, 1955). Though functional analyses of urban structure were primarily developed by economists and geographers, very similar work, also stressing the perceptual problems, has been carried out in a sociological context, for example, in relation to the social areas of Paris (Chombart de Lauwe *et al.*, 1952).

Whether one analyses spatial structure through the study of particular sub-areas (e.g. the slum) or through a multivariate approach, in terms of separation or of functional units, the relationship between spatial structure and urban social structure remains confused. Is there indeed, even in principle, a separate *urban* social structure? How can one start defining or measuring it? For example does the generally rapid movement into, out of and within cities lead to the 'blurring' of any stratification system? Beshers (1962, Reading 9) examines a number of such problems. He suggests that there is likely to be some overall, city-wide system based on easily observable symbols (of which residence is the most obvious), but that within this there are likely to be subcultures, acknowledging the overall system but not accepting it. On either basis, however, it is likely that social stratification will be associated with spatial segregation. People who are grouped together in the social structure in terms of income, education, or occupation, tend also to be spatially concentrated. This is particularly true where unskilled occupations, low incomes, poor housing, and lack of education combine to form a cycle of deprivation which confines those involved to particular parts of the city for long periods of time. Conversely, though high incomes permit and encourage mobility it is evident that in other parts of the city there is a cycle of affluence which effectively reinforces the territorial strengths of those in the upper and middle ranks of the social structure. Thus there are physical, economic, social and political barriers to mobility and the formation of urban sub-areas is much more than a physical process. Location theory and spatial structure analysis are essential tools for describing segregation, but they do not go far enough in explaining the processes by which individuals and groups determine their interests and exercise power (or in some cases fail to do so).

IV The urban process: community and interest

The concept of community has a central place in the development of urban theory but equally it has been argued that the idea of a single 'urban community' is untenable. A number of the readings in this volume (Burgess, Beshers, and Buttimer, for example) demonstrate that cities are likely to contain sub-communities with identifiable, stable patterns of relationship, both locally and non-locally based. Much of the earlier part of this introduction is devoted to the questions of how individuals choose particular locations, and how it is possible to define and describe the various sub-areas of cities, the purpose being to demonstrate that the differentiation of areas cannot be described or explained in purely 'physical' terms. In other words the local physical arrangements are clearly not the main determinants of the life styles of particular urban communities. Of course, such physical arrangements are not irrelevant to the way in which individuals or groups behave, and there has been a considerable volume of research on the extent to which social interaction is influenced by life in high flats, the availability of open space, the grouping of buildings, the local environment etc. Considerable effort, as Willis (1969) shows, has been put into establishing at what areal level various facilities (primary schools, or shops, for example) should be provided. In addition there have been numerous studies both in America and Britain of local status systems – who speaks to whom, who visits whom, what are the real or perceived social distances between households of similar occupation, income, class etc. All of these studies say something about 'neighbourhood communities' and 'local interaction' and the discussion by Buttimer (Reading 10) illustrates the extent to which various interpretations of community overlap in relation to spatial and social planning. Nevertheless there is widespread acceptance that there remains little validity in the concept of an urban neighbourhood, or a local community, seen as a self-contained unit comprising jobs, shops, recreational and cultural facilities, delimited by physical boundaries and functioning in terms of the spatial arrangement of the buildings (Keller, 1969; Dennis, 1958).

Indeed there is an entirely contrary view of community, which stems from changing communications technology. Webber has argued (1963, 1964) that the specific location of urban 'places' is increasingly irrelevant and that accessibility, in terms of a communications network, is a more necessary condition for 'community'. In his 'community without propinquity' various interest groups maintain webs of contact and these interest communities together form a number of non-place urban realms which are in turn characterized by 'spatial discontinuity, continuous variation, persisting disparity, complex pluralism and dynamic ambiguity'. Variations on these ideas can be seen in the work of Friedmann and Miller (1965) with their concept of the urban field and Meier

(1962) whose communications theory of growth stemmed from an assumption that the urban public communications network and the transactions through that network were useful indicators of growth. These non-place concepts of community can at least partially be related back to the definitions of urban sub-areas as functional areas – Meier's suggestion of measuring the time consumed in receiving information represents a crude form of time-budget, and as such has parallels in the work of Chombart de Lauwe on Paris. The implication is, therefore, that 'community' cannot properly be seen in terms either of an area, within which certain interaction takes place, or of an areal base to which certain people belong and from which they spread a web of contacts. It is more appropriate instead to look at the actual patterns of relationship which can be observed and thence to judge first the extent to which they may be locality or non-locality based and second the extent to which this base is or is not significant. Thus the stress is on networks of relationships or linkages, and on the association between such relationships and social economic structure.

The measurement of social networks raises numerous methodological problems. Are the relationships in question those of one person or of a set of persons? Are they unidirectional or reciprocal? Do they exist at one point in time or over time? How are relationships defined – in terms of conversation, visits to other people's houses or exchange of goods? How does one compare the intensity and value of the contact? Because of these and other similar problems the empirical content of social network analysis, in the context of western cities of the mid-twentieth century, is limited. Indeed the majority of research in this area has related to developing countries in Africa and South America, and to cases of migrants to cities from rural areas. In such examples the change from a tribal or peasant society to an urban society can involve both constraints upon migrants as old networks are maintained and opportunities as new ones are formed. The closest analogy with developed countries lies obviously with the migration of low-income and/or coloured workers from rural areas to the inner areas of major cities, and with the way in which such migrants are assimilated into the urban system or remain largely outside it. There are, however, a variety of forms of linkage related to work, education, religion, the family, recreational activities, or sport and these are likely to vary in intensity and frequency both between various social classes and over time and space. Family ties for example have often been held to be particularly important for working class families (Young and Wilmott, 1967), but it is also clear that the links within middle class families, whilst maintained less frequently, can be both strong in terms of inter-generational dependence, and permanent, in that links may be taken up at some time of crisis even though the relationship has been apparently dormant for some time (Bell, 1969).

Though many of these networks are conveniently assessed from a residential basis – the links between households for example – it is equally appropriate to measure the linkage between businesses, and the concept of industrial linkage is in many ways directly analogous to the social network concept. Linkages too can be defined in a number of ways; as the flow of goods between manufacturing plants (Keeble, 1969); as inter-plant contacts arising from research, marketing or sales; as attachments to particular types of labour; or as a wide variety of information flows both between and within firms. Indeed these 'ideas' linkages are increasingly regarded as the most important for future planning (Lasuen, 1969; Cowan, 1969). There are arguments that industrial policies or urban redevelopment projects should not destroy but should rather seek to recreate and strengthen systems of linkage, whether these be related to communication patterns (Goddard, 1971) or organizational linkages between plants and firms (Townroe, 1969).

This raises methodological questions similar to those raised above. How far does the existence of a 'link' imply that it should not be broken? What costs can be attached to the maintenance of, for example, sub-contracting facilities? How can the quality as well as the quantity of linkage be assessed? How far does the inertia which has already been noted in location decision-making breed and maintain linkage? Do particular business organizations see the existence of linkage (or other external economies which may arise from concentration and agglomeration) as a justification for forming a community of interest in order to further their own ends? This raises issues relating to the role of business organizations in modern society quite apart from urban situations but it also suggests that one way of assessing the importance of social relationships, linkage, or other forms of association is through analyses of the extent to which particular groups seek to foster or maintain such links. Such an approach to 'community' is clearly interdisciplinary in that it provides a common framework within which sociological, economic and political concepts of community are integrated. The specifically urban element arises since interest communities are likely to be concerned about the way in which planning allocates scarce resources and particularly the characteristically scarcest urban resource – geographical space. Thus claims to space are likely to be central in the strategies of different communities, segregation will arise from the relative ability or inability of particular urban individuals or groups to choose their location, and pressure will be exerted in order to influence the distribution of resources, particularly public spending, between different parts of the city. The urban structure that arises (identifiable spatial groupings with differentially articulated and achieved objectives relating to community 'homogeneity', or the provision of public services, etc.) will both stem from and consolidate the existence of locality-based interest groups. The different characteristics of these groups, however, will also be likely to encourage some urban residents to make a specific choice about the 'community' or area to which they would like to belong and thus attempt to change their location within the city. To some extent, immigrants to the city will also have preferences about where they wish to live or work, despite the possible constraints of lack of information and income.

This indeed is the basis of one model, discussed in the Margolis (Reading 11) and Harvey (Reading 16) readings, which relates the provision of public goods to personal preference and mobility (Tiebout, 1956). Individuals decide upon the services/tax mix which suits them best and opt to reside in the area in question. They associate with individuals who have similar preferences (even though this may in theory involve very small communities) and the whole system, according to Tiebout, operates like a market. The problem is that there are a number of imperfections in this market. There is unlikely to be universal knowledge of all the service/tax packages available; there will inevitably be limits upon the size and number of communities and individuals will face heavy adjustment costs so that the move to a new community will only be possible on rare occasions. Moreover, some individuals face constraints preventing them from moving at all, and most important the decisions of individuals concerning residence (and of firms over industrial location) will be influenced by many factors other than the availability and cost of public goods. A market type solution is therefore unlikely to be efficient and the urban fiscal question becomes characterized by problems such as those of spatial disparity (people paying in one area and benefiting in another), spillovers (the provision of goods to one area in fact spreading out to other areas), the non-excludability of some public goods (if the urban environment is improved it is difficult to prevent everyone from enjoying the benefit), differential areal requirements, and differential ability to raise finance. Central and/or local governments will clearly wish to concern themselves with the implications of these problems and the urban process can thus be seen as being concerned with two of Musgrave's (1959) three classic functions of the budget – distribution and allocation.

It can be reasonably argued that the main redistributive functions of government are best carried out at a national level by the central authority (Richardson, 1969). At the same time local taxation and expenditure policies are bound to have redistributive impacts (which may or may not be foreseen by central government). It is increasingly argued that various urban policies have significant effects upon the distribution of real income through their impact upon the spatial pattern of public resources (Pahl, 1971; Harvey, Reading 16). The most obvious distributional problems arise from the disparities between the suburbs and the central cities (Brazer, 1964), problems which – allowing for the differing roles played by various central governments – are common to many western cities. Disparities arise not only because higher income groups tend to reside further out, but also because the requirements of inner areas are greater due to the need to replace obsolete physical social capital, and because many services consumed by suburban residents have to be provided at the centre. There are therefore inevitable questions of who pays for, and who benefits from, the provision of urban services. The extent of redistribution which actually occurs within or between local communities depends upon the methods of financing expenditure (user charges, local taxation, or government grants), and upon the size of the areas involved (larger areas tend to involve more extensive redistribution).

The question of the size of the area for which facilities are provided is at least as important for efficiency as for redistribution. It is fashionable to argue that as the scale of provision of public goods increases, the unit cost falls and that, as a result, 'larger' areas are required. This was, for example, a crucial element in the thinking behind the recommendations of the Maud report on local government reorganization in England and Wales (Redcliffe-Maud, 1969). However, the empirical evidence is largely inconclusive apart from suggesting that in very general terms the average cost curve is of the normal U shape as a result of diseconomies setting in at a certain size threshold (Cameron, 1970). Not only does the minimum cost size vary from a population of 30,000 to one of a million but also it is impossible to isolate the effects of different mixes of services between areas and of different quality in the services provided. Because of such mix and quality factors the concept of an 'optimum size of area' for the efficient provision of services is artificial, and in any case planning will be concerned with the costs and benefits of expanding or reducing services at the margin rather than with the average cost of provision. These considerations (together with the facts that the technology of public service production changes over time, that cities grow and decline, and that extensive redistribution of population between parts of cities occurs) explain why such questions of efficiency and size produce a variety of public policy approaches. In brief these encompass enlarging the role of central government (and so taking the whole question away from the local level), reorganizing local government (which may in the short run produce more sensible areas without fundamentally tackling the problems inherent in efficiency and redistribution) or establishing multiple governments (with special districts, local boards, functional authorities etc.). Whatever the approach favoured, however, it is evident that the question of the proper size of areas is one which crosses the traditional disciplinary boundaries, in that the issues are at least as much political as economic.

Political scientists are of course concerned with size in relation to the functions of government and administrative efficiency, and in this sense their interests are very similar to those of economists. The areal basis of government, however, raises other political issues. Wood, for example (Reading 12) argues that in the American context the stress on function has meant that there has been 'little real attention paid to the construction of meaningful political communities'. 'Meaningful' here implies a concern for allowing public participation in government, for ensuring political responsibility, and for understanding the impact of the political process on individual values. It involves considering the organization of government in relation to the ability of individuals and groups to properly express their preferences (an analogy is with the 'community participation potential' discussed by Isard (1960)). However, Wood also emphasizes the point already made above that a static conception of a locality-oriented community is likely to be inadequate and inappropriate in relation to current urban situations and he suggests the political process may be strengthened by various interest groups pursuing particular objectives in relation to special functions or groups of functions (e.g. transportation). Clearly, if such groups have a city-wide base their influence can become large. This in turn can produce a political process dominated by pressure groups, which may be lively and influential but not particularly responsible to any identifiable element in the urban population.

In the United Kingdom the impact of such pressure groups has been seen both in relation to the siting of the third London airport (a regional issue, where the pressures of middle and upper class local residents were sufficient to tip the Government's final choice against that of the independent Roskill Commission) and to the proposal to build motorways in London (where again an articulate middle class Motorway Action Group had the finance and professional expertise to mount a powerful political campaign against urban motorways). A key question is whether the interest group/pressure group thesis provides a better explanation of urban politics than a more traditional approach based on formal local government organization. It can of course be argued that the immense difficulties involved in reforming local government and in amalgamating numerous small authorities into larger ones are indicative of the liveliness and strength of politics at the local level. This was certainly the conclusion of the research on community attitudes to local politics undertaken for the Royal Commission on Local Government (Redcliffe-Maud, 1969). Equally the unwillingness of suburban local authorities to be absorbed into metropolitan areas is the strongest available proof of the existence of 'community identity'. Nevertheless it is clear that in large urban areas there are a variety of interest groups whose areal base does not conform to any single area of government, and that the urban political process involves the exercise of influence and power by such groups. The question of power in cities is covered more fully later but some typical interest groups have already been identified. There are those, for example, which stem from residential location behaviour. Though the likelihood of non-locality based communities has been stressed, the possibility of local communities, whose common aim is to preserve the residential identity of an area, still remains. Indeed some of the strongest interest groups are those whose influence produces racial, class, or occupational segregation of the type discussed earlier. A second example is the business community whose aim might be to expand the central area, to ensure extra space for industrial expansion and possibly to jeopardize the environmental or residential goals of the city at large. A further influential group is likely to be that involving landowners, property developers and construction firms, since it is their willingness to undertake schemes which determines at least in part the rate and nature of physical change in cities. The role of the developer has been demonstrated to be important, both at the expanding edge of the city where new building takes place (Craven and Pahl, 1967) and in the central areas where urban renewal schemes are undertaken. The interaction of groups of this type, together with the local government machine which to some extent mediates between groups, is illustrated in Form's article on the influence of socia structure in the determination of land use (Reading 13). The article is primarily concerned with political and economic issues rather than with the traditional social ones. Form also points out that legal procedures have an important part to play both in determining urban spatial structure and in forming and preserving communities.

In both America and Britain the use of land is subject to fairly strict control, though the philosophy of control has varied greatly between the two countries. American control derives primarily from the law of nuisance which in general terms relates to cases where the user of one piece of land causes 'nuisance' to the users of neighbouring land. Economists recognize the concepts of externalities and social costs in nuisance law and its derivative, zoning law, but the main characteristic of zoning regulations is that they have set a limiting framework for individual action rather than a prohibitive one (Mandelker, 1965). Mandelker (Reading 14) also points out that zoning regulations are now being challenged as being discriminatory on racial as well as on economic grounds. In Britain planning law has been more positive and at the same time more directly restrictive (Haar, 1960). There has been greater emphasis laid upon the role of the community at large with the appropriation of property under powers of 'eminent domain' and the procedure is a bureaucratic one rather than a judicial one. Nevertheless legal processes have in many cases had similar effects in both countries. The exclusion of lower-priced accommodation from high-income suburbs is one example (though in Britain the scale of local authority building has produced a greater spatial dispersion of low income families). Legal powers can and do ease the task of public authorities undertaking urban renewal, whilst at the same time hindering them if the compulsory purchase procedures are too complex and long drawn out (Hart, 1968). A final issue is that the whole nature of planning control is determined by the right to participate or object possessed by various groups. Whether the process is judicial or bureaucratic, there will be some who are better equipped, either financially or in terms of expertise, to utilize the system efficiently. This is an argument that applies to the formulation of plans as well as to their implementation.

The existence of a legal framework within which individual decisions have to be taken illustrates the interrelationship between the various themes of this section and the previous one on location and structure. Thus locational decisions can only be explained within the context of zoning regulations or planning permission. One of the main problems in relating empirical observation of location behaviour to location theory arises from the need to isolate the effects of planning policy.

While it is possible to describe the structure of cities in terms of the use of urban physical space, and even though to some extent this structure can be explained by behaviour which takes account of space constraints, there remain a number of urban processes which are only marginally influenced by the physical characteristics of cities. The social scientist must understand this overlap between spatial and non-spatial problems, and be aware of those situations where spatial policies (which have been largely favoured by planners in the past) may be relevant and of those where non-spatial policies may be more appropriate. There will be various points in the urban process towards which intervention can be directed; the concern of the following section is to discuss the questions of where the social sciences would suggest that intervention (or planning in its widest sense) is likely to be both feasible and efficient.

V Planning and the social sciences

The extent to which an urban system can be changed depends upon the ability of the planner to isolate those points at which intervention is possible, to pick the most suitable means of intervention, and to predict the effects of intervention upon the system as a whole. In principle there is a wide range of economic, social, and political options open to the planner, and the extent to which such policies are physically oriented will obviously vary greatly. Since, however, it is clear that not all urban problems and processes are necessarily locality based, it follows that locality-oriented intervention (or physical planning) can only be partially successful. The initial presumption of all planning has already been noted; if left to follow their own preferences, individuals will not act in a way which maximizes the welfare of the city as a whole. Thus a basic question of intervention is how far, and by what means, can the urban collectivity limit the freedom of individuals. Some of the circumstances in which the community might wish to intervene have already been touched upon (spillovers and externalities, exclusionary action by particular groups, inefficiency in the provision of public services).

The major practical issue involved is a legal one. This stems from constitutional rights and their interpretation in law, and relates to the extent to which the state can determine the use of property, or alternatively expropriate it, with or without compensation (Dunham, Reading 15). As Delafons (Reading 2) points out there are fundamental differences on this issue between the United States and Britain. In the former case there has traditionally been greater stress laid upon the right of the individual to acquire and retain property, and the bulk of 'planning' legislation has been directed towards the protection of property rights and of the expectations which derive from property holding. Thus nuisance law, zoning law, and in analogous fields much anti-trust and environmental law, seek to protect particular people or groups from the encroachment of others rather than to specify limits on the action of these others, and the retention of freedom of action for the individual has been central in American planning procedures. This philosophy has weakened somewhat in recent years with the growing scale of acquisition of private property (Edens, 1970) (e.g. in order to allow highway construction), and with the establishment of numerous special boards and authorities (often with special powers) to provide a variety of urban public services. The most significant extension of compulsory purchase in the United States, however, has been in relation to urban renewal, with extensive public (federal) funds available to assist the financing of renewal schemes. Yet even here the concern for private property is demonstrated by the fact that after completion of renewal the redeveloped property (often commercial) is sold back to private owners.

The emphasis in British law has been more towards the power of eminent domain – the right to take private property without the owner's consent – and also towards the retention of property rights by public authorities. Compensation – whether to give it, and if so how to assess it – is too complex a question for this volume as indeed are the various changes in statutory planning procedures in Britain from the 1947 Town and Country Planning Act up to the latest amendments to the 1968 Act. It is only possible, to note the three basic characteristics of planning law in the last twenty-five years.

1. There is the obligation for every authority to produce a plan. The content of the plan has varied from the specific land use plans required under the 1947 Act to the more flexible strategic plans yet to be drawn up under the 1968 Act, but there is still a statutory plan on which individual proposals can be assessed.

2. There is a system of application for planning permissions under which proposals for development are put to the local authority, and thence if an appeal is made, to an inquiry, and to the Minister. There is therefore a bureaucratic procedure which can prescribe individual action.

3. There is the use of compulsory purchase and public ownership, not only for public housing which is of course far more extensive in Britain than in America, but also for redevelopment in inner city areas and for New Town development on green field sites.

Thus the legal processes allow considerable scope for planning action both in Britain and, to a lesser extent, in America. Altering the law may be, however, at one and the same time too easy and yet too difficult. It may be too easy in the sense that whilst legal regulations should reflect certain objectives for the community at large it is all too simple for the objectives never to be made explicit by the lawmakers. It may be too difficult, not only in so far as changing the law can be a lengthy process within which all sorts of political pressures can distort the main purpose of the exercise (Cleaveland et al., 1969), but also in that the law, once set, may be inflexible and indeed may be interpreted in an unforeseen way by the judiciary.

There are, however, many urban processes which occur quite independently of any legal framework, and one of these – the rate of economic growth or decline in a city – is central to the context within which planning operates. If one compares the impact that changing levels of economic activity have had on cities with the impact that planning has had, it is clear that the influence of the planner can be relatively meagre. Over the long term (the last two centuries) there have been numerous examples of the relative growth and decline of different cities due to technological innovation, the decline of traditional industries, the growth of new ones, and alterations in the competitive positions of cities. The relative decline of Baltimore and the growth of Washington is one example; the poverty, overcrowding, and lack of facilities in a number of the Lancashire cotton towns another. Over the short term 'planning' can have little effect, as the perennial problems of regional planning in Britain illustrate, and the future is highly uncertain. Even during the preparation of this book the discovery of oil in the North Sea has created unforeseen growth pressures on a number of east coast towns in Britain. Planned events such as industrial location decisions can have unexpected spillovers or can fail to achieve their intended results, and the planner's ability to change existing patterns is strictly limited as the experiences of many metropolitan areas suggests. The north east of the United States (Megalopolis) and the London Metropolitan Region are the best, but not the only, examples. In this context, the lack of any treatment of the processes of urban growth in this volume might be criticized. It is, however, precisely because many of these processes – investment, growth of incomes, wages and prices, in and out migration flows, continued urbanization – cannot be dealt with solely, or in some cases even partially, by the urban planning machinery that they have been omitted, and as was pointed out much earlier, this volume is not primarily concerned with the question 'What can the nation do about its cities?' but rather with the question 'What can the city do about its problems?' Of course there are national pressures operating upon local urban systems – the rate of economic growth, the national political climate, broad alterations at the national level in social structure – but there nevertheless remain a number of local processes which operate in individual cities and ensure that the system there does not resemble the national system, writ small. It is likely for example, that local voting behaviour will not exactly follow national patterns due to the existence of local issues or local personalities; also, where market forces determine the allocation of resources there are likely to be numerous local submarkets – for local jobs or housing – which only partially reflect the national situation. Thus there will be within a country a number of complex urban systems of the type analyzed by Harvey (Reading 16) and the interest of this book is with intervention *within* rather than *between* these systems (or with the single city sub-system rather the national system of cities).

In both British and American cities much resource allocation occurs through market mechanisms, and many urban problems, of which poverty is but one example, stem largely from market forces. It is characteristic of cities that markets do not work very efficiently with urban economic activity typically being conducted in circumstances of distorted (or absent) prices, monopolistic provision of goods, externalities and spillovers and absence of information. The most efficient method of correcting such imperfections is by relating prices as far as possible to user costs (marginal social costs rather than private costs (Vickrey, 1963)). Proper pricing methods could, for example, produce a more efficient balance between public and private transport if congestion charges were imposed upon the users of scarce urban road space (Ministry of Transport, 1964). Where pricing is impracticable the blunter instruments of taxation and subsidy can achieve similar ends.

Planning has an important function to fulfil in improving the supply of information upon which urban decisions are made – the sort of function exercised in relation to the decentralization of offices from London in recent years by the Location of Offices Bureau (LOB, 1971). Market improvement measures of this type are, however, essentially designed to alter the environment within which decisions are taken rather than to impinge directly upon private decision-taking, though there is a very fine distinction between this form of planning and that which seeks to control more directly the actions of individuals or firms in urban society. In fact the whole issue of the control of market forces raises the same questions as those discussed in relation to the role of law in planning (the fact that zoning law has its justification in the externality concept has already been mentioned).

It is equally possible to take the whole resource allocation process outside the market. In the discussion on community it was argued that the characteristics of many public goods (police and fire protection, education, health) suggest that they can be more efficiently and more equitably supplied by the public than by the private sector. It is difficult to establish empirically exactly how far this assertion about the public sector is in fact true. This is partly because the problems of measuring output and comparing it over time or between areas prevent any clear view of how far different cities achieve greater economies or encourage greater redistribution. If there have been various studies which demonstrate inter-state or inter-authority differences in expenditures

(Hirsch, 1968; Davies, 1968) these have necessarily fallen short of taking full account of the differing quality of services or of identifying and measuring benefits. Even less has been done in identifying variations in the intra-urban distribution of services, although the presumption that inner areas have been starved of social capital is central to a number of studies which highlight the declining tax base of inner areas and the need to adopt equalization procedures (e.g. revenue sharing) to facilitate the allocative and distributive functions of government.

Intervention can be, and has been, also directed at the areas of jurisdiction of urban governments. Reform of local government is a current concern in Britain following the Government's modification of the Redcliffe-Maud (1969) and Wheatley (1969) proposals, and a recent major experience was the 1963 change in the structure of government in London. Smallwood's case study of the London reforms (Reading 17) is not only one of the few depth studies of reorganization but also makes a number of telling comparisons between London reform and that of American cities. In Britain reform is largely instigated and implemented by the central government but the main differences between the UK and USA stem from the different structures of local government. In Britain there are proportionally fewer local authorities, they are stronger, and more open in their handling of issues; there is less pressure-group activity and few special boards. By contrast American city government is fragmented, there is an immense variety of pressure-group activity and the formal authority is often weak (Newton, 1969). These differences explain the relative emphasis on political science and power studies in America as opposed to the concern with administration and function in Britain. Altering the organization of government may therefore appear to be an attractive policy option, but in terms of one of the criteria for intervention – that the effects of intervention on the system as a whole should be predictable – it is in many ways unsatisfactory. Again like changing the law, changing the structure of government can be a long drawn out, and even inconclusive, process.

All of the approaches to planning so far discussed have some spatial implications. Market mechanisms can be improved in order to remove externalities or spatial monopolies, or ease the friction of space on the transmission of information; the public provision of services can combat spatial disparities and spillovers; the reform of local government can be directed at rationalizing areas of jurisdiction. Despite this spatial content, however, the approaches suggested obviously fall into a different category from the traditional methods adopted by planners – control of land use, improvements in the physical environment etc., and in the sense that they relate to the fundamental economic and political processes of the city are more likely to offer a genuine potential for altering the urban system. In this rejection of the primarily physical approach they echo some of the thinking of Gans (Reading 18) and indeed many of the areas of concern he identifies for social planning are covered in the paragraphs above. For example, in remarking that the planner 'is inevitably allocating scarce resources among sectors of the population providing benefits to some and costs to others' Gans is quite obviously raising issues of welfare economics and redistribution. The emphasis in social planning in fact lies in the identification of particular individuals and groups and in the need to adopt selective intervention in the system to help such groups. Problems of poverty, lack of education, poor access to health services, poor housing, etc., tend, as the analysis of urban structure demonstrates, to be concentrated in particular areas and on particular groups, leading to multiple deprivation and social immobility. To remedy this the social planner has to present policies which not only relate to spatial groupings but are capable of differentiating between them. Exactly how far this is either possible or desirable is open to argument. Many economists, for example, would argue that redistribution must be undertaken nationally, though within the context of knowledge of what local redistribution also takes place. The nature of social planning has been extensively covered elsewhere both in relation to America (Marris and Rein, 1967; Sharrard, 1968; Frieden and Morris, 1968) and Britain (Pahl, 1970b), and although not everyone would share Gans' almost total indictment of physical planners, it is clear that the 'geographical/sociological imagination' contrast has been to a large extent overcome in the development of social planning. However the main point in Gans' essay, and the point which links forward to the remainder of this volume, is that planning must be consumer oriented and that it must represent the wishes of the people who are being 'planned'. Who plans, and for whom, is central to the issue of power and legitimacy in urban planning.

VI Power and legitimacy

The nature of power and influence in cities has attracted considerable attention (at least in America) over the last two decades

(Hawley and Wirt, 1968) and the study of urban power raises a number of interesting interdisciplinary questions concerning the relationship between the various social science disciplines. Why some disciplines (political science and sociology) have concerned themselves with power whilst others (economics and management science) have ignored it, is discussed at a later stage. Initially, however, it is necessary to point out that even where power studies have been carried out, there has been considerable disagreement over approach, methodology and findings.

There have been three broad approaches to the study of community power.

1. The *positional* approach, assumes that the power structure consists primarily of certain persons holding objectively determined positions – bank presidents, business managers, judges, etc. – and infers that this observed elite adopts a common strategy towards the maintenance and use of power (Schulze, 1958).

2. The *reputational* approach is very similar except that the elite is identified not by objective positional criteria but by repute, on the basis of judgements by various members of the community about who does or does not have influence (Hunter, 1953).

3. The *pluralist* approach, however, rejects the methodology and conclusions of the two elitist theories and concentrates not upon the sources of power but upon its exercise. Pluralists suggest that it is necessary to focus on issues in order to understand where power lies, and that such a focus demonstrates that there is a separate power or interest group involved in each key issue so that the structure of power is a fluid one with individuals and groups combining and separating as different issues arise. Thus there is no single power elite (Dahl, 1961; Polsby, 1959).

All these approaches are open to criticism. The positional one does not distinguish between the holding of a position and the use of that position to exert influence, the reputational approach fails to take any account of the influence exerted by non-elite groups (e.g. negroes), and the pluralist one does not specify how the issues to be examined can be chosen nor how it is possible to assess how far the non-emergence of issues also reflects the exercise of power (Bachrach and Baratz, 1962).

Not only do the different methodologies of these approaches prevent the drawing of useful comparative conclusions between American cities, but also the contrasting theories present a rather artificial and polarized picture of the distribution of power. Finally the methods have given rise to only limited comparative research in relation to Britain and America probably owing to the very different structures of government (Newton, 1969) with the comparative studies of Bristol and Seattle being the significant exception (Miller 1958a, 1958b). Instead it is more useful to stand back from the many studies undertaken in the 1950s and 1960s and to look at the historic evolution of power. In America it is possible to distinguish various stages, often overlapping in time; the setting up in the late eighteenth and early nineteenth centuries of state and city governments on a checks and balances system analogous to the federal one, the era of the elected council, the machine and boss period, the emergence of the strong mayor and of the city manager. Throughout the twentieth century one can in fact trace a trend towards good government with efficient city management as a generally accepted aim. This trend is reviewed briefly by Salisbury (Reading 19) whose analysis suggests that a new convergence of power emerged in the 1960s between the mayor, the businessman and the technical expert. It is with the last of these that we are particularly concerned. Scott (1969) has described the evolution of American city planning from the mid-nineteenth century up to the point in the early 1960s when the planner was possessed of an expertise which gave him a significant volume of power – if he wished to exercise it. This coincided with the development of comprehensive planning and with the debate over the nature of planning – Altshuler's (1965) discussion of the issues and Friedmann's (1965) response to him are typical contributions. It is less easy to trace either the changing structure of urban politics or the growing influence of the planner in Britain, partly due to great continuity in local government, to the absence of boss or machine politics and to the non-emergence of the city manager. Even the 1947 and 1959 Planning Acts raised no major new issues over the role of the planner in society and it is only in recent years that any debate on this issue has developed (Webber, 1969).

Before discussing the key question of this debate, should planning confine itself to objective, value-free analysis on behalf of politicians or should it use its technical expertise in shaping policies, it is necessary to pose a second set of questions – is objective planning possible? can rational techniques prevail? or is value-free planning a myth? These questions bring back the crucial interdisciplinary issue of why some social sciences (politics and sociology) have become involved in power studies whilst others (economics and management science) have largely disregarded them. Power is not irrelevant to economic theory as Rothschild (1971) has shown, but economists have tended to regard competition as a sufficient limitation upon the exercise of power. It is possible to introduce concepts of power into economic analysis as the theory of monopoly illustrates, but the major contribution of economics to urban planning is in relation to the potential for rational decision-taking in situations where problems of power distribution are either irrelevant or, more likely, assumed away. Thus the problems inherent in public sector investment appraisal have led to the development of a variety of planning techniques such as cost benefit analysis (or variations upon it), the somewhat overrated threshold analysis (Hughes and Koslowski, 1968) and the planning-balance sheet (Lichfield, 1964). Such techniques are particularly appropriate for appraising schemes within a plan (e.g. a bridge, a drainage scheme, even an airport) where the strategic framework of the plan remains unchanged and the scheme is small enough to have little effect upon the plan as a whole. As Prest and Turvey (1966) point out 'cost-benefit analysis is only a technique for taking decisions within a framework which has to be decided in advance, and which involves a wide range of considerations, many of them of a political or social character'.

A different and more difficult situation arises in relation to a comprehensive urban (or regional) strategy where some form of systems approach on the lines suggested by McLoughlin (1969) becomes necessary and where the problem is one of multi-objective alternatives incorporating both complementary and conflicting objectives and requiring some form of programming, or systems analysis approach towards evaluation. Lichfield (1971) reviews a number of such approaches, many of which derive from the theory of cost-benefit/planning-balance sheets. It is possible to see the increasing sophistication of urban and regional (land use) planning evaluation as analogous to the development of PPBS (Planning, Programming, Budgeting Systems) (McKean, 1958; Schulze, 1968), Corporate Planning (Ackoff, 1970) and Strategic Choice systems (Friend and Jessop, 1969) as planning tools for public expenditure, the large public or private corporation, and local government, respectively. The general management functions of local government in Britain (whether these be land-use or expenditure-management functions) are thus becoming increasingly rationalized (not unrelated to the coming change in organization). Eddison (Reading 20) traces the evolution of this rationality in local government activity, and also points out that it has been subject to a good many criticisms.

It has been argued that the pure rationality approach is inappropriate simply because public sector decision-making is not (and presumably cannot be) undertaken in that way. Instead there is the science of muddling through (Lindblom, 1959) involving fragmented and distorted decisions, remedial and marginal action, risk minimization and short-term planning (if any). Clearly this is a description of things as they are, not as they might be, but there are valid arguments over whether long-term comprehensive planning is possible. It has been shown, for example (Boyce *et al.*, 1970), that in a number of American metropolitan land use and transportation plans the methods used 'were largely inadequate for the complexity of multi-functional alternatives proposed to fulfil diverse and often conflicting objectives' and similar conclusions on the problems inherent in evaluating very broad aims programmes have been drawn both elsewhere in America and in Britain, and in regional, as well as urban, contexts (Weiss and Rein, 1969; South-East Joint Planning Team, 1971). Finally even were it both politically and technically possible to adopt systematic and rational approaches to long-term planning, involving strategic objectives set within a framework of implementation and monitoring, there would remain a basic question of identifying those objectives to be adopted and here we return to a key question – who is being planned for? On whose behalf does intervention occur? In a sense the whole debate about PPBS, disjointed incrementalism, and rational planning is irrelevant if the underlying questions of values and welfare are not also explicitly handled. It is on this point that the polar positions of the social science disciplines become apparent. Political science and sociology by concentrating on power can fail to recognize the role that objective, quantitative analysis should play in informing decision-taking processes. Economics and management science are equally exclusionary by emphasizing rational appraisal techniques at the expense of political reality. All however, have to some extent failed to take account of their interdependency in relation to the problem of allocating scarce resources between competing groups in an urban system. Thus the allocation problem, like the concept of community, is a central theme in the interdisciplinary approach, and both themes are dominated by the question discussed particularly by Gans, Eddison, and Rein

(Readings 18, 20, 21); how far is it possible for the planning process to incorporate into itself the preferences and values of the community, or communities, of the city. Participation in planning is, in the early 1970s, extremely fashionable. The desire for participation stems in part from an awareness that the administrative machinery is breaking down, and in part from a growing concern about the preservation of the urban environment. It has been felt that the ever increasing technical complexity of the planning process (and thus the increasing inability of individuals to make any effective impact on the process) might be offset by greater public participation at various stages in the making and implementing of plans. The official recognition in Britain of this desire for participation was seen both in the 1968 Planning Act and more explicitly in the Skeffington Report on People and Planning (Skeffington, 1969). Less than three years after Skeffington, however, it is apparent that participation is easier to discuss than to actually create.

In a review of the movement towards participation in planning, Damer and Hague (1971) suggest that disillusionment has set in because the main philosophy behind the movement has not been to encourage the insertion into planning of the choices and preferences of various groups but has instead been to ensure that planners' existing values and preferences are reinforced. Participation is seen as 'the education of the public into the planners perspective' rather than the reverse, as Gans for example, would wish. Thus instead of highlighting the existence of differing preferences and priorities and so sharpening conflict in the city, it has instead been seen as a means of dampening down public involvement in planning. It is scarcely surprising, therefore, that participation (as officially defined) has had a lukewarm reception from the public, but there are of course, other ways in which local interest groups can become involved in changing the city. In America community development schemes, with heavy financial support from the federal government, have sought quite successfully, to involve local residents in the planning of small areas. A different development has been the growth, primarily in America, of advocacy planning (Peattie, 1968) which involves the exercise of the planning function not on behalf of some general public interest but rather on behalf of specified individuals or groups. Similar to this are the activities of planners who are prepared to make a public stand, often against the authority employing them, on the grounds that the 'official' plan (e.g. the New York Plan, or the Covent Garden proposals in London) is unsound, value laden and contrary to the interests of the local community. These various approaches to participation and the reactions they generate within the planning professions are related to Rein's article on legitimacy and planning (Reading 21), in which he seeks to assess where the reform oriented planner (or social scientist) gets his authority to propose change. Rein points out that there is no single source of legitimacy, that there are indeed likely to be conflicting sources, and that planning raises difficult moral problems for all who become involved in it. He does not however carry the argument further to suggest that the problem of conflicting values and different sources of legitimacy are likely to be so great as to totally debase the planning process, although this is the apparent implication of some studies (Dennis, 1970) which demonstrate the extent to which planners foist their values upon the public. In fact the debasement of planning may well occur. If involvement of the public (participation in any of its forms) proves to be blatantly purposeless, if rational analysis is impossible, if the imperfections in the system become worse rather than better, then it seems likely that for at least some groups in the city direct action will become a valid mechanism of change.

Urban violence is of course a common phenomenon in American cities and it is a phenomenon which is becoming more frequent as the 1969 follow-up to the Kerner Commission on Civil Disorders demonstrated. The extensive evidence presented in the Commission's own report (Kerner Commission, 1968) suggests that whilst grievances over the local physical environment may be culminating, precipitating incidents, urban violence is primarily the consequence of a long-term process of frustration, leading to aggression, and thence to violence. There are numerous theories of urban violence – the conspiracy theory, the recent migrant theory, the youth rebellion theory, and the police brutality theory, for example, but the roots of violence are clearly historical, lying in generations of rejection of and discrimination against negroes in the United States. It is held, however, that it is as societies become more equal that minorities observe and react to the remaining inequalities more violently. While continuing relative deprivation is a contributory cause of urban violence, the basic reasons are likely to be political ones revolving around the distribution of power in cities (Lupsha, Reading 22). It is the more alarming, therefore, that as the Kerner Commission follow-up again shows, the main reaction to the Kerner Report itself has been the strengthening of police resources rather than an attack upon the underlying *causes* of violence – be these social, economic or political.

The Kerner Commission devoted itself to urban riots primarily as manifestations of current racial problems in American cities. Violence has, however, been a recurrent theme in American urban history, and at various times has been seen as a legitimate form of political action for certain groups (Drake, 1968). The abolition movement, the labour movement, and the suffrage movement all involved urban violence to some degree and it is certainly wrong to regard racial conflict as the sole origin of city rioting. Violence is a product of anger directed at the inadequacy of the urban system in general to live up to expectations and promises, and in particular at the inability of political, economic, and social processes to satisfy community preferences, allocate resources efficiently and equitably, and reduce inequalities and offer social mobility. Thus the premium on understanding urban processes, urban change and the mechanisms of intervention, is that failure to do so can endanger the whole system and lead to the breakdown of law and order.

References

ABERCROMBIE, P. (1945), *Greater London Plan*, HMSO.
ACKOFF, R. L. (1970), *A Concept of Corporate Planning*, Wiley Interscience.
ALONSO, W. (1960), 'A theory of the urban land market', *Papers and Proceedings of the Regional Science Association*, Vol. 6, pp. 154–9.
ALONSO, W. (1970), 'What are new towns for', *Urban Studies*, vol. 7, pp. 37–55.
ALONSO, W. (1971), 'Beyond the inter-disciplinary approach to planning', *J. of the Amer. Inst. of Planners*, vol. 37, pp. 169–73.
ALTSHULER, A. (1965), 'The goals of comprehensive planning', *J. of the Amer. Inst. of Planners*, vol. 31, pp. 186–95.
BACHRACH, P., and BARATZ, M. S. (1962), 'Two faces of power', *Amer. Pol. Sci. Rev.*, vol. 56, pp. 947–52.
BARLOW (1940), *Royal Commission on the Distribution of Industrial Population Report*, cmnd. 6153, HMSO.
BAUMOL, W. J. (1967), 'Macroeconomics of unbalanced growth: the anatomy of urban crisis', *Amer. Econ. Rev.*, vol. 57, pp. 415–26.
BELL, LADY (1901), *At the Works*, Edward Arnold.
BELL, C. R. (1969), *Middle Class Families; Social and Geographical Mobility*, Routledge & Kegan Paul.
BERRY, B. J. L. (1967), *The Geography of Market Centers and Retail Distribution*, Prentice-Hall.
BERRY, B. J. L., and HORTON, F. E. (1970), *Geographic Perspectives on Urban Systems*, Prentice-Hall.
BESHERS, J. M. (1962), *Urban Social Structure*, Free Press.

BLUMENFELD, H. (1954), 'The tidal wave of metropolitan expansion', *J. of the Amer. Inst. of Planners*, vol. 20, pp. 3–14.

BLUMENFELD, H. (1967), in P. D. Spreiregen (ed.), *The Modern Metropolis: Its Origin, Growth, Characteristics, Planning*, MIT Press.

BOGARDUS, E. S. (1925), 'Social distance and its origins', *J. of appl. Sociol.*, vol. 9, pp. 216–26.

BOOTH, C. *et al.* (1891), *Life and Labour of the People in London*, Williams & Norgate.

BOURNE, L. S. (1969), 'A spatial allocation–land use conversion model of urban growth', *J. of Regional Sci.*, vol. 9, pp. 261–72.

BOYCE, D. E., DAY, N. D., and MCDONALD, C. (1970), *Metropolitan Plan-Making*, Regional Science Research Institute.

BRAZER, H. E. (1964), 'Some fiscal implications of metropolitanism', in B. Chinitz, (ed.), *City and Suburb*, Prentice-Hall.

BRIGGS, A. (1968), *Victorian Cities*, Penguin Books.

BURGESS, E. W. (1925), 'The growth of the city', in R. E. Park *et. al.*, *The City*, University of Chicago Press.

BURGESS, E. W., and BOGUE, D. J. (ed.), (1964), *Contributions to Urban Sociology*, University of Chicago Press.

BURKHEAD, J., and CAMPBELL, A. K. (1968), 'Public policy for urban America', in H. S. Perloff, and L. Wingo, (eds.), *Issues in Urban Economics*, Johns Hopkins.

BUTTIMER, A. (1971), 'Sociology and planning', *Town Planning Rev.*, vol. 42, pp. 154–68.

CAMERON, G. C. (1970), 'Growth areas, growth centres and regional conversion', *Scottish J. of Pol. Econ.*, vol. 17, pp. 19–38.

CAMERON, G. C., and CLARK, B. D. (1966), *Industrial Movement and the Regional Problem*, Oliver & Boyd.

CHECKLAND, S. G. (1964), 'The British industrial city as history: the Glasgow case', *Urban Studies*, vol. 1, pp. 34–54.

CHOMBART de LAUWE *et al.* (1952), *Paris et l'agglomération Parisienne*, Presses Universitaires de France.

CHRISTALLER, W. (1933), *Central Places in Southern Germany*, translated by C. W. Gaskin, Prentice-Hall, 1966.

CLEAVELAND, F. N. *et al.* (1969), *Congress and Urban Problems*, Brookings Institution.

CLINARD, M. B. (1966), *Slums and Community Development*, Free Press.

COOLEY, C. H. (1909), *Social Organization*, Charles Scribner & Sons.

COWAN, P. (1969), *The Office–A Facet of Urban Growth*, Joint Unit for Planning Research.

CRAVEN, E. A., and PAHL, R. E. (1967), 'Residential expansion: the role of the private developer in the South-East', *J. of the Town Planning Inst.*, vol. 53, pp. 137–43.

DAHL, R. A. (1961), *Who Governs?*, Yale University Press.

DAMER, S., and HAGUE, C. (1971), 'Public participation in planning: a review', *Town Planning Rev.*, vol. 42, pp. 217–32.

DARWENT, D. F. (1969), 'Growth poles and growth centers in regional planning–a review', *Environment and Planning*, vol. 1, pp. 5–32.

DAVIES, B. (1968), *Social Needs and Resources in Local Services*, Michael Joseph.

DAVIS, O. A., and WHINSTON, A. B. (1961), 'The economics of urban renewal', *Law and Contemporary Probs.*, vol. 26, pp. 105–17.

DELAFONS, J. (1969), *Land Use Controls in the USA*, MIT Press.

DENNIS, N. (1958), 'Popularity of the neighbourhood community idea', *Sociol. Rev.*, vol. 6, pp. 191–206.

DENNIS, N. (1970), *People and Planning*, Faber & Faber.

DRAKE, St. C. (1968), 'Urban violence and American social movements', *Proceedings of the Academy of Political Science*, vol. 29, pp. 13–24.

DUNHAM, A. (1964), 'Property, city planning, and liberty', in C. M. Haar, (ed.) *Law and Land*, Joint Center for Urban Studies, Harvard University and MIT Press.

DURKHEIM, E. (1893), *The Division of Labour in Society*, translated and edited by G. Simpson, Macmillan, 1933.

EDENS, D. (1970), 'Eminent domain, equity, and the allocation of resources', *Land Econ.*, vol. 46, pp. 314–22.

ENGELS, F. (1845), *The Condition of the Working Class in England*, translated and edited by W. O. Henderson, and W. H. Chaloner, Macmillan, 1958.

FORM, W. H. (1954), 'The place of social structure in the determination of land use', *Social Forces*, vol. 32, pp. 317–23.

FRANKENBERG, R. (1957), *Village on the Border*, Cohen & West.

FRIEDEN, B. J., and MORRIS, R. (eds.) (1968), *Urban Planning and Social Policy*, Basic Books.

FRIEDMANN, J. R. P. (1965), 'A response to Professor Altshuler', *J. of the American Inst. of Planners*, vol. 32, pp. 31–3.

FRIEDMANN, J. R. P., and MILLER, J. (1965), 'The urban field', *J. of the Amer. Inst. of Planners*, vol. 31, pp. 312–20.

FRIEND, J. A., and JESSOP, W. N. (1969), *Local Government and Strategic Choice*, Tavistock.

GANS, H. J. (1962), *The Urban Villagers*, Free Press.

GANS, H. J. (1969), 'Planning for people, not buildings', *Environment and Planning*, vol. 1, pp. 33–46.

GARNER, B. (1967), 'Models of urban geography and settlement location', in R. J. Chorley, and P. Haggett, *Socio-Economic Models in Geography*, Methuen University Paperbacks.

GEDDES, P. (1915), *Cities in Evolution*, Williams & Norgate.

GLASS, R. (1955), 'Urban sociology in Great Britain', *Current Sociol.*, vol. 4, pp. 5–19.

GODDARD, J. B. (1971), 'Office communications and office location', *Regional Studies*, vol. 5, pp. 263–80.

GOLDNER, W. (1955), 'Spatial and locational aspects of metropolitan labour markets', *Amer. Econ. Rev.*, vol. 45, pp. 113–28.

GOODEY, B. (1971), 'A small space for small-space', *Area*, vol. 3, pp. 93–5.

GOTTMANN, J. (1961), *Megalopolis*, Twentieth Century Fund.

GREATER LONDON COUNCIL (1969), *Greater London Development Plan, Report and Studies*, HMSO.

GRIGSBY, W. G. (1963), *Housing Markets and Public Policy*, University of Pennsylvania Press.

HAAR, C. (1960), 'Planning law', in *Land Use in an Urban Environment*, Liverpool University Press.

HAIG, R. M. (1926), 'Towards an understanding of the metropolis', *Q. J. of Econ.*, vol. 40, pp. 179–208.

HALL, P. G. (ed.), (1966), *Von Thünen's Isolated State*, Pergamon.

HARRIS, C. D., and ULLMAN, E. (1945), 'The nature of cities', *Annals of the Amer. Acad. of Pol. and Social Sci.*, vol. 242, pp. 7–17.

HART, T. (1968), *The Comprehensive Development Area*, Oliver & Boyd.

HARVEY, D. (1970), 'Social processes and spatial form: an analysis of the conceptual problems of urban planning', *Papers and Proc. of the Regional Sci. Assoc.*, vol. 25, pp. 47–69.

HARVEY, D. (1971), 'Social processes, spatial form, and the redistribution of real income in an urban system', in M. Chisholm, A. E. Frey, and P. Haggett (eds.), *Regional Forecasting*, Butterworth.

HAWLEY, A. H., and DUNCAN, O. D. (1957), 'Social area analysis: a critical appraisal', *Land Econ.* vol. 33, pp. 337–45.

HAWLEY, W. D., and WIRT, F. M. (1968), *The Search for Community Power*, Prentice-Hall.

HERBERT, D. T. (1967), 'Social area analysis: a British study', *Urban Studies*, vol. 4, pp. 41–60.

HIRSĊH, W. Z. (1968), 'The supply of urban public services', in H. S. Perloff and L. Wingo, *Issues in Urban Economics*, Johns Hopkins.

HOWARD, E. (1902), *Garden Cities of Tomorrow*, Swan Sonnenschein & Co.

HOYT, H. (1938), *The Structure and Growth of Residential Neighbourhoods in American Cities*, Chicago University Press.

HOYT, H. (1964), 'Recent distortions of the classical models of urban structure', *Land Econ.*, vol. 40, pp. 199–212.

HUGHES, J. T., and KOSLOWSKI, J. (1968), 'Threshold analysis–an economic tool for town and regional planning', *Urban Studies*, vol. 5, pp. 132–43.

HUNTER, F. (1953), *Community Power Structure*, University of North Carolina Press.

ISARD, W. (1960), *Methods of Regional Analysis*, MIT Press.

JACOBS, J. (1961), *The Death and Life of Great American Cities*, Random House, Penguin edition, 1965.

JACOBS, J. (1970), *The Economy of Cities*, Jonathan Cape.

KEEBLE, D. E. (1969), 'Local industrial linkage and manufacturing growth in outer London', *Town Planning Rev.*, vol. 40, pp. 163–88.

KELLER, S. (1969), *The Urban Neighbourhood: a Sociological Perspective*, Random House.

KERNER COMMISSION (1968), *Report of the National Advisory Commission on Civil Disorders*, US Government Printing Office, Bantam Books.

LASUEN, J. R. (1969), 'On growth poles', *Urban Studies*, vol. 6, pp. 137–61.

LAUMANN, E. O. (1966), *Prestige and Association in an Urban Community*, Bobbs-Merrill.

LEE, T. R. (1968), 'Urban neighbourhood as a socio-spatial schema', *Human Rels.*, vol. 21, pp. 241–67.

LICHFIELD, N. (1964), 'Cost-benefit analysis in plan evaluation', *Town Planning Rev.*, vol. 39, pp. 160–69.

LICHFIELD, N. (1971), 'Evaluation methodology of urban and regional plans: a review', *Regional Studies*, vol. 4, pp. 151–65.

LIEBERSON, S. (1963), *Ethnic Patterns in American Cities*, Free Press.

LINDBLOM, C. E. (1959), 'The science of "Muddling Through"', *Pub. Admin. Rev.*, vol. 19, pp. 79–88.

LOCATION OF OFFICES BUREAU (1971), *Location of Offices Bureau, Annual Report*, 1970–71.

LONDON SCHOOL OF ECONOMICS (1930), *New Survey of London Life and Labour*.

LUPSHA, P. (1969), 'On the theories of urban violence', *Urban Affairs Q.*, vol. 4, pp. 273–296.

LYNCH, K. (1960), *The Image of the City*, MIT and Harvard University.

MCELRATH, D. C. (1962), 'The social areas of Rome: a comparative analysis', *Amer. Sociol. Rev.*, vol. 27, pp. 376–91.

MCIVER, R. M. (1937), *Society*, Macmillan.

MCKEAN, R. N. (1958), *Efficiency in Government through Systems Analysis*, Wiley.

MCLOUGHLIN, J. B. (1969), *Urban and Regional Planning: A Systems Approach*, Faber.

MAINE, H. J. S. (1884), *Ancient Law*, Murray.

MANDELKER, D. R. (1965), 'The role of law in the planning process', *Law and Contemp. Probs*, vol. 30, pp. 26–37.

MANDELKER, D. R. (1970), 'A rationale for the zoning process', *Land Use Controls Q.*, vol. 4, pp. 1–7.

MARGOLIS, J. (1968), 'The demand for urban public services', in H. S. Perloff and L. Wingo (eds.), *Issues in Urban Economics*, Johns Hopkins.

MARRIS, P., and REIN, M. (1967), *Dilemmas of Social Reform*, Atherton.

MASTERMAN, C. F. (1909), in J. I. Boulton (ed.) *The Condition of England*, Methuen, 1960.

MEIER, R. L. (1962), *A Communications Theory of Urban Growth*, Joint Center for Urban Studies, Harvard University and MIT Press.

MILLER, D. C. (1958a), 'Industry and community power structure', *Amer. Sociol. Rev.*, vol. 23, pp. 9–15.

MILLER, D. C. (1958b), 'Decision-making cliques in community power structures', *Amer. J. of Sociol.*, vol. 64, pp. 299–310.

MINISTRY OF TRANSPORT (1964), *Road Pricing: The Economic and Technical Possibilities*, HMSO.

MUMFORD, L. (1961), *The City in History*, Secker & Warburg.

MUSGRAVE, R. A. (1959), *The Theory of Public Finance*, McGraw-Hill.

NEWTON, K. (1969), 'City politics in Britain and the United States', *Pol. Studies*, vol. 17, pp. 208–18.

PAHL, R. E. (1966), 'The rural–urban continuum', *Sociologia Ruralis*, vol. 6, pp. 5–23.

PAHL, R. E. (1969), 'Urban social theory and research', *Environment and Planning*, vol. 1, pp. 143–53.

PAHL, R. E. (1970a), *Patterns of Urban Life*, Longman.

PAHL, R. E. (1970b), *Whose City?*, Longman.

PAHL, R. E. (1971), 'Poverty and the urban system', in M. Chisholm and G. Manners (eds), *Spatial Policy Problems of the British Economy*, Cambridge University Press.

PARRIS, J. H. (1970), 'Congress rejects the President's urban department', in F. N. Cleaveland *et al.* (1969), *Congress and Urban Problems*, Brookings Institution.

PEATTIE, L. (1968), 'Reflections on advocacy planning', *J. of the Amer. Inst. of Planners*, vol. 34, pp. 80–88.

PERLOFF, H. S., and WINGO, L. (eds.) (1968), *Issues in Urban Economics*, Johns Hopkins.

PERROUX, F. (1950), 'Economic space, theory and applications', *Q. J. of Econ.*, vol. 64, pp. 89–104.

PIRENNE, H. (1925), *Medieval Cities*, Doubleday Anchor Books, 1956.

POLSBY, N. (1959), 'The sociology of community power: a reassessment', *Social Forces*, vol. 37, pp. 232–36.

PREST, A. R., and TURVEY, R. (1966), 'Cost benefit analysis: a survey', *Econ. J.*, vol. 75, pp. 683–735.

REDCLIFFE-MAUD (1969), *Royal Commission on Local Government in England*, 3 volumes, cmnd. 4040, HMSO.

REDFIELD, R. (1941), *The Folk Culture of Yucatan*, University of Chicago Press.

REIN, M. (1969), 'Social planning: the search for legitimacy', *J. of the Amer. Inst. of Planners*, vol. 35, pp. 233–43.

REISSMAN, L. (1964), *The Urban Process*, Free Press.

REITH (1964), *New Towns Committee, Final Report*, cmnd. 6876, HMSO.

RICHARDSON, H. W. (1969), *Regional Economics*, Weidenfeld & Nicholson.

RICHARDSON, H. W. (1971), *Urban Economics*, Penguin Books.

ROBSON, B. (1969), *Urban Analysis*, Cambridge University Press.

ROTHENBERG, J. (1967), *Economic Evaluation of Urban Renewal*, Brookings Institution.

ROTHSCHILD, K. W. (1971), *Power in Economics*, Penguin Books.

ROWNTREE, B. S. (1901), *Poverty: A Study of Town Life*, Nelson.

ROWNTREE, B. S. (1942), *Poverty and Progress*, Longmans.

SALISBURY, R. H. (1964), 'Urban politics: the new convergence of power', *J. of Pol.*, vol. 26, pp. 775–97.

SCHULZE, R. O. (1958), 'The role of economic dominants in community power structure', *Amer. Sociol. Rev.*, vol. 23, pp. 3–9.

SCHULZE, C. L. (1968), *The Politics and Economics of Public Spending*, Brookings Institution.

SCOTT, M. (1969), *American City Planning*, University of California Press.

SEELEY, J. R. (1959), 'The slum: its nature, use and users', *J. of the Amer. Inst. of Planners*, vol. 35, pp. 7–14.

SHARRARD, T. D. (ed.) (1968), *Social Welfare and Urban Problems*, Columbia University Press.

SHAW, C. (1929), *Juvenile Delinquency in Urban Areas*, Chicago University Press.

SHEVKY, E., and BELL, W. (1955), *Social Area Analysis: Theory, Illustrative Application and Computational Procedure*, University of California Press.

SHEVKY, E., and WILLIAMS, M. (1949), *The Social Areas of Los Angeles: Analysis and Typology*, University of California Press.

SJOBERG, G. (1960), *The Pre-Industrial City*, Free Press.

SKEFFINGTON (1969), *People and Planning, Report of the Committee on Public Participation in Planning*, HMSO.

SMALLWOOD, F. (1965), *Greater London: the Politics of Metropolitan Reform*, Bobbs-Merrill.

SOMMER, R. (1969), *Personal Space: The Behavioural Basis of Design*, Prentice-Hall.

SOUTH-EAST JOINT PLANNING TEAM (1971), *Strategic Plan for the South-East, Studies Volume* 4, HMSO.

STACEY, M. (1969), 'The myth of community studies', *Brit. J. of Sociol.*, vol. 20, pp. 134–46.

TAUEBER, K. E., and TAUEBER, A. F. (1965), *Negroes in Cities: Residential Segregation and Neighbourhood Changes*, Aldine.

THRASHER, F. (1927), *The Gang*, University of Chicago Press.

TIEBOUT, C. M. (1956), 'A pure theory of local expenditures', *J. of Pol. Econ.*, vol. 64, pp. 416–24.

TÖNNIES, F. (1877), *Community and Association*, translated and edited by C. P. Loomis, Routledge & Kegan Paul, 1955.

TOWNROE, P. M. (1969), 'Locational choice and the individual firm', *Regional Studies*, vol. 3, pp. 15–24.

TOWNROE, P. M. (1971), *Industrial Location Decisions: A Study in Management Behaviour*, Center for Urban and Regional Studies, University of Brimingham.

VICKREY, W. S. (1963), 'General and specific financing of urban services', in H. G. Schaller (ed.), *Public Expenditure Decisions in the Urban Community*, Johns Hopkins Press.

WEBBER, M. M. (1963), 'Order in diversity, community without propinquity', in L. Wingo (ed.), *Cities and Space*, Johns Hopkins.

WEBBER, M. M. (1964), 'The urban place and the nonplace urban realm', in M. M. Webber *et al.*, *Explorations into Urban Structure*, Pennsylvania University Press.

WEBBER, M. M. (1969), 'Planning in an environment of change', *Town Planning Rev.*, vol. 39, pp. 181–95 and 277–95.

WEBER, M. (1921), *The City*, translated and edited by D. Martindale and G. Neuwirth, Free Press, 1958.

WEBER, M. (1922), *The Theory of Social and Economic Organization* T. Parsons (ed.), Free Press, 1966.

WEISS, R. S., and REIN, M. (1969), 'Problems of evaluating broad aim programmes', *Annals of the Amer. Acad. of Pol. Sci.*, vol. 385, pp. 133–42.

WHEATLEY (1969), *Report on the Royal Commission on Local Government in Scotland*, cmnd no. 4150 HMSO.

WHITE, M., and WHITE, L. (1964), *The Intellectual versus the City*, Joint Center for Urban Studies, Harvard University and MIT Press.

WILLIS, M. (1969), 'Sociological aspects of urban structure', *Town Planning Rev.*, vol. 39, pp. 296–306.

WILSON, J. Q. (1968), *City Politics and Public Policy*, Wiley.

WINGO, L. (1961), *Transportation and Urban Land*, Washington, Resources for the Future.

WIRTH, L. (1928), *The Ghetto*, University of Chicago Press.

WIRTH, L. (1938), 'Urbanism as a way of life', *Amer. J. of Sociol.*, vol. 44, pp. 1–24.

WOOD, R. C. (1959), 'A division of powers in metropolitan areas', in A. Maas (ed.), *Area and Power*, Free Press.

YOUNG, M., and WILLMOTT, P. (1957), *Family and Kinship in East London*, Routledge & Kegan Paul, Penguin Books.

Part One
Perspectives

One of the main themes running through the introduction to this
reader is that of anti-urbanism – the unwillingness of both social
scientists and planners to concern themselves explicitly with the
problems of cities. Glass (Reading 1) traces the history of this
bias in the British context, whilst Delafons (Reading 2) provides
an historical perspective to the growth of intervention in the
American urban system, raising some of the same issues
concerning attitudes to urban planning. Coming closer to the
present day, Pahl's essay (Reading 3) is of interest in a number
of ways. Not only does it raise some of the questions which are
central to this reader – for example the relationship between
spatial and social planning – but it does so through a review of
the relevance of a major American contribution – Gans' *People
and Plans* – to the British urban context. Indeed perhaps the main
point of this reading is that it points out both the benefits and
dangers in comparing British and American experience. The
excerpt from Burkhead and Campbell's essay (Reading 4)
discusses the future direction of American urban policy within a
context which includes social objectives and political realities as
well as economic analysis.

1 R. Glass

Anti-Urbanism

Excerpt from the Introduction to 'Urban sociology in Great Britain:
a trend report and annotated bibliography', *Current Sociology*, vol. 4,
1955 pp. 5–19, reprinted in R. E. Pahl (ed.), *Readings in Urban Sociology*,
Pergamon Press, 1968, pp. 63–73.

[. . .] British anti-urbanism has a long history. A large anthology
could be devoted to writings on this subject, and an extensive
treatise to comment and explanation. When we read the history
of Roman Britain and that of Victorian England, we find that
during the centuries the attitude of Britons towards the town has
hardly changed. Collingwood and Myres (1936) writing of the
first to fourth centuries, describe the contrast between the
Graeco-Roman and the British concept of the town.

Deep in the mind of every Roman, as in the mind of every Greek, was
the unquestioned conviction which Aristotle put into words: that what
raised man above the level of barbarism, in which he was a merely
economic being, and enabled him to develop the higher faculties which
in the barbarian are only latent, to live well instead of merely living,
was his membership of an actual, physical city. Man's body and animal
existence might be satisfied by the country; his spiritual needs could
only be satisfied by the town (p. 186).

But 'for the northern peoples, public life needs no town. Its
elements already exist in every man's household; and its higher
forms crystallize into shape round a tree or a stone where men
meet together, and culminate in the court of a king who lives
nomadically from manor to manor'. Northern men were 'con-
ceiving the towns as a mere economic fact, a place where man only
makes a livelihood and finding room for the development of his
higher faculties only in the country' (p. 187). Already by the third
century it was evident that 'the first attempt to romanize British
life, by imposing upon it the civilization of the town, had failed.
It was when its failure was most complete that the second attempt,
based on the spontaneous development of the country house,
began to display its most brilliant successes' (p. 207).

During the new urban colonization of the nineteenth century,
there was the same failure to accept the concept of urban civilization, as summed up brilliantly by G. M. Young (1936).

In correspondence with its traditional structure, the traditional culture and morality of England were based on the patriarchal village family of all degrees: the father worked, the mother saw to the house, the food and the clothes; from the parents the children learnt the crafts and industries necessary for their livelihood, and on Sundays they went together, great and small, to worship in the village church. To this picture sentiment clung. . . . It inspired our poetry; it controlled our art; for long it obstructed, perhaps it still obstructs, the formation of a true philosophy of urban life (pp. 21–2).

Even now this anti-urbanism is unabated; indeed, it gained new impetus during the nineteenth century. The rising urban middle class fused with the landed gentry and aristocracy and emulated their modes of living. And for the maintenance of the balance of power in society this fusion was all to the good. For that reason it was welcomed by Escott, that shrewd observer of the Victorian scene. 'The fact that the great country landlord is also, in many cases, the great proprietor of mines and factories, is at once a guarantee, and a sign of the fusion between the different elements of English life, and the diverse sources of our national power' (1885, p. 79). And again: 'There are typical country gentlemen in the House of Commons and in society, but the country interest is no longer the sworn enemy of the urban interest. Our territorial nobles, our squires, our rural landlords great and small, have become commercial potentates; our merchant princes have become country gentlemen. The possession of land is the guarantee of respectability, and the love of respectability and land is inveterate in our race' (p. 315).

Not all, of course, regarded the fact that the upper classes were mere parasites in the towns with approval and equanimity. Should they be allowed to abandon their own creations – these new 'whirlpools' and 'monster clots of humanity', where 'the working man is pacing wearily the low, dim, swampy habitation good enough for the creation of all wealth?'[1] Should they not admit their responsibility for the sufferings of the urban poor who had made them rich, instead of letting children with 'their grandfathers or grandmothers huddle and die in the same miserable dustbins?'[2] Several decades before Escott's hey-day, such views were frequently expressed with differing degrees of indignation, for instance, by Dr Kay in 1832, in reporting on his investigations in Manchester.

1. See Jones (1851, p. 242).
2. See Hollingshead (1861, pp. 72–3).

That the evils of poverty and pestilence among the working classes of the close alleys, the crowded courts, the overpeopled habitations of wretchedness, where pauperism and disease congregate round the source of social discontent and political disorder in the centre of our large towns . . . that these evils should have been overlooked by the aristocracy of the country, cannot excite surprise. Very few of their order reside in, or near, our large provincial towns. . . . Their parks are not often traversed by those who are capable of being the exponents of the evils endured by the working classes of large towns, and the hoarse voice of popular discontent disturbs not the Arcadian stillness of the scene. . . . (p. 8).

Again, a contributor to the *Quarterly Review*, in commenting on the social protest literature, made a rather moderate complaint. There were many, he said,

who withhold the co-operation which we might expect from their humanity, and which their wealth and intelligence would render highly important and efficient. Many of the wealthier classes treat their periodical visits to London as a mere episode in their existence, and regard their country homes as the allotted scene of their duties (1855).

The country house certainly remained the symbol of social success, 'an important point of convergence between society and politics', the centre of the cultural life of a carefully assembled elite, though not of a closed clique. 'It was said by Moore, the poet, that there was no receipt for taming a radical like an invitation to Bowood' (1885, pp. 341–2). In most parts of Britain, the town was but a station on the journey to social status symbolized by the country seat.[3] It was not, as in other societies, the home of reason, intellect and a symbol of civic pride, but merely a place of new resources for the impoverished landed upper classes, and one where manufacturers and merchants could make money to buy their tickets of admission into the polite circle of the shires. And if the peerage and squirearchy were inaccessible, there were still their many imitations all down the social scale: those who could not reach the manor house could always retreat to the stronghold of a suburban villa, or at least to a semi-detached, jerry-built, mock-Tudor *Mon-repos*.

Retreat appeared certainly to be advisable. Those who left the towns went in search of safety as much as for the sake of social advancement, though their exodus brought to the towns themselves increasing misery and accelerated decay. Throughout the

3. There are, of course, exceptions – in Scotland, for example – which it would be well worth while to study closely.

nineteenth century, the towns, the domain of the new industrial might, while growing in confusion, become more hideous and more unhealthy – physically and socially. Above all, they represented a formidable threat to the established social order: the more the towns were deserted by the upper and middle classes, the more plainly were they also the barracks of a vast working class whose lessons in the power of combination had already begun, and whose sporadic riots were portents of latent insurrection. The industrial town was thus identified with the working class: it was feared so strongly because the working class was so frightening. This was the persistent theme of Victorian literature as of Victorian movements for social reform. Superimposed upon a tradition according to which the individual home – humble or distinguished – is the castle, the country seat the symbol of social status, the countryside – idealized though occasionally real – the inspiration for emotion and the arts, and the town a mere place for earning money, the memory of this fear has continued to be a reason for British animosity against urbanism.

The Victorians expressed their anxiety in unmistakable terms. Cooke Taylor in his *Notes of a Tour in the Manufacturing Districts of Lancashire* in 1842 had this to say of Manchester:

As a stranger passes through the masses of human beings which have been accumulated round the mills and print-works in this and the neighbouring towns, he cannot contemplate those 'crowded hives' without feelings of anxiety and apprehension almost amounting to dismay. The population . . . is hourly increasing in breadth and strength. It is an aggregate of masses, our conceptions of which clothe themselves in terms that express something portentous and fearful. We speak of them . . . as of the slow rising and gradual swelling of an ocean which must, at some future and no distant time, bear all the elements of society aloft upon its bosom, and float them – heaven knows whither. There are mighty energies slumbering in those masses (p. 6).

Over sixty years later, Masterman (1904), writing on the growth of cities, used similar expressions.

To some observers the change excites only a lament over a past that is for ever gone. They mourn the vanishing of a vigorous jolly life, the songs of the village alehouse, existence encompassed by natural things and the memories of the dead – the secure and confident life of 'Merrie England'. To others, again, the change is one charged with a menace to the future. They dread the fermenting, in the populous cities, of some new, all-powerful explosive, destined one day to shatter into ruin all their desirable social order. In these massed millions of an obscure life, but dimly understood and ever increasing in magnitude, they behold a danger to security and all pleasant things (p. 61).

Throughout the nineteenth century, this apparent danger was intensified not only by the flight from the cities, but also by the increasing separation of the social classes within cities. The middle and upper classes who did not leave the towns altogether, at least locked themselves up in separate quarters of their own. By doing so, they not only accentuated the actual social cleavages, but also their own fear of the other 'nation': they were left with a distorted image of the poor. It was Cooke Taylor again who saw these implications of class segregation quite early and very clearly. 'Another evil of fearful magnitude arises from this separation of Manchester into districts in which relative poverty and wealth form the demarcation of the frontiers. The rich lose sight of the poor, or only recognize them when attention is forced to their existence by their appearance as vagrants, mendicants, or delinquents' (1842, p. 14).

Though the fear of the working class persisted, it became less acute during the last two decades of the nineteenth century. By that time, in some quarters at least, imagination was already dulled: there had been so many false alarms. The heterogeneity of the British working class was discovered and encouraged. 'This diversity of thought, belief, and aim among the toilers of England is at once the consequence and the cause of exceptional national advantages.' Thus Escott could say: 'We have faith in the good sense, the good feeling, and the political docility of the English working man' (1885, pp. 79–80 and 130).

The chain reaction of social imitation, moreover, had already started. The working classes themselves began to join the exodus from the cities, partly out of choice, and partly because they were compelled to do so as their homes crumbled around them and their standards rose. Suburbia tamed their radicalism. When Masterman in 1909 asked why London, unlike other European capitals, had not produced any revolutionary programmes, he saw a partial answer, at least, 'hidden in these strings and congestions of little comfortable two-storeyed red and grey cottages . . . proclaiming with their cleanliness and tiny gardens and modest air of comfort a working population prosperous and content' (p. 100). And while Masterman himself realized that his spectacles were perhaps too rosy and too much focused on London as compared with the industrial north – he also felt it still necessary to say that '"poverty" is the foundation of the present industrial order' – he had nevertheless quite correctly recognized a new trend.

It is one which the utopians and community reformers of the nineteenth century would regard with mixed feelings. Though their dreams have not been realized, their ideas – modified and distorted in compromise – have gained belated importance. The actual flight from the cities was and is not as complete nor as radical as they would have wished, for on such a scale it is impracticable. Ideologically, however, the flight goes on all around us: all strata of society take an active part in it, and since the turn of the century none of them has spoken plainly against it.

Robert Owen, James Silk Buckingham, J. Minter Morgan, the Reverend Henry Solly, William Morris and Ebenezer Howard had all felt the menace of the towns. And so had the founders of model communities – of Saltaire, Bournville and Port Sunlight, to name only the most prominent ones, apart from the creations of the utopians themselves. They all thought, like Solly, that 'the remedy, unquestionably, seems to be to turn back the tide from the town to the country by finding these folks [the working classes] employment, profitable to themselves and the community, where they can be decently housed and fairly well remunerated' (1884, pp. 8–9) – and where they could, moreover, be under the close supervision of a paternalistic employer. Though these reformers believed that 'certainly the reluctance of debased, or spirit-broken, hapless victims of an un-christian civilization to exchange darkness for light, will have to be reckoned with' (p. 7), they all had an indomitable confidence in the influence of environment on human character. Robert Owen, in writing on the New Lanark Establishment, predicted that, if its principles were 'generally adopted, the consequences will be, that not only our manufacturing but our entire population will gradually change its character' (1812, p. 22). And J. Minter Morgan (1850), in advocating *The Christian Commonwealth*, expressed surprise because 'no modern Government seems to have perceived that men are as clay in the potter's hand' (p. 9). These schemes, the 'New Institution', model towns, Christian colonies, industrial villages and garden cities, were all supposed to combine the best of both worlds – the past and the present, individualism and socialism, town and country. In fact, they were based on unhistorical fiction, and likely to combine the worst of both worlds, being neither. They were certainly regarded as the antidote to harsh social change, as 'a peaceful path to real reform'.

Another movement at the end of the century – that of the university settlements – had the object of combining 'the latent power in the masses' with 'the latent knowledge and the latent ability in the men and women of culture' (Knapp, 1895, p. 15). It was the dominant idea of the 'Oxford settlers' in the East End 'to give the poorest and most densely populated working-class districts the benefit of a resident gentry such as, in the clergyman or the squire, is generally commanded in rural parishes'. While the authors of the utopias and community experiments had advocated the dispersal of working men to model villages under the aegis of their 'masters' as a means of dispelling the danger of working-class combination, the new 'squires of the East End' – more realistically – were trying to meet the same danger by the dispersal of the 'classes' among the masses in the cities. It was their ambition to become not only the social, but also the political leaders of the workers, and this was one which they have occasionally realized. They felt, as Canon Barnett said, in 1895, in his contribution to a symposium on the settlements in East London: 'The two nations, that of the rich and that of the poor, are very evident. Each grows strong, and the danger of collision is the great danger of our time' (Knapp, p. 55). This danger, as Sir John Gorst explained in his introduction to the same book, could be averted.

If the people had wise counsellors whom they trusted, the trade unionists would gladly accept their co-operation, and take their views into consideration, and the selfish agitators would probably disappear. Such a position University men and women settled amongst the poor have every prospect of attaining . . . they have better chances than their poorer neighbours of arriving at a right judgment; and their advice, when the confidence of the people is gained, is likely to be sought and followed (pp. 16, 17).

In the settlement movement, too – both in Britain and America – there was the same tendency as in the other schemes for community reform to break up the large urban aggregates, not only by the infiltration of the upper classes among the lower, but also by the return to the comfort of the face-to-face group – the neighbourhood. Chalmers' 'principle of locality', formulated in the 1820s, was once again accepted – his scheme for splitting up 'the vast overgrown city' into separate parochial units so as to prevent the people 'forming into a combined array of hostile feeling and prejudice' (1821–6, vol. 2, pp. 39–40).

These ideas again, though perhaps not of great practical success in the settlements themselves, have become influential in other fields. In current town planning – as shown, for instance, by the emphasis on decentralization, low density development, new towns and neighbourhood units – the thought of the utopias and their relatives, such as model communities and university settlements, is still very much alive. Indeed, the mixture is as before; only the container – the language – is different. And as there has been no new genesis of ideas, this is hardly surprising. Twentieth-century Britain has not only inherited but also re-experienced the distaste for towns.

In sociology, the influence of anti-urban thought has been less direct than in town planning. Here, it has had mainly negative results ever since the close association between sociology and social policy, which inevitably drew the attention of investigators to urban social ecology and pathology, was dissolved. Since that time, just as British society has rejected the town as an object of affection, British sociology has rejected the town as an object of inquiry. Nowadays, British sociologists are concerned with odd corners, but hardly with the general contours, of urbanism.

It is unlikely to be a mere coincidence that the small-scale phenomena with which sociologists are now frequently concerned are precisely those which play so large a part in the make-up of British anti-urbanism, and also in its schemes and literature. Sociologists certainly share the nostalgia for the intimate, apparently discrete groups – the family, kinship and neighbourhood. They, too, find comfort in the collection of bric-à-brac.

Such interests, however, exist in other countries as well. The absence of any general British texts on urbanism, on the other hand, is undoubtedly in keeping with the native dislike of towns. It remains a characteristic feature of British sociological literature, even if allowance is made – as it should be made – for the general scarcity of resources for social research in this country, and also for the shortage of adequate source material.[4] As in Britain, especially, the stereotype images of urbanism – picturing the city as a soulless, frigid, menacing aggregate of people and buildings – have been retained, the diversity of habitat and society hidden behind these images has rarely been explored. Instead,

4. The conclusions here reached were derived not only from a review of published studies, but also from information on current and projected research. However, in considering these conclusions, the lack of opportunities for social research in Britain – compared, for example, with the United States – should be kept in mind, and also the fact that basic data – historical, statistical and geographical – on urbanism in Britain are comparatively meagre and certainly rather scattered and patchy.

social investigators, conditioned by such fixed ideas, have turned their attention increasingly to the trivial aspects of urbanism. And so the stereotypes persist.

Recently, this vicious circle has become very noticeable. The few, isolated attempts to view the urban social scene in wide perspective belong to the Victorian and Edwardian eras. Since the thirties, especially, there has been a total lack of comparative studies devoted to the characteristics of towns, to their diversity and changes. Neither their demographic and historical traits, nor their class relations, economy and culture have been systematically investigated; these aspects have not even been broadly mapped out. Indeed, in Britain, the most urbanized country in the world, we know so little about our contemporary towns – largely, it appears, because here they have not yet been accepted.

References

CHALMERS, T. (1821–6), *The Christian and Civic Economy of Large Towns*, 3 volumes, Collins.

COLLINGWOOD, R. G., and MYRES, J. N. L. (1936), *Roman Britain and the English Settlements*, Clarendon Press.

ESCOTT, T. H. S. (1885), *England*, Chapman-Hall.

HOLLINGSHEAD, Y. S. (1861), *Ragged London of 1861*, Smith, Elder.

JONES, E. (1851), *Notes to the People*, vol. 1,

KAY, J. P. (1832), *The Moral and Physical Condition of the Working Classes Employed in the Cotton Manufacture in Manchester*, James Ridgway.

KNAPP, Y. M. (ed.) (1895), *The Universities and the Social Problem*, Rivington Percival.

MASTERMAN, C. F. (1904), *The English City*, Johnson.

MASTERMAN, C. F. (1909), *The Condition of England*, Methuen.

MORGAN, I. M. (1850), *The Christian Commonwealth*, Gilpin.

OWEN, R. (1812), *A Statement Regarding the New Lanark Establishment*, Moir

SOLLY, H. (1884), *Rehousing of the Industrial Classes*, Swann, Sonnenschein.

TAYLOR, C. (1842), Notes of a Tour in the Manufacturing Districts of Manchester, Duncan & Malcolm.

YOUNG, G. M. (1936), *Victorian England: Portrait of an Age*, Oxford University Press.

2 J. Delafons

Land Use Controls in the USA

J. Delafons, 'Context', in *Land Use Controls in the USA*, MIT Press, 1969, ch. 1, pp. 1–15.

The land and its development

Land has never been a scarce resource in America. Its great abundance has been a powerful influence on American attitudes toward the land, its development and attempts by government to control its use. The total area of the United States (excluding Hawaii and Alaska) is 1904 million acres. England and Wales, with a population about one quarter that of the United States, have a land area less than 2 per cent of this. In an early Congressional debate on public land policies in 1796, Gallatin remarked that 'If the cause of the happiness of this country was examined into, it would be found to arise as much from the great plenty of land in proportion to the inhabitants, which their citizens enjoyed, as from the wisdom of their political institutions.'

The whole population of the United States could be housed within view of the Pacific Ocean. All cities and villages occupy only ten million of the total 1904 million acres. Of course, the fact that there are thousands of square miles of undeveloped land in, say, Arizona or Wyoming does not help the people living in metropolitan Philadelphia or New York. The population density in New Jersey and Massachusetts is greater than in most European countries. Rhode Island is almost as densely populated as the Netherlands. But the lack of any urgent concern for preserving open land as such, which has always been a dominant objective of British planning policies, is very characteristic of American attitudes. The cities of Dallas and Fort Worth are about thirty miles apart. Dallas has about 650,000 inhabitants, Fort Worth about 380,000. In the past five years the town of Arlington midway between the two has grown from 8000 to over 40,000 and is still growing rapidly as the result of being selected by a group of New York developers for the site of Great Southwestern Industrial Estates, 'the largest planned industrial development in the world'. In England a similar situation would probably be met by a determined attempt to keep the three communities from growing into one, and to preserve some vestige of a green belt. But there is no such concern in America. The growth of Arlington is applauded. As a Fort Worth businessman remarked to me, 'Why try to stop it? In twenty minutes' drive in any direction I can be on a lake in my boat, fishing'.

But the problems of land-use planning do not diminish in relation to the quantity of land. They increase in relation to the amount of development, and the pace of development in America is fantastic. The editors of *Fortune* have calculated that 3000 acres a day are bulldozed for new development of all kinds. In England and Wales urban development takes about 30,000 acres a year. Housing production in America for the past five years has been running at the rate of about 1,300,000 units a year, of which the vast preponderance are single detached homes (and less than 2 per cent are public housing). Other types of development are on a proportionate scale. In Phoenix, Arizona, from 1950–57 over six million square feet of shopping centers were built; four million square feet are under construction and ten million are in the planning stage.

Between 1950 and 1960 the population of the United States increased by over twenty-eight million. Bureau of Census projections for 1980 range from 230 million to 272 million, an increase over 1960 of at least fifty million and possibly nearly 100 million. At current densities the urban population of 1980 will absorb at least twice the amount of land used today. In many areas this growth can be absorbed without encroaching too noticeably on the surrounding wilderness of land. But in some regions open space has been annihilated. The Los Angeles urban area is already fifty miles wide and twenty-six miles long. By 1975 it may well have linked up the chain of settlements from Santa Barbara on the north to San Diego on the Mexican frontier, a distance equal to that from London to Manchester. Los Angeles County has grown from 3500 persons in 1850 to over four million in 1950, and incredibly, to over six million in 1960. Similarly, the New York conurbation is already 110 miles long, and by 1975 the east coast from Boston to Washington, a distance of over 450 miles, will probably form a single urban mass. As anyone knows who has driven route US 1 between these two cities, the effect is achieved already by the unbroken string of roadside development. This is the 'linear city' which some see as the American norm for the future, and which has been christened Megalopolis.

The attitude to growth

Despite this rampant growth, it is very rare in America to encounter any antipathy to new development. Quite the opposite is
usually the case. We were in west Texas when the first returns of
the 1960 census were released. There was jubilation among communities that had grown, and indignation and despondency
among those that had remained static or declined. In Sweetwater,
the city council held an emergency session to pass a 'motion of
protest' at the fact that their population had barely shifted in the
past decade.

There is general sympathy in America for the man who builds
something, and especially for the man who builds a business. The
bigger the building the more genuine the admiration, but even the
most precarious enterprise in the most makeshift accommodation
is accepted in a generous spirit, and be the advertisements ever so
blatant (they get larger as the success of the enterprise diminishes)
there is little urge to pull them down. As Professor Brogan has
observed, the average American is not the sucker who buys
wooden nutmegs but the guy who sells them.

Along with this acceptance of growth goes a thriving speculation in land. In 1959 a book with the engaging title *How I Turned
a Thousand Dollars into a Million in Real Estate – in My Spare
Time* remained high on *The New York Times* bestseller list for
thirty-eight weeks. Popular magazines advertise the attraction of
investment (on hire purchase principles) in Florida real estate –
'*not* under water' runs a reassuring phrase in the blurb. Quick
fortunes are, in fact, still made in the land market. Land in
Houston that was bought ten years ago for $400 an acre can be
sold today for $4000 or, in some parts of the city, for $40,000.
Large landholders are still powerful in this part of the country.
One of Houston's pioneer families still owns a 60,000-acre ranch
which now lies within the city limits and is being released in calculated amounts for development. Speculation in land has been a
tradition in America and was in fact a major motivating force in
opening the West. It was not the prerogative of the rich (none of
the great American fortunes derived from real estate) but in an
undeveloped country was available to all comers. This speculative
bent still colors American attitudes toward the land and is a factor
to be reckoned with in attempting to control its use.

Prairie psychology

The general unconcern for the rate at which land is consumed by new development, born of the confidence that the supply is virtually unlimited, has been called the 'prairie psychology'. And it is not altogether fanciful to see a persistence of the log-cabin tradition in the overwhelming American preference for the detached one-story house on a large plot. The customs and attitudes of the frontier still flourish. Even thirty miles outside of Boston, small townships have all the boisterous determination to expand and the indifference to the look of things that might characterize a pioneer settlement. New businesses are welcomed, and the developer barely bothers to clear the brushwood from the site before throwing up a flimsy shelter for his trade. Within a few years it will be replaced by something more substantial, if not more permanent, or it will be pushed aside by a competitor. One of the most marked characteristics of American development is its impermanence. Even settlements which have been staging posts on major routes west for a hundred years or more show no signs of historical continuity. The gas stations, motels, and other buildings on Main Street could have been (and probably were) built within the last ten years or less. Only in towns which have outlived their original purpose – like Tombstone, Arizona, 'the town too tough to die' – does the physical appearance of the frontier remain. But the attitudes of a rapidly developing community in virgin territory still prevail. Except in the old communities on the Atlantic seaboard, an aggressive individualism remains a lively reminder that people came to America as a land of opportunity. There is a real antagonism toward anyone who presumes to limit a man's right to do as he pleases with his own property. Between 1860 and 1900, 14 million immigrants entered America; between 1900 and 1940 there were 19 million. One of the fascinations of America is to see what men made of this huge country in a hundred years. The run-down, blighted neighborhoods which cover the older cities are in fact the residue of the first wave of urban settlement in the New World.

The new mobility

The factor which has changed the whole context of development within a generation is, of course, the automobile. There are now 65 million cars on American roads. The forecast is two more cars for every three new Americans. By 1975 there will be over 100 million cars.

The result has been a revolution in the pattern of development. The location of new industry, homes, and shopping centers is no longer dependent on predictable or traditional requirements. Anything can locate anywhere, since the automobile provides the necessary link. Some new location factors are beginning to emerge, but they are not necessarily a reflection of desirable land use. The market has decided that major street intersections are the best place for shopping centers, and city planners replace the strip commercial zoning of an earlier era with an equal superfluity of commercial zones at every intersection, which from the traffic flow and safety aspects seems the worst possible location. Accessibility, which might have imposed restraint on strip development, is no longer an important factor, and nothing is more typical of the American urban scene than the marginal commercial enterprises that string out for ten or twenty miles along the approaches to major cities.

Similarly, housing need not be adjacent to shopping or community facilities. The 1960 Parade of Homes sponsored by the homebuilders of Houston and various utility companies and magazines (and liberally blessed by civic leaders) chose a site ten miles out of downtown Houston on a barren plain, miles from any similar development, where the only landscape feature was a flood protection ditch.

The American's idea of recreation also revolves around the car. Hunting is far more typical than hiking (despite a handful of honorable exceptions like the Appalachian Trail Club); two-thirds of all the deer taken are shot within half a mile of a main road. When the American family goes out for the day, it loads up the station wagon with fishing gear, portable barbecue, icebox, water skis, and perhaps a speed boat on a trailer, and heads at sixty miles an hour to the nearest State Park or National Forest. And these are surprisingly generous and accessible. Nearly 20 per cent of California is reserved for state or national parks and forests. There are almost no neighborhood parks in which to take the dog for a walk or knock a ball about, but once in the car the most constricted urbanite is within relatively easy reach of the great outdoors.

A barrier of distrust

Another characteristic American attitude that exercises a fundamental influence on the methods and scope of land-use control, as on other types of governmental authority, is distrust of politicians.

Americans expect corruption in government and to a remarkable degree accept it. When a recent Chicago police scandal broke (police patrol cars were being used to cart off the loot from burglarized premises), a newspaper editorial exclaimed, 'there is a limit to the amount of corruption that decent citizens will tolerate'. In a seminar at the Harvard Graduate School of Public Administration, the professor asserted flatly that government without corruption ('gravy') is impossible. Professor H. J. Morgenthau, writing in *The New York Times* on the payola quiz scandal, remarked that 'Pecuniary corruption in the political and commercial spheres must be expected. For since the ultimate value of these fields is power, and wealth is a source of power, the possibility of pecuniary corruption is built into these spheres.' Since the values conferred or denied by land-use controls are great, their administration affords exceptional opportunities for graft and by the same token exposes them to exceptionally strong pressures. The result, in America, has been a determination to eliminate the scope for discretion in land-use controls by formalizing them in a set of standard regulations and by laying down in advance the conditions under which, if at all, change may be allowed.

Free enterprise

It is at least a basic assumption, if not entirely a fact, that the American economic system – or, as the Chambers of Commerce prefer, the American way of life – is founded on unwavering adherence to the tenets of the free market and the private enterprise system. Although the massive intervention by the federal government in, for example, agriculture or house purchase finance shows that the system is less free and less enterprising than it is usually represented, there is in fact a very strong prejudice against government control over any aspect of the economy. In matters of land planning it is generally assumed that land uses are most efficiently organized if the decisions are made by the market and the objective of control under these circumstances is simply to moderate the maladjustments of the process. The reasons why, in the face of this antipathy, land-use controls have gained the hold they have in America and the motives and objectives of American land-use planning are considered elsewhere. It is sufficient at this stage to note the dominance of this economic credo, and to observe that one important result is that American planners are much more diffident about interfering with the process of private development and the choices made by the market mechanism than British planners have been.

Agriculture

No one in America feels any great concern for protecting agricultural land from urban development. The government's problem has been to hold down farm production. For twenty-five years farmers have been subject to restrictions on acreage but have been protected by a massive price support system which is currently costing the government 9 billion dollars. The alternative policy now favored is to extend greatly the land retirement program which dates back to 1933. Under this system the government 'rents' land from farmers for five- to ten-year periods and places it in a conservation reserve or 'soil bank'. From 1956–59, some 22–500,000 acres were removed from production by this method. The aim is to adjust supply more nearly to demand, and remove the need for government storage, quotas or price support except when sudden collapse threatens. Agricultural economists stress that to be really effective the soil bank must attract highly productive farms and not merely the marginal or inefficient ones.

If the farmer can sell his land to a builder, that is so many acres less to burden the soil bank. In the New England region, despite the vast amount of development in the past ten years, the amount of unused land has actually increased. The farmer finds it more profitable to sell out to speculators and retire to Florida or move west to the farm belt; the land remains idle until suburbanization catches up with it.

In a few areas, where specialist crops are grown and the productive value of land is very high, there have been attempts to protect it by adapting urban land-use controls to the needs of the agricultural community.

Local government

Planning and land-use control are carried out by municipalities, incorporated units of local government. There were 3164 municipalities in the United States in 1952. Other powers of local government are divided among the municipalities and a bewildering array of unincorporated units, school districts, and special districts – *ad hoc* authorities, usually serving one purpose (fire protection, drainage, soil conservation, etc.).

None of the 168 standard metropolitan areas is governed by a single, all-purpose authority. In 1900 there were 1521 cities in these areas; by 1950, 1354 new cities had been created, and half of these were in only sixteen areas. The five largest metropolitan areas include 748 municipalities. The total number of local government units in these five areas is even more bewildering (see Table 1):

Table 1 **Total number of local government units in the five largest metropolitan areas**

New York	1071
Chicago	960
Philadelphia	702
Pittsburgh	616
St Louis	420

The next six areas in size have around 300 authorities apiece.

There are no effective planning authorities covering more than one local government unit; each municipality is its own planning agency, and the power of land-use control is one activity which is never relinquished to another authority. Inevitably it is made to serve essentially local interests, and, by very general admission, private interests are more likely to be observed than any conscious public objective. The reasons for this and the relationship between public and private interests are discussed elsewhere.

Outside the incorporated areas, the counties may exercise similar planning powers to those of the cities. This is a comparatively recent development; ten years ago only a handful of states granted zoning and subdivision control powers to the counties; now all states but one have granted powers to at least some of their counties. This is important since, despite the flood of incorporations, the population of unincorporated parts of the standard metropolitan areas has increased much more rapidly than that of incorporated areas. A few of the more urban counties have developed the controls available to the cities, and in a very few cases joint city-county regulations have been adopted. But the county planning function does not survive incorporation, and all powers of land-use control pass to the municipality whether its population is 50,000 or 500.

Whatever the effect of this multiplicity of units on the efficiency and economy of local government and its services (many cities contract with the county for all their services, simply retaining for themselves the right to say yes or no – particularly in matters of land use), the effect is to render impossible any consistent or widely based planning policies for the metropolitan area.

There are a handful of 'Regional Planning Authorities' of an advisory character set up on an *ad hoc* basis by state legislatures, but none have any powers of control and their influence seems to be minimal. In the 1930s an attempt was made to build up state planning agencies but they disintegrated in nearly every state during the war years. More recently they have been revived as part of the federal government's policy for administering its grants in aid for planning by smaller communities, but they exert little authority and only one or two engage in state-wide planning studies.[1]

Finally, the role of the federal government in land-use planning is at the present time insignificant and intentionally so. During the New Deal the National Resources Planning Board carried out a major program of research which demonstrated the inadequacy of traditional land-use controls and the need for plans and policies to guide the use of available controls. But the antagonism to any suggestion of federal dominance in what is regarded as essentially a local concern has defeated more recent legislative attempts to establish a 'Department of Urbiculture' that would give Cabinet status to urban affairs.[2] Even where the federal government under its '701 program' contributes half the cost of preparing master plans for smaller communities (under 25,000 population) administration of the program is left to the state planning agencies and no requirements are laid down even for the contents or character of such a plan. Similarly, federal officials emphasize that the urban renewal program (in which the federal government pays two-thirds of the net cost of the project) is a 'local program locally administered'. In fact the federal agency plays an important part in the program, but it is true that the important decisions are left to the local authority, and the initiative rests entirely with them. The Housing and Home Finance Agency exercises far more influence over the institutions of private enterprise (the mortgage market and the homebuilding industry) than it does over local governments.

1. There has since been a revival of interest in the state governments as planning agencies, and the Department of Housing and Urban Development is encouraging the formation of metropolitan planning agencies.
2. The Department of Housing and Urban Development, with Cabinet status, became the eleventh executive department of the United States Government on 9 September 1965.

Organization for planning

Although every municipality has the power to control land use and private development, the decision may be to do without it. There is no obligation to exercise control (unless the city wants to participate in the federal urban renewal program) and although most communities of any size have adopted a rudimentary zoning ordinance, the chances are that it will be thirty years or more out of date and be readily amended to admit any new tax-producing development. But even the rudiments are by no means universal. Of the 1378 cities of over 10,000 population listed in the *Municipal Year Book*, only 791 had comprehensive zoning ordinances in 1953. Subdivision control, which is regarded by many planning officials as a more effective control was used in only 509 of those cities. The total may well have increased since that date, but there are certainly many communities which get along without any public control over private land use.

The planning agency within the city government has traditionally been a city planning commission appointed by the mayor from among leading citizens, not themselves members of the council. The commission has usually been vested with power to advise in the planning and programming of public improvements, and responsibility for administering the subdivision regulations which usually allow little scope for discretion. The commission has generally also been charged with preparing a 'master plan', which is not so much a plan for land use as a broad picture of how the city might improve itself by a program of public works. The city council often reserves to itself the most influential function – that of approving changes in the zoning map, on which the planning commission might or might not be invited to comment. The planning commission has generally been expected and disposed to remain 'above politics'. Consequently it has never exerted much influence in city government or in major development decisions. More recently planning has begun to assume an important place in city management partly because of the need to control both public and private development, partly because it can serve a useful co-ordinating function, and partly because politicians saw in it a source of good publicity which they were reluctant to leave to the ineffective planning commission. It is very clear that many city planning departments, particularly those with a lavish budget and the glossiest publications, serve primarily as a public relations service for the city government – or, in the parlance, 'front men for the mayor'. Planning staffs are absorbed into the managerial hierarchy and the planning commission usually survives in an even more exiguous position than before. Its survival, even in this attenuated form, only serves to obscure the proper role of planning as an executive arm of government, and to blur the relationship between the planning function and political responsibility.

Finally, land-use control, like every other activity of government in America, has to stand the test of the Constitution as interpreted by the courts. Whereas in Britain land-use planning remains entirely within the control of the executive and legislature, in America the courts, not a Minister, are the final arbiters in disputed decisions. The courts will not substitute their judgment for that of the locally appointed body, provided that it has not acted unreasonably or gone beyond its acknowledged authority. But the American attorney is a resourceful character and the amount of litigation on planning decisions is formidable. Any student of the American system of land-use control can soon find himself sunk in a deluge of ingenious law journal articles from which there is no recovery.

The outer limits of control

A crucial difference between the American and British systems of land-use controls is that in America no compensation is payable to owners whose property loses value as the result of a planning decision.

In very brief outline, the British system confers compensation only where the land affected by the planning decision had development value before the present system of control was introduced.[3] If the land has acquired development value since then, no compensation is payable except where the decision cancels 'existing use' rights. If, however, the land has become 'incapable of reasonably beneficial use' as a result of a planning decision, then the owner can require the local authority to purchase the land. The compensation position in Britain and America is now

3. The system introduced in Britain in 1947 also provided that persons wishing to carry out development should purchase the development value of the land from the state by paying a 'development charge'. This attempt to recoup betterment to offset the cost of compensation was abandoned in 1952, but a similar charge was introduced by the Land Commission Act 1967. The position now is that the developer generally has to pay a betterment levy if he obtains planning permission to develop his land but he gets no compensation if he is refused permission (except in the cases already referred to).

somewhat similar, i.e. in general, no compensation for planning decisions. But whereas in Britain the introduction of the control system was accompanied by massive compensation (a fund of £300 million was established for the purpose), in America the system has never been accompanied by any provision for compensation. It is essential to understand the reasons for this, since the lack of power to pay compensation, and the absence of any 'once and for all' settlement on the lines of the British system, obviously curtails the scope of land-use control in America.

The originators of the zoning system in America had to decide on which of two quite distinct governmental powers these new controls should be based: eminent domain or the police power. If property rights were condemned under the power of eminent domain (compulsory acquisition), then compensation would have to be paid. If on the other hand these controls could be brought under the police power (the general residual power of government to pass laws in the interests of the general public health, safety, and welfare), then no compensation would be payable and the controls would be analogous to fire or structural regulations. Casting its shadow over this problem, and causing the lawyers involved in this long debate to move with extreme caution, has been the Fifth Amendment: 'No person . . . shall be deprived of life, liberty, or property, without due process of law; nor shall private property be taken for public use without just compensation.'

This was the key problem facing the Commission on the Height of Buildings which was set up in 1913 to advise the city of New York on the means of controlling private development. The commission's report is a basic document in the history of American planning. The choice facing the Commission was an extremely difficult one, but they had no doubt about the answer. In practical terms proceeding by the slow and cumbrous method of eminent domain was impossible, and though the limits of the police power in this field were almost uncharted, it was the only hope of securing simple and uniformly effective control. The Commission concluded:

It is theoretically conceivable that a general plan of building restriction and regulation might be entered upon by resort to the power of eminent domain, but, practically, such a resolution is out of the question. The expense and burden of condemnation proceedings and litigation in multitudinous cases would create a tax burden that would increase rather than compensate for the injury to property interests. Moreover, the kinds of regulation under consideration are not such as to justify individual compensation. While they restrict individual liberty to a certain extent, they do it in such a way as to conserve individual and public interests and rights. They subject the use of urban land to such restrictions as are appropriate and reasonable in the nature and history of this class of property.

This decision determined the direction and limits of planning controls in America. The controls had to be such as would not justify compensation to individual owners, and they must bear a clearly demonstrable relation to the public health, safety, or welfare. There was no knowing how the courts might interpret this relation, but it was clear that the controls could not extend very far beyond the basic objectives of separating out grossly incompatible uses and establishing minimum standards of development.

3 R. E. Pahl

Whose City?

R. E. Pahl, 'Whose city?', in *New Society*, January1969, reprinted in
Whose City? Longmans, 1970, ch. 12, pp. 201–208.

What is to become of the city? Intellectuals scorn the neatness and
order of skilled manual worker or lower-middle-class housing in
new towns or spec-built estates, and deplore huge, 'inhuman'
blocks of flats. But at the same time they feel angry or guilty
about overcrowding and poverty in Notting Hill or Sparkbrook.
They are not sure whether the car must adapt to the city or the
city to the car. Their attitude to the London motorway box seems
to depend more on whether it affects their local area or on whether
they have recently been ensnarled in crawling traffic for hours,
rather than on any clear vision of what the city might or should
be.

The attitudes of middle-class radicals to many other urban
problems are highly ambivalent. Commuting, urban renewal, the
location of the third London airport, urban poverty, mobility and
congestion are all irritatingly confused issues on which the progressive line is not at all clear. Attempts to stay in London, by
making such areas as Islington fashionable, are a potential source
of guilt ('taking away houses from those in greater need'). The
only comfort is·that those who have done up cottages in the
country are probably suffering from a similar sort of guilt.

There has been a recent spate of television programmes and
articles by various pundits giving 'personal views' about the
dreary creations of the planners and architects, particularly when
seen in contrast to the lively, human, squalor of the streets of
Soho and Chelsea or the excitement of the great mobile life of
California. There is a pathetic demand for a visionary, who can
explain in one Sunday supplement how we should all live; and
yet at the same time there is a sort of underlying resentment that
the richness, diversity, variety, etc., of 'real human life' should be
squashed into the moulds devised by planners who, by implication,
are all unimaginative technocrats. Planners are expected to make
our life 'better', but if they succeed they may be resented –

because people are thereby being deprived of the freedom to plan their lives for themselves.

It seems that we are as uncertain of the problems as we are of the solutions. We know that there are slums; we know that the population is increasing; we know that the basic physical infrastructure is ageing and will have to be renewed; we know that our urban roads are congested; and yet we don't know which aspect of these various issues is 'the real problem'. New towns and new cities can help siphon off young, skilled, energetic people from existing cities. But they are far from complete solutions, since it is those most in need of help who are left behind. When the transportation technocrat is not sure what to feed into his computer, and the playwrights' and novelists' visions don't go much farther than a few bustling streets in certain parts of London, maybe the third culture, sociology, will provide the answers?

Surely the sociologist can tell us what people will want – not only now, but in 1984, the year 2000, or whatever year it is to which we have to fix the long-term financial budgeting? But the sociologist wriggles. He argues that it is for him to analyse the implicit goals of different groups in society – how they conflict and what the unintended consequences of planning decisions might be – but not for him alone to prescribe these goals. He is a member of society as much as anyone else.

However, if pressed, the sociologist will say that physical arrangements have very little effect on social arrangements. Renewing the physical environment of the urban poor does not eliminate the causes of their poverty. The poverty is largely the result of the distribution of power in society and this distribution is preserved by powerful interest groups and finds expression in spatial and physical terms in the city. The elimination of poverty necessitates a voluntary abdication of some power by the affluent majority in favour of the poor minority.

Even though buildings and land use have very little effect on people's behaviour, this is not to say that the actual house that people live in is not very important. It is hardly an agent of social change, but it is still a much more important environment than the locality. People's *social world* is best conceived of as a social network of linkages, which is not necessarily based on locality.

However, physical planners have enough of the conventional wisdom to know that ultimately they must be concerned with social welfare in the broadest sense. Certainly, some might argue that planning is simply an end in itself rather than a means to an end. Neatness, tidiness, orderliness and planning in general may be defined as good, in some abstract sense, no matter what the people being planned may think. But the current vogue is 'participation': the Skeffington committee's report on public participation in planning has had wide publicity, and so even the most enthusiastic 'drains man' or rule-book backwoodsman is probably prepared to make some small gesture towards public participation.

I have been stimulated to consider these issues by reading *People and Plans*, a collection of essays on urban problems and solutions, by Herbert J. Gans. It seems to me that, particularly for us in Britain, Professor Gans's essays could not have been published at a more opportune time. As both a sociologist and a qualified planner Professor Gans has had a long and distinguished record of research, and his two books, *The Urban Villagers* (1962) and *The Levittowners* (1967) were valuable contributions to the ethnography of contemporary America. More recently he has been actively engaged in advising government committees on the nation's so-called 'urban' crisis. Few people are as well qualified, either here or in America, to discuss the relationship between people and plans.

Furthermore, Gans is prepared to forsake academic detachment and make clear suggestions on policy. He argues consistently that planning must be *user*-oriented – it is for people, not for planners; it ought to be *compensatory*, so that those who get the fewest rewards from the private sector ought to get most from the public sector; finally, it ought to be more concerned with the established needs of *today* rather than with the hypothetical needs of the future. The problems of urban slums are greater than the problems of the aesthetics of urban sprawl. He is more concerned with the *processes* than with the symptoms they create, and traces back the causes of urban poverty to the social, economic and political structure of the society.

There are some thirty or so essays collected in this book ranging from satirical or polemical pieces aimed at a popular audience, to summaries of the sociological literature on a topic prepared for planners or social workers, and to scholarly papers, such as his critique of 'Urbanism and suburbanism as ways of life'. It is hard to think of a better book to recommend to all the planners and architects who are increasingly wanting to know what the contribution of the sociologist to their field is or could be. There is much that is wise; it is cogently expressed and it provides a fine contribution to the sociology of planning in its widest sense. Nevertheless, the book ends on a deeply pessimistic note, as Gans doubts whether the war on poverty and segregation can be won and raises the question whether the new, affluent suburbia has been achieved at the cost of withholding opportunities from the poor and non-white.

One fears that some British planners may be acting out a script which was written in the United States in the 1950s and is now increasingly outdated. The fashion in America was then to concentrate on transportation facilities, and teams of transportation experts, with economists and operation researchers, programmed their computers with alternative simulation models: thus, given the simplifying restraints of the exercise, they were able to formulate a number of alternative schemes. It would be sad if a decade later some British planners are still expecting too much from this new technical expertise, while a large part of the American planning profession has moved on to a greater concern with *social* objectives and the most rational and effective way of achieving them.

Professor Gans describes these changes in his essays on the 'Sociology of city planning' and on the 'Goal-oriented approach to planning'. In an essay on 'Culture and class in the study of poverty', Gans attacks the notion that the poor are condemned to remain so, trapped in a culture of poverty.

If the culture of poverty is defined as those cultural patterns which keep people poor, it would be necessary to include in the term also the persisting cultural patterns among the affluent which, deliberately or not, keep their fellow citizens poor. When the concept of a culture of poverty is applied only to the poor, the onus for change falls too much on them, when, in reality, the prime obstacles to the elimination of poverty lie in the economic, political and social structure that operates to increase the wealth of the already affluent (1968).

It is at this point that the British planner may begin to assume that the discussion is no longer relevant to him.

This is the tragedy of the British situation: it is tragic for the people that the planner sees his job in such a limited way; and it is tragic, too, for the planner that his best efforts are frustrated by forces which he defines as being outside his dominion. Thus he may build houses, only to find that those for whom they were built cannot afford to live in them because wages locally are low (Manchester Corporation reported early in 1969 that this is the situation in its newest estate at Whitefield); or he may help to create jobs, only to find that he has condemned those who fill them to overcrowded housing because local land values are so high that housing is scarce.

However, we in Britain are fortunate in that we have the example of America to learn from. There, too ready an acceptance both of the most easily applicable techniques and of the values of the most powerful groups has led to the situation in which they have, for example, splendid freeways, which simply enable the middle class to ride past the poor more rapidly. Making physical changes without parallel changes in the social structure may serve to add to the problem by drawing sections of the population farther apart. Clearly no one wants British cities to be centres of poverty and racial intolerance. However, there may be some danger that if British planners feel that their main task is to concentrate on the future and to spend their time worrying about the provision of motorways and yachting marinas in 1991, they may take attention away from present problems and so, indirectly, help to make them worse.

Similarly, if they concern themselves with large areas, which have no elected representatives – such as regions – they can avoid facing local problems by claiming that they are not relevant at the larger level. Thus planning as an activity can continue indefinitely, without having to face the conflicting goals of the present at the scale on which people live. Method-oriented planners can easily lose sight of the goals, and the question which Gans poses in the American situation is equally relevant here. 'Who plans, with what ends and means, for what interest group?'

Yet Gans is one sociologist who cannot be criticized for being negative and for providing no positive suggestions. If only for his chapter on 'Planning for everyday life and problems of suburban and new town residents', any New Town social relations officer should have the book on his desk. It should be standard reading for all community activists from Glenrothes to Solent City.

The British situation is very different from that in America, but is nevertheless disturbing. Not only are planners coming increasingly under attack through the mass media at the national level but also they may feel threatened and insecure at the local level as their professional isolation is invaded by public participation. There may thus be a retreat to defending bureaucratic procedures at the very time that a more outward-looking concern with social processes and social problems, is needed.

The planners are being urged to devise means to achieve social goals, but neither they (nor the sociologists) can determine a community's goals. These goals may be explicit – an economic growth rate of 4 per cent, a modern nation-wide transport network, a minimum standard of living which is above the poverty line; or they may be implicit – more choice for the affluent sections of society, fewer constraints placed on the poorer sections and so on.

The will of the community is mediated through the political process, so that those with the most power set the goals, which makes the planner simply the tool of the elite. This is why, in America, the profession is becoming politicized. The progressives want social planning to reduce economic and racial inequality, the conservatives want to defend traditional physical planning and the legitimacy of middle-class values. A third group wants to plan for all interest groups, but is split over whether to work for or against the establishment.

All planning is social planning, and while geographers and transportation experts have an important role in the planning process they should not be the tail that wags the dog. In America, as Gans says, 'the city planner is no longer a non-political formulator of long-range ideals, but is becoming an adviser to elected and appointed officials, providing them with recommendations and technical information on current decisions'. Urban renewal should be seen as a way of dealing with the processes which force people into slums: land-use studies are becoming less relevant as planners concern themselves with the provision and use of social services and the economic and political consequences of the policies they recommend.

The crucial lesson for British planners is to learn their limitations, and to make these limitations more widely known. The public, seeing, for example, the physical environment in decay, mistakenly assumes that the solution lies in physical renewal alone. However, the planner finds that the amelioration of one problem brings about a deterioration in another sphere, for he is dealing all the time with symptoms not causes.

If the planner analyses the social and economic origins of the problem, he might wish to suggest quite other solutions, even if it were outside his scope to implement these solutions. The danger is that his regard for his professional position will make him disregard the most relevant policies in favour of policies within his field of competence. The planner cannot be the *deus ex machina* of the urban condition. The trouble is that neither the planners nor the people are facing up to the fact that our power to alter the physical environment is greater than we can cope with. Participation implies that people should not only take part in making decisions about the physical environment, but should also take responsibility for the values implicit in planning decisions.

In this sort of situation it is simpler to do what can be done most easily, even if it is expensive. Enormous sums of money are being spent by planners on traffic surveys and transportation studies, but as we concentrate on physical mobility we completely ignore social mobility. Hence we do not know whether our urban areas are collecting an unskilled rump with little opportunity for occupational mobility. We do not know how easily coloured immigrants are moving up the occupational hierarchy. Published plans make pious statements about social goals and social objectives but no long-term social research, such as a continuing monitoring programme on social mobility, is being planned. There are, however, signs that the Central Statistical Office will initiate work on social indicators and this would be a welcome and much needed task.

Professor Gans's book has prompted these thoughts because I feel that in Britain, too, the physical city with its physical problems has been overstressed. The city is essentially a social entity – the product of a particular society at a particular time. It is partly because the Americans saw the city in terms of accessibility, and urban renewal as a way to more profitable uses, that they have got into their present confusions.

In Britain we more readily accept positive discrimination – we already have the educational priority areas, the urban programme and so on. Despite this we still tend to get carried away by the discussions of the physical forms and sometimes neglect to discuss the social goals we are aiming to achieve. Professor Gans says, 'I want immediate change that improves the conditions of the deprived immediately'. Are we sure that we have our priorities right in this country? The city is what society lets it be.

References

GANS, H. J. (1962), *The Urban Villagers*, Collier-Macmillan.
GANS, H. J. (1967), *The Levittowners*, Allen Lane.
GANS, H. J. (1968), *People and Plans: Essays on Urban Problems and Solutions*, Basic Books, reprinted in Penguins, 1972.

4 J. Burkhead and A. K. Campbell

Public Policy for Urban America

Extract from J. Burkhead and A. K. Campbell, 'Public policy for urban America', in H. S. Perloff and L. Wingo (eds.), *Issues in Urban Economics*, Johns Hopkins Press, 1968, pp. 637–47.

New directions – incrementally

[. . .] In the polemics surrounding American urbanism and metro-politanism there is a persistent demand for a unified *federal urban policy*. It is argued that no such policy exists today, and that the present attacks on urban problems are piecemeal, frag-mented, inconsistent and unco-ordinated. An overriding urban policy would make possible, it is believed, the meshing of specific programs into a meaningful framework.

Such a condition will never exist. The American decision process simply does not work that way. Policy changes are incre-mental, not sweeping. New directions are tried, but with caution. Perhaps it is true, as Lindblom (1959) argues, that this concentra-tion on small incremental changes is reasonable '. . . given the limits on knowledge within which policy-makers are confined' (1959, p. 87).

Whether reasonable or not, American urban policy is made in this way. The bits and pieces of that policy are in those programs described here, together with a great many others. The others include scattered site public houses (more talked about than practiced), rent subsidies (little money), air and water pollution control (beginning to move), and the more grandiose, just-enacted metropolitan planning requirements and Demonstration Cities program. A more complete list would include, as well, the long-established programs for mortgage guarantees and for public housing.

Obviously overall national economic and employment policies have significance, too, for urban policy. The federal commitment to high levels of employment makes a contribution to the well-being of metropolitan areas. But the need for specific urban social policies is one measure of the degree of failure of national macro-policy. Fiscal and monetary policies that are successful in the aggregate do not guarantee sufficient employment or sufficient income to maintain all people in society at a minimal economic level. Further, the private market, particularly in land, has not produced a distribution of human activities within metropolitan areas which is satisfying to very many. That market, often influenced by government policy, has unleashed forces contributing to the deterioration of the central city and the dispersal of population across the adjoining countryside. Transportation, pollution, social segregation and fiscal problems are among the results.

It is not surprising that these consequences have created a demand for a national urban policy. The difficulty with the demand is that it assumes agreement about what the problems are, their causes, and the kind of urban society desired. There is, in fact, no general agreement on any of these prerequisites to an urban policy and it is, in part, this lack of agreement which has produced the variety of *ad hoc* approaches to urbanism and metropolitanism that today, together, constitute urban policy.

Although a single national policy produced by rational analysis and proclaimed as binding is not possible, it is useful to examine what the content of such a policy might be and the process by which it could be formulated. The first step in such an analysis must be identification of the forces responsible for the problems.

There are two broad classes of forces and although the classes overlap they are sufficiently distinct for separate analysis. One class might be described as the physical or hardware problems. These relate to the present distribution of activities within metropolitan areas – where people work, live, and recreate, and the movement from one activity to another.

The second class relates to the social or 'soft' problems produced by the low living standards imposed on a significant portion of the population living in metropolitan areas. Tying these two classes of problems together is housing. This has both physical dimensions, the maintenance of minimum structural standards, and social dimensions, the behavior patterns of neighborhood groups.

Since these two classes of problems have different impacts in cities and suburbs it is sometimes useful to distinguish between the two. On the whole, however, there is too much overlap in this classification. The 'soft–hard' dichotomy serves better.

The distribution of activities

The redistribution of activities throughout large urban areas has produced what has become called the Spread City.[1] Market forces

1. See Regional Plan Association of New York, *Spread City*, Bulletin 100, 1962.

in land use are spreading urban activities over a wider and wider area. The new spread pattern, although traditional wisdom deplores it, has its champions. One student, for example, finds 'in the dissolution of the urban settlement a liberation of human energies and a proliferation of opportunities for human interaction'.[2] Those opposed to the present pattern claim its costs are too high relative to the needed public investment in social overhead and, further, that it tends to eliminate the cultural and social advantages of a more compact city. It is argued that it is technologically possible, today, to build highly compact, densely populated cities. Only in cities, it is contended, is it possible to have fine symphony orchestras, great libraries, dynamic museums, quality educational institutions and first-rate theatres. Without a healthy, compact center these activities will die or disperse, and disperson will inevitably lower quality and availability. Further, the social heterogeneity represented by the city is seen as preferable to the presumed dull, unimaginative conformity of the communities in a spread city pattern.

Both market forces and governmental fragmentation promote the spread city. But even if these are allowed to operate unhindered, it does not follow that there is no need for physical development policy. The champions of a decentralized urbanism do not defend the present unorganized pattern which has been produced by the new spread pattern. Some kind of multi-centred urban area is more often advocated with resulting communities resembling the long-championed New Towns.

What the New Town is supposed to provide is what the standard suburb leaves out: good transportation, good timing of community facilities, good public utilities, good open space, and good overall design. Above all it is concerned with the better use of land.[3]

If there is to be a preferred physical pattern, New Towns or otherwise, it can be accomplished only if present functional policies in such areas as transportation, utilities, urban renewal and land use controls are designed to accomplish that pattern. The difficulty, of course, is that the present arrangement of governmental institutions does not permit a hard decision to be made about whether it is compact cities or spread cities, or something in between, that government policy should promote. It may be

2. See Webber (1963, p. 18).
3. See Huxtable (1964, p. 28). There is a vast literature on New Towns. A good overall view is contained in Osborn and Whittick (1963).

that the issue is not what urban policy ought to be, but rather the provision of a mechanism for making that decision.

Requirements for comprehensive planning, which are integral parts of more and more federal programs (highways, airports, open spaces, urban renewal, mass transit) represent a recognition of this need. In the Housing Act of 1966, this comprehensive planning requirement has been generalized. After June 30th, 1967 any local government jurisdiction seeking federal aid for physical improvement will have to advance its aid request through a metropolitan planning agency. In the words of the Act,

All applications made after June 30th 1967 for federal loans or grants to assist in carrying out open space land projects, or for the planning or construction of hospitals, airports, libraries, water supply distribution facilities, sewerage facilities and waste treatment works, highways, transportation facilities, and water development and land conservation projects within any metropolitan area shall be submitted for review to any area-wide agency which is designated to perform metropolitan or regional planning for the area within which the assistance is to be used. (Title II, Sec. 204.)

The passage of this provision culminates a long-time effort by Senator Muskie to encourage metropolitan-wide regional planning with real power. The Act does not require the regional unit to approve the plan of the local jurisdiction, but if it comments unfavorably it goes back to the local jurisdiction who may either change it to meet the criticisms or it may be passed on with the unfavorable comments to the appropriate granting agency in Washington. That agency, according to the Act, shall review the comments and recommendations 'for the sole purpose of assisting it in determining whether the application is in accordance with the provisions of federal law which govern the making of the loans or grants'. In other words, if there is no requirement for comprehensive planning in the specific federal grant programs under which the local government is applying, the Washington agency has no legal power to consider the recommendations of the metropolitan planning agency. Even with this limitation, however, a seemingly significant power grant is made by the Act. Many specific federal programs do have comprehensive planning requirements. Further, the Act will establish on a permanent basis many metropolitan planning agencies. These agencies will compete for power with other units and will, on occasion, win.

The development policies that may be adopted by these regional planning agencies are, of course, not known. They must have representation on their governing boards from the elected officials within the area. These officials are not likely to approve any drastic revision in present patterns. Nevertheless, these new requirements do represent one of the first efforts by the federal government to influence governmental structure at the local level.

Instead of a hard decision for spread or compact cities, direct attacks within specific functional areas will continue to be made. Highways will be built, and perhaps a few mass transit systems. Pollution will be partially controlled and some downtown rebuilding will continue. In the suburbs there is a possibility that new communities will come to take on more recognizable shape than has been true of the leapfrogging spread of the past. It is possible that private industry will find the creation of New Towns a profitable enterprise. Already Reston, in Virginia, and Columbia, in Maryland, are pointing the direction. The federal government policy, which has already attempted to make easier the creation of New Towns through providing grants to local jurisdictions for borrowing ahead for public utilities, is helping. That help will probably increase.

New Towns in-town, essentially to help cope with the social problems of the central city, have also been suggested.[4] In this case, the proposal is for the creation of well-serviced, reconstructed 'new' communities within cities. Not only would such towns provide new and improved housing but, in addition, new and improved community facilities – schools, playgrounds, neighborhood centers, shopping areas and the like.

The New Towns in-town concept might well become attached to the currently discussed public-private corporation for the rebuilding of certain sections of cities. The administrative model most often cited is Comsat. The hope is to combine, as in the case of Comsat, private and public capital for the rebuilding of depressed sections of cities. The advantage such an approach would have over present urban renewal is greater administrative flexibility and, perhaps, more use of the supposed innovative spirit of the private sector. Although it is not clear why this could not be done through a full-fledged public corporation, such as TVA, the American bias in favor of the private sector may be controlling. The only thing really new about the proposal is the administrative device it would create. The need for massive public subsidy would remain.

4. See Perloff (1966), reprinted as Reprint no. 57, Resources for the Future.

None of this discussion of new approaches to physical development is meant to imply that a new national urban policy is about to be established. Rather, there will continue to be a variety of approaches, incremental in their impact. It is possible, however, that the increments will evolve into a new package of programs which will move policy in a new direction. As is evident from programs already tried, whatever is done will be costly. There is no way to remake or even to maintain urban America at its present standards without substantial public resources. Most of these resources will have to be provided by the national government.

Socially sick cities

Living throughout America but concentrated in its great central cities are families and individuals whose income is inadequate to maintain a minimum standard of well-being. The urban poor are characterized by poor education, bad health, inadequate housing and an apathy encouraged by the environment. The poor have been trapped. The Anti-Poverty Program and federal aid to education are two approaches for dealing with the problems created by these conditions; other approaches are obviously necessary.

Government policies to increase aggregate demand reduce the numbers of persons in poverty. But the success of programs specifically designed to provide training for the kinds of skills needed in an urban society is less clear. Many of those who are unemployed, and particularly Negro teenagers, may be victims of a vague and ill-defined alienation that is a product of slum living, discrimination, low motivation and the apparent anti-Calvinist attitudes of the culture of poverty itself. If this is the case – and it is impossible to document – the improvement of skill levels, which is the aim of all the training programs, will bring very modest results and indeed may only increase the level of frustration.

The Demonstration Cities Program, proposed by the Administration and enacted by Congress in 1966, is an effort to bring together the various social approaches of the federal government into a concentrated attack on the central city conditions which, it is believed, produces this environment. The purpose of the Demonstration Cities approach is, in the words of Congress,

to improve their [cities'] physical environment, increase their supply of adequate housing for low and moderate income people and provide educational and social services vital to health and welfare.

J. Burkhead and A. K. Campbell 97

In more specific terms, Congress says that

the purposes of this title are to provide additional financial and technical assistance to enable cities of all sizes . . . to plan, develop and carry out locally-prepared and scheduled comprehensive city demonstration programs containing new and imaginative proposals to rebuild or revitalize large slum and blighted areas, to expand housing, job and income opportunities, to reduce dependence on welfare payments, to improve educational facilities and programs, to combat disease and ill health, to reduce the incidence of crime and delinquency, to enhance recreational and cultural opportunities, to establish better access between homes and jobs, and generally to improve living conditions for the people who live in such areas, and to accomplish these objectives through the most effective and economical concentration and coordination of federal, state and local public and private efforts to improve the quality of urban life.

Again, the federal government, as in the metropolitan planning provisions of the same Act, is attempting to force local communities to think through and plan their own programs. Unable to organize a comprehensive attack from the federal level, the national government is attempting to provide the incentive necessary to accomplish such co-ordination at the local level.

In order to encourage such comprehensive planning the federal government is making aid available for such planning. Thus far no money has been appropriated for the actual conduct of programs, only for their planning. It remains to be seen whether Congress will respond once the local communities have formulated their own plans.

Even assuming money will be made available to local communities, the issue of whether enough is known about causation to make such plans effective is an open question. Theories are abundant; practical successes are few. The difficulty of providing educational services in a meaningful way to the disadvantaged has already been examined. The issue of motivation remains unsolved. Perhaps it is true that the present generation of disadvantaged is different from past generations. 'Was there any evidence other than impressions that the immigrants of fifty years ago had aspiration and hope in addition to their economic poverty, while the present poor lack aspiration and tend to pass on their impoverished economic and spiritual state from one generation to another?'[5] The evidence is not conclusive.

The problems are so serious that small-scale experimentation

5. See Seligman (1965, p. 15).

is insufficient. Massive undertakings are necessary. The politicians must be prepared for failures and they, in turn, must prepare the public. Thus far no new generation of metropolitan leaders has appeared willing to take the kinds of political risks implied.

The new technology and cities

Modern technology has been blamed as the cause of the problems of urban America and, in turn, is often offered as the solution. If only the resources and energies that have gone into the development of the new technology necessary for modern defense systems and for space exploration had been applied to cities, it is argued, their problems by now would be solved. In addition, there are those who maintain that there is a substantial technological spin-off from the advances in defense and space which, if applied to city problems, would make a major contribution to their solution.[6]

There have been, perhaps, a few by-products of space research which have some relevance to city problems. They are not many and they are not spectacular. As John H. Rubel (1966), vice-president of Lytton Industries, suggests, 'It would be wholly accidental if technologies valuable to space projects should turn out to be economically valuable in cities' (p. 7).

It has been suggested, however, that even though there has been no substantial technological spin-off from space research and development, it is possible that the space program does indicate a method by which new city technology might be developed. Again, quoting Rubel,

Missiles and space projects use systems analysis. They require multi-disciplinary teams. The problems of space are very complex. Likewise cities and city problems are complex, in many ways much more so. Surely they too, call for multidisciplinary teams. Ergo, runs this argument, why not use the systems approach? (p. 7).

Arguing that this is too simple a translation of the space experience into city development, Rubel urges that a market place for urban technology be created.

Out of this market will grow a new technology for specific kinds of urban development. Rubel suggests that:

In short, if you could set up a project for the creation of a new city from scratch and offer the job to private industry and set up project goals in terms of the performance of a dynamic system, you would see new industry spring up within the framework of existing firms to meet the

6. See NASA (1963).

new needs. Soon the multidisciplinary teams would be assembled. The relevant analytical techniques would be applied; the new methods, the new technologies, the new insights would begin to emerge. The new insights and the new technologies would include wholly new species of engineering and technology (1966, p. 13).

Rubel argues that such a development could take place only in new cities. It could not be done with old cities. There are simply too many obstacles in the way. Further, he maintains that his experiment will work only in a situation in which 'the project owns or effectively controls the ownership of virtually all the land in the city and surrounding it for a considerable distance. This is an absolute requirement.'

Rubel's insistence upon new cities and public ownership of lands points to the major political difficulties which face the re-building of urban America. The space technicians would not have had the success they have had if they faced some of the political obstacles that stand in the way of urban redevelopment.

If there were citizens on the moon who owned real estate and who voted and possessed other political resources, the space pro-gram would not have proceeded as smoothly as it has.

All of this does not mean that technology cannot make a major contribution to the solution of urban problems. One wonders if the money now being expended by the Department of Housing and Urban Development (HUD) for the perpetuation of the old technologies in cities might not be better spent in research and development. There is no provision in the American system, in either the private or the public sector, to supply basic or applied research to the problems of cities. The resources entering this field are minimal and even those H U D has tried to secure from Con-gress have been denied. The housing industry, the automobile industry, and other established interests in the market sector fear the possible consequences of major research in these areas and often erect effective barriers.

Government and politics of urban redevelopment

The metropolitan planning provisions in last year's housing bill may point the direction in which the federal government will move in attempting to influence the structure of local govern-ment. These provisions are a beginning in the establishment of one kind of significant region-wide governing institution. If the federal government decides to move further in this direction, the Heller–Pechman proposal of general grants provides a possible means.[7] Governmental reorganization, as has already been suggested in a bill filed by Representative Henry S. Reuss, could be tied to such a general grant system. Much of the criticism of the general grant proposal lies in the insistence that state and local governments are not strong enough, good enough, or innovative enough to deserve these grants. The Reuss bill suggests that no grants be provided to any state until it submits a plan for the modernization of its state-local governmental system.

Beyond the politics of reforming local government structure is the politics surrounding the various functional areas relevant to city building. Highways are politically strong. They will continue to be built and, in many instances, will be the principal influence determining urban form. Education has its political strength and will undoubtedly continue to receive more funds, but whether education aid will be pointed in the direction of solving central city ills is by no means clear. Welfare and anti-poverty are weak politically. Urban renewal has changed its political support from the liberal to the chamber of commerce community. Whether this weakens or strengthens the program is not clear, but it does mean that it will be directed to saving downtown rather than providing housing to low-income families.

Emerging political configurations do not bode well for many urban programs, but these configurations do possess greater potential at the federal level than at state and local levels. The federal constituency does provide a base which makes it possible, particularly for the President, to move in new directions without sacrificing his potential for re-election. As has already been demonstrated, federal politics do not limit innovation to the extent that state and local politics do.

There are a variety of explanations for the difference between state and local and federal politics, but perhaps most significant is the fiscal bind in which state and local governments find themselves. The result is that state and local politics tend to be tax politics, while federal politics are more nearly program politics. Further, a local office-holder and, to a somewhat lesser extent, a state office-holder must constantly fear the creation of 'a pocket of opposition'. A president, because of the size of his constituency, can balance off opposing groups with favoring groups. This is not easy at the state and local level. The local official may create a vigorous opposition group by the placement of a physical facility – a highway or a garbage disposal unit, or by sponsoring a social

7. See Heller (1966). See also Heller, Ruggles, *et al.* (1968).

program such as a police review board. The opposition group may vote in the next election on the basis of this one issue. The creation of the opposition group does not, however, automatically create a countervailing group. The rest of the community is likely to vote on a variety of issues and thereby the political future of the local office-holder is threatened by the 'pocket of opposition'.

These political facts of life make it inevitable that within the present structure of metropolitan governing institutions urban policy leadership will have to come from the federal level. Such leadership will not create a unified single urban policy for America. It may move, however, in the direction of co-ordinating present programs, modifying conflicting ones, and perhaps even grasping a new idea like New Towns – both in-and-out-of-town – and perhaps even new cities.

There is not, however, a single large pro-city pressure group with much political muscle. In order to create policy in this field the politician must bring together disparate political forces, often with no interests in common, and try to build a substantive package which has sufficient appeal across pressure group lines to be politically acceptable. In many cases these programs will be designed by the bureaucracy, as was the case with the poverty program. But in every case there must be strong political support, existing or emergent, to overcome the conflicting and anarchic influences that now make every urban policy exclusively incremental.

References

HELLER, W. W. (1966), *New Dimensions of Political Economy*, Harvard University Press.

HELLER, W. W., RUGGLES, R. *et al.* (1968), *Revenue Sharing and the City*, Johns Hopkins Press.

HUXTABLE, A. L. (1964), 'First light of new town era is on horizon', *New York Times*, 17 February.

LINDBLOM, C. E. (1959), 'The science of "Muddling Through",' *Pub. Admin.*, vol. 19, no. 2, p. 79–88.

NASA (1963), *Conference on Space Science and Urban Life*, US Government Printing Office.

OSBORN, F. J., and WHITTICK, A. (1963), *The New Towns: The Answer to Megalopolis*, Hill & Leonard.

PECHMAN, J. A. (1965), 'Financing state and local government', in *Proceedings of a Symposium on Federal Taxation*, American Bankers Association.

PERLOFF, H. S. (1966), 'New Towns intown', *J. of the Amer. Inst. of Planners*, vol. 32, pp. 155–61.

RUBEL, J. H. (1966), 'Defining the role of the private sector in overcoming barriers to urban "betterment"', *Harvard Program on Technology and Society*, unpublished.

SELIGMAN, B. B. (ed.) (1965), 'Introduction', in *Poverty as a Public Issue*, Free Press.

WEBBER, M. M. (1963), 'Order in diversity: community without propinquity', in L. Wingo (ed.), *Cities and Space, the Future Use of Urban Land*, Johns Hopkins Press.

Part Two
The Urban Process:
Location and Structure

Alonso's (Reading 5) analysis of the theory of the urban land
market represents a statement of the way in which different urban
activities compete for space and of how both individuals and the
market as a whole can reach equilibrium. His formulation
produces an urban structure of concentric zones, and it is
interesting to link this with the earlier work of Burgess (Reading
6), whose concentric zone model arose from ecological rather
than economic theory. Burgess' article (from the historic
volume on *The City* edited by Robert Park) is included not only
because the Chicago ecologists' adoption of the concepts of
Darwinian biology remains an excellent example of the nature of
interdisciplinary work – the ability to take an idea from one
discipline and apply it in a totally different context – but also
because human ecology demonstrates in a number of ways the
link between spatial and social structure. The possibility of
analysing urban problems at a micro-spatial level is illustrated
by the analysis of blight and slums (Rothenberg, Reading 7)
which discusses the nature of slums, their role in providing low-
cost housing, the factors which operate to bring about social
costs and inefficiencies in the housing market. The Duncans'
article (Reading 8) describes the analysis of a large number of
urban sub-areas and, although fifteen years old, remains one of
the clearest examples of the systematic consideration of the
spatial aspects of stratification phenomena. A theme which runs
through all four of these readings is that of residential segregation
and the relationship between residential area and social structure
is one of the concerns of Beshers' article (Reading 9) on urban
social structure. Beshers' contribution is significant in this
collection of readings, since not only does it link backwards to
the other readings in this section but it also raises some of the
issues relating to status, community and interest which are the
concern of Part Three of these Readings.

5 W. Alonso

A Theory of the Urban Land Market

W. Alonso, 'A theory of the urban land market', *Papers and Proceedings of the Regional Science Association*, vol. 6, 1960, pp. 154–9.

The early theory of rent and location concerned itself primarily with agricultural land. This was quite natural, for Ricardo and Malthus lived in an agricultural society. The foundations of the formal spatial analysis of agricultural rent and location are found in the work of J. von Thunen (1826) who said, without going into detail, that the urban land market operated under the same principles. As cities grew in importance, relatively little attention was paid to the theory of urban rents. Even the great Marshall provided interesting but only random insights, and no explicit theory of the urban land market and urban locations was developed.

Since the beginning of the twentieth century there has been considerable interest in the urban land market in America. R. M. Hurd (1903) and R. M. Haig (1927) tried to create a theory of urban land by following von Thunen. However, their approach copied the form rather than the logic of agricultural theory, and the resulting theory can be shown to be insufficient on its own premises. In particular, the theory failed to consider residences, which constitute the preponderant land use in urban areas.

Yet there are interesting problems that a theory of urban land must consider. There is, for instance, a paradox in American cities: the poor live near the center, on expensive land, and the rich on the periphery, on cheap land. On the logical side, there are also aspects of great interest, but which increase the difficulty of the analysis. When a purchaser acquires land, he acquires two goods (land and location) in only one transaction, and only one payment is made for the combination. He could buy the same quantity of land at another location, or he could buy more, or less, land at the same location. In the analysis, one encounters, as well, a negative good (distance) with positive costs (commuting costs); or, conversely, a positive good (accessibility) with negative costs (savings in commuting). In comparison with agriculture, the urban case presents another difficulty. In agriculture, the location is extensive: many miles may be devoted to one crop. In the urban case the site tends to be much smaller, and the location may be regarded as a dimensionless point rather than an area. Yet the thousands or millions of dimensionless points which constitute the city, when taken together, cover extensive areas. How can these dimensionless points be aggregated into two-dimensional space?

Here I will present a non-mathematical over-view, without trying to give it full precision, of the long and rather complex mathematical analysis which constitutes a formal theory of the urban land market.[1] It is a static model in which change is introduced by comparative statics. And it is an economic model: it speaks of economic men, and it goes without saying that real men and social groups have needs, emotions and desires which are not considered here. This analysis uses concepts which fit with agricultural rent theory in such a way that urban and rural land uses may be considered at the same time, in terms of a single theory. Therefore, we must examine first a very simplified model of the agricultural land market.

Agricultural model

In this model, the farmers are grouped around a single market, where they sell their products. If the product is wheat, and the produce of one acre of wheat sells for $100 at the market while the costs of production are $50 per acre, a farmer growing wheat at the market would make a profit of $50 per acre. But if he is producing at some distance – say five miles – and it costs him $5 per mile to ship an acre's product. his transport costs will be $25 per acre. His profits will be equal to value minus production costs minus shipping charges: $100 − $50 − $25 = $25. This relation may be shown diagrammatically (see Figure 1). At the market, the farmer's profits are $50, and five miles out, $25; at intermediate distance, he will receive intermediate profits. Finally, at a distance of ten miles from the market, his production costs plus shipping charges will just equal the value of his produce at the market. At distances greater than ten miles, the farmer would operate at a loss.

In this model, the profits derived by the farmer are tied directly to their location. If the functions of farmer and landowner are

1. A full development of the theory is presented in my doctoral dissertation (Alonso, 1960).

viewed as separate, farmers will bid rents for land according to the profitability of the location. The profits of the farmer will therefore be shared with the landowner through rent payments. As farmers bid against each other for the more profitable locations, until farmers' profits are everywhere the same ('normal' profits), what we have called profits becomes rent. Thus, the curve in Figure 1, which we derived as a farmers' profit curve, once we distinguish between the roles of the farmer and the landowner, becomes a 'bid rent function', representing the price or rent per acre that farmers will be willing to pay for land at the different locations.

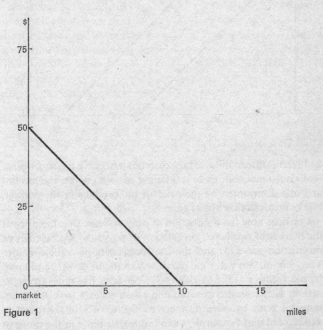

Figure 1

We have shown that the slope of the rent curve will be fixed by the transport costs on the produce. The level of the curve will be set by the price of the produce at the market. Examine Figure 2. The lower curve is that of Figure 1, where the price of wheat is $100 at the market, and production costs are $50. If demand increases, and the price of wheat at the market rises to $125 (while production and transport costs remain constant), profits or bid rent at the market will be $75; at five miles, $50; $25 at ten miles,

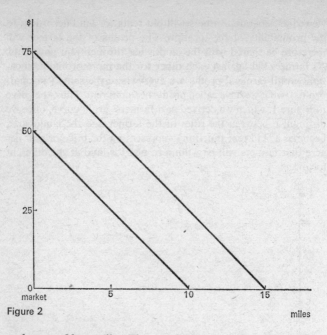

Figure 2

and zero at fifteen miles. Thus, each bid rent curve is a function of rent *vs* distance, but there is a family of such curves, the level of any one determined by the price of the produce at the market, higher prices setting higher curves.

Consider now the production of peas. Assume that the price at the market of one acre's production of peas is $150, the costs of production are $75, and the transport costs per mile are $10. These conditions will yield curve *MN* in Figure 3, where bid rent by pea farmers at the market is $75 per acre, five miles from the market $25, and zero at seven and a half miles. Curve *RS* represents bid rents by wheat farmers, at a price of $100 for wheat. It will be seen that pea farmers can bid higher rents in the range of zero to five miles from the market; farther out, wheat farmers can bid higher rents. Therefore, pea farming will take place in the ring from zero to five miles from the market, and wheat farming in the ring from five to ten miles. Segments MT of the bid rent curve of pea farming and TS of wheat farming will be the effective rents, while segments RT and TN represent unsuccessful bids.

The price of the product is determined by the supply–demand

relations at the market. If the region between zero and five miles produces too many peas, the price of the product will drop, and a lower bid rent curve for pea farming will come into effect, so that pea farming will be practiced to some distance less than five miles.

Abstracting this view of the agricultural land market, we have that:

1. Land uses determine land values through competitive bidding among farmers;
2. Land values distribute land uses, according to their ability to pay;
3. The steeper curves capture the central locations. (This point is a simplified one for simple, well-behaved curves.)

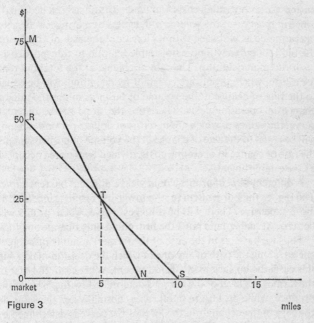

Figure 3

Abstracting the process now *from* agriculture, we have:

1. For each user of land (e.g., wheat farmer) a family of bid rent functions is derived, such that the user is indifferent as to his location along any *one* of these functions (because the farmer, who is the decision-maker in this case, finds that profits are everywhere the same, i.e., normal, as long as he remains on one curve);

2. The equilibrium rent at any location is found by comparing the bids of the various potential users and choosing the highest;

3. Equilibrium quantities of land are found by selecting the proper bid rent curve for each user (in the agricultural case, the curve which equates supply and demand for the produce).

Business

We shall now consider the urban businessman, who, we shall assume, makes his decisions so as to maximize profits. A bid rent curve for the businessman, then, will be one along which profits are everywhere the same: the decision-maker will be indifferent as to his location along such a curve.

Profit may be defined as the remainder from the volume of business after operating costs and land costs have been deducted. Since in most cases the volume of business of a firm as well as its operating costs will vary with its location, the rate of change of the bid rent curve will bear no simple relation to transport costs (as it did in agriculture). The rate of change of the total bid rent for a firm, where profits are constant by definition, will be equal to the rate of change in the volume of business minus the rate of change in operating costs. Therefore the slope of the bid rent curve, the values of which are in terms of dollars per unit of land, will be equal to the rate of change in the volume of business minus the rate of change in operating costs, divided by the area occupied by the establishment.

A different level of profits would yield a different bid rent curve. The higher the bid rent curve, the lower the profits, since land is more expensive. There will be a highest curve, where profits will be zero. At higher land rents the firm could only operate at a loss.

Thus we have, as in the case of the farmer, a family of bid rent curves, along the path of any one of which the decision-maker – in this case, the businessman – is indifferent. Whereas in the case of the farmer the level of the curve is determined by the price of the produce, while profits are in all cases 'normal', i.e., the same, in the case of the urban firm, the level of the curve is determined by the level of the profits, and the price of its products may be regarded for our purposes as constant.

Residential

The household differs from the farmer and the urban firm in that satisfaction rather than profits is the relevant criterion of optimal location. A consumer, given his income and his pattern of tastes, will seek to balance the costs and bother of commuting against the advantages of cheaper land with increasing distance from the center of the city and the satisfaction of more space for living. When the individual consumer faces a given pattern of land costs, his equilibrium location and the size of his site will be in terms of the marginal changes of these variables.

The bid rent curves of the individual will be such that, for any given curve, the individual will be equally satisfied at every location at the price set by the curve. Along any bid rent curve, the price the individual will bid for land will decrease with distance from the center at a rate just sufficient to produce an income effect which will balance to his satisfaction the increased costs of commuting and the bother of a long trip. This slope may be expressed quite precisely in mathematical terms, but it is a complex expression, the exact interpretation of which is beyond the scope of this paper.

Just as different prices of the produce set different levels for the bid rent curves of the farmer, and different levels of profit for the urban firm, different levels of satisfaction correspond to the various levels of the family of bid rent curves of the individual household. The higher curves obviously yield less satisfaction because a higher price is implied, so that, at any given location, the individual will be able to afford less land and other goods.

Individual equilibrium

It is obvious that families of bid rent curves are in many respects similar to indifference curve mappings. However, they differ in some important ways. Indifference curves map a path of indifference (equal satisfaction) between combinations of quantities of two goods. Bid rent functions map an indifference path between the price of one good (land) and quantities of another and strange type of good, distance from the center of the city. Whereas indifference curves refer to tastes and not to budget, in the case of households, bid rent functions are derived both from budget and taste considerations. In the case of the urban firm, they might be termed isoprofit curves. A more superficial difference is that, whereas the higher indifference curves are the preferred ones, it is the lower bid rent curves that yield greater profits or satisfaction. However, bid rent curves may be used in a manner analogous to that of indifference curves to find the equilibrium location and land price for the resident or the urban firm.

Assume you have been given a bid rent mapping of a land use, whether business or residential (curves brc$_{1,2,3}$, etc. in Figure 4). Superimposed on the same diagram the actual structure of land prices in the city (curve SS). The decision-maker will wish to reach the lowest possible bid rent curve. Therefore, he will choose that point at which the curve of actual prices SS will be tangent to the lowest of the bid rent curves with which it comes in contact brc$_2$. At this point will be the equilibrium location L and the equili-

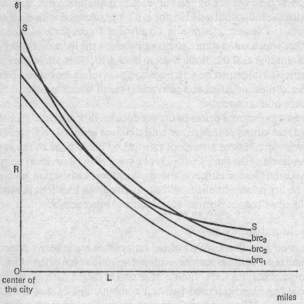

Figure 4

brium land rent R for this user of land. If he is a businessman, he will have maximized profits; if he is a resident, he will have maximized satisfaction.

Note that to the left of this point of equilibrium (toward the center of the city) the curve of actual prices is steeper than the bid rent curve; to the right of this point (away from the center) it is less steep. This is another aspect of the rule we noted in the agricultural model, the land uses with steeper bid rent curves capture the central locations.

Market equilibrium

We now have, conceptually, families of bid rent curves for all three types of land uses. We also know that the steeper curves will occupy the more central locations. Therefore, if the curves of the various users are ranked by steepness, they will also be ranked in terms of their accessibility from the center of the city in the final solution. Thus, if the curves of the business firm are steeper than those of residences, and the residential curves steeper than the agricultural, there will be business at the center of the city, surrounded by residences, and these will be surrounded by agriculture.

This reasoning applies as well within land use groupings. For instance, it can be shown that, given two individuals of similar tastes, both of whom prefer living at low densities, if their incomes differ, the bid rent curves of the wealthier will be flatter than those of the man of lower income. Therefore, the poor will tend to central locations on expensive land and the rich to cheaper land on the periphery. The reason for this is not that the poor have greater purchasing power, but rather that they have steeper bid rent curves. This stems from the fact that, at any given location, the poor can buy less land than the rich, and since only a small quantity of land is involved, changes in its price are not as important for the poor as the costs and inconvenience of commuting. The rich, on the other hand, buy greater quantities of land, and are consequently affected by changes in its price to a great degree. In other words, because of variations in density among different levels of income, accessibility behaves as an inferior good.

Thus far, through ranking the bid rent curves by steepness, we have found the relative rankings of prices and locations, but not the actual prices, locations, or densities. It will be remembered that in the agricultural case equilibrium levels were brought about by changes in the price of the products, until the amount of land devoted to each crop was in agreement with the demand for that crop.

For urban land this process is more complex. The determination of densities (or their inverse, lot size) and locations must be found simultaneously with the resulting price structure. Very briefly, the method consists of assuming a price of land at the center of the city, and determining the prices at all other locations by the competitive bidding of the potential users of land in relation to this price. The highest bid captures each location, and each bid is related to a most preferred alternative through the use of bid rent curves. This most preferred alternative is the marginal combination of price and location for that particular land use. The quantities of land occupied by the land users are determined by these prices. The locations are determined by assigning to each successive user of land the location available nearest the center of the city after the assignment of land quantities to the higher and more central bidders.

Since initially the price at the center of the city was assumed, the resulting set of prices, locations and densities may be in error. A series of iterations will yield the correct solution. In some cases, the solution may be found by a set of simultaneous equations rather than by the chain of steps which has just been outlined.

The model presented in this paper corresponds to the simplest case: a single-center city, on a featureless plain, with transportation in all directions. However, the reasoning can be extended to cities with several centers (shopping, office, manufacturing, etc.). with structured road patterns, and other realistic complications, The theory can also be made to shed light on the effects of economic development, changes in income structure, zoning regulations, taxation policies, and other. At this stage, the model is purely theoretical; however, it is hoped that it may provide a logical structure for econometric models which may be useful for prediction.

References

ALONSO, W. (1960), *A Model of the Urban Land Market: Locations and Densities of Dwellings and Businesses*, University of Pennsylvania.
HAIG, R. M. (1927), *Regional Survey of New York and its Environs*, New York City Plan Commission.
HURD, R. M. (1903), *Principles of City Land Values*, The Record and Guide.
THUNEN, J. von (1826), *Der Isolierte Staat in Beziehung auf Landwirtschaft und Nationalekonomie*, 1st vol. 1826, 3rd vol. and new edn 1863.

6 E. W. Burgess

The Growth of the City

E. W. Burgess, 'The growth of the city', in R. E. Park *et al.*, *The City*, University of Chicago Press, 1925, ch. 2.

The outstanding fact of modern society is the growth of great cities. Nowhere else have the enormous changes which the machine industry has made in our social life registered themselves with such obviousness as in the cities. In the United States the transition from a rural to an urban civilization, though beginning later than in Europe, has taken place, if not more rapidly and completely, at any rate more logically in its most characteristic forms.

All the manifestations of modern life which are peculiarly urban – the skyscraper, the subway, the department store, the daily newspaper and social work – are characteristically American. The more subtle changes in our social life, which in their cruder manifestations are termed 'social problems', problems that alarm and bewilder us, as divorce, delinquency, and social unrest, are to be found in their most acute forms in our largest American cities. The profound and 'subversive' forces which have wrought these changes are measured in the physical growth and expansion of cities. That is the significance of the comparative statistics of Weber, Bücher and other students.

These statistical studies, although dealing mainly with the effects of urban growth, brought out into clear relief certain distinctive characteristics of urban as compared with rural populations. The larger proportion of women to men in the cities than in the open country, the greater percentage of youth and middle-aged, the higher ratio of the foreign-born, the increased heterogeneity of occupation increase with the growth of the city and profoundly alter its social structure. These variations in the composition of population are indicative of all the changes going on in the social organization of the community. In fact, these changes are a part of the growth of the city and suggest the nature of the processes of growth.

The only aspect of growth adequately described by Bücher and

Weber was the rather obvious process of the *aggregation* of urban population. Almost as overt a process, that of *expansion*, has been investigated from a different and very practical point of view by groups interested in city planning, zoning and regional surveys. Even more significant than the increasing density of urban population is its correlative tendency to overflow, and so to extend over wider areas, and to incorporate these areas into a larger communal life. This paper, therefore, will treat first of the expansion of the city, and then of the lesser known processes of urban metabolism and mobility which are closely related to expansion.

Expansion as physical growth

The expansion of the city from the standpoint of the city plan, zoning and regional surveys is thought of almost wholly in terms of its physical growth. Traction studies have dealt with the development of transportation in its relation to the distribution of population throughout the city. The surveys made by the Bell Telephone Company and other public utilities have attempted to forecast the direction and the rate of growth of the city in order to anticipate the future demands for the extension of their services. In the city plan the location of parks and boulevards, the widening of traffic streets, the provision for a civic center, are all in the interest of the future control of the physical development of the city.

This expansion in area of our largest cities is now being brought forcibly to our attention by the Plan for the Study of New York and Its Environs, and by the formation of the Chicago Regional Planning Association, which extends the metropolitan district of the city to a radius of fifty miles, embracing 4000 square miles of territory. Both are attempting to measure expansion in order to deal with the changes that accompany city growth. In England, where more than one-half of the inhabitants live in cities having a population of 100,000 and over, the lively appreciation of the bearing of urban expansion on social organization is thus expressed by C. B. Fawcett (1922):

One of the most important and striking developments in the growth of the urban populations of the more advanced peoples of the world during the last few decades has been the appearance of a number of vast urban aggregates, or conurbations, far larger and more numerous than the great cities of any preceding age. These have usually been formed by the simultaneous expansion of a number of neighboring towns, which have grown out toward each other until they have reached a practical coalescence in one continuous urban area. Each such conurbation still has within it many nuclei of denser town growth, most of which represent the central areas of the various towns from which it has grown, and these nuclear patches are connected by the less densely urbanized areas which began as suburbs of these towns. The latter are still usually rather less continuously occupied by buildings, and often have many open spaces.

These great aggregates of town dwellers are a new feature in the distribution of man over the earth. At the present day there are from thirty to forty of them, each containing more than a million people, whereas only a hundred years ago there were, outside the great centers of population on the waterways of China, not more than two or three. Such aggregations of people are phenomena of great geographical and social importance; they give rise to new problems in the organization of the life and well-being of their inhabitants and in their varied activities. Few of them have yet developed a social consciousness at all proportionate to their magnitude, or fully realized themselves as definite groupings of people with many common interests, emotions and thoughts (pp. 111–12).

In Europe and America the tendency of the great city to expand has been recognized in the term 'the metropolitan area of the city', which far overruns its political limits, and in the case of New York and Chicago, even state lines. The metropolitan area may be taken to include urban territory that is physically contiguous, but it is coming to be defined by that facility of transportation that enables a businessman to live in a suburb of Chicago and to work in the loop, and his wife to shop at Marshall Field's and attend grand opera in the Auditorium.

Expansion as a process

No study of expansion as a process has yet been made, although the materials for such a study and intimations of different aspects of the process are contained in city planning, zoning and regional surveys. The typical processes of the expansion of the city can best be illustrated, perhaps, by a series of concentric circles, which may be numbered to designate both the successive zones of urban extension and the types of areas differentiated in the process of expansion (see Figure 1).

This represents an ideal construction of the tendencies of any town or city to expand radially from its central business district – on the map 'The Loop'. Encircling the downtown area there is normally an area in transition, which is being invaded by business and light manufacture. A third area is inhabited by the workers in industries who have escaped from the area of deterioration but who desire to live within easy access of their work. Beyond this zone is the 'residential area' of high-class apartment buildings or of exclusive 'restricted' districts of single family dwellings. Still farther, out beyond the city limits, is the commuters zone – suburban areas, or satellite cities – within a thirty- to sixty-minute ride of the central business district.

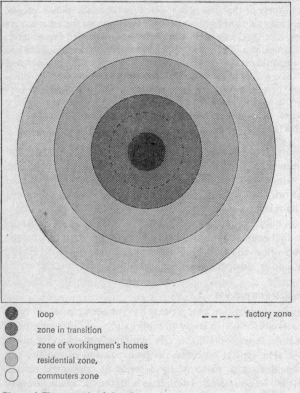

loop

zone in transition

zone of workingmen's homes

residential zone,

commuters zone

_ _ _ _ _ factory zone

Figure 1 The growth of the city

This chart brings out clearly the main fact of expansion, namely, the tendency of each inner zone to extend its area by the invasion of the next outer zone. This aspect of expansion may be called *succession*, a process which has been studied in detail in plant ecology. If this chart is applied to Chicago, all four of these zones were in its history included in the circumference of the inner zone, the present business district. The present boundaries of the area of deterioration were not many years ago those of the zone now inhabited by independent wage-earners, and within the memories of thousands of Chicagoans contained the residences of the 'best families'. It hardly needs to be added that neither Chicago nor any other city fits perfectly into this ideal scheme. Complications are introduced by the lake front, the Chicago River, railroad lines, historical factors in the location of industry, the relative degree of the resistance of communities to invasion, etc.

Besides extension and succession, the general process of expansion in urban growth involves the antagonistic and yet complementary processes of concentration and decentralization. In all cities there is the natural tendency for local and outside transportation to converge in the central business district. In the downtown section of every large city we expect to find the department stores, the skyscraper office buildings, the railroad stations, the great hotels, the theaters, the art museum and the city hall. Quite naturally, almost inevitably, the economic, cultural and political life centers here. The relation of centralization to the other processes of city life may be roughly gauged by the fact that over half a million people daily enter and leave Chicago's 'loop'. More recently sub-business centers have grown up in outlying zones. These 'satellite loops' do not, it seems, represent the 'hoped for' revival of the neighborhood, but rather a telescoping of several local communities into a larger economic unity. The Chicago of yesterday, an agglomeration of country towns and immigrant colonies, is undergoing a process of reorganization into a centralized decentralized system of local communities coalescing into sub-business areas visibly or invisibly dominated by the central business district. The actual processes of what may be called centralized decentralization are now being studied in the development of the chain store, which is only one illustration of the change in the basis of the urban organization.[1]

Expansion, as we have seen, deals with the physical growth of the city, and with the extension of the technical services that have made city life not only livable, but comfortable, even luxurious. Certain of these basic necessities of urban life are possible only through a tremendous development of communal existence. Three millions of people in Chicago are dependent upon one

1. See E. H. Shideler, *The Retail Business Organization as an Index of Community Organization.*

unified water system, one giant gas company, and one huge electric light plant. Yet, like most of the other aspects of our communal urban life, this economic co-operation is an example of co-operation without a shred of what the 'spirit of co-operation' is commonly thought to signify. The great public utilities are a part of the mechanization of life in great cities, and have little or no other meaning for social organization.

Yet the processes of expansion, and especially the rate of expansion, may be studied not only in the physical growth and business development, but also in the consequent changes in the social organization and in personality types. How far is the growth of the city, in its physical and technical aspects, matched by a natural but adequate readjustment in the social organization? What, for a city, is a normal rate of expansion, a rate of expansion with which controlled changes in the social organization might successfully keep pace?

Social organization and disorganization as processes of metabolism

These questions may best be answered, perhaps, by thinking of urban growth as a resultant of organization and disorganization analogous to the anabolic and katabolic processes of metabolism in the body. In what way are individuals incorporated into the life of a city? By what process does a person become an organic part of his society? The natural process of acquiring culture is by birth. A person is born into a family already adjusted to a social environment – in this case the modern city. The natural rate of increase of population most favorable for assimilation may then be taken as the excess of the birth-rate over the death-rate, but is this the normal rate of city growth? Certainly, modern cities have increased and are increasing in population at a far higher rate. However, the natural rate of growth may be used to measure the disturbances of metabolism caused by any excessive increase, as those which followed the great influx of southern Negroes into northern cities since the war. In a similar way all cities show deviations in composition by age and sex from a standard population such as that of Sweden, unaffected in recent years by any great emigration or immigration. Here again, marked variations, as any great excess of males over females, or of females over males, or in the proportion of children, or of grown men or women, are symptomatic of abnormalities in social metabolism.

Normally the processes of disorganization and organization may be thought of as in reciprocal relationship to each other, and as co-operating in a moving equilibrium of social order toward an end vaguely or definitely regarded as progressive. So far as disorganization points to reorganization and makes for more efficient adjustment, disorganization must be conceived not as pathological, but as normal. Disorganization as preliminary to reorganization of attitudes and conduct is almost invariably the lot of the newcomer to the city, and the discarding of the habitual, and often of what has been to him the moral, is not infrequently accompanied by sharp mental conflict and sense of personal loss. Oftener, perhaps, the change gives sooner or later a feeling of emancipation and an urge toward new goals.

In the expansion of the city a process of distribution takes place which sifts and sorts and relocates individuals and groups by residence and occupation. The resulting differentiation of the cosmopolitan American city into areas is typically all from one pattern, with only interesting minor modifications (Figure 2). Within the central business district or on an adjoining street is the 'main stem' of 'hobohemia', the teeming Rialto of the homeless migratory man of the Middle West.[2] In the zone of deterioration encircling the central business section are always to be found the so-called 'slums' and 'bad lands', with their submerged regions of poverty, degradation, and disease, and their underworlds of crime and vice. Within a deteriorating area are rooming-house districts, the purgatory of 'lost souls'. Near by is the Latin Quarter, where creative and rebellious spirits resort. The slums are also crowded to overflowing with immigrant colonies – the Ghetto, Little Sicily, Greektown, Chinatown – fascinatingly combining old world heritages and American adaptations. Wedging out from here is the Black Belt, with its free and disorderly life. The area of deterioration, while essentially one of decay, of stationary or declining population, is also one of regeneration, as witness the mission, the settlement, the artists' colony, radical centers – all obsessed with the vision of a new and better world.

The next zone is also inhabited predominatingly by factory and shop workers, but skilled and thrifty. This is an area of second immigrant settlement, generally of the second generation. It is the region of escape from the slum, the *Deutschland* of the aspiring Ghetto family. For *Deutschland* (literally 'Germany') is the name given, half in envy, half in derision, to that region beyond the Ghetto where successful neighbors appear to be imitating German Jewish standards of living. But the inhabitant of this area in turn

2. For a study of this cultural area of city life see Anderson (1923).

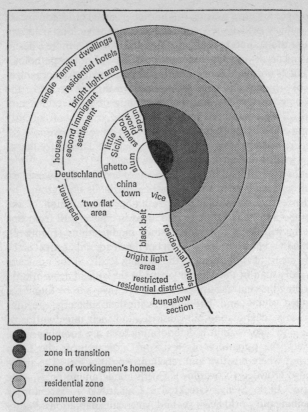

single family dwellings
residential hotels
bright light area
houses
second immigrant settlement
apartment houses
Deutschland
'two flat' area
little Sicily
ghetto
under world
roomers
slum
china town
vice
black belt
bright light area
restricted residential district
residential hotels
bungalow section

● loop
● zone in transition
◐ zone of workingmen's homes
◯ residential zone
○ commuters zone

Figure 2 Urban areas

looks to the 'Promised Land' beyond, to its residential hotels, its apartment-house region, its 'satellite loops', and its 'bright light' areas.

This differentiation into natural economic and cultural groupings gives form and character to the city. For segregation offers the group, and thereby the individuals who compose the group, a place and a role in the total organization of city life. Segregation limits development in certain directions, but releases it in others. These areas tend to accentuate certain traits, to attract and develop their kind of individuals, and so to become further differentiated.

The division of labor in the city likewise illustrates disorganization, reorganization and increasing differentiation. The immigrant from rural communities in Europe and America seldom brings with him economic skill of any great value in our industrial, commercial or professional life. Yet interesting occupational selection has taken place by nationality, explainable more by racial temperament or circumstance than by old-world economic background, as Irish policemen, Greek ice-cream parlors, Chinese laundries, Negro porters, Belgian janitors, etc.

The facts that in Chicago one million (996,589) individuals gainfully employed reported 509 occupations, and that over 1000 men and women in *Who's Who* gave 116 different vocations, give some notion of how in the city the minute differentiation of occupation 'analyzes and sifts the population, separating and classifying the diverse elements'.[3] These figures also afford some intimation of the complexity and complication of the modern industrial mechanism and the intricate segregation and isolation of divergent economic groups. Interrelated with this economic division of labor is a corresponding division into social classes and into cultural and recreational groups. From this multiplicity of groups, with their different patterns of life, the person finds his congenial social world and – what is not feasible in the narrow confines of a village – may move and live in widely separated, and perchance conflicting, worlds. Personal disorganization may be but the failure to harmonize the canons of conduct of two divergent groups.

If the phenomena of expansion and metabolism indicate that a moderate degree of disorganization may and does facilitate social organization, they indicate as well that rapid urban expansion is accompanied by excessive increases in disease, crime, disorder, vice, insanity and suicide, rough indexes of social disorganization. But what are the indexes of the causes, rather than of the effects, of the disordered social metabolism of the city? The excess of the actual over the natural increase of population has already been suggested as a criterion. The significance of this increase consists in the immigration into a metropolitan city like New York and Chicago of tens of thousands of persons annually. Their invasion of the city has the effect of a tidal wave inundating first the immigrant colonies, the ports of first entry, dislodging thousands of inhabitants who overflow into the next zone, and so on and on until the momentum of the wave has spent its force on the last urban zone. The whole effect is to speed up expansion, to speed up

3. Weber (1899, p. 442).

industry, to speed up the 'junking' process in the area of deterioration (II). These internal movements of the population become the more significant for study. What movement is going on in the city, and how may this movement be measured? It is easier, of course, to classify movement within the city than to measure it. There is the movement from residence to residence, change of occupation, labor turnover, movement to and from work, movement for recreation and adventure. This leads to the question: What is the significant aspect of movement for the study of the changes in city life? The answer to this question leads directly to the important distinction between movement and mobility.

Mobility as the pulse of the community

Movement, *per se*, is not an evidence of change or of growth. In fact, movement may be a fixed and unchanging order of motion, designed to control a constant situation, as in routine movement. Movement that is significant for growth implies a change of movement in response to a new stimulus or situation. Change of movement of this type is called *mobility*. Movement of the nature of routine finds its typical expression in work. Change of movement, or mobility, is characteristically expressed in adventure. The great city, with its 'bright lights', its emporiums of novelties and bargains, its palaces of amusement, its underworld of vice and crime, its risks of life and property from accident, robbery, and homicide, has become the region of the most intense degree of adventure and danger, excitement and thrill.

Mobility, it is evident, involves change, new experience, stimulation. Stimulation induces a response of the person to those objects in his environment which afford expression for his wishes. For the person, as for the physical organism, stimulation is essential to growth. Response to stimulation is wholesome so long as it is a correlated *integral* reaction of the entire personality. When the reaction is *segmental*, that is, detached from, and uncontrolled by, the organization of personality, it tends to become disorganizing or pathological. That is why stimulation for the sake of stimulation, as in the restless pursuit of pleasure, partakes of the nature of vice.

The mobility of city life, with its increase in the number and intensity of stimulations, tends inevitably to confuse and to demoralize the person. For an essential element in the mores and in personal morality is consistency, consistency of the type that is natural in the social control of the primary group. Where mobility is the greatest, and where in consequence primary controls break down completely, as in the zone of deterioration in the modern city, there develop areas of demoralization, of promiscuity and of vice.

In our studies of the city it is found that areas of mobility are also the regions in which are found juvenile delinquency, boys' gangs, crime, poverty, wife desertion, divorce, abandoned infants and vice.

These concrete situations show why mobility is perhaps the best index of the state of metabolism of the city. Mobility may be thought of in more than a fanciful sense, as the 'pulse of the community'. Like the pulse of the human body, it is a process which reflects and is indicative of all the changes that are taking place in the community, and which is susceptible of analysis into elements which may be stated numerically.

The elements entering into mobility may be classified under two main heads: (1) the state of mutability of the person, and (2) the number and kind of contacts or stimulations in his environment. The mutability of city populations varies with sex and age composition, the degree of detachment of the person from the family and from other groups. All these factors may be expressed numerically. The new stimulations to which a population respond can be measured in terms of change of movement or of increasing contacts. Statistics on the movement of urban population may only measure routine, but an increase at a higher ratio than the increase of population measures mobility. In 1860 the horse-car lines of New York City carried about fifty million passengers; in 1890 the trolley-cars (and a few surviving horse-cars) transported about 500 million; in 1921, the elevated, subway, surface, and electric and steam suburban lines carried a total of more than 2500 million passengers.[4] In Chicago the total annual rides per capita on the surface and elevated lines were 164 in 1890; 215 in 1900; 320 in 1910; and 338 in 1921. In addition, the rides per capita on steam and electric suburban lines almost doubled between 1916 (23) and 1921 (41), and the increasing use of the automobile must not be overlooked.[5] For example, the number of automobiles in Illinois increased from 131,140 in 1915 to 833,920 in 1923.[6]

4. Adapted from W. B. Monro (1923, p. 377).
5. *Report of the Chicago Subway and Traction Commission* (p. 81), and the *Report on a Physical Plan for a Unified Transportation System* (p. 391).
6. Data compiled by automobile industries.

Mobility may be measured not only by these changes of movement, but also by increase of contacts. While the increase of population of Chicago in 1912–22 was less than 25 per cent (23·6 per cent), the increase of letters delivered to Chicagoans was double that (49·6 per cent) – (from 693,084,196 to 1,038,007,854).[7] In 1912 New York had 8·8 telephones; in 1922, 16·9 per 100 inhabitants. Boston had, in 1912, 10·1 telephones; ten years later, 19·5 telephones per 100 inhabitants. In the same decade the figures for Chicago increased from 12·3 to 21·6 per 100 population.[8] But increase of the use of the telephone is probably more significant than increase in the number of telephones. The number of telephone calls in Chicago increased from 606,131,928 in 1914 to 944,010,586 in 1922,[9] an increase of 55·7 per cent, while the population increased only 13·4 per cent.

Land values, since they reflect movement, afford one of the most sensitive indexes of mobility. The highest land values in Chicago are at the point of greatest mobility in the city, at the corner of State and Madison streets, in the Loop. A traffic count showed that at the rush period 31,000 people an hour, or 210,000 men and women in sixteen and one-half hours, passed the southwest corner. For over ten years land values in the Loop have been stationary, but in the same time they have doubled, quadrupled, and even sextupled in the strategic corners of the 'satellite loops'[10] an accurate index of the changes which have occurred. Our investigations so far seem to indicate that variations in land values, especially where correlated with differences in rents, offer perhaps the best single measure of mobility, and so of all the changes taking place in the expansion and growth of the city.

In general outline, I have attempted to present the point of view and methods of investigation which the department of sociology is employing in its studies in the growth of the city, namely, to describe urban expansion in terms of extension, succession, and concentration; to determine how expansion disturbs metabolism when disorganization is in excess of organi-

7. Statistics of mailing division, Chicago Post Office.
8. Determined from *Census Estimates for Intercensual Years*.
9. From statistics furnished by Mr R. Johnson, traffic supervisor, Illinois Bell Telephone Company.
10. From 1912–23, land values per front foot increased in Bridgeport from $600 to $1250; in Division-Ashland-Milwaukee district, from $2000 to $4500; in 'Back of the Yards', from $1000 to $3000; in Englewood, from $2500 to $8000; in Wilson Avenue, from $1000 to $6000; but decreased in the Loop from $20,000 to $16,500.

zation; and, finally, to define mobility and to propose it as a measure both of expansion and metabolism, susceptible to precise quantitative formulation, so that it may be regarded almost literally as the pulse of the community. In a way, this statement might serve as an introduction to any one of five or six research projects under way in the department. The project, however, in which I am directly engaged is an attempt to apply these methods of investigation to a cross-section of the city – to put this area, as it were, under the microscope, and so to study in more detail and with greater control and precision the processes which have been described here in the large. For this purpose the West Side Jewish community has been selected. This community includes the so-called 'Ghetto', or area of first settlement, and Lawndale, the so-called 'Deutschland', or area of second settlement. This area has certain obvious advantages for this study, from the standpoint of expansion, metabolism, and mobility. It exemplifies the tendency to expansion radially from the business center of the city. It is now relatively a homogeneous cultural group. Lawndale is itself an area in flux, with the tide of migrants still flowing in from the Ghetto and a constant egress to more desirable regions of the residential zone. In this area, too, it is also possible to study how the expected outcome of this high rate of mobility in social and personal disorganization is counteracted in large measure by the efficient communal organization of the Jewish community.

References

ANDERSON, N. (1923), *The Hobo*, Chicago.
FAWCETT, C. B. (1922), 'British conurbations in 1921', *Sociol. Rev.*, vol. 14, pp. 111–12.
MONRO, W. B. (1923), *Municipal Government and Administration*, Macmillan.
WEBER, A. (1899), *The Growth of Cities in the Nineteenth Century*, Macmillan.

7 J. Rothenberg

Elimination of Blight and Slums

J. Rothenberg, 'Elimination of blight and slums', in *Economic Evaluation of Urban Renewal*, Brookings Institution, 1967, ch. 3, pp. 32–57.

As the discussion so far has indicated, this study seeks to trace the positive and negative effects of urban renewal on the well-being of all involved individuals. No amendment need be made to this for the treatment of so-called 'social goods'.[1] This study is not a manipulation of theory for its own sake, however. It seeks to fashion a technique that will facilitate empirical measurement and thus the need to deal with 'social goods' will require some modification.

Urban renewal projects do not simply change the amount and quality of some goods and services; they may bring about extensive changes in the whole pattern of urban living activities. As has long been recognized, human-environmental interactions may be changed. Indeed, the possibilities of such profound and subtle changes rank high among the reasons for which urban renewal has been championed by its advocates.[2] Many of these effects can be only vaguely delineated. Quantitative distinctions will be rudimentary. Furthermore, for some of these and even for other kinds of consequences that are more capable of being delineated, their action is so diffuse that it is difficult to separate the affected from the unaffected portions of the population. The influence on urban architecture, for example, is probably of this sort. Finally, some portions of the population who may not themselves be directly affected by the project nevertheless have strong preferences about how others fare under it – for example, the concern in the general population about how impoverished or racial minority groups are treated. Urban renewal involves 'social goods' in this double

1. The term 'social goods' is used in the spirit of Paul A. Samuelson's 'public goods', but is somewhat broader, as will be indicated briefly below. For an explanation of Samuelson's concept, see Samuelson (1954).

2. Much of the theoretical and empirical work in this area is in the sociological and social psychology literature. It is a large and controversial field.

sense of extensive, subtle external interactions and a broad concerned audience.[3]

These social-good effects are considered not only extensive but also very important foci of the urban renewal program. They may prove ultimately to be either measurable but trivial, or entirely intractable; but at the outset the kinds of effects that are likely to be involved must be examined, as well as their order of magnitude and the methods by which they can be measured. The complexity of some of these interactions has been mentioned above. An implication of this complexity is that since the environment of an individual cannot be controlled in order to measure his state of well-being, it is not *a priori* obvious which indices should be looked at to find the consequences of renewal activity. A desideratum of the procedure being formulated is operational feasibility. The admonition to observe everything fails this test.

A short-cut way to seek at least some of the directions of significant influence is to consider the purposes of the urban renewal program. The more significant of the many purposes – both explicit and tacit – that have been ascribed to it are:

1. Elimination of blight and slums
2. Mitigation of poverty
3. Provision of decent, safe and sanitary housing in a suitable environment for all
4. Revival of downtown business areas of the central cities
5. Maintenance and/or expansion of universities and hospitals
6. Achievement and/or maintenance of an adequate middle-income household component in the central city
7. Attraction of additional 'clean' industry into the central city and
8. Enhancement of the financial strength of the central city government.

The redevelopment portion of urban renewal has been deemed to have all of these same purposes; and all but numbers 4, 5, and

3. The term 'collective goods' also relates to highly diffused externalities, but not where these externalities are distributed with notable inequalities. Moreover, the externalities subsumed are of physical effects, and not of interdependence in the utility functions of individuals whereby one individual's well-being is a function of another's well-being, not of the other's particular consumption pattern. These are the major differences between 'public goods' and 'social goods' as used here.

7 have been variously ascribed to residential redevelopment. Rehabilitation and 'community renewal', two other renewal approaches under the overall program, have had the same list ascribed to them. Each item in the list will be examined in turn to discover its relationship with urban renewal and the nature of the benefits thereby generated.

The nature of blight and slums

What is the purpose of the federal urban renewal program? Possibly the major target of the program is to eliminate 'blight and slums'. There are at least two ambiguities in this objective, one associated with the meaning of 'blight' and 'slum', the other with the purpose to be achieved by their elimination.

'Blight' and 'slum' are not rigorously defined in the federal statutes, nor in most discussions of the subject. The conventional meanings are in terms of the physical characteristics of dwellings in relation to their occupancy. The closest to an official definition is found in the Housing Act of 1937: '"Slum" means "any area where dwellings predominate which, by reason of dilapidation, over-crowding, faulty arrangement or design, lack of ventilation, light, or sanitation facilities, or any combination of these factors, are detrimental to safety, health or morals".'[4] To use more recent terminology, the dwellings do not provide housing that is 'decent, safe, and sanitary'. Slum dwellings are usually filthy and vermin infested and are fire hazards. 'Dilapidation', in the above definition, has been given content by the Census Bureau in the 1950 Census as follows: 'A dwelling unit should be reported as dilapidated if, because of either deterioration or inadequate original construction, it is below the generally accepted minimum standard for housing and should be torn down, extensively repaired or rebuilt.'[5] This usage would certainly seem to be ambiguous for measurement purposes; yet the Census Bureau has apparently used it successfully.[6]

'Blight' is not ordinarily sharply distinguished from 'slum'. It often refers simply to the process, stage, or state that characterizes a slum but is more general in that it can apply to single structures as well as to clusters. It is more frequently applied to

4. Sections 2 and 3. Cited in Rumney (1951, p. 69).
5. US Bureau of the Census, *The 1950 Enumerator's Manual*. Cited in Rumney (1951, pp. 75–76).
6. Rumney (1951).

non-residential structures than is the term 'slum'. Another difference is that 'blight' sometimes is used to indicate the process by which property becomes substandard. So property may exhibit different degrees of blight, whereas the cluster of structures in a slum exhibits well-advanced stages of blight.

These definitions are based essentially on conventional judgment – judgment about what kind of housing is decent or safe or sanitary. Sometimes this is supplemented by a criterion that is more operational, the criterion of 'standard' versus 'substandard' housing. This criterion was formulated by the Census Bureau for the 1940 Census. A dwelling unit is defined as 'substandard' if 'it is in need of major repairs, or lack[s] a private bath, or private indoor toilet, or running water' (1951, p. 75). The first part of this definition is highly judgmental (as it turns out, more variably so than the later-defined 'dilapidated'), and the remainder has been characterized as a criterion of architectural obsolescence rather than of disrepair.[7] Houses that are hampered today because they are of older architectural fashion and standards may in all other respects be in good condition.

Ambiguity about the definition of slums is bothersome but not decisive. Slums do exist, and most observers would agree on the classification of areas into slums and non-slums. Ambiguity introduces slippage into the consensus and makes fuzzy the enumeration of the critical dimensions of the problem.

Slums and resource allocation

Under the definitions so far, slum and blight refer to poor housing – housing of low quality.[8] In addition, overcrowding means that the per capita accommodations are small. In this sense they refer also to housing of low quantity. It is not surprising that slums are typically inhabited by poor families.

The 'demand' for slums

What if these low-income families, given their poverty, want low-quality, low-quantity housing as part of a utility-maximizing pattern of expenditure? What if, given such a demand and considering the conditions of supply for housing, the continued existence of a stock of low-grade housing is part of an optimal overall use of resources? Then a policy goal of eliminating low-grade

7. See Greer (1965).
8. The discussion at this point is confined to residential renewal. Some of the analysis will be relevant to non-residential blight as well.

housing can yield benefits only if some further goal will thereby be facilitated.

Slum removal in itself can yield social benefits only if at least one of the following is true: low-income groups do not demand low-grade housing because of their small budgets; or demand and supply conditions together do not make low-grade housing an efficient resource use; or slums are something more than simply low-grade housing – that is, either they are themselves something more, or they have unintended consequences not easily controlled by consumers and others. Therefore the question must be raised whether slums can be said to be part of an optimal (given an assumed pattern of poverty) equilibrium situation. This must be investigated in some detail to put into better perspective the arguments of those who, on the one hand, assert that the housing market can in effect 'do everything' if left undisturbed and those who, on the other, say that it can in effect 'do nothing' unless radically disturbed.

If there is poverty, this means that some people are living a 'substandard' way of life. Such a way of life must necessarily contain some 'substandard' elements – perhaps inadequate food, or clothing, or recreation, or shelter, or various combinations of these. Poor housing may easily be seen as an effective way to economize desperately scarce purchasing power. Moreover, it may be the easiest sacrifice to make. Hunger and cold are immediate pains and are barriers against holding gainful employment in a way that dirty, old, overcrowded living quarters are not. The 'decency' of housing rests on conventional value premises that vary widely among groups with different economic, ethnic and urban-rural backgrounds, and with differences in other dimensions of culture. Urban slums are occupied disproportionately by first-generation immigrant families; many of these migrated away from housing conditions so bad that the urban slum represented an improvement.

Thus, on the demand side it is conceivable that low-grade occupancy is part of the preferred expenditure pattern for many impoverished families. If these families nonetheless dislike such occupancy, and if the general public dislikes it for them as well, then the problem here is not slums but poverty. Subject to what determines the supply response of the housing industry (discussed below), one could argue that the eradication of poverty would eradicate slum occupancy, and indeed that 'artificially' destroying particular slums without making an attack on poverty would not eradicate slum occupancy, since other slums would be created elsewhere. But the eradication of slum occupancy by dealing with poverty would be simply a symptom or a by-product of the improvement in the overall standard of living of poor people. The overall improvement is accounted as the benefit of the program. The slum elimination should not be accorded any additional benefits.[9]

Factors affecting supply

The supply function for housing is influenced heavily by the durability of residential structures and the relative ease with which quality changes in either direction can be incorporated in existing structures. At any one time the marginal cost of providing some conventional unit of given quality of housing service during the next accounting period from the existing stock of housing is typically considerably less than from a newly built structure. Further, the difference in expected present value of net returns between an existing structure in tolerably good condition and a comparable new structure almost always favors the former – considering relative quality of service and its value, the cost of incorporating quality changes, remaining expected lifetime, and expected maintenance cost, and counting acquisition cost as zero for the former. It rarely pays to build new housing explicitly to replace parts of the existing housing stock that are in at least fairly good condition.[10] New construction usually functions to expand the size of the overall stock. Where dwelling units are retired from the existing stock to offset the effect of new construction on size of stock, this retirement does not occur in the same part of the market that is primarily affected by the new construction. Rather, retirements come mostly from the low end of the stock – the dilapidated, lowest-quality structures. In any one year new construction forms only a small percentage of the total stock and is typically fashioned to the housing demands of middle-income and upper middle-income consumers. Public housing is a well-known exception, but of course it is not part of the private market response; even as an exception, moreover, it is a very small part of new construction.

Housing accommodations for lower-income households are

9. Later analysis in this chapter suggests that this is not the whole story.
10. Housing in tolerably good condition is likely to be directly replaced only if dramatic changes in land use are involved – for example, if a few single family dwellings are to be replaced by a large high-rise structure.

typically made available by converting dwellings from use by higher-income households. This is known as 'filtering'.[11] Sometimes, the conversion requires more or less extensive physical alteration of the structure – as, for example, the installation of new partitions and walls and additional plumbing and electrical wiring if more occupants are to inhabit the same area. Sometimes conversion requires no physical change at all, but involves the amount and kinds of services that the property owner provides his tenants. Where conversion consists simply in a transfer of home ownership, no change in capital or services is involved at all. Since mobility within the housing market is apt to be greater at higher levels of income than at lower levels,[12] filtering is initiated largely by middle-income and higher-income groups releasing their present accommodation in favor of newly constructed dwellings. Conversion occurs via changes in vacancy rates and relative prices. Thus, the housing stock gradually passes downward from one income group to a lower one. The private housing industry has generally not found it profitable to construct new dwellings for the lower-income groups in competition with the existing stock filtering down.

Thus a stock of typically old, worn housing, cut up in the process of downward conversion in order to decrease the size of the dwelling unit, is the type of accommodation that the housing industry provides to the poor. Unless one can show that such housing is still above the slum level, or that, while at slum level, the supply response reflects externalities that are not heeded in the market, one is led to the position that inferior housing for the poor may well be an equilibrium situation representing optimal resource use. In such a case, a policy devoted to direct eradication of slums produces no benefits on that score at all. It does so only if other goals are simultaneously met in the program.

Suboptimality of slum housing: market externalities

In the analysis so far, slums and blight have been treated as though they referred simply to housing in a late stage of filtering –

11. This discussion depends heavily on Grigsby (1963, chs 2–3). The concept of 'filtering' is controversial.

12. It should be noted, however, that the wealthiest families are probably more fixed in domicile than any other group, including the poorest. The probability is a function of upward social mobility and dissatisfaction, as well as of wealth and insecurity; so there is a mixture of motives operating on any income class.

an orderly equilibrium market response to normal demand and supply forces. But *is* this what was described above as blight and slums? Low quality, low quantity is one problem; dilapidation, filth, and unsafe and unsanitary conditions may well be another. There are a number of reasons for believing that slums are not an optimizing response to normal market forces.

There are at least three respects in which slums may represent suboptimal resource use:

1. There are important 'neighborhood effect' externalities in land use. These are likely to be especially significant in slum areas.

2. The profitability incentives to produce the particular type of low-quality housing that characterizes slums rest upon market biases that are either ethically disapproved or are the inadvertent result of public policies.

3. The functioning of slums entails the creation of important social costs that are externalities to the people involved.

Neighborhood effects

There are important externalities in the nature of housing services and hence in the value of the property that provides them.[13] The housing consumed by a household consists not only in occupancy of a specific dwelling but also in the location of the dwelling and its neighborhood. The neighborhood consists of other residential dwellings, of commercial and industrial establishments, of public services like schools, street lighting, and police protection, of recreational and cultural amenities, and, perhaps most of all, of people. Consider the simple model presented in Davis and Whinston (1961, pp. 106–12). The quality of the housing services associated with a particular dwelling depends on the character of the dwelling and the amount of maintenance and repair devoted to it; also on the character of dwellings in the neighborhood, together with their state of maintenance-repair. For each of the n pieces of property comprising the neighborhood, the owner obtains the highest return if his property is undermaintained while all or most others are well maintained. He gets a smaller return if his, as well as all or most of the others, is well maintained, less if his and all or most others are poorly maintained, and least if his

13. This contention is widespread and has been current for some time. Two recent works make this the cornerstone of a theory of urban renewal: Davis (1960, pp. 220–26); Davis and Whinston (1961, pp. 105–17).

is well maintained while all or most others are poorly maintained. This is the payoff matrix of the 'Prisoner's Dilemma' type of strategic game. Each owner has an incentive to let his property be undermaintained while others maintain their property well. But the very generality of this incentive means that it cannot be realized. All property will tend to be undermaintained. Yet this outcome is less satisfactory to all owners than the only other attainable outcome, namely high maintenance for all. The latter could not be attained by atomistic behavior, since each owner singly would shy away from high maintenance. But it is an outcome that all could agree to bring about simultaneously. That is, each could agree to it contingent on everyone else's agreeing to it.

Private response to externalities

The private market could achieve an optimal response in the face of these externalities by either of two means:

1. By voluntary agreements among property owners to coordinate their behavior so as to achieve mutually satisfactory results

2. By an integration of resource decisions over neighborhoods through large-scale private assembly of land.

Both means are likely to be inadequately used, however. Voluntary agreements of the sort envisaged are difficult to bring into being and even more difficult to maintain successfully. Often quite a large number of property owners is involved in any externality. It is an extremely onerous task to get voluntary agreement from enough of them to make a difference in the market. More important though, in order for such an agreement to be successful, some enforcement mechanism is needed, since without it each individual has an incentive to pretend to be abiding by the agreement in order to induce compliance by others and then to violate it by undermaintaining his property. Widespread violations are likely to result.

The integration of resource decisions through land assembly also faces obstacles. The large number of property owners who must be dealt with imposes very costly bargaining burdens on a would-be private assembler. The process of assembly is a sequence of bilateral monopoly confrontations, with each potential seller eager to squeeze out the full amount of profit to be obtained from the assembler's integrated decision-making. The result for the latter is a very high cost in both time and money – a formidable obstacle when the number of necessary transactions is large.

Thus, the important externality of neighborhood means that the outcome arrived at by atomistic choice will typically be sub-optimal, in the sense that non-atomistic co-ordinated choice would make all owners better off than when they are acting atom-istically.

The notion of this type of externality is deemed so important by Davis and Whinston that they base their entire analysis of urban renewal on it and indeed redefine 'blight' in terms of it. 'Blight is said to exist whenever (1) strictly individual action does not result in redevelopment, (2) the co-ordination of decision-making via some means would result in redevelopment, and (3) the sum of benefits from renewal could exceed the sum of costs' (1961, pp. 111–12). Moreover, blight is sharply distinguished from slums. Slums are characterized by physical attributes, blight is a process of suboptimal land use. Under their analysis some slums need not reflect blight – they may represent optimal resource use. On the other hand, areas that are not slums may be blighted. To eradi-cate slums that are not blighted produces no benefits in terms of aggregate national product.

This analysis substantially complicates the discussion up to now. The immediate policy goal of the urban renewal program being the elimination of blight and slums, the two have been dealt with as near synonyms and in recognizably physical terms. If blight is the evil to be tackled and it bears no particular relation to slums, why are slums relevant at all? The problem of blight under this conception stems from the existence of externalities (in production and consumption) – the influence of the neighbor-hood. But this is a very general kind of influence and may be supposed to affect property in all areas. Moreover, neighborhood effects may not everywhere be such that low maintenance is sub-optimal. There may well be situations where high maintenance is suboptimal. Is the market any better able to adjust land uses to the complicated pattern of such externalities in upper-income areas than it is in lower-income areas? At first glance, it would seem that one would have to be willing to say that suboptimal land use can occur anywhere, at any level, in any direction, and to any extent, depending only on accident; and that one would apply the term 'blight' to only those areas whose misallocation could be corrected at smaller 'redevelopment' cost than the degree of misallocation.

It should be made clear that land misuse can take many forms: undermaintenance *or* overmaintenance; or the very character of the housing services, such as single versus multiple occupancy dwellings, high-rise versus walkup apartment buildings, attached versus detached structures, etc.; or even the residential-commercial-industrial use mix. The very diversity of these misuse patterns seems to push residential slums further into the background.

Social action and slums

Yet there is a special correlation between this type of market suboptimality and slum areas. Neighborhood effects are generally recognized, and special social mechanisms have been devised to minimize their adverse consequences. Building codes, health codes, and zoning are examples of measures that seek to moderate some of the worst effects of land-use externalities. They set lower limits on housing quality to avoid the sheer physical dangers of fire and disease; they forbid a degree of heterogeneity of use that would have significant nuisance value; and through residential zoning, they stipulate quality and quantity minima above that of avoiding physical inconvenience to preserve a desired homogeneity of social status. It should be noted that most of these involve setting lower limits but never upper limits. Overmaintenance and 'inappropriate' upward conversion are not controlled by zoning and building codes.[14] Undermaintenance and downward conversion are the objects of control.

While the scope and enforcement of these control instruments vary widely, there is much in the planning and renewal literature that suggests that zoning and building codes are less effective for low-quality areas than for high-quality areas.[15] There are a number of reasons for this. First, slum homeowners are likely to have low incomes. But depreciation on their old dwellings makes necessary substantial maintenance expenses, sometimes major repairs. Their own resources are likely to be too meager, and their

14. However, it is argued below that such upward conversion, while by assumption a more expensive use of the land than is warranted, may well mean significant external economies to the rest of the community – that is, heterogeneity produced through selective upward conversion can result in community benefits that heterogeneity through selective downward conversion may not.

15. See for example, Rhyne (1960, pp. 685–704).

efforts to borrow from private sources are almost invariably frustrated. Loans through conventional channels are very nearly unobtainable. When they can be obtained, interest rates are likely to be quite high,[16] thus cutting down the demand. The credit available for housing in these areas is typically undercover financing at very high interest rates for dealers in speculative housing. This encourages not maintenance but conversion of dwellings to slum use (Jacobs, 1961).

Second, the situation is somewhat the same for landlords. Low-income rentals often involve tenants who have only slight stakes in the community, often recently migrated from rural, culturally different societies, with little appreciation of the necessary disciplines involved in urban living. Their occupancy is very likely to accelerate markedly the depreciation of their dwelling units. Again adequate maintenance is likely to be very expensive, and, when major repairs are needed, it is likely to be thwarted by the unavailability of credit. Thus, the rapid, even accelerated, depreciation of property makes upkeep onerous. This is enough to induce some homeowners to skimp on maintenance and to risk code violations. For landlords it provides a temptation to skimp; but this temptation is not enough to provoke violation, if to do so would mean weakening their market position *vis-à-vis* tenants. But tenants in these poor areas are likely to have very low bargaining power in the market. They have little wealth, little mobility, highly inadequate knowledge of alternatives, and – as is disproportionately true in slums – they are discriminated against in housing as in employment, education and political influence. Their alternatives are meager. Finally, they have often migrated to the urban area from an even poorer environment, so that the building code standards are apt to seem to them like high standards and not absolute minima. In short, they do not often either notice, or complain of, or take effective action against poor maintenance and code violations.[17] The uneven political as well as economic contest between landlord and tenant makes code enforcement politically unpopular. In addition, it is unusually expensive in a high-density area, where improvement can be

16. See Jacobs (1961, ch. 16).
17. Of course, what may be tolerable housing, from the point of view of both individual and group, in rural areas may be intolerable in a city, because it creates externalities. The individual does not see its effects on third parties who have no power to affect the terms of the transaction. This is discussed at considerable length below.

forced legally in many instances only by the costly, cumbersome process of the city taking over property from impecunious or dishonest owners, sometimes evicting poor tenants in the process. The frequent result is widespread lack of code enforcement.

Thus, the kind of misallocation of resources dealt with by Davis and Whinston *is* likely to have unusually heavy incidence in slum areas. Slums are likely to represent suboptimal land use.

Biases in the profitability of slum creation

Slums do not simply happen. They represent a pattern of resource use that is man made. They are produced because they are profitable. It is argued here that this profitability stems partly from a kind of market situation that is not 'normally approved' but rather generally desired by the electorate to be publicly rectified. It also stems partly from certain existing public policies, which are also capable of correction. Thus, the profitability of slums is not inevitable, nor does it rest on market forces that are ethically neutral. In a special sense it can be said that it is 'socially inadvertent'.

Slums are produced both intensively and extensively. Intensive production means converting property to lower and lower use and then, for lowest uses, to lower and lower quality levels of service. Extensive production means extending the spatial boundaries of slum concentrations. The two often go hand in hand. The most important kinds of intensive production are to convert dwellings to increasingly overcrowded occupancy and to allow the state of the property to deteriorate progressively.

To say that slums are profitable to produce is not to say that all property owners get excess returns. It means rather that high rewards are available to 'innovators', and, initiative having already been taken, it pays others to follow suit, sometimes against their personal preferences. Profitable opportunities exist, and the dynamics of contagion through neighborhood effects magnifies the drift. There are profitable opportunities because of the characteristics of the demand for inferior housing and because of legal and financial policies.

The effect of demand

On the demand side urban slums have historically been occupied by those who are in the lowest income groups. As was argued above, they have typically been recent immigrants into the area and members of what were at that time minority groups. They have often come to the area in large, concentrated numbers and have been poor. They have been seriously uninformed about housing alternatives and too poor to seek such information. They have been self-conscious about their differences from the rest of the urban community and have therefore been anxious to live in close proximity with members of their own group. They have been largely ignorant of their civil rights, of their rights as tenants, and of the housing code and other aspects of the law.

Such groups would have poor economic leverage on these grounds alone. On top of these bargaining disabilities, however, the rest of the community has often imposed the artificial disability of discrimination. This has become especially onerous in the present generation, when the Negro is preponderantly the slum dweller. The problem of slums is not at present solely a problem of race, but the fact that the Negro disproportionately inhabits the slums aggravates the problem. Discrimination against Negroes in employment and housing has been especially severe. In housing it takes the form of segregation.[18] Large areas of the city are effectively closed to Negro occupants, even when they are able and willing to pay the stipulated rents or acquisition costs.

As a result of all this, there is, especially under tight housing conditions, a strong uninformed, highly inelastic[19] demand for low-quality housing in concentrated areas. Expansion of the quantity supplied most profitably comes from conversion to overcrowding. Moreover, the owners, instead of making up the higher cost of accelerated depreciation by increasing rents, make it up in a less noticeable way by neglecting to maintain the property up to legally required standards. Thus, conversion to slum use often increases revenues without increasing costs and may even actually decrease costs. It is not at all unusual for property to be run down profitably to a state where the cost of bringing the structure up to the legally required minimum level exceeds the value of the property. The property in this sense has *negative* social value.[20]

Slum profitability stemming from these demand characteristics

18. Interestingly, there has been more housing segregation in northern than in southern cities. This does not imply that there has been more prejudice in the North. In the North, segregation by housing has been the only way that social, political, and educational segregation could be maintained. In the South, segregation was long maintained by custom and by law.

19. Inelastic because of a paucity of known, feasible alternatives.

20. See Dagen and Cody (1961, pp. 70–84). Compare this with other treatments of the profitability of slums: Rapkin (1959, p. 120); Metropolitan Housing and Planning Council of Chicago (1954); Nakagawa (1957, p. 45).

is a dynamic phenomenon. It does not represent a permanent source of surplus. The supply of housing is quite competitive, and the relative shortages that especially favor slum creation tend gradually to be made up. But the high durability of structures, the substantial lead time required for new construction, and discrimination combine to keep the relevant housing stock limited for significant periods of time, although conversions of existing stock down to slum use do partly offset this. A gradually decreasing profitability of slum ownership as the supply increases relative to demand tends to diminish further downward conversions. Besides, longer-run trends in population and construction can moderate slum creation over time.

But such moderation is not equivalent to reversal. It is easier to create dwellings suitable to slum occupancy than to 'uncreate' them. One reason is an asymmetry in the functioning of neighborhood effects. The existence of spots of low-quality occupancy in an otherwise higher-quality neighborhood is more likely to depress occupancy levels downward than is the existence of high-quality occupancy spots in an otherwise low-quality area to raise levels. This is because the minority spots are a nuisance calling for majority adjustment in the former situation but not in the latter. Thus, any incentive on the part of property owners to enhance the competitive attractiveness of their slum units when the market loosens tends to take the form of price cuts rather than extensive physical upgrading or outright replacement. Moreover, the attempt to offset these neighborhood effects by elaborate private redevelopment and large-scale simultaneous replacement tends to be discouraged by the very heavy transaction and bargaining costs of large-scale land assembly. Thus, overcrowding often takes place in periods of tight housing, especially when substantial in-migration of minority groups is taking place. Subsequently, in periods when housing is much looser, higher-quality housing options come from other areas (predominantly through filtering), and the slum area experiences not an upgrading but simply a higher vacancy rate and lower rental levels. Slum occupancy decreases, but slum property remains (except where vacancy becomes so great as to warrant abandonment). In sum, while slum-creating forces are sporadic, their effects are asymmetric: once formed, slum structures tend to persist. Indeed, there are additional forces, to be mentioned below, that help induce slum owners to keep their property in existence longer than the age and condition of the property would ordinarily warrant.

This dynamic impetus to slum creation may be likened to the profitability from fraud and adulteration in ordinary markets, since both depend to some extent on consumer ignorance and other disabilities. In the latter kind of situation the market response is not considered to be the product of 'normally approved' market forces. The consumer is considered to be 'unfairly' disadvantaged, and government action is typically called upon to offset the disadvantage. To the extent that such protection is not yet forthcoming, the market outcome is 'socially inadvertent'. And slum creation too has this element of 'social inadvertency'.

Supply effects

On the supply side the profitability of slum production is significantly enhanced by a number of 'artificial' factors – artificial in the sense that they are inadvertent consequences of certain public policies rather than inherent characteristics of the market. They are remediable. Federal and local tax systems are important factors of this kind.

Income and capital gains taxes. The federal income and capital gains tax system plays an important role here. A landlord can report accelerated depreciation on his property, thereby obtaining a substantial deduction from taxable income. This depreciation is not offset by maintenance outlays. When the property has been completely depreciated for tax purposes, it is still habitable, despite a lack of physical maintenance of the property, with little impairment of its competitive market position relative to the rest of the neighborhood, due to the neighborhood effects and the bargaining disabilities characteristic of the tenants. The property can then profitably be sold, because the new purchaser can subsequently take depreciation on the property anew, while failing to maintain it, and can in turn resell it profitably. The same property, many times dilapidated, is pressed into lower and lower occupancy use while continuing to be depreciated for tax purposes. Thus, where market conditions permit undermaintenance of property – as occurs in slums due to the characteristics of demand and the absence of code enforcement by government – the income tax provides an incentive to keep the property in existence longer and at a much lower level of quality than its age would warrant in the absence of the tax. This does not mean that the tax makes slum property (or indeed any old property) more profitable than non-slum (or new) property. It means simply that property already in existence is *no less profitable, regardless of its age,* than new property, so long as its owner is not forced to maintain it well (the increasingly onerous costs of upkeep being a principal reason for the replacement of old by new housing).

Where transactions can be carried out on a large scale, it is often the capital gains advantage that predominates. Speculators are led to initiate a sizable amount of deliberate conversion of non-slum structures to slum use. They buy non-slum dwellings relatively inexpensively and refashion them for the overcrowding that increases revenues and sets the stage for faster deterioration. Then they sell them. The prospects for high-income flows from slum property and subsequent capital gains enable them to realize large present capital gains, which are subject to the advantageous capital gain tax rates.[21]

There is another pattern in which primary attention to income flows through depreciation allowances induces each owner to hold onto a given piece of property for only a few years before selling it and buying another property. The rapid turnover is encouraged by the fact that depreciation allowances are greatest in the early years of ownership. The same property does continue in existence under different owners, as above. Even with this structure of depreciation, however, primary attention to capital gains will induce each owner to hold a property for a longer period when no reconversion is involved.[22] Here again the property is allowed to deteriorate badly. As with the pattern noted above, both these procedures stem from the fact that gains – whether income flows or capital gains – do not depend on adequate maintenance of the property. On the contrary, systematic neglect of maintenance increases the amount of net gains (Schorr, 1963).

Real estate taxes. The local property tax under existing appraisal practices also encourages slum use and discourages elimination of slums. Tax assessments do not take into account the (partly illegal) profitability of slum use; but assessments *would* be raised for

21. See Laidler (1964); Schorr (1963, p. 91).
22. Before 1964, owners were able to treat sales prices in excess of the depreciated value of most real property as capital gains. The Revenue Act of 1964, however, restricted this practice. Under present law, the taxpayer is required to treat as ordinary income a percentage of the excess of depreciation actually taken over straight-line depreciation. The percentage declines gradually from 100 per cent on property held two years or less to zero on property held over ten years.

conversion upward. Assume, for example, that property in slum use earns profits of x. Now suppose that, despite the neighborhood effects dragging down the quality of property use, additional investment in maintenance and renovation would succeed in increasing profits to $x + a$. But the higher value of the improved property would result in higher property tax assessments, thereby reducing total profits to some $x + a - b$, where b is the additional tax; and the additional tax b may be greater or less than the additional profits a. This asymmetric assessment response acts as a drag on capital expenditures to improve the quality of both slum and non-slum property. Thus, even in the especially favorable case assumed here, the property tax biases resource use toward less capital-intensive uses of land. Of two land uses that, aside from the property tax, would yield equal returns, there is an incentive to choose the less capital-intensive use – lower-maintenance, lower-quality use.[23]

Credit problems. Capital rationing to slum and near-slum areas has an even stronger effect. The essential unavailability of credit for remodeling and repairs discourages speculators from attempting to upgrade the neighborhood as a whole and also discourages homeowners from attempting to maintain quality or remove slums (Jacobs, 1961, chs 15–16). Credit sources apparently base their judgements on marginal considerations: each single effort on its own is likely to fail to offset downward neighborhood pressure. They fail to allow for the effect of the pattern that would be created if all applications for credit were approved as part of an explicit policy.[24] The credit freeze contributes to the production of slums in yet another way; the inability to upgrade dwellings in declining but non-slum areas means that homeowners can usually obtain higher-quality or even comparably well-maintained dwellings only in other – usually outlying – areas. This tends to increase the supply of dwellings for cheap, and often quick, sale in the

23. See Mitchell (1959, pp. 1–6); Walker (1959); Rawson (1961); Schorr (1963).

24. It is admittedly difficult to demarcate empirically what is here referred to as an *imperfection* in the capital market, and the tighter credit conditions that can reasonably be expected in view of the poorer risk or greater uncertainty situation of many property owners in slums. I am indebted to Richard Muth for emphasizing this point. On the other hand, in the case of poor risk and uncertainty, a perfect capital market would respond in terms of higher interest rates on available loans. The actual response is simply to make loans unavailable at any rate of interest.

declining areas. The purchasers for such bargains are more than likely to be speculators who buy for the purpose of converting large numbers of dwellings to slum use. Their efforts are abetted by the fact, noted above, that the neighborhood effects work asymmetrically. Low-income minority groups are undesirables to higher-income 'majority' groups, but not vice versa. Speculative provision to admit the former is nearly unbeatable, since the former can drive out the latter just by their presence; speculative attempts to do the opposite *could* succeed, but strong enough attractions would have to be provided to offset the often-considerable antipathy to the presence of the indigenous group.

Prejudice. Ethnic prejudice encourages slum creation in two ways. The first, which has already been mentioned, involves the disabilities, the immobility, and the poverty of groups that can be herded into concentrated ghetto areas and constrained to remain there. The second is that the expected result of such concentration pressure is differentially higher housing costs for given quality within the segregated area. There is generally a pent-up demand for better quality and less expensive housing. This demand occasionally presses into 'majority' areas when the prejudice of sellers is offset by the prospects of profits due to the weak bargaining power of minority group members. But a single successful incursion often results in panic flight by the indigenous majority, followed by a large-scale migration of the minority group into the area. The pent-up demand pressure of the minority group is often so great that, whatever the original character of the area was, it becomes profitable to convert dwellings to slum use. Initial panic sales create bargains for speculators, even though ultimately prices are likely to rise at least to previous levels.[25] Rapid turnover of property favors slum creation, since it destroys the stable neighborhood expectations that could anchor land-use patterns to the previous style.

This last factor concerns the extensive rather than intensive production of slums – its spatial spread rather than its effect on worsening quality in any one area. The profitability of spread stems from the same factors that favor its intensive production. Spread takes place because of higher real prices for housing of given quality within the slum area than outside, which create incentives to increase the supply of housing available to slum

25. See Laurenti (1960); Downs (1960, pp. 181–88).

dwellers.[26] The greater the facility with which this is accomplished, the less is the profit obtainable from the intensive production of slums. On the other hand, constraints on external spread, such as from segregation, enhance the profitability of intensive production. In this process one must distinguish between the spatial spread of minority groups and the spatial spread of slums. The former predisposes to the latter, but they are not identical.

Underlying this discussion of the profitability of slum creation has been the assumption that the overall housing supply is tight. Some differential pressure on the supply between slum and non-slum is to be expected even in the absence of such tightness, just because of the tendency toward segregation. But an overall buyer's market in housing, or even a relative paucity of demand in the slum sector, can substantially reduce the production of slums. Filtering may proceed faster, the degree of overcrowding may lessen, dwellings may be retired from the stock sooner. The effect will be an improvement in the average quality of housing; some slums will be eliminated. Thus, the discussion above should not be taken to mean that slums are constantly and relentlessly being produced, regardless of the state of the supply and demand for housing. There are dynamics in the creation of slums such that the process tends to feed on itself and to have asymmetric features; but a reduction in slum occupancy can be brought about by important changes in the tightness of the market.

If a period of relative oversupply does occur, one consequence is likely to be a spatial spread in minority group housing. Here the spread of minority housing would not be tantamount to a spread of slums, unlike what was described above as the 'typical' situation.

There is some indication that the general tightness of housing of the 1940s through the late 1950s accompanied by substantial interregional migration (especially from rural to urban areas), a situation which favored production of slums, is gradually being reduced. Some diminution in the intensity and extent of new slum creation can be expected while such a trend continues; and there may possibly even be some 'natural' decrease in its overall reach.

To summarize, slums are not simply low-quality housing. There are forces on the demand side other than mere poverty (ignorance,

26. For an example of an explicit model of this type, see Bailey (1959, pp. 288–92).

minority status, concentrated migration, etc.), forces on the supply side (tax bias, capital market imperfections, ethnic prejudice, etc.), and more general market forces (neighborhood externalities) that together raise the real prices of low-quality housing in concentrated areas relative to those outside. These higher real prices systematically result from a quality level lower than legal minima, whether or not quality depreciation is accompanied by higher money prices as well (the case of exploitation). In other words, *within the stock of low-quality housing*, there are forces that tend to produce a clustering toward the lowest end of the quality scale without tending to increase comparably the overall stock of low-quality housing.

In cases where there is no exploitation, a reduction in quality and an increase in money prices are alternative forms that higher real prices may take. It might be supposed that in these cases it makes no real difference which form they take. But this is not so. If housing price pressure in this part of the market takes the form of overcrowding and dilapidation – that is, slums – this may have great social significance, for it has been strongly argued that the mere physical existence of slums involves substantial social costs. These are costs imposed both on slum dwellers themselves and on outsiders. Both types result from externalities and are therefore inadvertent in that they were not taken into account in the market transactions that determined patterns of housing occupancy and use. To the extent that the existence of such costs can be substantiated, they establish the suboptimality of slums in overall resource allocation. This social cost of slums will be considered below.

The point to be made here is that, among the market forces that are responsible for creating slums, there are some situations that either are socially disapproved or are the inadvertent result of remediable public policies. There are, for example, a serious lack of information, low mobility, prejudice, systematic tax biases and capital market imperfections. With respect to the first three, our society has shown a willingness to overrule consumer sovereignty when the exercise of self-choice imposes considerable damage either to the choosers themselves, to market partners, or to third parties. As for the last two, capital market imperfections and public policy biases are by no means believed to be exempt from public scrutiny. They are not typically considered to be necessarily desirable or ineradicable. In short, slums are not natural; they are not inevitable; and they may not be desirable.

The social costs of slums

It was indicated above that the existence of slums and hence their eradication could well have far-reaching effects on living patterns in the city. For many years the existence of slums has been alleged to generate important social evils:[27] physical, psychological, and health hazards to inhabitants and passers-by; and heavy resource costs to inhabitants of the rest of the city. These ills are believed to be due not only to the low quality of each dwelling in the slum, but perhaps more to the heavy clustering of a relatively homogeneous poor population in poor housing. The concentration generates serious enough external diseconomies to produce the alleged ills. The diagnosis in much of this literature is as follows:

1. Slum dwellings are likely to be fire traps, significantly increasing the likelihood and extent of fire damage.

2. Given overcrowding, filth, and inadequate sanitary facilities, slum areas are likely to be a health menace, increasing the frequency and severity of illness for both inhabitants and outsiders (through contagion). Insofar as slum dwellers receive subsidized medical care, moreover, some of these costs are borne by the general taxpayer. Additional costs are borne at large through the effect of illness on the overall productivity of the economic system.

3. Slums breed crime. Admittedly, crime stems partly from poverty. But slum living itself adds to the incidence of crime. Overcrowding and lack of privacy – especially in the context of general economic deprivation – tend to generate lack of respect for the individual and frustration over the constant obtrusion of others. Human teeming aggravates many kinds of externalities. This is amplified because the individual is surrounded by a pattern of life and values in the slums that contrasts greatly with the dominant values of the broader culture. Opportunities for crime and recruitment into criminal subcultures are aided by the closeness and swarming of life.

4. Slums generate personality difficulties. For example, beyond poverty, slums can create subcultures of despair, or bitterness, or violence, because the degree of overcrowding makes it possible to obtain a critical mass for many such movements. Many of these groupings of mutual dependency result in vicious circles: the surrounding examples provoke and support a collapse of socially functional aspiration levels, the outside culture with its achieve-

27. See Seeley (1959).

ment orientation is too far away. Recent social science emphasizes the effect of the environment of culture on the socialization of the individual. Inevitably the ethos of the slum becomes a significant part of personality development and hinders many in their attempts in later life to join the dominant culture of the society.

These are examples of the costs alleged to stem from slums, though their existence is by no means generally agreed upon.

For the present, it must be emphasized that these claims are not contravened by evidence that the housing is actually chosen by its residents or that the behavior giving rise to the alleged 'social costs' is deliberately engaged in. For example, the causative patterns that are said to be operating are often extremely subtle and difficult for direct participants to observe. For another, many of the processes involve significant external effects. Each individual may or may not be disadvantaged by his own action; but it imposes disturbances on others considerably greater than any disturbance to himself. This general type of relationship can be seen in the following example. An additional motorist entering a congested highway adds to the total congestion. He thus inconveniences himself slightly by his own action. But the sum of the discomfort he adds to all others is a large multiple of this. Similarly, most of the discomfort he feels is the result of the action of others. So it is also in slum living.

A final pattern involved here is that the individual is caught in a dynamic circle of interaction with others – a vicious circle. At each step he takes what seems to be the best possible action for him, given admittedly poor circumstances. The similar choices of each under the same circumstances in fact worsen the circumstances and thus call for further action on the part of each. This carries the progressive deterioration of the living environment further and further. Each is trapped into a marginal response that assumes the environment to be beyond his own power to change. No one can break the pattern as a whole. Thus, the overall pattern is unwanted by all or most, yet the marginal response which unalterably contributes to this pattern is deliberately chosen. The situation is suboptimal.

Summary

A major purpose of the urban redevelopment program, it has been indicated, is to eliminate blight and slums. To a degree, slums provide a type of commodity that is desired by poor households – low-quality, low-quantity housing. As a first approximation, slums represent an economically efficient way to produce this commodity. Elimination of slums by large-scale demolition would interfere with this warranted response of the market. It would generate not benefits, but costs on balance, even if none of the costs of elimination are considered.

Slum elimination can be considered to produce gross benefits only if slums represent an inefficient market response. It has been argued here that substantial externalities and 'artificial', socially questionable incentives in the housing market tend to bring about the particular type of land use known as a slum in contradistinction to simply low-cost housing. Therefore, the slum may not be an efficient market response after all. Moreover, the existence of a slum, however brought about, may engender important social costs to society at large. For these reasons the elimination of slums could well produce gross benefits. The desirability of eliminating them is measured, of course, by comparing these benefits with the real costs of bringing them about. The redevelopment type of project under the urban renewal program is one way of eliminating slums. One of the fruits of this long analysis, however, has been to cast light on the reasons why slum elimination might bring benefits, and therefore on the sources of suboptimality in slum land use. The advantage of this procedure is that it helps to specify an alternative, or set of alternatives, to redevelopment for eliminating the sources of inefficiency in slums. Such alternative policies would either prevent slums from forming, or help them to be transformed, or aid in mitigating whatever social ills they generate. Thus, rehabilitation, spot clearance, code enforcement, credit and tax policies, and income supplements to the poor, may also contribute in producing benefits of this sort.

References

BAILEY, M. (1959), Note on the economics of residential zoning and urban renewal, *Land Econ.*, vol. 35 August, pp. 288–92.

DAGEN, I., and CODY, E. C. (1961), 'Property *et al. vs.* nuisance *et al.*', *Law and Contemporary Problems*, vol. 26, pp. 70–84.

DAVIS, O. A. (1960), 'A pure theory of urban renewal', *Land Econ.*, vol. 36 May, pp. 220–26.

DAVIS, O. A., and WHINSTON, A. B. (1961), 'The economics of urban renewal', *Law and Contemporary Probs.*, vol. 26, pp. 105–17.

DOWNS, A. (1960), 'An economic analysis of property values and race' *Land Econ.*, vol. 36 May, pp. 181–8.

GREER, S. (1965), *Urban Renewal and American Cities; the Dilemma of Democratic Intervention*, Bobs-Merrill.

GRIGSBY, W. G. (1963), *Housing Markets and Public Policy*, University of Pennsylvania Press.

JACOBS, J. (1961), *The Death and Life of Great American Cities*, Random House.

LAIDLER, D. (1964), 'The effects of federal income taxation on owner-occupied dwellings', unpublished Ph.D. thesis, University of Chicago.

LAURENTI, L. (1960), *Property Values and Race*, University of California Press.

METROPOLITAN HOUSING AND PLANNING COUNCIL OF CHICAGO (1954), *The Road Back—The Slums*, Chicago.

MITCHELL, G. W. (1959), 'The financial and fiscal implications of urban growth', *Urban Land*, vol. 18, July–August, pp. 1–6.

NAKAGAWA, A. (1957), 'Profitability of Slums', *Synthesis*, April.

RAPKIN, C. (1959), *The Real Estate Market in an Urban Renewal Area*, New York City Planning Commission.

RAWSON, M. (1961), *Property Taxation and Urban Development*, research monograph 4, Urban Land Institute.

RHYNE, C. S. (1960), 'The workable program—a challenge to community improvement', *Law and Contemporary Probs.*, vol. 25, pp. 685–704.

RUMNEY, J. (1951), 'The social costs of slums', *J. of Social Issues*, vol. 7, p. 69.

SAMUELSON, P. A. (1954), 'The pure theory of public expenditure', *Rev. of Econ. and Stats.*, vol. 36, November, pp. 387–9.

SCHORR, A. L. (1963), *Slums and Social Insecurity*, US Department of Health, Education and Welfare.

SEELEY, J. (1959), 'The Slum; its nature, use and users', *J. of Amer. Inst. of Planners*, vol. 35, pp. 7–14.

WALKER, M. (1959), 'Tax responsibility for the slum', *Tax Policy*, vol. 32, October.

8 B. Duncan and O. D. Duncan

Residential Distribution and Occupational Stratification

B. Duncan and O. D. Duncan, 'Residential distribution and occupational stratification', *American Journal of Sociology*, vol. 60, 1955, pp. 493–503.

The idea behind this paper was forcibly stated – in fact, somewhat overstated – by Robert E. Park:

It is because social relations are so frequently and so inevitably correlated with spatial relations; because physical distances so frequently are, or seem to be, the indexes of social distances, that statistics have any significance whatever for sociology. And this is true, finally, because it is only as social and psychical fact can be reduced to, or correlated with, spatial facts that they can be measured at all.[1]

This study finds a close relationship between spatial and social distances in a metropolitan community. It suggests that a systematic consideration of the spatial aspect of stratification phenomena, though relatively neglected by students of the subject,[2] should be a primary focus of urban stratification studies. Aside from demonstrating the relevance of human ecology to the theory of social organization, the study offers further evidence for the suitability of a particular set of methodological techniques for research in comparative urban ecology.[3] These techniques are adaptable to a wide variety of problems in urban ecological structure, permit economical and objective comparisons among communities, and thus overcome some of the indeterminacy of a strictly cartographic approach. The techniques are here applied to only one metropolitan community, Chicago; however, comparative studies, conducted on an exploratory basis, indicate their ability to produce significant results.

Data and method

The sources of data for this study, except as noted otherwise, were the published volume of 1950 census tract statistics for Chicago

1. See Park (1926, p. 18).
2. See Rowener, the discussion of 'drilling area', in Warner (1949, pp. 151–54).
3. See Duncans (1955, p. 72); Bogue (1949); Redick (1954).

and adjacent areas[4] (coextensive with the Chicago Metropolitan District, as delineated in 1940), and the census-tract summary punch cards for this area obtained from the Bureau of the Census. The ecological analysis pertains to employed males fourteen years old and over, classified into the eight major occupation groups listed in the tables below. The occupation groups disregarded in this analysis (farmers and farm managers, farm laborers, private household workers, and occupation not reported) include only twenty-one thousand of the one and a half million employed males in the Metropolitan District.

A portion of the analysis is carried through with the census tract as the area unit. There are 1178 census tracts in the Metropolitan District, of which 935 are in the city of Chicago and 243 in the adjacent area. The remainder of the analysis rests on a scheme of zones and sectors, delineated rather arbitrarily. Tracts were assigned to circular zones, concentric to the center of the city at State and Madison streets, with one-mile intervals up to fourteen miles, two-mile intervals up to twenty-eight miles, and with residual categories of tracts more than twenty-eight miles from the city center and tracts in the adjacent area too large to be classified by zones. The latter category contains only 1·4 per cent of the employed males. Five sectors were established, with boundaries approximating radial lines drawn from the city center. The North Shore sector runs along Lake Michigan through such suburbs as Skokie, Evanston, Lake Forest and Waukegan; the Northwest sector extends through Park Ridge and Des Plaines to Arlington Heights; the West sector includes the suburbs of Cicero Oak Park and Berwyn, running out as far as Wheaton and Naperville; the Southwest sector is approximately bisected by a line running through Blue Island, Harvey and Chicago Heights to Park Forest; and the South Shore sector runs along Lake Michigan through the Indiana suburbs of East Chicago, Hammond, Gary and East Gary. Combining the zone and sector schemes yielded a set of 104 zone-sector segments; that is, area units averaging about ten times the size of a census tract, though with considerable variation in area and population.

The spatial 'distance' between occupation groups, or more precisely the difference between their areal distributions, is measured by the *index of dissimilarity*.[5] To compute this index,

4. *U S Census of Population*, Bulletin P-D 10.

5. For the use of the index of dissimilarity as a 'coefficient of geographic association', see National Resources Planning Board (1943, p. 118).

one calculates for each occupation group the percentage of all workers in that group residing in each area unit (tract or zone-sector segment). The index of dissimilarity between two occupation groups is then one-half the sum of the absolute values of the differences between the respective distributions, taken area by area. In the accompanying hypothetical example the index of dissimilarity between occupations A and B is 20 per cent (i.e. 40/2). This may be interpreted as a measure of displacement: 20 per cent of the workers in occupation A would have to move to a different area in order to make their distribution identical with that of occupation B.

Table 1	Area	A	B	Diff.
		%	%	%
	1	10	15	5
	2	20	15	5
	3	40	25	15
	4	30	45	15
Total	%	100	100	40

When the index of dissimilarity is computed between one occupation group and all other occupations combined (i.e., total employed males except those in the given occupation group), it is referred to as an *index of segregation*.[6] An equivalent and more convenient means of computing the segregation index is to compute the index of dissimilarity between the given occupation group and total employed males (i.e., all occupations), 'adjusting' the result by dividing by one minus the proportion of the total male employed labor force included in that occupation group.

The indexes of segregation and dissimilarity were computed on both a tract basis and a zone-sector segment basis to determine the effect of the size of the area unit on the results. While the indexes for tracts are uniformly higher than for zone-sector segments, this effect can be disregarded for purposes of determining the relative positions of the occupation groups. The product-moment correlation between the two sets of segregation indexes in Table 3 is 0·96. The correlation between the two sets of dissimilarity indexes in Table 4 is 0·98, with the segment-based index s related to the tract-based index t by the regression equation

$$s = \cdot 8t - 1 \cdot 3.$$

6. See Duncan and Duncan (1949).

These results indicate that for the kind of problem dealt with here the larger, and hence less homogeneous, unit is as serviceable as the smaller one. This suggests that some of the recent concern about census-tract homogeneity may be misplaced.[7]

The *index of low-rent concentration* is obtained by

1. Classifying tracts into intervals according to the median monthly rental of tenant-occupied dwelling units;

2. Computing the percentage distribution by rent intervals for each occupation group and for all occupations combined;

3. Cumulating the distributions, from low to high rent;

4. Calculating the quantity

$$\Sigma X_{i-1} Y_i - \Sigma X_i Y_{i-1}$$

where X_i is the cumulated percentage of the given occupation through the ith rent interval, Y_i is the cumulated percentage of all occupations combined, and the summation is over all rent intervals;

5. 'Adjusting' the result (as for the segregation index) to obtain an index equivalent to the one obtained by comparing the given occupation group with all other occupations combined. This index varies between 100 and -100, with positive values indicating a tendency for residences of the given occupation group to be in areas of relatively low rent and with negative values indicating relative concentration in high-rent areas.

The *index of centralization* is computed in the same fashion, except that tracts are ordered by distance from the center of the city, that is, are classified according to the zonal scheme. A negative index of centralization signifies that the given occupation group tends to be 'decentralized', or on the average located farther away from the city center than all other occupations, while a positive index is obtained for a relatively 'centralized' occupation.[8]

Occupation and socioeconomic status

Selected non-ecological indicators of the relative socioeconomic status of the major occupation groups are shown in Table 2. The

7. See Myers (1954, pp. 364–6); Smith (1954, pp. 201–7).

8. The indexes of low-rent concentration and of centralization are formally identical with the index of urbanization proposed in Duncan (1952, pp. 267–7). The formula given here is a simplification of the one presented there and the area units and principle, are of course, different.

professional and managerial groups clearly have the highest socioeconomic rank, while operatives, service workers, and laborers are clearly lowest in socioeconomic status. The ranking by socioeconomic level would probably be agreed on by most social scientists. The major occupation groups correspond roughly with the Alba Edwards scheme of 'social-economic groups'. Edwards does not separate sales workers and clerical workers by

Table 2 **Selected indicators of socioeconomic status of the major occupation groups**

Major occupation group[a]	Median income in 1949[b]	Median school years completed[c]	Edwards' socio-economic groups[d]	Per cent non-white[e]
Professional, technical, and kindred workers	$4387	16+	1	2·7
Managers, officials, and proprietors, except farm	4831	12·2	2	2·2
Sales workers	3698	12·4 ⎫		⎧ 2·8
Clerical and kindred workers	3132	12·2 ⎬	3	⎨ 7·4
Craftsmen, foremen and kindred workers	3648	9·5	4	4·9
Operatives and kindred workers	3115	8·9	5	12·4
Service workers, except private household	2635	8·8	5–6	23·0
Laborers, except farm and mine	2580	8·4	6	27·4

a Does not include farmers and farm managers, private household workers, farm laborers, and occupations not reported.

b For males in the experienced labor force of the Chicago Standard Metropolitan Area, 1950. Source: *1950 US Census of Population*, Bulletin P-C13, Table 78.

c For employed males twenty-five years old and over, in the North and West, 1950. Source: *1950 US Census of Population*, Special Report P-E No. 5B, Table 11.

d Approximate equivalents. Source: Alba M. Edwards, *Comparative Occupation Statistics for the United States, 1870 to 1940* (Washington, DC: Government Printing Office, 1943).

e For employed males in the Chicago Metropolitan District, 1950. Based on non-whites residing in census tracts containing 250 or more non-white population in 1950. These tracts include 95·8 per cent of all non-white males in the Metropolitan District.

'social-economic group', and the group of service workers, except private household, contains individual occupations variously classified by Edwards as skilled, semiskilled, and unskilled, predominantly the latter two.

A ranking in terms of median income results in two reversals in rank. The 1949 median income of male managerial workers in the Chicago Standard Metropolitan Area was about $500 greater than that of professional workers, although both were substantially above that for sales workers. The median income for the craftsmen–foremen group was about $500 higher than that for clerical workers. In fact, the median income for the craftsmen-foremen group was only slightly below that for sales workers, whereas the median income for clerical workers was only slightly above that for operatives.

However, in median school years completed, professional workers clearly rank first, while there is little difference in the medians for the managerial, sales and clerical groups. The median drops sharply, over 2·5 years, for the craftsmen-foremen group and declines further for each group in the order of the initial listing

In the Chicago Metropolitan District the proportion of non-whites in an occupation group appears to be closely related to its socio-economic status. The proportion is very low in the professional, managerial, and sales groups, but it is somewhat higher for clerical workers than for the craftsmen-foremen group. Increasing proportions are observed for operatives, service workers, and laborers, in order.

The suggested ranking is in general conformity with the National Opinion Research Center's data on popular attitudes toward occupations, except that sales occupations appear to rank below clerical and craft occupations in the NORC results.[9] An inadequate sampling of occupational titles within the sales group may account in part for the low prestige rating of sales workers obtained by the NORC. Furthermore, their data do not differentiate prestige ratings by sex. Particularly in a metropolitan area, the male sales worker group is more heavily weighted with such occupations as advertising, insurance, and real estate agents and sales representatives of wholesale and manufacturing concerns than is the case for female sales workers, among whom retail sales clerks are the large majority.

The failure of different bases of ranking to give identical results has been discussed by writers on stratification in terms of 'dis-

9. See NORC (1947, pp. 3–13).

affinity of strata' and 'status disequilibrium'.[10] The reversals in rank between the professional and managerial groups and the clerical and crafts workers are most frequent. The upshot seems to be that no one ranking can be accepted as sufficient for all purposes. The examination of residential patterns discloses other instances of disequilibrium, which are of interest both in themselves and as clues to the interpretation of those already noted.

Residential patterns

Four aspects of the residential patterning of occupation groups are considered. The first is the degree of residential segregation of each major occupation group with respect to all others, that is, the extent to which an occupation group is separated residentially from the remainder of the employed labor force. The second is the degree of dissimilarity in residential distribution among major occupation groups, that is, the extent to which pairs of occupation groups isolate themselves from one another. The third aspect is the degree of residential concentration of each occupation group in areas characterized by relatively low rents. Finally, the degree of centralization of each major occupation group (i.e., the extent to which an occupation group is concentrated toward the center of the metropolitan community) is examined. In each case the spatial patterning of the residences is considered in relation to socio-economic level.

A clear relationship of the ranking of major occupation groups by socio-economic status and by degree of residential segregation is shown in Table 3. Listed in the order given there, the indexes of residential segregation form a U-shaped pattern. The highest values are observed for the professionals and the laborers and the lowest value for the clerical workers. The degree of residential segregation varies only slightly among the professional managerial and sales groups; however, it declines markedly for the clerical workers and then increases regularly for each successive group.

This finding suggests that residential segregation is greater for those occupation groups with clearly defined status than for those groups whose status is ambiguous. The latter groups are necessarily subject to cross-pressures from the determinants of residential selection; for example, the clerical group has an income equivalent to that of operatives but the educational level of managerial workers.

10. See Sorokin (1947, pp. 289–94); Benoit-Smullyan (1944, pp. 154–61); Kaufman (1946).

Table 3 Index of residential segregation of each major occupation group, for employed males in the Chicago metropolitan district, 1950

Major occupation group[a]	By census tracts	By zone-sector segments
Professional, technical, and kindred workers	30	31
Managers, officials, and proprietors, except farm	29	20
Sales workers	29	20
Clerical and kindred workers	13	9
Craftsmen, foremen, and kindred workers	19	14
Operatives and kindred workers	22	16
Service workers, except private household	24	20
Laborers, except farm and mine	35	29

a Does not include farmers and farm managers, private household workers, farm laborers, and occupation not reported.

To check the hypothesis that spatial distances among occupation groups parallel their social distances, the indexes of dissimilarity in residential distribution among major occupation groups are shown in Table 4. As previously indicated, a listing of major occupation groups by socio-economic level can at best only roughly approximate a social distance scale. Similarly, a measure of dissimilarity in residential distribution can only approximate the spatial distance between groups – the index measures only the dissimilarity of the residential distributions with respect to a particular set of areas and is insensitive to other important aspects of the spatial pattern such as proximity of areas of concentration.

Nonetheless, the data in Table 4 indicate the essential correspondence of social and spatial distance among occupation groups. If it is assumed that the ordering of major occupation groups corresponds with increasing social distance (e.g., the social distance between professional and sales workers is greater than that between professional and managerial workers), and if it is assumed that the index of residential dissimilarity approximates the spatial distance between the two groups, the expected pattern would be the following: starting at any point on the diagonal, the indexes would increase reading up or to the right (down, or to the left, in the case of the indexes below the diagonal, based on zone-sector segments). It is clear that the expected pattern, though not perfectly reproduced, essentially describes the observed pattern.

Table 4 Indexes of dissimilarity in residential distribution among major occupation groups, for employed males in the Chicago metropolitan district, 1950

(Above diagonal, by census tracts; below diagonal, by zone-sector segments)

Major occupation group[a]	Major occupation group							
	Prof., tech., kindred	Mgrs., offs., props.	Sales wkrs.	Clerical, kindred	Craftsmen, foremen, kindred	Operatives, kindred	Service, exc. priv. hshld.	Laborers, exc. farm and mine
Professional, technical, kindred workers	—	13	15	28	35	44	41	54
Managers, officials, and proprietors, except farm	8	—	13	28	33	41	40	52
Sales workers	11	7	—	27	35	42	38	54
Clerical and kindred workers	20	18	17	—	16	21	24	38
Craftsmen, foremen, kindred workers	26	23	25	12	—	17	35	35
Operatives, kindred workers	31	29	30	16	14	—	26	25
Service workers, except private household	31	31	30	19	25	19	—	28
Laborers, except farm and mine	42	41	42	32	30	21	24	—

a Does not include farmers and farm managers, private household workers, farm laborers and occupations not reported.

The exceptions are few and for the most part can be explained hypothetically; such hypotheses provide clues for additional research.

The least dissimilarity is observed between professional and managerial workers, managerial and sales workers and professional and sales workers. Furthermore, the dissimilarity of each of these groups with each other occupation group is of approximately the same degree. In fact, three of the inversions of the expected pattern concern the comparison between the managerial group and sales workers; that is, the residential dissimilarity of sales workers with craftsmen-foremen, operatives, and laborers is slightly greater than that of the managerial group, although their difference in terms of socio-economic level is presumably less.

The residential distribution of clerical workers is more dissimilar to the distribution of sales workers, professional and managerial workers than to that of the craftsmen or the operatives. Hence, although clerical workers are often grouped with professional, managerial and sales workers as 'white-collar', in terms of residential distribution they are more similar to the craftsmen and operatives than to the other white-collar groups.

The remaining inversions of the expected pattern involve service workers, except private household. One-fifth of these are 'janitors and sextons'. Presumably a substantial proportion of the janitors live at their place of work in apartment buildings housing workers in the higher status occupation groups.[11] It is hypothesized that this special circumstance accounts for the tendency of service workers to be less dissimilar to the higher status groups than expected on the basis of socio-economic status.[12] At the same time the color composition of the service group presumably acts in the opposite direction. In so far as residential segregation on basis of color, cutting across occupational lines, exists within the metropolitan community, occupational status is rendered at least partially ineffective as a determinant of residential location. These factors, however, probably do not wholly explain the largest single deviation from the expected pattern, the much larger index of dissimilarity between craftsmen-foremen and service workers than between clerical and service workers.

The first column of Table 5 shows the indexes of low-rent con-

11. See Gold (1952, pp. 486–93).
12. This effect has been definitely noted in data, not shown here, for female private household workers, about one-fourth of whom 'live in'.

Table 5 Indexes of low-rent concentration and of centralization for major occupation groups, Chicago metropolitan district, 1950

Major occupation group[a]	Index of low-rent concentration (total employed persons)	Index of centralization (Employed Males)					
		Sector Metropolitan district	North shore	North-west	West	South-west	South shore
Professional, technical, and kindred workers	−32	−14	−15	−20	−29	−20	5
Managers, officials, and proprietors, except farm	−30	−12	−20	−16	−19	−15	1
Sales workers	−25	−5	−15	−12	−12	−9	8
Clerical and kindred workers	−9	5	7	2	1	5	9
Craftsmen, foremen, and kindred workers	11	−8	6	−6	−7	−5	−26
Operatives, kindred workers	29	10	21	16	18	8	−4
Service workers, except private household	7	21	16	18	20	16	36
Laborers, except farm and mine	32	7	9	21	30	16	−1

a Does not include farmers and farm managers, private household workers, farm laborers and occupations not reported.

centration of the occupation groups. Some caution must be exercised in interpreting them, since the tabulation on which they are based did not distinguish between male and female workers, and the indexes had to be computed for total employed persons rather than males. It is clear, nonetheless, that the degree of low-rent concentration is inversely related to the socio-economic status of the occupation groups. All four of the white-collar occupation groups have negative indexes, signifying relative concentration in high-rent areas, whereas all four of the blue-collar groups have positive indexes. Again, there is a relatively sharp break between the clerical and the other three white-collar groups. The managerial group has a slightly greater index of low-rent concentration than the professional group, despite the higher income level of the former. It is even more striking that the low-rent concentration of craftsmen-foremen is substantially higher than for clerical workers, again the reverse of the relative positions on income. It can be shown that in 1940 the combined clerical and sales group tended to spend a larger proportion of its income for rent than did the group of craftsmen, foremen and kindred workers. For example, for tenant families with wage and salary incomes between $2000 and $3000 in 1939, and without other income, 63 per cent of the families headed by a clerical or sales workers paid $40 per month or more rent, as compared with only 38 per cent of families whose heads were craftsmen, foremen, or kindred workers.[13]

The index of low-rent concentration for service workers, although positive, is low compared to the other blue-collar groups. This exception to the expected pattern no doubt has the same explanation as advanced above; that is, that a substantial proportion of service workers live in comparatively high status areas in connection with their place of employment.

The indexes of centralization of the occupation groups are given in Table 5, both for the Metropolitan District as a whole and within each of the five sectors. According to the Burgess zonal hypothesis, there is an upward gradient in the socio-economic status of the population as one proceeds from the center to the periphery of the city. Hence one would expect the degree of residential centralization of an occupation group to be inversely related to socio-economic status. The data provide general support for this hypothesis, although there are some significant exceptions. Thus, for the Metropolitan District as a whole, three of the

13. Data for the Chicago Metropolitan District, 1940, from Table 11; *Families: Income and Rent, Population and Housing, 16th Census of the US.*

four white-collar indexes are negative (indicating relative decentralization), and three of the four blue-collar indexes are positive (indicating relative centralization). The exceptional cases are again the clerical and craftsmen-foremen groups.

In three of the five sectors (Northwest, West and Southwest), the hypothesized pattern of centralization indexes is perfectly reproduced, except for the inversion between clerical workers and the craftsmen-foremen group, which appears in all sectors. For the North Shore sector the principal deviation from the pattern is the comparatively low degree of centralization of service workers and laborers. In this sector the managerial group is somewhat more decentralized than the professional group, as is also true in the South Shore sector. The latter sector exhibits a quite marked departure from the expected pattern, in that the only decentralized occupations are those in the blue-collar category. There is a small measure of confirmation for the hypothesized pattern, in that within the white-collar category the least centralized groups are the professional and managerial, and within the blue-collar category the most decentralized is the craftsmen-foremen group. The high index for service workers is doubtless due to the relatively high proportion of non-whites in this occupation, and the relatively central location of the South Side 'Black Belt', a large portion of which falls in the South Shore sector. The decentralization of the other blue-collar groups is attributable to the presence of the Indiana industrial suburbs on the periphery of the South Shore sector. A similar effect of some industrial suburbs at the northern end of the North Shore sector is observable in the low centralization index for laborers in that sector. It is apparent that expectations based on the zonal hypothesis must be qualified by recognizing distortions of the zonal pattern produced by peripheral industrial concentrations. Such concentrations appear only in certain sectors, and, where they are absent, the zonal hypothesis leads to a realistic expectation concerning the pattern of residential centralization by socio-economic status.

Residential separation and dissimilarity of occupational origins

There are good reasons for supposing that residential patterns are related to occupational mobility. For example, ecologists have noted a tendency for advances in socio-economic status to be accompanied by migration toward the city's periphery. Residential segregation is doubtless one of the barriers to upward mobility, in so far as such mobility is affected by the opportunity to observe and imitate the way of life of higher social strata. Among the findings reported above, at least one may have an explanation that involves mobility. It is surprising that the residential patterns of sales workers do not differ more than they do from those of professional and managerial workers; since the income of sales workers is well below that of either, they rank lower in prestige, and their educational attainment is substantially less than that of professional workers. But there are data which suggest that a sizable proportion of sales workers are moving to a higher occupational level, or aspire to such a move, anticipating it by following the residential pattern of the higher group. The Occupational Mobility Survey found that for males employed in both 1940 and 1950 there was a movement of 23 per cent of the men employed as sales workers in 1940 into the group of managers, proprietors, and officials by 1950. This is the largest single inter-occupational movement in the mobility table, except that 23 per cent of laborers moved into the group of operatives and kindred workers.[14] Another aspect of occupational mobility is illuminated by the data in Table 6, which shows indexes of dissimilarity among the major occupation groups with respect to the distribution of each group by major occupation group of the employed male's father.[15] These indexes, therefore, pertain to differences among the major occupation groups in background, origin, or recruitment. The hypothesis to be tested is that, the greater the dissimilarity between a pair of occupation groups in occupational origins, the greater is their dissimilarity in residential distribution.

The pattern of Table 6 is clearly like that of Table 4. The indexes of dissimilarity with respect to residence, computed on the zone-sector segment basis, correlate 0·91 with the indexes for occupational origin. The correlation is 0·94 for the residential indexes based on census tracts, with the regression of the tract-

14. Based on unpublished Table W-56 of the Occupational Mobility Survey, taken in six cities in 1951. For description of the sampling and enumeration procedures see Palmer (1954, ch. 1).

15. These indexes are based on the aggregated results of sample surveys in six cities in 1951. Although separate data are available for Chicago, these were not used here, because the sample was too small to produce reliable frequencies in most of the cells of the 8 × 9 table from which the dissimilarity indexes were computed. (In the inter-generation mobility table the classification of father's occupations included the group 'farmers and farm managers' as well as the eight major occupation groups listed in Table 6. This was desirable, since a significant proportion of fathers – though very few of the sons in this urban sample – were farmers.)

Table 6ᵃ Indexes of dissimilarity in distribution by father's occupation among major occupation groups for employed males in six cities in the United States, 1950

Major occupation groupᵇ	Major occupation group						
	Mgrs., offs., props.	Sales wkrs.	Clerical, kindred	Craftsmen, foremen kindred	Operatives, kindred	Service, incl. priv. hshld.	Laborers, exc. mine
Professional, technical and kindred workers	20	16	27	38	39	34	46
Managers, officials, and proprietors, except farm	—	11	28	31	34	30	42
Sales workers	—	—	26	35	37	35	47
Clerical and kindred workers	—	—	—	18	20	28	39
Craftsmen, foremen, kindred workers	—	—	—	—	14	25	31
Operatives, kindred workers	—	—	—	—	—	22	23
Service workers, including private household	—	—	—	—	—	—	20

a Source: Unpublished data from Occupational Mobility Survey, Table W-9. For description of sampling and enumeration procedures see Palmer (1954).
b Does not include farmers and farm managers and occupation not reported. A small number of private household workers are included with service workers, and a small number of farm laborers with laborers, except mine.

based index t on the index of dissimilarity in occupational origin u being $t = 1 \cdot 2u - 1 \cdot 8$. The hypothesis is thereby definitely substantiated.

In Table 6 all but one of the inversions of the pattern expected on the assumption of an unequivocal ranking of the occupation groups involve the sales and service workers. Sales workers are closer to professional workers with respect to occupational background than are the managerial workers and farther from each of the blue-collar groups. Actually, a more consistent pattern would be produced by ranking sales workers second in place of the managerial group. In this respect the data on occupational origins are more consistent with the ecological data than are the data on socio-economic status in Table 2. In terms of the indexes of dissimilarity in occupational origins, service workers are closer to the first three white-collar groups than are any of the other blue-collar groups. However, in comparisons among the clerical and blue-collar groups, service workers clearly rank next to last, or between operatives and laborers. Again, the factor of occupational origins is more closely related to residential separation than are the indicators of socio-economic status.

The last point deserves emphasis. Not only do the indexes of dissimilarity on an area basis have the same general pattern as those on an occupational origin basis but also the deviations from that pattern occur at the same points and in the same direction. This cannot be said regarding the several indicators of socio-economic status. If income determined residential separation, managers would outrank professionals, and clerical workers would be virtually identical with operatives in their separation from other groups. If education determined residential separation, there would be substantial differences between the indexes for professional workers and managerial workers. Neither of these hypotheses is borne out by the data, whereas differences in occupational background lead to accurate, specific predictions of the pattern of differences in residential distribution.

The ecological analysis has provided strong support for the proposition that spatial distances between occupation groups are closely related to their social distances, measured either in terms of conventional indicators of socio-economic status or in terms of differences in occupational origins; that the most segregated occupation groups are those at the extremes of the socio-economic scale; that concentration of residence in low-rent areas is inversely related to socio-economic status; and that centralization of residence is likewise inversely related to socio-economic status. These results are in accord with accepted ecological theory, provide support for it, and demonstrate the relevance of ecological research to the theory of social stratification.

These generalizations, however, are perhaps no more significant to the advancement of knowledge than are the instances in which they do not hold and the additional hypotheses advanced to account for the exceptions. Conventional measures of socio-economic status do not agree perfectly as to the rank order of the major occupation groups, nor do the several ecological indexes. The prime case in point occurs at the middle of the socio-economic scale, at the conventional juncture of white-collar and blue-collar occupations. Clerical and kindred workers have substantially more education than craftsmen, foremen, and kindred workers, and the clerical occupations are usually considered of greater prestige than the craft and related occupations. However, craftsmen-foremen have considerably higher incomes on the average, and, among males, their non-white proportion is smaller. The pattern of the indexes of dissimilarity in residential distribution clearly places the clerical group closer to the other white-collar groups than the craftsmen-foremen are, and the clerical workers' index of low-rent concentration is less than that of the craftsmen and foremen. But in terms of residential centralization the clerical group tends to fall with the lower blue-collar groups, and the craftsmen-foremen group with the other white-collar groups. In general, it would appear that 'social status' or prestige is more important in determining the residential association of clerical with other white-collar groups than is income, although the latter sets up a powerful cross-pressure, as evidenced by the comparatively high rent-income ratio of clerical families. To account fully for the failure of clerical workers to be residentially decentralized like the other white-collar groups, one would have to consider work-residence relationships. Data on work-residence separation for a 1951 Chicago sample show that clerical workers resemble craftsmen, foremen and kindred workers in the degree of separation much more than they do sales, managerial or professional workers.[16]

Perhaps the most suggestive finding of the study in the dissimilarity in occupational origins is more closely associated with dissimilarity in residential distribution than is any of the usual indicators of socio-economic status. This result can only be inter-

16. See B. Duncan (1953).

preted speculatively. But one may suppose that preferences and aspirations concerning housing and residential patterns are largely formed by childhood and adolescent experiences in a milieu of which the father's occupation is an important aspect.

The discovery that 'status disequilibria' are reflected in inconsistencies in the ordering of occupation groups according to their residential patterns provides a further reason for distinguishing 'class' from 'social status' elements[17] within the complex conventionally designated as 'socio-economic status'. Apparently, attempts to compound these two can at best produce a partially ordered scale; at worst, they may obscure significant differences in life-style, consumption patterns, and social mobility.

There is one important qualification of the results reported. Like census tracts, broad occupation groups are not perfectly homogeneous. The managerial group includes proprietors of peanut stands as well as corporation executives, and night-club singers are classified as professional workers along with surgeons. One would therefore expect to find a much sharper differentiation of residential patterns if more detailed occupational classifications were available. In particular, the points at which cross-pressures on residential location develop should be more clearly identified.

Further research should seek other forces producing residential segregation. Ethnic categorizations other than race are doubtless relevant though difficult to study directly for lack of data. In general the patterns described here would be expected to hold for females, but significant deviations might also occur, in part because the residence of married females is probably determined more by their husbands' occupation than by their own, and in part because the occupations that compose each of the major occupation groups are different for females from those for males (as mentioned above in regard to sales workers). Both race and sex would bear upon residential patterns of private household workers, who are predominantly female and non-white. A final class of especially important factors is the effect of the location of workplaces on residence. There is evidence that residences are not distributed randomly with respect to places of work. If location of work is controlled, an even sharper differentiation of residential patterns than that described here may be revealed.

17. See Gerth and Mills (1946).

References

BENOIT-SMULLYAN, E. (1944), 'Status, status types and status interrelations', *Amer. Sociol. Rev.*, vol. 9, pp. 154–61.

BOGUE, D. J. (1949), *The Structure of the Metropolitan Community*, University of Michigan.

BURGESS, E. W. (ed.) (1926), *The Urban Community*, University of Chicago Press.

DUNCAN, B. (1953), 'Factors in work-residence separation: wage and salary workers, Chicago 1951', paper presented at the annual institute of the Society for Social Research.

DUNCAN, O. D. (1952), 'Urbanization and retail specialization', *Social Forces*, vol. 30, pp. 267–71.

DUNCAN, O. D., and DUNCAN, B. (1949), 'A methodological analysis of segregation indexes', *Amer. Sociol. Rev.*, vol. 20, pp. 210–27.

GERTH, H. H., and MILLS, C. W. (eds) (1946), 'Class, status, party', in *From Max Weber*, Oxford University Press.

GOLD, R. (1952), 'Janitors *vs.* tenants: a status–income dilemma', *Amer. J. of Sociol.*, vol. 57, pp. 486–93.

KAUFMAN, H. F. (1946), *Defining Prestige in a Rural Community*, Sociometry monograph no. 10, Beacon House.

MYERS, J. K. (1954), 'Note on the homogeneity of census tracts: a methodological problem in urban ecological research', *Social Forces*, vol. 32, pp. 364–6.

NATIONAL OPINION RESEARCH CENTER (1947), 'Jobs and occupations: a popular evaluation', *Opinion News*, vol. 9, pp. 3–13.

NATIONAL RESOURCES PLANNING BOARD (1943), *Industrial Location and National Resources*, p. 118, Government Printing Office.

PALMER, G. L. (1954), *Labor Mobility in Six Cities*, Social Science Research Council, New York.

PARK, R. M. (1926), 'The urban community as a spatial pattern and a moral order', in Burgess, E. W. (ed.), *The Urban Community*, University of Chicago Press.

REDICK, R. W. (1954), 'A study of differential rates of population growth and patterns of population distribution in central cities in the U S: 1940–50', paper presented at the 1954 annual meeting of the American Sociological Society, Urbana, Illinois.

SMITH, J. (1954), 'A method for the classification of areas on the basis of demographical homogeneous populations', *Amer. Sociol. Rev.*, vol. 19, pp. 201–7.

SOROKIN, P. A. (1947), *Society, Culture and Personality*, Harper.

WARNER, L. W. *et al.* (1949), *Social Class in America*, Science Research Associates.

9 J. M. Beshers

Urban Social Structure

Extract from J. M. Beshers, 'Urban social structure', in *Urban Social Structure*, Free Press of Glencoe, 1962, pp. 39–60.

[. . .] The traditional sociological literature is relevant to urban social structure. Little specific attention has been paid to the city itself, but the omission is symptomatic of the difficulties lying ahead. In general, the nineteenth century sociologists took a macroscopic point of view and described the social structure of whole societies as revealed by historical data. Recent sociologists, however, have more often dealt with the social structure of small, self-contained communities as revealed by interview and systematic observation. Most recent work falls into a microscopic point of view, save for several major nationwide surveys of opinions. In either case, most of the literature is either too broad or too restricted to enable us to focus on urban social structure directly. On the whole, stratification has been given the major emphasis in recent discussions of social structure and will be examined most carefully here.

The macroscopic view of social structure viewed historically is a descendant of Marx's theories of social and economic organization. Marx tended to reduce most aspects of stratification to the economic basis of class; the fundamental distinction lies in whether one is bourgeois or proletarian, that is, in one's relationship to the means of production. All of his structural concepts are organized around this distinction. The bourgeois control of economic matters implies bourgeois control of political matters. Further, all functional consequences of structure are implied by the economic organization of society – namely, the capitalist society in which such a distinction exists – and by the inevitable conflict between classes, which, coupled with the concepts of class consciousness and solidarity, provides a social psychology of social relationships. Thus, the Marxian synthesis relates stratification to economic structure and power structure, states the functions of stratification, and contains a social psychology of stratification. Much subsequent sociological writing has tended away from this synthetic view.

The critics of Marx, such as Pareto, Durkheim and Weber, retained broad syntheses in their own formulations of social structure (Parsons, 1949). For example, Pareto's cyclical theory of history based on notions of circulation of elites and of fundamental, slowly changing residues is a direct attack upon Marx's view of social change; Pareto considers alternative functions for stratification and an alternative social psychology. Weber decomposed stratification into class, status and party, yet he accepted the obligation to state the relationships among these components. Durkheim attempted to escape from the obligation of a social psychology, yet his analysis of the division of labor ranges from ecological and demographic considerations on one hand to the relationship between normative integration and psychological integration on the other.

But most recent macroscopic endeavors have come to regard stratification as a thing apart from social structure, with correlates instead of functions, and with few social-psychological aspects. Current interest is focused upon describing multiple dimensions of social structure but often without reference to a larger synthetic context of theory and analysis.

Seven specific criticisms of contemporary macroscopic theory will be considered here:

1. Stratification is abstracted from other structural concepts. The relationship between culture and stratification has been reduced to a descriptive listing of the different customs that are found in different social classes. Even the relationship between the ethnic group and the social class is considered only in a restricted sense. To sum up, stratification has been posed as a special topic of inquiry that can be pursued in a vacuum; stratification can be defined and measured independently of other social concepts. Much technical progress in scale construction has been made within this narrow conception but little theoretical interpretation of the results is possible.

2. The functions of stratification have been neglected, as is already implied in the first criticism. Not merely have the relationships among structural elements been neglected but the processes that underlie these relationships have been largely ignored. Stratification has been investigated as a self-perpetuating mechanism, as in Hollingshead's *Elmtown's Youth*, but little light has been

thrown upon the more general consequences of these processes (Hollingshead, 1949). The need for dynamic models is indicated by these omissions.

3. Survey methods and data have been emphasized while historical and anthropological data have been neglected. Perhaps this point accounts for the first two, for the survey method tends to tear data out of context unless it is skillfully employed. Structure is not easily inferred from the responses of individuals. Context or structural considerations must be imposed during the survey design or it will never enter the study.

4. Prestige ranking has been considered a sufficient object of stratification studies. The Warner studies (Warner and Lunt, 1941; Warner et al., 1949) and the North–Hatt study (North and Hatt, 1947) are specific examples, but this tendency is visible in most of the other studies in the 1930s and 1940s. A literature in power structure has been inspired by Hunter's research (1953) and Mills' writing (Mills, 1946); while Centers (1949) investigated psychological identification and social class. However these are recent and as yet tangential developments in the stratification literature. What are the functions, or consequences, of high prestige? The listing of correlates at one point in time will not do as an answer to this question.

5. Some sort of 'mass' society concept is apparently needed for the macroscopic view of stratification. Ranking seems to exist as an abstract property of society completely apart from concrete social relationships and devoid of psychological content. Theoretical discussion by Davis and Moore (1945) has stressed a relationship between ranking and the division of labor by applying an economic analogy of the scarcity of commodities to the sociological problem of the allocation of positions in society, as brought out by Simpson (1956). However, this argument does not explicitly delve into concrete social relationships. The social-psychological aspects of social relationships are largely neglected. Clearly, Radcliffe-Brown's view of social structure retains social-psychological elements in social structure, and unless we can demonstrate empirically that all social relationships are impersonal or anonymous, we had better include social psychology in our theories.

6. No locale nexus for social relationships is provided by this macroscopic view of stratification. Some stability of actors and

interactions in a social system is necessary before social relationships can be said to exist. Although stability of interaction can be conceived of without reference to any specific locale, most stable interactions do take place within a specific locale, and the characteristics of the locale influence the characteristics of the interaction.

7. The macroscopic view ignores the variations in stratification within society – variations among regions, among subcultures between rural and urban areas, and even within social strata. Perhaps references to a single system of stratification in the United States are valid when crude comparisons with rather different stratification systems are intended; otherwise the notion of a single stratification system in the United States is likely to be misleading. True, if mass culture has an extreme homogenizing influence upon the United States, then this objection will no longer hold. But as yet the internal variations are quite striking.

Let us turn to the microscopic approach to social structure. This approach tends to be more concrete than the macroscopic one. Radcliffe-Brown's conception of social structure and social relations is typically concrete. The field methods employed in the analysis of these kinds of social relations permit direct observation of the social relationship. Weber's conception of a social relationship as existing in the probability that individuals act toward each other in characteristic ways is quite close to Radcliffe-Brown's concern with empirical regularities (Weber, 1947).

Radcliffe-Brown also placed a holistic stamp upon the microscopic approach, though he recognized that complex modern societies could not readily be studied in these terms. His concern for institutional analysis in particular derived from his holistic emphasis. Indeed, within a relatively small, self-contained homogeneous society this microscopic approach is actually equivalent to a macroscopic one. However, in larger societies the microscopic approach is not feasible, so that some other approach must be used to study social relationships.

An alternative social-psychological approach defines social structure in terms of role, norm and expectation. Studies of socialization, conformity and deviation often employ this terminology (Parsons, 1951). This approach and the previous one may be linked together by the expectations concept. We may define 'role' as a set of norms specific to a position, and define 'norm' in terms of shared expectations. The shared expectations determine social relationships. Within a particular group we can identify roles with reciprocal social relationships. In this way, one can translate-statements about social relationships into statements about roles (Bates, 1956).

Studies of stratification in the United States using a microscopic approach have tended to restrict their scope to prestige ranking, for example, the community studies of the 1930s. Therefore, the functional criticisms of the macroscopic approach also apply to the microscopic approaches. However, anthropological studies of social structure deal with kinship structure and its relationships to other aspects of social structure, thereby escaping these criticisms.

The microscopic approaches assume a common body of actors in mutually meaningful interaction or with stable social relationships among themselves. This assumption is often reasonable for societies with little migration, homogeneous cultures and little social change. Small numbers of population are implied if the common body of actors, or at least some of them designated as judges, are expected to be in interaction with most of the rest of the population. Most of the specifically anthropological research techniques are feasible only for small populations.

All of the assumptions listed in the previous paragraph are invalid with respect to the urban United States. Of course, the structure of certain parts of a city, as well as the structure of certain cliques in a city, may be examined with these assumptions considered as valid. *Family and Kinship in East London* (Young and Willmott, 1957) illustrates the first kind of study, while Floyd Hunter's *Community Power Structure* (1953) illustrates the second. But if there is any single social structure containing all of the inhabitants of the city, it will not be found in this way.

How can the merits of the macroscopic and the microscopic approach be combined? Will such a combination be appropriate to urban social structure? Let us indicate some merits of each approach.

The macroscopic approach can include the insights of historical research and of social anthropology. Both of these bodies of literature are organized around an institutional approach. Historical research stresses the relationship among institutions over great periods of time while social anthropology expresses the relationship among institutions at a particular time as revealed by social relationships. By placing the context of stratification in society as a total system this approach encourages a multi-functional analysis of stratification. Prestige itself is one of the less important aspects of stratification in such an analysis. Power, values, social interests and economic consequences can all receive greater attention. Indeed, prestige itself can be regarded as a manifestation of values.

Some deficiencies of the macroscopic approach stem from the lack of information on concrete social relationships obtained in empirical research in large heterogeneous social units. Once the anthropological methods break down one is left mainly with demographic and historical data. Neither of these kinds of data is easily related to the specific structures and specific behavioral systems that we would like to analyze in our society. The survey method as yet has not been used with such formulations. The survey measures individual responses directly, not social structure. The mechanism of reference groups may be employed to relate individual responses to social or demographic categories, but this device still does not yield direct evidence about social relationships, only evidence of identification.

The microscopic approaches have desirable properties for empirical research, but, save for the anthropological approach, they have not developed equally significant theory. Role, norm, deviation, expectation and sanction must be placed within a broader context of social structure before they enable us to analyze any large heterogeneous social units. These concepts have, for the most part, been used descriptively. Empirical research in small communities has tended to be highly community specific, that is, the man is ranked in terms of a local interaction system but the implications for his rank in some other community are not investigated, and therefore we cannot generalize the results.

Next let us consider the main problems presented by urban social structure:

1. Limitations of time alone suggest that close personal relationships cannot be established and maintained among all the inhabitants of a city. Impersonal relationships may be numerous among those people involved in many interactions. In brief casual contacts between persons only superficial information can be communicated, yet this kind of information will commonly be the basis for evaluating and ranking them. Reliance upon symbols to communicate this information leads to a certain standardization of ranking criteria within impersonal relationships. Address, car,

dress, speech and manners as symbols become important criteria. Of course, within personal relationships, the esteem of role performance (Davis, 1948, pp. 93–4) and the repute of personal evaluations (Gordon, 1959, pp. 245–6) will still be found. Nevertheless, if we are to refer to a reputational stratification system for the entire city, we will probably have to describe the system in terms of highly visible, standardized symbols. These symbols do not communicate the type of evaluations implied by esteem or repute.

2. The degree of cultural homogeneity and the extent to which channels of communication link together the various groups in the population affect the extent to which an over-all stratification system can be described. The existence of sub-cultures, which may or may not follow the boundary lines of the stratification system, tends to obliterate any precise overall ranking system. While some subcultures may be ranked as aggregates in a crude way, comparisons between any two persons in two different subcultures may have little meaning.

3. The stability of the population of a city affects the extent to which a stratification system can be described. Newcomers are only slowly absorbed into the existing network of social relationships that anthropoligists seek to describe. Rapid social change engendered by rapid technological change serves as a stimulus to population movement and to the development of new occupations, which cannot readily be interpreted in terms of a previous stratification system. Thus, the economic system, as the source of technological change, may lead to flexibility or blurring in an overall stratification system.

The movement of population confronts us with further problems of similarities among the social structures of different cities. If a family moves, how is it placed in the new stratification system? Are characteristics such as size of city or economic base of city crucial in this problem? To what extent is there a national stratification system that can guide us to an answer to this question? These questions must be dealt with before we can speak of a characteristic urban social structure, as opposed to the social structure of specific cities. The heterogeneity of values within a city has already posed difficulties for us; now we must deal with the heterogeneity of values on a national level as well. For the newcomer must necessarily be judged by superficial symbols, and the meanings attached to these symbols can be similar only if the systems of values in the various cities are similar.

To this point numerous difficulties have been indicated in any attempt to create a satisfactory schematization of urban social structure. Let us now sketch out a possible solution to these problems. There are undoubtedly several systems of social structure within each city. Of these, two must be distinguished now. We may refer to the overall system of superficial symbols used to rank persons in a city as the 'urban stratification system'. This is the only system that is shared by the inhabitants of the city and participated in by most members of the city. The system can be described in terms of prestige, though the significance of the system is by no means summarized in these terms.

We may also think of the city as composed of numerous subcultures, some following social class lines and some following racial or ethnic lines as well as others. Within the subcultures, the urban stratification system will be recognized, but it will not be regarded in the same way in the different groups. In general, those persons in an advantageous position in the system will tend to sanctify the system and argue for the *status quo*. Those not so fortunate will take a different view.

These two systems of social structure may be studied by different research methods. The urban stratification system may be directly measured by survey techniques. The abstractness of the survey technique will not be harmful, since a symbolic system is under investigation, not relationships among persons. The urban subcultural system may be studied directly by anthropological techniques. Data pertinent to both systems will be found in the census tract tabulations. If surveys measure the different views of the overall stratification system held within the different subcultures then these two systems can be linked.

We have, then, an abstract, overall system and a set of concrete subsystems. We may borrow Leach's model for the analysis of the subsystems in their relationship to the overall system: the differential meaning and value placed on the overall system within the subsystems can be used to construct a dynamic model of social stratification. This dynamic model should express the processes by which the overall stratification is maintained as well as the processes that tend toward making changes in the system.

Within the subcultures we can investigate concrete social relationships. The esteem of role performance and the repute of personal evaluations will be pertinent here. While esteem will be involved in all performances of roles, the most important situation for heads of household will be found in work, with family roles almost as important. Thus, the knowledge of esteem will generally be restricted to rather small, but perhaps highly stable, social systems. Similarly, the knowledge of repute will be restricted to family, peer groups and others within primary social relationships. The social systems in which esteem and repute are operative will ordinarily be much smaller than subcultures. Systems of repute will tend to be entirely within single subcultures, but systems of esteem may cross subcultural boundaries.

The existence and the meaningfulness of esteem and repute in the urban setting may be challenged from two points of view. First, the amount of mobility, previously mentioned, will tend to disrupt the establishment of primary or close social relationships within which these concepts are meaningful. Second, the existence of social disorganization, or anomie, within a subculture would have the same disruptive effect. This possibility has been suggested for the lower classes in general and the recent migrants to the city in particular, especially those migrants marked out by ethnic or racial distinctions.

Recent research, however, indicates that greater stability of social relationships exists in the city than had been previously believed. In particular, the importance of kinship ties among those groups formerly believed to be disorganized has been emphasized. Although esteem and repute probably may not have the same significance in urban social structure that they have in a small, stable community, they may have more significance than the classical treatment of urban social structure suggests.

The overall urban stratification system may also be interpreted in social-psychological terms. The concept of *social distance* (Bogardus, 1928) may be used to express prestige ranking as it affects social relationships concretely. Social distance need not be restricted to the social relationships among racial and ethnic groups but may be used to describe relationships among social classes, occupational groups or any other grouping. Social distance may be measured behaviorally – who marries whom, who lives near whom and so forth; or it may be measured psychologically by the traditional social-distance scale in which persons are asked to rank various ethnic and racial groups according to a series of hypothetical social relationships – would you marry an X, eat meals with an X, have an X in your neighborhood, in your school, at your job and so forth.

Social distance is a useful concept because it describes an aspect of interaction that can take place within any social relationship and it also describes this interaction in terms of participation in different institutional settings. These merits can be retained in the generalized view which we are taking. Although social distance has been traditionally associated with caste distinctions, the inclusion of social classes on a social-distance scale should also prove illuminating. The occupations that North and Hatt ranked by prestige might be ranked on a social-distance scale as well as the social-class categories of Centers. A comparison between these rankings and those of various racial and ethnic groupings should be illuminating. In particular, occupational, ethnic and racial combinations should be ranked (such as Negro doctor) in order to determine the relative importance of each component in assigning social distance. By this approach, the survey technique can help us to describe the overall stratification system in terms that will simplify the further study of subcultures. The determination of boundaries in a stratification system is especially aided by social-distance measures. The fact that much behavior in specific situations cannot be predicted from knowledge of the symbolic aspects of stratification does not detract from the significance of this approach.

So far we have included elements of both macroscopic and microscopic approaches to social stratification and have begun to delineate a dynamic model for explaining overall patterns of stratification. The criticisms of the macroscopic approach as lacking social-psychological context are met by the inclusion of elements from both approaches in the system model. The main criticism of the microscopic approach, its lack of applicability, is also met. But the functional criticisms of the current macroscopic approach as lacking economic and political relevance deserve more attention.

The total effect of the functional criticisms is to call attention to the narrow focus on prestige ranking in recent work. The general institutional, structural or functional context of stratification has been neglected. But how does the approach described above escape these criticisms?

We must sketch out the institutional context of stratification before we can answer this question. Let us consider first the economic system, the political system and the cultural system.

The economic system has been correctly emphasized in the stratification literature. The dominance of economic institutions in the culture of the West, and especially of the United States, is sufficient to justify this emphasis. But the relationship between the economic system and the stratification system is not so simple. The overall stratification system is based on symbols. Weber's notion of status as 'style of life' (Weber, 1946) and Veblen's notions of invidious distinction and conspicuous consumption (Veblen, 1931) represent similar conceptions of stratification. Some symbols cost money and are therefore restricted to those persons who can afford them; other symbols, however, stand for the person's position in the productive processes, specifically his occupation; still other symbols denote racial or ethnic position.

Various empirical studies have underscored the importance of occupation in predicting prestige ranking in the United States. Since symbols reflect values we may note that such intrinsic characteristics of occupation as skill and responsibility relate to the prestige system more closely than do the extrinsic rewards (Barber, 1957). Thus, the significance of position in the productive processes is not solely a matter of financial return but reflects more general cultural evaluations.

We have already noted that economic processes related to technological change can result in a shifting occupational structure, and therefore in a shifting stratification system. We may further note that the organization of economic activities into firms or bureaucracies affects the occupational system and stratification system. Such popular works as *The Organization Man* (Whyte, 1956) dwell on the rigidifying effects of bureaucracy upon stratification. In particular, the reliance upon academic degrees for entrance into the management hierarchy may increase the rigidity of stratification or the presence of boundaries.

The development of labor unions as counters to the power of management further affects the stratification system. Paradoxically, the pooling of the economic interests of workers in unions has not led to generalized class conflict. The ultimate effects of unionization upon the rigidifying tendencies of class is by no means clear.

In summary, the relationship between the economic system and the stratification system is as follows. Many consequences for the stratification system stem from the economic system. However, these economic consequences in no sense entirely define or determine the stratification system. Many other factors affect stratification including those self-maintaining factors found within stratification. Any predictions as to the future state of the stratification system must take account of economic factors, but these economic factors are not sufficient to allow prediction by themselves.

The specific relationship between the economic system and the social structure of a particular city is not simple. When a single, locally owned industrial concern dominates the economy of a small city, then the patriarchal, not to say feudal, effects upon the social structure will be quite clear. In Elmtown, for example, approximately 35 per cent of the adult males were employed by one locally owned industrial concern (Warner, *et al.*, 1949, pp. 101–114). Of course, the textile-mill towns of New England and the South are extreme examples of this situation. But when the economic base of the community is more diversified, the effects upon the stratification system are not so clear. Possibly a white-collar city, such as Washington, DC, would tend toward a system different from an industrial city. In fact, social structure must reflect economic variations of place as well as economic variations of time if there are any economic effects at all.

When we turn to the political system quite a different set of problems awaits us. Although the prestige ranking system contains some hints as to the overall distribution of power in society, the actual controls of power are invested in large organizations. For the most part, he who has power in our society is he who has a strategic position in a giant organization, be it political, military, industrial, labor union, or whatnot. Therefore, many high ranking persons, such as those in the medical profession, may have little power (save through their own mass organization, the AMA) while some low ranking persons may have considerable power. The American political system, national and local, is a mediator between the conflicts and pressures of numerous organizations; therefore control over these organizations provides access to power.

The maintenance of overall power relations, however, has a good deal to do with stratification. In our democratic system, voting has very definite long-run effects upon the overall structure of power relations. But the phenomenon of voting itself is greatly affected by the stratification system, as shown by numerous studies of voting behavior (Lipset, 1960).

On the other hand, the effects of power upon the stratification system are less clear. Certainly, shifts in the power structure will affect the stratification system; certainly, rigidity of the power structure will also affect the stratification system, as suggested by the position of the Negro in the North and South. But there is no objectively visible link, such as occupation, in relation to the economic system, through which we can establish these connections. In part, the phenomenon of power thrives on secrecy, the data are not available. But in part also, the relationship may simply not be as close as that between the economic system and the stratification system. The study of power should focus more closely upon the relations between large organizations than upon stratification.

Within a particular city there may be an informal power structure presiding over community-wide decisions, especially those of a community welfare nature. This power structure wields decisive influence when a project requiring volunteer financing is involved, for the persons in the controlling positions are those who normally provide large lump sums. Hunter's examples of decisions in *Community Power Structure* are mainly of this sort, so that the degree of control over other community activities is less clear. In *Middletown*, the Lynds found a more stringent control wielded by the power structure, but the size of community and dominance of a single, locally owned industry account in part for the difference (Lynd and Lynd, 1929).

When we turn to the relationship between the stratification system and the system of symbols and values, we are really dealing with the internal mechanisms of the stratification system itself. For the overall stratification system consists of symbols, not persons, and the symbols reflect the values of society. Thus, the definition of a stratification system is dependent upon a certain minimum of common values. The persistence of the stratification system therefore depends upon the communication of these values to subsequent generations.

Suppose we turn to the further question, what are the consequences of the ranking system for behavior? While some of the symbols, such as occupation, represent activities, we can still ask, is the ranking system merely an ordering of behavioral differences, or does the ranking system itself affect behavior? By our definitions, the ranking system must affect behavior to be a stratification system. But how are these consequences expressed?

The most direct answer involves values and information.

Different values are found among the different subcultures. These values govern the ways in which the persons in subcultures act toward one another – that is, the social relationship between persons in different subcultures, which leads us back to the initial definition of social structure. The symbolic information permits individuals to perceive the rank and then act according to values. Now, the stratification system must explain not merely the existence of social relationships among subcultures but also the persistence of these social relationships. Thus, the communication of values to subsequent generations must be bounded so that the subcultures themselves persist. The stratification system, by affecting social relationships, can affect communication among subcultures and therefore can perpetuate itself.

The view outlined above is essential to the interpretation of the correlates between stratification and behavior that have been reported by the various survey analysts. It is the distribution of values that frequently enables us to interpret stratification theoretically, not the distribution of prestige itself. Clearly, prestige is defined by values, and is itself a value. The 'status seekers' are those who emphasize this value in their decision-making.

The socialization process becomes a key process for the maintenance of the stratification system. The crucial boundaries in the maintenance of the stratification system become the boundaries affecting the content of the socialization process, the channels of communication of values to particular subcultures in subsequent generations.

The emphasis upon subculture can be employed in the relating of stratification to racial and ethnic groups. The latter groups often have been treated as subcultures; as such they stand on the same footing as social classes. Many investigators have pointed out that such racial and ethnic subcultures are often concentrated in the lower social strata, especially in their initial period of immigration. The characteristic rise and diffusion of these people throughout the stratification system has been regarded as the outcome of an assimilation process over several generations. The differential success of various groups in rising has been attributed to their different arrival dates and to social distance between these groups and the dominant groups in society. Social distance is expressed in terms of symbolic differentials between these groups. Some authors define ethnic symbols as cultural symbols and racial symbols as biological symbols. Thus, ethnic symbols may be erased by a cultural assimilation process, whereas biological symbols cannot be. In particular, the position of the Negro is partially explained in terms of the biological character of racial symbols (Broom and Selznick, 1955, ch. 12).

Several community studies have revealed that a stratification system exists within the racial and ethnic groups roughly paralleling the stratification system among the dominant groups. Thus, social distance exists among members of these groups and is organized around the same symbolic referents as are found within the dominant groups. But contrary evidence is presented by William Foote Whyte (1955). The stratification system within ethnic groups may have features quite unlike the system within the dominant groups, especially with respect to the position of racketeers, politicians, entertainers and so forth.

The importance of subcultures in the present context stems from two sources. First, they will be regarded as essential elements in a stratification system. Second, they will enable us to construct a dynamic model of social structure.

The result of this institutional survey is to define values, symbols, ethnic groups and racial groups as parts of the stratification system, but to regard economic and power phenomena as external to the stratification system.

Let us relate this discussion to urban social structure. In particular, let us turn our attention to the relationship between residential area and urban social structure. In doing so we will be concerned more about the social structure of specific cities and less about general societal social structure or the related institutional structure.

The residential area of a city is distinctively a part of the city; as occupation, car, or other status symbols are not. As a symbol, the residential area, or address within the residential area, places a person within the context of a particular urban social structure. It is specific to the city in a way that none of the other familiar indexes of social stratification is.

Earlier we noted that mutual social relationships among all persons in a city was an impossibility; indeed, most inhabitants must remain anonymous to any particular inhabitant. But residential areas may be widely known, and their general social characteristics may also be a matter of common knowledge. A survey could easily provide us with relevant information on this point. Certainly, the residential areas and their social positions are far less anonymous than the individuals in the city. It is likely that any one person's social map of the city would reveal his own position, much as the humorous maps entitled *A New Yorker's View of the United States* or *A Bostonian's View of the United States* reflect both geographical and social factors. But the distortion might be only a stretching and shrinking of the residential areas with the essential geographical relations remaining in the same order throughout.

The residential area presumably reflects values in that the residence itself is a consumers' item. More evidence on the relative weight of different aspects of residential area as a factor in the decision to purchase or rent a home is needed to enlighten us on this point. Relative homogeneity of residential areas with respect to social characteristics is assumed in this statement. The residence itself is a more useful index of social stratification than most other consumers' goods; for the residence as symbol has much the same prestige significance throughout the social scale. This is not to say that the meaning of residence is the same at all levels, but that residence itself is a meaningful symbol in prestige terms at all levels. By contrast, the make and model of automobile, while a prominent issue among the lower classes, may be subordinate to housing desires in the restricted budget of the lower white-collar members of the middle class (such as university professors). Most of the symbols of greatest use in differentiating members of the upper classes are inaccessible to, if not invisible to, members of the lower classes. The public character of residence, the necessity of residence and the high cost of residence, leads to its importance as a symbol of social position.

The usefulness of residential area as a predictor of social characteristics has been attested to by many community studies, and has been given close attention by the Warner group (Warner, Meeker and Eells, 1949). Indeed, this group has included residential area in its summary index of social class. This index is intended for use in any urban area of the United States. Its validation rests on its relationship to the stratification system that Warner has studied with a reputational interview.

The residential area is also related to subcultures. Data from newly constructed housing projects suggests that spatial location is an important determinant of clique structure. Further, the congregation of various ethnic subcultures in particular areas may have resulted partly from discrimination by the outside world and partly from preference of the insiders, but the fact remains that once they are concentrated in a single area, the spatial proximity can serve to reinforce the characteristics of the subculture. Perhaps the extreme example of proximity reinforcing culture can be found in the old order Amish of Lancaster County, Pennsylvania, in which isolation plays a role as inverse proximity (Kollmorgen, 1943). Maximum proximity among ingroup members plus minimum proximity to outgroup members yields maximum cultural stability if (1) cultural stability is an end of the ingroup culture (2) static environment (3) proximity determines interaction patterns.

Nevertheless, residential area is only tangentially related to many aspects of social structure. We can learn very little about a power structure from residential areas alone. One aspect of the economic system is expressed in land values, but an aspect only distantly related to the industrial system and occupational structure. Even the socialization process, the heart of the stratification system, is not directly revealed in residential area data. Why, then, its importance in this essay?

Two answers can be given. Let us return to the aggregate problem posed elsewhere. A central problem of sociology is the description of supra-individual aggregates.

1. While it is true that residential areas reflect only part of social structure, it is also true that if social structure exists as an aggregate, its effects must be revealed in residential areas. While observations on residential areas are not substitutes for observations on individuals in research, the consequences of social structure can be expressed in terms of their effects upon the social characteristics of areas, and these consequences can be tested by observations on residential areas. The reality of social structure is attested to by the fact that social characteristics of residential areas are not randomly distributed, but are clustered in ways that one might readily predict from the discussion earlier in this chapter.

2. Residential area data can reflect aggregate effects as processes. The Chicago school's adaptation of Simmel's social processes has been widely, and correctly, accused of having only descriptive merit (Alihan, 1938). Accommodation, conflict, invasion, succession, these are certainly descriptive terms. But they need not remain so. Imbedded in a theoretical system they can become theoretical concepts. At the same time, such a theoretical system will be process oriented. Dynamic models might explain these residential area processes. The static view of social structure could be supplemented in this way.

In this chapter the theoretical orientation of the book has been presented. Three tasks were undertaken; these were: (1) definitions of concepts, (2) a critique of current theory and research, and (3) a formulation of synthetic theoretical approach combining elements from diverse traditions.

References

ALIHAN, M. A. (1938), *Social Ecology: A Critical Analysis*, Columbia University Press.

BARBER, B. (1957), *Social Stratification*, Harcourt, Brace.

BATES, F. L. (1956), 'Position, role and status: a reformulation of concepts', *Social Forces*, vol. 34, May.

BOGARDUS, E. S. (1928), *Immigration and Race Attitudes*, D. C. Heath & Co.

BROOM, L., and SELZNICK, P. (1955) *Sociology*, Row Peterson.

CENTERS, R. (1949), *The Psychology of Social Classes*, Princeton University Press.

DAVIS, K. (1948), *Human Society*, Macmillan.

DAVIS, K., and MOORE, W. E. (1945), 'Some principles of stratification', *Amer. Sociol. Rev.*, vol. 10, pp. 242–9.

GORDON, M. (1959), *Social Class in American Sociology*, Duke University Press.

HOLLINGSHEAD, A. B. (1949), *Elmstown's Youth*, Wiley.

HUNTER, F. (1953), *Community Power Structure*, University of North Carolina Press.

KOLLMORGEN, W. (1943), 'The agricultural stability of the Old Order Amish and the Old Order Mennonites of Lancaster County Pennsylvania', *Amer. J. of Sociol.*, vol. 49, pp. 232–41.

LIPSET, S. M. (1960), *Political Man*, Doubleday & Co.

LYND, R. S., and LYND, H. M. (1929), *Middletown*, Harcourt, Brace & World.

MILLS, C. W. (1946), 'The middle classes in middle-sized cities', *Amer. Sociol. Rev.*, vol. 11, pp. 520–29.

NORTH, C. C., and HATT, P. K. (1947), 'Jobs and occupations: a popular evaluation', *Opinion News*, 1st September, pp. 3–13.

PARSONS, T. (1949), *The Structure of Social Action*, Free Press.

PARSONS, T. (1951), *The Social System*, Free Press.

SIMPSON, R. L. (1956), 'A modification of the functional theory of social stratification', *Social Forces*, vol. 35, pp. 132–7.

VEBLEN, T. (1931), *The Theory of the Leisure Class*, Viking Press.

WARNER, R. L., and LUNT, P. S. (1941), *The Social Life of a Modern Community*, Yale University Press.

WARNER, R. L., *et al.* (1949), *Democracy in Jonesville*, Harper.

WARNER, R. L., MEEKER, M. M., and EELLS, K. (1949), *Social Class in America*, Science Research Associates.

WEBER, M. (1946), 'Class, status and party', in H. Gerth and C. W. Mills (eds), *Max Weber: Essays in Sociology*, Oxford University Press.

WEBER, M. (1947), *The Theory of Social and Economic Organization*, Free Press.

WHYTE, W. F. (1955), *Street Corner Society*, University of Chicago Press, 2nd edn.
WHYTE, W. H. Jr (1956), *The Organization Man*, Simon & Schuster.
YOUNG, M., and WILLMOTT, P. (1957), *Family and Kinship in East London*, Routledge & Kegan Paul.

Part Three
The Urban Process:
Community and Interest

Probably no terms have given rise to greater confusion between
sociologists and planners than those of 'neighbourhood' and
'community'. The confusion stems partly from the contrast
between the geographical and sociological imaginations (as
outlined in the introduction to this reader) and partly from the
history of planning in the nineteenth century. If the excerpt
'Community' (Reading 10) from Buttimer's article on Sociology
and Planning is still fairly oriented towards the physical
implications of the concept of community it nevertheless
provides a current perspective which relates back to the earlier
article by Beshers (Reading 9) and forward to that of Gans
(Reading 18). Margolis (Reading 11) on the other hand
approaches the question of community via the problem of public
goods, goods which 'if available to anyone are equally available
to others'. He considers the questions of how much to provide,
who is to pay and who is to benefit, not only in terms of welfare
economics but also of political processes. The breakdown of
locality based communities, the variations in the types of demand
for public goods and the inherent potential conflict between
various urban sub-areas are all reflected in the patterns of urban
government. Wood (Reading 12) accepts that there are too many
urban governments but argues that the important point is
the emphasis laid on functional reorganization and administrative
convenience which has made it almost impossible to see any
valid areal division of power. Form's article (Reading 13) belies
its title; it is of course concerned to some degree with social
structure but his argument is that local political influence and
power over resources can influence the use to which land is put.
Form illustrates this view by reference to zoning decisions and
this is taken further by Mandelker (Reading 14) in his brief
review of the evolution of zoning in the USA and of its rationale

as a tool for planning. The links here are not only back to
Delafons' (Reading 2) perspective on urban problems, but to all
of the readings on community and interest, since it is clear that
the use of the law to enforce segregation or to preserve
homogeneity is an important element within the urban process.

10 A. Buttimer

Community

A. Buttimer, 'Community', extract from 'Sociology and planning',
Town Planning Review, vol. 42, no. 2, 1971, pp. 154–168.

[. . .] The obvious occasion for a convergence of interest between
sociologist and planner is in the elucidation of society's relationship to its physical environment. The planner is involved in
shaping and remoulding the physical setting; the sociologist is
interested in the social groups who inhabit that setting. One very
logical area of sociological research which should have enormous
interest for planners, then, should be the 'Community Studies'
tradition. Within this tradition a set of generalizations – necessarily complex given the changing nature of spatially circum-
scribed communities – has emerged.

The demise of socially autonomous and spatially-circumscribable social groups, however, has raised questions about the viability of 'community' as a conceptual framework. Social change
and geographical mobility have tended to splinter social groups
and disaggregate their impact on, and relationship to, a particular
physical environment. The logical direction for sociological
investigation has thus been to explore individual dimensions of
'community' for example, changes in working class life styles,
the emergence of suburban 'communities' and the changing
significance of the neighbourhood. Generalizations about these
dimensions of community can provide useful practical guidelines
for planning policy.

The 'community studies' tradition
The literature

In Britain and the USA, two predominant parent streams of research in community studies can be discerned. On the one hand
there are the studies which tried to grasp the total institutional
structure and behavioural systems of whole communities within
their environmental context; on the other hand there are the
problem-inspired analyses of urban sub-communities which
endeavoured to place a specific set of behavioural problems within

a community context. While the latter naturally appear to have more direct relevance to planning, the former also have yielded important insights into the nature of social behaviour and social change.

These distinct and contrasting sources help to explain the different approaches used in Britain and their different degrees of relevance to planning. Studies of whole communities, often modelled on anthropological research procedures, tended to select identifiable and spatially-circumscribed settlement groups at various stages of socio-economic development and analyze their nature, internal dynamics and life styles. The micro-sociological orientation, on the other hand, tended to focus on specific problem areas, for example, poverty-stricken sections of industrial cities, and examine these areas as far as possible from the perspective of the occupants. The former in general are intellectually exciting explorations done in detached academic fashion with little or no references to planning implications; the latter tended to be *postfacto* evaluations or critiques of planned or unplanned urban situations.

With regard to the first type, Frankenberg's (1966) interpretation of British community studies in terms of a general conceptualization of social change should provide a very useful document for scrutiny by planners. This comparative approach which uses a 'morphological continuum' model seeks to identify the social concomitants of increasing technological complexity; elaborating and qualifying the time-honoured hypothesis of a rural-urban continuum. The notion of 'rôle redundancy', borrowed from communications theory, also helps to bridge the conceptual gap between the social contrasts at both ends of the continuum (1966, pp. 237–96).

The demise of spatially-circumscribable communities in Britain and elsewhere has evoked voluminous questioning among sociologists regarding the viability of this approach to social research. In general, modern community studies in Britain have tended to concentrate on institutions as these are manifested in a locality (Young and Willmott's kinship studies, Rosser and Harris's family studies), or study of the interrelationships between institutions in one locality (for example, Stacey's *Banbury*, Williams' *Gosforth*, etc.).[1] From these two distinct but often overlapping fields of enquiry, important generalizations have been derived.

1. See Stacey (1969); Rex and Moore (1962); Williams (1964); Stacey (1960).

Young and Willmott's studies of working class residents of Bethnal Green,[2] for example, has altered several traditional notions about the effects of relocation upon kinship structure, and has questioned the oft-repeated planning device of trying to ameliorate the quality of social life through careful urban design.

... even when ... planners have set themselves to create communities anew as well as houses, they have still put their faith in buildings, sometimes speaking as though all that was necessary for neighbourliness was a neighbourhood unit, for community spirit a community centre. ... But there is simply more to a community than that. The sense of loyalty to each other amongst the inhabitants of ... Bethnal Green is not due to buildings. It is due far more to ties of kinship and friendship which connect the people of one household to the people of another. In such a district community spirit does not have to be fostered, it is already there. If the authorities regard that spirit as a social asset worth preserving, they will not uproot more people, but build the new houses around the social groups to which they already belong (Young and Willmott, pp. 198–9 Penguin edition).

The effects of time, however, were often omitted from community studies. As was seen later in Willmott's study of Dagenham various adaptive mechanisms can be developed by residents in their new residential environments.

In America, community studies also followed rather separate lines. Urban sub-communities were studied in terms of their 'ecological' setting on the one hand, while rural and small-town communities were studied from an anthropological perspective on the other hand. Chicago's mosaic of ethnic neighbourhoods provided an ideal empirical basis for testing some of the classical conceptualizations about the nature and dynamics of 'community' life. Community and sub-community studies constituted the core of Park's urban sociology.[3] He seemed particularly keen on testing and developing Durkheim's ideas about social change within and among communities. Like Durkheim, Park recognized the possibilities for personal disorganization arising from rapid change in standards and opportunities, but he also noted the creative potentialities of these processes as well as their potentially destructive ones.

Several classical case studies in the Chicago tradition revealed important dimensions of urban life.

2. See Young and Wilmott (1957) and (1963).
3. See Park (1964); Stein (1964). Some of the most relevant of these studies criticized by Stein are Zorbaugh (1929); Wirth (1928) and Whyte (1955).

Zorbaugh's *The Gold Coast and the Slum* (1929) explored a socially-complex neighbourhood in the lower North Side of Chicago, where several natural areas existed in close physical proximity but utter social isolation. He raised the question of how to design a social organization in which the disparate needs and interests of these groups could be co-ordinated. While the distinctiveness of these sub-areas, and the social distance between them, was unique to Chicago, the definition of problems involved in forming variegated neighbourhoods into coherent political units remains a very pertinent one in other contexts. Louis Wirth's *The Ghetto* (1928) showed how the ideologies, social patterns and personality types of the ghetto provided a basis for ethnic solidarity under almost any circumstances. He also introduced a valuable insight into the nature of upward mobility, by tracing the succession of neighbourhoods into which Jews tended to move as they moved out of the original ghetto.

An alternative approach to community study endeavoured to apply a time-tested technique of anthropological research to the study of urban communities. The Lynds' study of Muncie, Indiana (1929), and R. Lloyd Warner's *Yankee City* studies (1947) focused on the effects of industrialization and bureaucratization as processes shaping American community life.[4] Each of these community studies became, then, a study of transitional processes rather than an ecologically-orientated analysis of society's relationship to a particular environment.

While various charges regarding *raison d'être*, methodological efficacy, and scientific accuracy can be and have been raised against community studies, there are certain strengths evident in the approach which appear to be particularly relevant for planners.[5] The comprehensive perspective on social life taken in a community study parallels the comprehensive perspective on physical planning for social life which a planner has to adopt. Community sociologists usually look at the full range of institutional participation as each aspect of it affects every other aspect. The individual's total life space – his modes of participating in major institutional areas – is usually the main focus of attention.

Generalizations about 'community'

What conclusions seem to emerge from this rich body of substantive research? What insights or generalizations can the planner

4. See also Anderson (1937); Seeley *et al.* (1956).
5. See Vidich *et al.* (1964); Stacey (1969); Anderson (1971).

glean as guidelines for practical policy? The evidence falls naturally into sociological categories, that is, generalizations have been
reached about sociologically defined aspects of community,
rather than directly about planning implications. The literature
yields generalizations about people's relationships to their social
rather than physical environment. However, since these two kinds
of environmental web are intricately interwoven, insights about
one provide valuable guidelines for shaping the other. In an attempt to reduce such generalizations to operationally testable
propositions, Margaret Stacey has recently outlined the 'state of
the arts' on community studies (1969). Her propositions deal
primarily with the necessary pre-conditions for the development
of local social systems, the implications of adding or subtracting
certain local institutions, the interplay of roles and 'power points'
within the system, and the complex interweaving of local and non-
local systems within one area.

The central implication for planning concerns the relationship
(if any) between people's differential participations in social systems and the kind of physical organization of space which would
facilitate such participations. People's subjective perceptions and
attitudes toward distance often distort the 'objective' (geodesic)
measures of distances; their participation in various kinds of
social sub-systems reflects the interplay of local and non-local
influences on their lives. The critical point is that no one physical
organization of space, no one kind of community service provision could satisfy all these varying needs. The locally-orientated
type will demand different kinds of services and institutions close
to his residence; the non-locally-orientated may prefer *not* to have
the same facilities close to his home. The implication then is to
provide for both types, and for as many variations in between as
possible.

The social composition of population in a planned residential
area also poses questions for which community studies have some
insights to offer. The ratio of host to migrant population may
well determine the probability that a local social system could
develop. The planner cannot add or subtract institutions (such as
employment) from an area without expecting certain predictable
social concomitants. Finally, the scale of development, that is, the
size of the area to be taken as a whole for redevelopment, should
reflect the scale and degree of development within and among
local social systems.

In general, community studies indicate two contrasting kinds of social participation in space which have significance for planning. First, there is the spatially-circumscribed 'home area' type of identity, as ghettoes, 'urban villagers' and ethnic neighbourhoods, and secondly, the nodally-organized network of spatial influences radiating from key institutions like work, school, recreation centre and others. While the former tends to orientate people primarily toward local loyalties and a degree of local independence, the latter tends to expand spatial horizons and produce outward orientations and interdependence. Both types of influence probably co-exist within every locality. Physical planning can influence the balance of these two kinds of force, and the investment of effort should reflect the socio-cultural characteristics of the people being planned for. As John Rex suggests:

It is the task of the planner and the sociologist to work out what kinds of community the economic circumstances will allow in each particular case and, having done this, to provide for the kind of physical facilities which will make it possible (1968, pp. 28–33).

Working class life styles

The nature of the working class and the dynamics of social life within working class areas have consistently evoked the intellectual curiosity of community sociologists and social anthropologists.[6] To the urban planner, the working class has become more than an object of intellectual curiosity. In many senses, working class communities have become the 'fly in the ointment' for many of his idealistic redevelopment renewal plans. Assumptions about human behaviour which stemmed either from models of middle-class life styles or stereo-typical models of the working class have continually been called into question because of the limited success and often failure of efforts to design for the social needs and tastes of working class people.[7]

A two-fold motivation, then – frustrated idealism on the part of the planner, heightened intellectual curiosity on the part of the sociologist – underlies the growing interest in working class behaviour evident in post-war Britain. Dennis's *Coal is Our Life* (1956), Firth's *Studies of Kinship in London* (1956), Young and Willmott's *Family and Kinship in East London* (1957) and *The Evolution of a Community* (1963) and a host of evaluative studies

6. See Goldthorpe *et al.* (1969), Dennis (1956); Stacey (1960, pp. 101–5, 112–14).
7. See Young and Willmott (1957); Blair (1969); Dennis (1970).

of planning endeavours within 'twilight' areas all constitute a mine of information on the nature of working class life styles.

There are certain obvious processes of secular social change which have deeply affected working class life styles and values in recent times. Most of these processes would seem to point to a general demise of a monolithic cohesive working class stratum within or opposed to society. These changes could be subsumed roughly under three major headings:

1. Economic: rising income and living standards which appear to give workers an *entrée* to middle class consumption patterns.

2. Technological: changes in industrial technology which alter the nature of work and the salaries paid for labour, and are associated with changing attitudes toward work and restructuring of social relationships at shop floor level.

3. Ecological: the movement of workers from rural to urban and from urban to suburban residential environments with the consequent dilution of old life styles and place-orientated ties.

Individuals are thus freed from traditional social networks and exposed to a wide variety of choices and influences, so working class consciousness is reduced from internal and external influences. Changes in employment, the break-up of traditional work-based communities, geographical mobility, bureaucratization of trade unions and the institutionalization of conflict have all tended to reduce the solidary nature of communal attachments and the feeling of working class consciousness. As old attachments and values are gradually eroded, they tend to be replaced by a more individualistic outlook in terms of expenditure, use of leisure time and aspiration level (Goldthorpe *et al.*, 1969, pp. 1–29). A similar set of forces has influenced white collar groups, but in different ways. Bureaucratization of the white collar worker situation, for instance, has led to more depersonalized working conditions and lowered chances of upward mobility. As a result some white collar groups have tended to lose faith in the virtues of 'individualism' and have turned to collective trade union action of an apolitical or instrumental kind.

Marxist interpretations of these changes stress the enduring alienation of workers despite superficial changes in life styles. Other interpretations include the *embourgeoisement* thesis, for example, which suggests that changes in the economic situation of workers (increased earnings, increased ownership of consumer durables, etc.) have led to the adoption of a middle class outlook and way of life among large sections of the working class.[8] Primary emphasis is focused on the economic aspects of class, that is, they have taken that similarity of income and living standards among members of the working class and the middle class would automatically lead to similar attitudes and behaviour. A contrasting thesis suggests a convergence between certain 'affluent workers' and lower middle class workers. Goldthorpe and Lockwood's critique of the *embourgeoisement* thesis, for example, holds that the economic situation is presumably only a necessary, not sufficient condition in class membership (Goldthorpe, 1969). Equally important in their view are the normative (what is valued and how it is to be achieved) and relational (the pattern of social life, acceptance or rejection by middle class) aspects of class. In their empirical research they found little evidence that the working class was actually becoming 'middle class' either in terms of their values or their patterns of social participation. They found directions of change in working class life styles which seemed to be leading away from the traditional pattern, but *not* towards assimilation with the middle class. Rather they were leading to what they called convergence in the normative orientations of certain sections of the working class and some white-collar groups. Changes away from traditional working class and middle class patterns of life were leading certain groups (on the margins of both classes) in the same direction in terms of similarity of outlook and aspiration.[9]

Certain social characteristics of middle-class people, family and home-centredness, may not mean an adoption of middle-class ways, but rather an adaptation of traditional patterns to accommodate changing situations (such as, movement to new estates and separation from traditional ties). More important still – in view of planning implications – changes in standards and styles of living may not mean there has been a concomitant change in the nature of social relationships between workers and other groups within society. Finally, there is still insufficient evidence as to whether in fact working class people actually wish to be associated with middle class groups in social relationships.[10]

Young and Willmott's studies of kinship systems among rehoused working class people in East London provide a uniquely

8. See Marshall (1950); Bendix (1964, 1965); Geiger (1949).
9. See Kerr *et al.* (1960); Lipset (1964); Goldthorpe (1964).
10. See Abrams (1960); Butler and Rose (1960).

valuable set of insights into these differential rates of change in working class life styles. Family and kin continued to play a highly significant rôle in the behaviour and life aspirations of working class communities. In a sense, the East London case epitomizes the rather consistent syndrome of behaviour and attitudes found among working class communities in several industrial cities through Britain, Continental Europe and North America, where ties of kinship and neighbourhood traditionally provided a warmth and security which seemed to compensate for the dreariness of the physical environment.[11]

Urban renewal and relocation of working class families, it appears, involve more than a potential rupture of social networks; they also involve a rupture with a particular place, – a home ground which has become invested with previous social memories and associations.[12] This two-fold link – physical and social – helps explain the traumatic effects of relocation on some working class families. In urban renewal, a rupture with physical location may be inevitable, but the break-up of social networks need not be. In Young and Willmott's Bethnal Green study, for example, a plea was made that whole communities or at least substantial blocks of a social network be relocated together rather than be allocated houses according to their positions on a waiting list. However, after a period of time, people can adjust to the process of urban renewal, though this adjustment does not necessarily have to lead to the adoption of middle class values. Willmott's Dagenham study showed that after forty years within their new housing environment, the residents showed remarkable social ease and identity with their environment, and traditional social patterns showed a remarkable resiliency and vitality (Young and Willmott, 1963).

Studies of working class communities in the USA reiterate this general finding, which lends empirical support to Goldthorpe and Lockwood's theoretical critique of the *embourgeoisement* thesis. Berger's *Working-Class Suburb* (1960) provided significant evidence that working class suburbanites do not adopt the behaviour patterns and beliefs characteristic of middle class suburbs. However, several studies of relocated slum families in some Eastern cities point to a rather different conclusion. Where relocation

11. See Mogey (1956); Kerr (1958).
12. See Bakke (1953); Ferguson and Pettigrew (1954); Schorr (1963); Gans (1959); Fried and Gleicher (1961); Hole (1959); Mogey (1955); HMSO (1967).

corresponded with an improvement in the physical surroundings, and an increase in cultural and educational opportunities, significant change in life style and aspiration took place among certain black families.[13]

Two clear sets of conclusions emerge from the empirical evidence: working class communities have a more resilient type of life style than was previously believed. First, their behaviour patterns are changing at different rates and in different directions, but certainly not all tending toward the model of middle class. Secondly, the two-fold attachments of working class people to (a) neighbourhood, and (b) to social networks, are intricately interwoven, and changes in one, as the removal from traditional home area, may cause a temporary rupture of the other, but over time these can again be repeated or substituted for.

What are some of the planning implications of these studies of working class communities? These are best considered in the context of some of the major problems posed by the older 'slum' areas and by the new housing estates to which working class people have been relocated. Problems associated with older working class areas have been fairly well documented: problems of health, crime, poverty and others; problems of the re-housed populations are not yet thoroughly known, but the commonly held lore includes such social problems as *anomie*, delinquency, 'unbalanced' age structure and lack of facilities (MHLG, 1967). Since the planner is presumably more in a position to influence the latter, the focus of discussion will rest on these. Basically, four sets of problems have been encountered in the planning of working class housing estates:

1. Problems of social composition.

2. Problems of control and decision-making.

3. Problems associated with the provision of employment, social services and other facilities.

4. Problems of physical design and layout.

The problems of class homogeneity and 'unbalanced' age-structure in housing estates have been well documented. Typically the first wave of migrants includes young families sometimes accompanied by older relatives. The associated needs for schools, recreational facilities and other amenities for young children have often been lacking. The provision of such facilities from the out-

13. See Millspaugh and Breckenfeld (1958).

set appears extremely important since they could provide opportunities for social interaction in an environment which lacks the traditionally established foci for social contact characteristic of the older areas from which these people have come. After some time, other needs develop: facilities for teenage and young adult populations and other kinds of provision arising out of the natural development of the population. Even if the housing estates are carefully designed to fit the social requirements of the first generation of residents, the initial programme cannot be considered as a *fait accompli*; as the population matures, social provision must also develop and expand to meet the normal concomitants of such evolution. Such provision involves primarily (a) job opportunities, namely, accessibility to suitable employment; (b) adequate range of choice in housing to fit the demands of households of varying age and class composition; (c) provision of transport, educational, recreational and other cultural facilities. In Dagenham, for example, an exodus of the 'second generation' became inevitable because of the lack of housing and other provision. This left a high proportion of older people often living alone in large houses which could have been occupied by young couples. This led to the curious anomaly of young people leaving the area because of a housing shortage while actually several houses were 'underoccupied' (Young and Willmott 1963, pp. 118–122).

While questions relating to demographic structure are reasonably predictable, however, the question of class composition poses greater problems. Despite a continuing ideological predilection for 'social balance', and 'integration' there is considerable empirical evidence on the wishes of people to live with people of their own class. The advantages of being socially at ease with one's neighbours appear more important to many people – particularly working class communities – than the loss of such social and cultural opportunities which might come as a result of class heterogeneity. Willmott therefore suggests that one should perhaps plan for one-class 'neighbourhoods' within mixed class communities – the neighbourhood being large enough to give the residents a sense of social ease, but not so large that they isolate people from those in other social classes (1963, p. 117). A similar recommendation also stems from American experience. Gans (1961) has argued for block homogeneity and community heterogeneity as one solution to the question of social integration in residential areas.

The political question of co-ordinating the control and allocation of houses also poses serious problems. From the viewpoint of planning, it is difficult to design physical provision for a population whose characteristics are not specifically known; from the viewpoint of some residents too, it is frustrating not to be consulted by the authorities who make decisions about their residential environment. Reforms of local government may well reduce or eliminate this problem; but there is a case for unifying or at least co-ordinating the control of housing estates. It would appear desirable that the same authority should handle the allocation of houses and the eventual administration of the estate. This leads to the question of community participation in the process of urban renewal and redevelopment.

To what extent do working class people know, or have any interest in knowing the mechanisms through which the planning process affects or determines their environment? There is little evidence of active public participation by working class people either in Britain or North America. Various case studies have revealed rather their passivity in the face of questions regarding environmental planning. The renewal/redevelopment process may appear clearly as a 'We-They' issue, and working class people may continue to be unwilling or incapable of participating actively in planning. This is not an argument for dismissing community participation; on the contrary it argues of a deliberate cultivation of the proper dispositions which would make such participation possible.[14]

Finally, there remains the question of physical design and the nature of social relationships. Willmott suggests that street layout can influence the extent to which people have neighbourly relations with each other in three ways:

1. The physical 'framing' of the housing unit: if this has a clear physical unity, people find it easier to feel a sense of identity with it and with their fellow residents;

2. The actual arrangement of the dwellings in relation to each other and to the transport lines;

3. The general housing density: the closer homes are to each other, other things being equal, the more likely it is that people become acquainted with their fellow residents.

The Dagenham study illustrated how the first two formulae affected social life. The Plan for a new town at Hook argued

14. See Dennis (1970, pp. 321–56); Ministry of Housing and Local Government (1969).

strongly for density control as a mechanism for promoting more social interaction among residents.[15] Several plans echoed a similar argument for higher densities, for example, the new town of Cumbernauld, but the effectiveness of such policy has not yet been fully proven.[16] It appears probable that communities like working class communities, which have always been used to high density in their traditional home areas, may wish comparatively higher densities in their new housing environment than others. However, the philosophical problem of how much and what kind of sociability is desirable in a residential area remains an open question. The general recommendation would be to provide for a choice; housing arrangements which facilitate frequent social interaction should co-exist on the same estate with arrangements for more privacy if such should be desired.

This leads finally to the question of location and distribution of local services and public amenities. Zoning of land uses has become such an entrenched policy among town planners that it is difficult to argue for scattered and diffuse types of distributions. However, if the social functions of shops, public houses, schools and other facilities were considered, a strong argument for wide dispersal could be made. Willmott's Dagenham study showed that corner shops and pubs can help to foster and maintain acquaintances among local people. Two kinds of locational network could presumably be designed: a spatially clustered set of major services and facilities where considerations of scale economies must enter, and a spatially diffuse set of minor services and facilities justified largely by their social functions.

Studies of working class communities in the context of urban renewal have thus two important messages for the planners. First, an explosion of the 'architectural determinism' myth, and secondly, an orientation to new dimensions in the traditional theories of working class behaviour.

How can the planner best apply these lessons in practical terms? To what extent can these aspirations of working class families be accommodated in redevelopment plans, and to what extent are they changing, changeable, and finally, how desirable or feasible is it to attempt to satisfy them? It is in the discussion and resolution of such issues that dialogue with sociology should be most beneficial. Sociological considerations should be part of the planner's argument in his effort to implement plans which must ulti-

15. See London County Council (1961, p. 41).
16. See McConnell (1969a).

mately be justified in terms of cost/benefit to society at large. But urban renewal is rarely if ever justifiable on grounds of purely economic cost/benefit: in the USA, for example, the federal government grants up to two thirds of the cost of redevelopment, and the criteria on which such subsidies are granted, are invariably social rather than economic (McConnell, 1969b).

Suburbia

Generalizations regarding the life styles of particular social groups rank among the most important contributions which sociologists have made to the planning enterprise. The declining importance of place-orientated communities and the increasingly ambiguous significance of class in the determination of particular or unique types of social behaviour became evident in the discussion of working class. Suburbia, however, has occasioned a reversal of many behavioural trends observable in urban society. To a certain extent, class-related life-styles – diluted and transformed in the process of urbanization – are reappearing in the suburbs; attachments to particular neighbourhoods are often consciously or unconsciously fostered by escapees from the anonymity of city life and by profit-seeking development agencies.[16]

Images of suburbia, and the research on which such images are based, reflect the socio-cultural context within which these studies have been done. In America, for example, there is a marked contrast between the old suburbs of the twenties and thirties and the privately-developed suburban tracts of post Second World War metropolitan areas. Similarly, a contrast appears between British public (local authority) suburban estates, privately built suburban estates, and new towns. It is difficult to derive generalizations which would cover the social characteristics of all suburbs.[17] In general, the British estates have been studied in terms of how they contrast and compare with old areas from which suburban residents come; whereas in America the standard polar types were 'urban' versus 'suburban' with some speculations on the rural-urban fringe. A contrast exists, too, between those sociologists who take a predominantly ecological view of the suburbs and those who explore suburban behaviour from the viewpoint of specific social characteristics. To the ecologist, for example, the

16. See Martin (1952, 1958); Douglas (1925); Fava (1958a, 1958b); Duncan and Reiss (1956); Harris (1943).
17. See Dobriner (1963); Wood (1958); Martin (1953); Spectorsky (1955); Schnore (1957); Whyte (1956).

two 'definitive' features of suburbia are, first, its physical location outside the political limits of the city; and secondly, its economic dependence on the city which generates commuting patterns (Martin, 1952). Examining the impact of these situational factors upon the structure of suburban communities, the ecologist hypothesizes that participation in downtown activities will decrease, and community participation in the residential area will also be curtailed because of the time spent in travelling to work. In practice, however, the relatively small scale and low densities of suburban residential communities have been conducive to certain types of association: neighbourhood and informal association.[18]

Besides, it has been questioned whether commuting is in fact a peculiarly suburban pattern at all. Hoover and Vernon's analysis (1959, p. 145) of commuting patterns between the various 'rings' of the New York Metropolitan region discovered that 'over 80 per cent work in the zone in which they live, while the remaining 15 per cent or so commute to a more central zone'. In America generally, more suburban commuters travel within the suburban zone than between zones; similarly, more core workers commute within the core than between zones. Suburbanization of manufacturing, the growth of suburban shopping centres, the continued expansion of employing satellites have created many jobs within the suburban zone, and thus suburbanites find employment within the suburban area itself. Implications for the planning of transport routes and traffic flows are rather obvious – more intrasuburban lateral routes may be needed than direct urban – suburban ones.

But the consequences of a commuting work force are seen mainly in the nature of social life among the non-employed members of suburban families. 'Women', the stereo-typical model suggests, 'are the force behind suburban organizations, indeed, behind the entire suburban ethic.' Several studies suggest that commuters participate less in the local community, but this may reflect age, recency of arrival and other characteristics rather than commuting *per se*. The relationship between commuting and participation in suburbia remains rather ambiguous. In general, the key to social participation can be found in the age and type of suburb and the social characteristics of the population.

To the sociologist, at least prior to the Second World War, the striking fact about the suburbs was their remarkably classless and

18. See Schaff (1952).

homogeneous character; a peculiarly monolithic model of suburban personality types and ways of life had emerged. The suburbanite, according to Douglas in 1925, is typically an escapee from the noise and congestion of city life to the open spaces and quiet pace of life on the fringe (p. 34). In a comparative study done during the thirties, Lundberg (1934) concluded that suburbanities differed psychologically from those who remained in the city: they had a great attachment to nature and the outdoor life, the neighbourhood, domestic and family life. In the fifties, Fava demonstrated that suburbia selectively attracted individuals who seek informal contacts and relationships which were not available in the city (1958b). The low-density and openness of suburban tracts also means a high degree of mutual visibility; as in the older working class districts, suburban neighbours know each other's life styles far better than apartment-living urbanities ever could. This 'visibility' principle indirectly promotes standardization: one could almost speak of the 'formalized informality' of suburban life styles.

But the apparent uniformity of the early suburbs may well have been a temporary phase in the process of further differentiation.[19] Gans's studies in Park Forest (1966) and Levittown (1967) suggest that the physical uniformity of suburbia does not necessarily reflect any social homogeneity.

In fact, Gans supplied ample empirical evidence to illustrate the transfer of urban and suburban life styles and class heterogeneity into a suburban context. The behavioural characteristics now manifest in suburbia, he postulates, have always been at least latently present in the urban context, just as the social patterns of some new working class housing estates in Britain reflect traditional patterns of the older areas (1966, pp. 549–620).

But contrasts between suburbs are also evident and enduring. Industrial suburbs or 'satellite cities' have little in common with residential suburbs. Dobriner (1963) shows how suburbs differ greatly in the circumstances of their creation, in the price and use of their real estate, their degree of transiency, their size and institutional complexity, and the income, life-style, occupation and educational level of their residents. Sociological reflection on the class structure of suburbs, he points out, has been based largely on a few case studies of middle class suburbs of the late forties, and in fact recent studies by Lazerwitz and Gans also show that the traditional middle class monopoly of suburban living is being

19. See Ktsanes and Reissman (1959–60).

broken by the out-migration of semi-skilled workers to the suburbs.[20] In fact, the life styles, ideologies, folk-ways, values, aspirations and child-rearing practices of suburbanites in general defy generalization to 'homogeneity'.

The American experience, in many ways a foreshadowing of what is appearing embryonically in Britain, reveals another important facet of suburban life. The role of real estate private development companies in designing residential suburbs has assumed increasing importance even in Britain. Craven and Pahl's study (1967) of residential expansion in south east England, for example, is currently investigating the private builder/developer as a major agent of suburban expansion (1967, pp. 137–43). Within the limits imposed by planning and other authorities the private developer, through his choice of sites, is seen as a major controller of residential growth patterns. Three important implications emerge from these general trends:

1. The changing and often convergent trends in social characteristics of suburban life, particularly the re-emergence of class and stage in the life cycle as the predominant determinants of social life.

2. The appearance of new 'factors' and forces in shaping suburbia such as private development interests, suburbanization of industry and growing autonomy of suburban, commercial and retail activities.

3. The expanding scale in which the analysis and planning of suburbia must be placed. It makes little sense to design plans for suburbs without placing them within the broader metropolitan-economic, social and cultural-context.

Before considering the planning implications of these social characteristics it is instructive to look at the kinds of problem which frequently occur in suburbia. Gans has specified six major types of problem which the planner should keep in mind (1968b).

1. *Social isolation*, particularly prevalent among young mothers, recent arrivals and those who find it difficult to make friends in their new home.

2. *Physical isolation*, particularly for those who do not own a car, or are not mobile.

3. *Financial problems* where incomes are inadequate to cover the

20. See Lazerwitz (1960); Gans (1968a).

costs of living in suburbia where new kinds of expenditure become necessary.

4. Adolescents' problems, particularly if recreational and other facilities are not available.

5. Community conflicts, – block conflicts between neighbours, economic conflict between the 'haves' and the 'have-nots', conflicting interests of old and new residents, political conflicts between residents and builders and between residents and government.

6. *Persistent individual and family problems*.

How is the planner to address himself to these problems? As in the case of working class communities, it appears that physical layout can significantly affect the nature of social life within a suburb. Here, however, the varying aspirations and life styles of individual family members assume perhaps more importance than the needs of the family unit. Each member participates in a network of social contacts which sometimes is quite distinct from the networks of other members. For all, however, accessibility ranks perhaps the highest priority: for men, access to work and to other men with shared interests; for the women, accessibility to friends, relatives and other women of shared interests; for youth, cultural and entertainment facilities with their contemporaries; for the elderly, an opportunity to interact with one another and to contribute in some way in the life of the community. For those whose feelings of isolation are related to the loss of frequent contact with kin and relatives, access to telephone and good public transportation should be provided; for the cultural minority group, adequate information on community organizations and activities should be available; for the elderly relatives, perhaps housing close to young families could be provided. The local social services, clinics, counselling agencies, churches and schools, could have a very valuable contribution to make in the resolution and prevention of problems related to social isolation. If planning could screen and supervise the kinds of personnel employed in these local institutions, perhaps suburbanites who normally do not attend could be attracted. Training in psychiatry and social psychology might sensitize the doctor, welfare worker, counsellor and others to the problems experienced by their clients and could thus be more effective agents in reducing the problems associated with social isolation.

Site planning and house design can also affect neighbouring and the evolution of neighbourhood life. A balance between involvement in the neighbourhood and privacy in family life has somehow to be realized. In general the house design should be such that household work routines are minimized, and people are free to interact with their neighbours as much or as little as they wish. Gans has argued for social homogeneity at the block level so as to reduce or eliminate conflicts and optimize the conditions for the development of neighbourly relations. The more homogeneous the block, he argues, the greater the opportunity for heterogeneity in neighbourhood and community life. On site planning specifically, he goes on to suggest:

1. A compromise between privacy and accessibility is necessary at the block-level; houses cannot be sited so as to put people on top of each other socially and visually. Small courts and narrow culs-de-sac are undesirable.

2. Social contact is determined to some extent by accessibility and, if the area is occupied by young families, by where children play; therefore, areas with young children should be well serviced with play areas, parks and meeting places.

3. Higher-priced houses should be socially and physically separated from lower-priced houses.

4. To prevent 'slum' development, strict performance standards on building need to be imposed.

5. Segregation of blocks by population characteristics might be feasible, – groups of houses for families with small children separate from other groups for retired couples.

6. Neighbourhood shopping areas should include cafés and other meeting places for youth and other special interest groups.

Financial problems are less amenable to 'planning' solutions, but certain measures could be taken: selection of tenants according to income right from the beginning; subsidies for those who are forced to commute to work, careful and restrained taxation policies. While conflict resolution may be beyond the control of the planner, careful site planning may, however, help to remove some of the sources of conflict, and careful co-ordination of responsibilities may clarify certain issues over which conflicts often arise. In general the availability of adequate information about the estate is highly important.

The specific planning implications of the suburban literature also vary according to the context. The British situation is still quite different from the American one, and planning guidelines designed for Columbia, Maryland, cannot be transposed en bloc to the Cumbernaulds and Milton Keynes of Britain. Several of Gans's recommendations, however, are still applicable in the British context. The need for a wider choice of housing, possibly including a range of sizes in dwelling units seems particularly appropriate in new estates designed for relocated communities within British cities so that if necessary extended families could live together. Measures to counteract or prevent social isolation may have to be quite different from those recommended for American suburbs and here is an area where sociological research is necessary; however, community centres and other loci for social interaction should be considered everywhere.

References

ABRAMS, M. (1960), 'New roots of working class conservatism', *Encounter*, May.

ANDERSON, E. E. (1937), *We Americans*, Harvard University Press.

ANDERSON, N. (1971), 'Diverse perspectives of community', *Inter. Rev. of Community Devel.*, no. 7, pp. 15–53.

BAKKE, E. W. (1953), *The Unemployed Man*, Nisbet.

BENDIX, R. (1964), 'Transformations of Western European societies since the eighteenth century', in *National Building and Citizenship*, Wiley.

BENDIX, R. (1965), *Work and Authority in Industry*, Wiley.

BERGER, B. M. (1960), *Working Class Suburb*, University of California Press.

BUTLER, D. E., and ROSE, R. (1960), *The British General Election of 1959*, Macmillan.

CRAVEN, E. A., and PAHL, R. E. (1967), 'Residential expansion; a preliminary assessment of the role of the developer in the South-East', *J. of Town Planning Inst.*, vol. 53, pp. 137–43.

DENNIS, N. (1956), *Coal is OUR Life*, Tavistock.

DENNIS, N. (1970), *People and Planning: The Sociology of Housing in Sunderland*, Faber & Faber.

DOBRINER, W. M. (1963), *Class in Suburbia*, Prentice-Hall.

DOUGLAS, H. (1925), *The Suburban Trend*, Appleton-Century Crofts.

DUNCAN, O. D., and REISS, Jr A. J. (1956), *Social Characteristics of Urban and Rural Communities*, Wiley.

FAVA, F. (1958a), 'Contrasts in neighboring: New York City and a suburban community', in W. M. Dobriner (ed.), *The Suburban Community*, Putnam.

FAVA, F. (1958b), 'Suburbanism as a way of life', *Amer. Sociol. Rev.*, vol. 25, p. 347.

FERGUSON, T., and PETTIGREW, M. G. (1954), 'Study of 718 slum families rehoused for upwards of ten years', *Glasgow Med. J.*, vol. 38, pp. 183–201.

FIRTH, R. (1956), *Studies of Kinship in London*, Athlone Press.

FRANKENBERG, R. (1966), *Communities in Britain. Social Life in Town and Country*, Penguin.

FRIED, M., and GLEICHER, P. (1961), 'Some sources of residential satisfaction in an urban slum', *J. of the Amer. Inst. of Planners*, vol. 27, pp. 305–15.

GANS, H. J. (1959), 'The human implications of current redevelopment and relocation planning', *J. of the Amer. Inst. of Planners*, vol. 25, pp. 15–25.

GANS, H. J. (1961), 'The balanced community: homogeneity or heterogeneity in residential areas', *J. of the Amer. Inst. of Planners*, vol. 27, pp. 176–84.

GANS, H. J. (1966), 'Popular culture in America', in H. S. Becker (ed.), *Social Problems: A Modern Approach*, Wiley.

GANS, H. J. (1968a), 'The suburban community and its way of life', in *People and Plans: Essays on Urban Problems and Solutions*, Basic Books, reprinted in Penguin 1972.

GANS, H. J. (1968b), 'Planning for the everyday life and problems of suburban and New Town residents', in *People and Plans: Essays on Urban Problems and Solutions*, Basic Books, reprinted in Penguin 1972.

GEIGER, T. (1949), *Die Klasse Gesellschaft im Schmelztiegel*, Cologne.

GOLDTHORPE, J. H. (1964), 'Social stratification in industrial society', in P. Halmos (ed.), *The Development of Industrial Societies*, Keele Sociol. Rev., monograph no. 8.

GOLDTHORPE, J. H. *et al.* (eds) (1969), *The Affluent Worker in the Class Struggle*, Cambridge University Press.

HARRIS, C. D. (1943), 'Suburbs', *Amer. J. of Sociol.*, vol. 49, pp. 1–13.

HOLE, V. (1959), 'Social effects of planned rehousing', *Town Planning Rev.*, vol. 30, pp. 161–73.

HOOVER, E., and VERNON, R. (1959), *Anatomy of a Metropolis*, Harvard University Press.

KERR, C. *et al.* (eds.) (1960), *Industrialism and Industrial Man*, Harvard University Press.

KERR, M. (1958), *The People of Ship Street*, Routledge & Kegan Paul.

KTSANES, T., and REISSMAN, L. (1959–60), 'Suburbia, new homes for old values', *Social Problems*, vol. 7, pp. 187–94.

LAZERWITZ, B. (1960), 'Metropolitan residential belts', *Amer. Sociol. Rev.*, vol. 25, pp. 245–52.

LIPSET, S. M. (1964), 'The changing class structure of contemporary European politics', *Daedalus*, vol. 60, p. 1.

LONDON COUNTY COUNCIL (1961), *The Planning of a New Town*, LCC.

LUNDBERG, G. *et al.* (1934), *Leisure: A Suburban Study*, Columbia University Press.

LYND, R. S., and LYND, H. (1929), *Middletown*, Harcourt Brace.

MARSHALL, T. H. (1950), *Citizenship and Social Class*, Cambridge University Press.

MARTIN, W. T. (1952), 'A consideration of differences in the extent and location of the formal associational activities of rural–urban fringe residents', *Amer. Sociol. Rev.*, vol. 17, April.

MARTIN, W. T. (1953), *The Rural–Urban Fringe*, University of Oregon

MARTIN, W. T. (1958), 'The structuring of social relationships engendered by suburban residence', in W. M. Dobriner (ed.), *The Suburban Community*, Putnam.

McConnell, S. (1969a), 'Residential density', *Official Architecture and Planning*, April, pp. 410–15.

McConnell, S. (1969b), 'Urban renewal', *Official Architecture and Planning*, March, pp. 309–21.

Millspaugh, M., and Breckenfeld, C. (1958), *The Human Side of Urban Renewal* (ed.), M. Colean, Baltimore.

Ministry of Housing and Local Government (1967), *The Needs of New Communities*, HMSO.

Ministry of Housing and Local Government (1969), *People and Planning*, HMSO.

Mogey, J. M. (1955), 'Changes in family life experienced by English workers moving from slums to housing estates', *Marriage and Family Living*, vol. 17, pp. 123–8.

Mogey, J. M. (1956), *Family and Neighbourhood*, Oxford University Press.

Park, R. E. (1964), *Human Communities*, University of Chicago Press.

Rex, J. (1968), 'Economic growth and decline—their consequences for the sociology of planning', *Town and Country Planning Summer School*, September, pp. 28–33.

Rex, J., and Moore, R. (1962), *Race, Community and Conflict: A Study of Sparkbrook*, Oxford University Press.

Schaff, A. H. (1952), 'The effect of commuting on participation in community organization', *Amer. Sociol. Rev.*, vol. 17, pp. 215–20.

Schnore, L. F. (1957), 'The growth of metropolitan suburbs', *Amer. Sociol. Rev.*, vol. 22, pp. 165–73.

Schorr, A. L. (1963), *Slums and Social Insecurity*, US Dept. of Health, Education and Welfare.

Seeley, J. R. *et al.* (1956), *Crestwood Heights*, Basic Books.

Spectorsky, A. C. (1955), *The Exurbanites*, Lippincott.

Stacey, M. (1960), *Tradition and Change*, Oxford University Press.

Stacey, M. L. (1969), 'The myth of community studies', *Brit. J. of Sociol.*, vol. 20, pp. 134–46.

Stein, M. (1964), *The Eclipse of Community: An Interpretation of American Studies*, Princeton University Press.

Vidich, A. J. *et al.* (1964), *Reflections on Community Studies*, Wiley.

Warner, R. L. (1947), *Yankee City*, Yale University Press.

Warner, R. L., and Lunt, P. S. (1947), *The Social Life of a Modern Community*, Yale University Press.

Whyte, W. F. (1955), *Street Corner Society*, 2nd edn., University of Chicago Press.

Whyte, W. H. Jr (1956), *The Organization Man*, Cape.

Williams, W. M. (1956), *The Sociology of an English Village, Gosforth*, Routledge & Kegan Paul.

Wirth, L. (1928), *The Ghetto*, University of Chicago Press.

Wood, R. C. (1958), *Suburbia*, Houghton Mifflin.

Young, M., and Willmott, P. (1957), *Family and Kinship in East London*, Routledge & Kegan Paul Pelican edn 1967.

Young, M., and Willmott, P. (1963), *The Evolution of a Community; Dagenham after Forty Years*, Routledge & Kegan Paul.

Zorbaugh, H. (1929), *The Gold Coast and the Slum*, University of Chicago Press.

11 J. Margolis

The Demand for Urban Public Services

Extract from J. Margolis, 'The demand for urban public services', in
H. S. Perloff and L. Wingo (eds), *Issues in Urban Economics*, Johns
Hopkins Press, 1968, pp. 535–56.

Demand for public services

[. . .] The demand for an urban public service is not an unambiguous concept. Consider the demand function for private goods. No matter how difficult it is to estimate demand functions for private goods, we usually have observations of amounts purchased during several periods at a reasonably well-identified set of prices. Often these gross observations can be supplemented with information about the attributes of purchasers – for example, their income, race, residence, occupation, etc. But how different it is in the public sector. The consumers of the goods are not the purchasers; the purchasers are a mix of elected and appointed officials who pay with tax revenues; the taxpayers may not be the users of the services and decision-makers may be neither tax-payers nor users. Observations on prices or quantity are rare; costly surveys are often necessary to tell us who uses the services; and the handful of studies of who pays for the services are highly oversimplified. Not only are there several steps between consumer and payer, but often the consumer may not be part of the political constituency which is doing the paying.

Demand analysis for private goods reaches back to individual preferences to motivate market behavior and also to provide a basis to evaluate market performance. Therefore, it is not surprising that the body of analysis developed to understand the demand for public services should also refer back to individual preferences. Certainly it is reasonable to attempt to apply private market analogies to public processes. If successful, we would have a rich body of theory to extend to the huge but neglected public sector; possibly the normative theorems might be transformable into administrative rules. Unfortunately, it is more difficult in the public sector to use predictive tests to judge the usefulness of abstract models and, therefore, discussions about the reasonableness of models will be more common. It is easy to sympathize with the critic who feels that his sensibility is being strained in being asked to accept refined arguments to explain why the resident of New York 'demands' more education for the resident of New Orleans, or more wilderness areas in California.

Since there is no body of studies of demand for urban public services, we shall deal with the problems of demand in a more indirect fashion. We shall critically survey some of the recent, more promising developments in economic analysis for the urban public sector and see how they contribute to our understanding of the demand for urban public services. Before turning to the new developments in analysis let us mention, albeit too briefly, the more traditional approaches to the market for public services.

Need rather than demand has been the more traditional basis of planning for public services. Need is sometimes defined in crude terms of 'requirements for a satisfactory urban society', but in serious studies it is derived from detailed surveys of service levels that governments are trying to achieve or more sophisticated studies of goals, priorities and costs.[1] Goals research is an old preoccupation of man. Preachers and political leaders have long felt that they had special insights into the goals of society. Leaders in professional groups, like librarians, planners, or sanitary engineers, felt that they could interpret the public welfare and the implied needs for their services; and now social scientists are joining the search for goals and priorities. The possible establishment of goals and the specification of needs by elites or social processes, though deserving of research, has been beyond the insights of economic analysis. Though the economist's decision-model has become increasingly sophisticated about the form in which to consider objectives, and how to use optimization techniques, it has not progressed in the domain of substantive objectives. The economist's focus is on the utility of individuals; therefore, let us turn to the demand for public service as revealed, though imperfectly, by the preferences of individuals, and to the analytical structures developed with individuals – acting individually or as groups – as major elements.

In the two decades since the end of the Second World War, there has been a many-pronged attack on the problems of analyzing the provision of public services. The special conditions associated with public, rather than private, supply of goods and services have begun to be subjected to intensive analysis. Brave souls have applied the model of *homo economicus* to explain the

1. See Lecht (1966).

political processes by which decisions are made. Welfare economists have extended their models to include public goods and to pay attention to public decision-making.

The analysis of public goods became deeply involved with the studies of the failure of decentralized market structures. It was clear that there was no decentralized market system by which to achieve Pareto optimal levels of public goods (Samuelson, 1958), and efforts to derive voting models for political choices have not been successful. Public *goods*, first formulated as the extreme case, is now considered as a special case of externalities, and the difficulties of providing optimal public goods are now attributed to a much broader range of public services. It is far too early to predict where this line of research will go, but it has already been a fruitful source of hypotheses for the study of urban public services. Public goods are provided through political processes, usually considered impervious to economic analysis and, though an optimal political decision-making process has not been devised, the study of optimal political systems may suggest hypotheses for the study of political decision-making in regard to public services. These two lines of investigation – public goods and economic theory of political decisions – have centered on mechanisms by which a society can be elevated into the welfare economists' utopian world of Pareto optimality.

Another tack – centering on cost-benefit analysis – has borrowed less from these developments in theory and has addressed itself to the more pressing operational questions of how to evaluate the public services and plans to alter them. Applied welfare economics in the form of benefit-cost analysis, which began as an oddity in the evaluation of certain kinds of public works, has merged with the more limited operations-research type of cost-effectiveness studies to form a loosely defined field of programming-planning-budgeting systems analysis of public operations. Though most of these developments have occurred at the level of the federal government, they have percolated down to the local levels. The analytical studies have gained the opportunity to demonstrate their value for the urban public decision-makers; they still have to prove themselves as useful techniques by which to evaluate urban public services or to plan them. At the moment, support for their extension is strong but far from universal.

I cannot present a report of the successful fusion of these traditions and their unraveling of problems of the demand for urban public services, but a partial survey of some of the developments in these new research areas does indicate progress, if too little to make us confident as to the obvious correctness of these approaches.

Public goods

The analysis of public goods is intimately tied to the welfare economists models of the optimally organized decentralized market economy. A specific allocation of resources would earn the welfare economists' accolade of optimal if the marginal rate of substitution of any two goods for any two consumers would be equal to the marginal rate of transformation in production of these two goods.[2]

The decentralized price-market economy would lead to this desirable outcome under a set of stringent conditions, including the absence of externalities. An externality is an unpriced effect. It may be a benefit received by those who do not pay for it, or a loss incurred by those who are not compensated. In any case the decision-makers, who produce the service or those who purchase it, will not make the proper determinations in production or consumption if they lack the pecuniary incentives or guides that 'price' supplies. A public good, in its pure form, is an extreme case of an externality. It is defined as a good which, if available to anyone, is equally available to all others. This pure case implies that there are no feasible ways to exclude any consumer from enjoying the good, and the consumption of the good by one consumer does not affect the amount available for all others. Classic illustrations would be a radio signal which blankets an area, a defense system which deters an attack, an act of charity which eases all our consciences.

The difficulty for demand analysis, based on individual preferences, posed by the treatment of public services as public goods, is that there is no voluntaristic procedure by which to signal the decision maker that the benefits of an increment of output are greater than the costs of that increment. The benefit of an increment is the sum of the benefits received by each member of the community. Citizen A is not inclined to offer to pay a sum for a public good if there is a subset of members of the community who benefit and hopefully will pay so that the good will be available to each member of the community, including citizen A. Since it is likely that a reasonably large number of persons will share in this strategic behavior, it is argued that the public goods will be under-

2. The clearest statement of the condition is in Bator (1957).

supplied – the true demand for the good will not be revealed by the consumers. Unfortunately, the same difficulties of revealing true preferences hold in the case of political decisions of any type of public service which is provided without a price.

The perplexing feature of a public good is that it relies on individual preferences for the evaluation, but without an optimal mechanism to aggregate the preferences. In fact, there may not be any observable individual actions directly attributable to the consumption of the public good. For instance, the community 'image' is a public good. Do citizens value the identification of their city as 'friendly', 'culturally progressive', 'an All-American City', a 'city of churches', 'a city with know-how', 'honest'? Certainly many, if not most residents, value these images and public officials' actions are affected thereby in many ways, but short of deciding where you are going to live it is difficult to identify individual behavior which reflects on individual values assigned to the 'image'. The insistence on individual valuation is perfectly understandable. The individual utility arguments in the evaluation of a public good create a complete, individually evaluated allocation of resources for private market and public political goods, but it is not clear that this is the best way to proceed to analyze the demand for public services or to evaluate the institutions by which public services are provided. Comparability of public provision with private market choice is a virtue, but it is not a necessity.

In the private sector, utility theory provides a preference mechanism for demand analysis; its usefulness lies in its contribution to prediction and to normative judgements about market solutions. For the latter objective, welfare judgements, individual preferences are insufficient since we must rely on a social welfare judgement for distributional rules. It is far from clear that the individualistic basis of public goods analysis contributes to the positive analysis of public services. This does not necessarily nullify its central role for normative analysis, but it does arouse suspicion that it may provide an incomplete basis, possibly a disastrously incomplete one. If these reservations have merit, public goods analysis would provide a weak source for positive or normative demand analysis of the public sector, but the whole field is in much too exploratory a stage for anyone to discourage this line of investigation. But just as it would be in error to prejudge the value of public goods concepts, it would be an error to neglect other approaches to explain or evaluate public services.

Public goods have been defined traditionally by the existence of non-excludability (e.g., the noise I hear from the adjoining freeway cannot be denied my neighbor), but there are at least two other categories which broaden the class and extend the problem of public goods to a major part of urban public services. Non-excludability need not derive from technological conditions of supply but it may be deemed efficient or desirable on some policy grounds.

Wherever the marginal cost of supplying another consumer is zero, it would be efficient to allow the consumer entry without assessing a charge, even if it were technically feasible to charge a price; for example, since no resources are diverted if another car is permitted upon an underutilized freeway, it should not be charged a price even if it were simple to collect the toll. Zero marginal cost is an extreme case of a more general category – marginal costs well below average costs. Many public services are characterized by a large ratio of capital to operating costs or by the establishment of a large network. The bridge or water supply would be an illustration of the first type and a police system illustrates the second. In both cases a very large capacity is required to meet certain peak conditions, but in off-peak periods the costs of another unit of output is very slight. If the system is to be efficiently used and entry is to be controlled by price, then the sum of revenues may be less than the costs though the sum of benefits, or the value of the demand, may be greater than costs. Under these conditions, efficiently designed, exclusion prices will not reveal the benefits of the increment of service.[3]

But the largest urban public service, education, would not qualify as a public good on the technical grounds either of non-excludability or of marginal costs far below average costs. In Musgravian language, public education satisfies merit wants (Musgrave, 1959, pp. 13–14). These services are supplied 'freely' to the qualified population and they are financed through the general fisc. They are 'private' goods which have become endowed with public interest. Though they are the bulk of urban public services, the literature on public goods is distressingly weak in analyzing them. There is a trend to incorporate them into the general class of public goods, which has both advantages and disadvantages.

One general characteristic of public services which greatly expands the applicability of public goods doctrine, though the goods

3. For a survey of possible pricing rules, see Vickrey (1963).

rarely satisfy the technical conditions, is the great value assigned to uniform treatment in the public sector. Possibly, uniformity of services is a 'halo' effect extending from the important doctrine of uniform treatment before the law, but whatever the source of the desire for uniformity, it is very widespread throughout the public services. The goal of uniformity is rarely directly analyzed, but it comes up indirectly in the case of specific public services, where equal treatment becomes one of the attributes of the merit want to be satisfied by the specific service.

Merit goods

The initial attitude towards merit goods was to see them as imposed on the population by a group of moralists or the intellectual elite or a pressure group with power, but with a recognition that the imposition might be a legitimate activity in a democratic society. Though there existed a modicum of respectability for merit goods, they were viewed with hostility. The absence of a link between the merit goods and the preferences of consumers meant that the individualistic normative model could not handle them and therefore they were outside the realm of normative analysis.

One response to the lacunae in analysis would be to explore more carefully the model of political organization, and to evaluate the role of groups in influencing allocations and the institutions by which the allocations are made. Hopefully, this search for explanation would give rise to insights about how to formulate a set of normative rules appropriate to group decision-making. A second response would be to find ways to transform merit goods to public goods and then apply the body of doctrine developed for public goods. The latter approach has been more common. It is understandable, but not necessarily best, that the economist turned in this direction. The first approach, an examination of the process of political decision, might have cast light on the mechanism by which conflicts are resolved or, in economists' language, resources are allocated, and therefore on the processes through which preferences are revealed. The interpretation of the latter phrase explains inhibitions in turning towards political models. It is likely that the political model, or the analysis of demand as it is revealed through political interchanges, would not reveal the only measure of demand considered meaningful for welfare judgement – a demand based upon individual preferences. But if the public sector is dominated by merit goods and if the analyses of merit goods were not amenable to individualistic models, then normative models based upon individual preferences would be irrelevant for policy and it might be more desirable to explore political models. The moral for research is that more work on the analysis of public institutions is necessary to develop a normative model for policy. But before going into political models, let us look at the transformation of merit goods to public goods – the extension of the traditional normative model to services associated with social values.

In the case of a merit good the individual receives more of the public service than the amount he would have purchased, e.g., he has more low-cost housing, more days in the hospital, or more years in school than he would be willing to pay for himself. Two arguments can be developed to permit this excess to be consistent with Pareto optimality. The first would argue that the receipt of goods by the underprivileged enters into the utility function of the privileged.[4]

The underprivileged, in terms of their preferences, would have been still happier if they had received the transfer in money rather than in kind, but this would not have been as satisfactory to the privileged. The privileged allocate their budget among commodities so as to maximize their utilities, and among the commodities are the incomes of the underprivileged and a set of specific commodities consumed by the underprivileged (merit goods).[5] There is an optimal combination of income transfer and merit goods transfers from the perspective of the privileged. From the perspective of the underprivileged these transfers are constraints, and they optimize within them. Therefore, a Pareto optimality is achievable, but there is one catch. If we assume that the transfers enter the budget functions of the privileged as disinterested charity – i.e., they are only interested in the welfare of the underprivileged and not in the grace of giving – then the utility of the donor increases as much with their neighbor's gifts as their own. Charity is a public good. A day in school for an underprivileged child gives satisfaction to all the privileged. My neighbor's joy does not diminish mine. Clearly, some, possibly most, of us will be tempted to let our neighbor pay for the com-

4. The most complete statement of these arguments deals with intergenerational transfers used in the defense of social discount rate. See Marglin (1963).

5. The underprivileged need not be the conventionally defined poor; they may be the young or the aged.

mon satisfactions. A common decision, a public act, is necessary to get the proper amount and mix of transfers. But the decision necessitates a political act, and again we face the difficulty of revealing 'true' preference for public goods via market or political processes.

Once we convert these merit goods it is difficult to know what should be the limit on the definition of a public good. One of the most ingenious conversions of a merit good to a public good is the assignment of direct benefits to non-users who are potential users. It has been proposed that we evaluate parks, museums, and similar facilities not only in terms of benefits to users, thereby treating it as a private good, but that we should assign a demand for the facility to non-users who might want to use it (Weisbrod, 1964a). Note that the commodity non-use is equally available to all and the amount of non-use by one party does not affect the amount of non-use by any other party. At first blush this would seem to be sleight of hand, but it is clear that persons would often pay for an option to purchase something they may never use and which they may hope never to use. An obvious example would be a local hospital. If there were insufficient local private demand the community might unanimously support a tax to represent the wishes of the healthy but fearful. To repeat, the transformation of the merit good to a private-plus-public-good is an illuminating bit of analysis but it still leaves us without a basis for 'revealed' preferences except for the actions of the political bodies.

An alternative transformation of merit goods is less extreme. Rather than searching out a public good dimension, a careful, exhaustive enumeration of all of the externalities is analyzed. From one perspective this is what is done in the preceding case, since a public good can be defined as the polar case of externalities, but the difference in form does make a great difference in the possibility of demand evaluation. Utility interdependence is peculiarly difficult to measure. Private charity provides only a lower limit and, of course, there is no private market counterpart. The externalities sought in this second approach are independent of the utility gains of the recipient of the merit good; one can often find market-type analogies for these types of goods; and, as in the case of public goods, the valuation of the externalities is based upon individual preferences.

Consider the following partial list of benefits of education, other than the increased income of the student:

1. Improved home environment of children of students,
2. Social and political stability of an informed electorate,
3. Less costly collections of taxes,
4. Mothers can work or enjoy their leisure,
5. Neighbors find the more socialized child more attractive,
6. Crime costs decline in community of child's residence and the community to which he migrates.[6]

Most of these gains accrue to specific parties, and they are gains which either reduce costs or increase incomes. They contain some benefits that are difficult to measure, such as improved citizenship, but most of the gains are susceptible of measurement. One of the most astute students of economics of education says that

in principle, the recipients of external benefits from some activity (for example, education) should be willing to subsidize the activity and, indeed, should seek to subsidize it. The voting mechanism and taxation provide the means for subsidization. Analysis of voting behavior may shed some light on the question of whether external benefits are recognized and have an effect on decisions. But regardless of whether or not subsidies are actually paid by 'outsiders', we need to identify and measure the magnitudes of external benefits to determine the returns on resources devoted to education (Weisbrod, 1964b, pp. 27–28).

Note the hypotheses of the quotation:

1. The beneficiaries of externalities should be willing to pay.

2. Voting and taxation behavior may reveal whether externalities are perceived and whether they affect decisions.

3. Analysis of benefits is important whether or not beneficiaries pay.

But note also the limitations:

1. Beneficiaries always prefer that someone else pay, and if they can shift burdens they will.

2. If voting were the major institutiona channel for public decision making this hypothesis might be reasonable, but voting is not the major institution.

3. As a scientific problem, the determination of the rate of return is of great interest, but its role as an index of demand is conditioned by the peculiar nature of merit goods, unpriced distribution and the values associated with the political organization.

6. See Weisbrod (1964b, pp. 24–37); and Hirsch (1966, p. 51).

I shall deal with the problems of measurement of benefits and the rate of return on investment in a later discussion of benefit-cost analysis. At this point, I want to explore briefly the implications that this decomposition of merit goods into groups of externalities has for hypotheses about the state of the public services. What are some of the 'idealized facts' that are part of this approach to merit goods? First, merit goods are supplied at zero prices to direct consumers, since it is desired that they consume an amount whose cost is greater than the value it holds for them. The fact of zero prices also holds for public goods, though there is no desire to subsidize the consumers of public goods. Secondly, an optimal supply of merit goods would require an optimally designed voting and taxing scheme or, if possible, a pricing scheme which would have the same results. Both of these sets of 'facts' are reasonable approximations. What do they imply for the provision of urban merit goods?

If a good is supplied at a zero price, we can expect an excess demand at that price or, as more commonly described in the 'view-with-alarm' literature, an insufficiency of supply. The response to excess demand is that some form of rationing, other than price, is adopted. Typical forms are: congestion (where some persons decide to avoid the service because of quality deterioration); administrative rules limiting access to the public service; an active market in other assets which gives one access to the public service. Let us consider each of the above response patterns.

Changes in land values are often associated with a public improvement. Consider, then, the construction of a park or a playground or a community center. Those who welcome the facility and are prepared to incur costs for them will pay more for a residential site located closer to them. Land values and rents will rise and the sites will be occupied by those who value the facility more.[7] Those who find less of an attraction in the facility and therefore do not value the convenience of living nearby will not be willing to pay the higher rent and will move elsewhere. We are all familiar with upgrading through urban renewal and the consequence to the poor, who were presumed to benefit, being forced to relocate to areas not blessed with the improved facilities.

7. A precise statement of the pattern of occupation and rent changes would involve an analysis of consumers surpluses, income elasticities of demand, value of time, density preferences and so on, which would take us beyond the scope of this paper.

Therefore, we may find the perverse effect: the consumers, who would have generated the greatest externality benefits for others, may not consume, and those citizens who 'subsidized' the merit good may find their well-intentioned subsidy captured in capital gains to land, with the consumers of the good paying an indirect price.

The 'perversity' phenomenon is only applicable to merit goods, not 'public goods' like transportation or fire-fighting systems. The same changes in land values will occur and the same rationing of use by changes in the price of housing will develop, but since the externality benefits are not anticipated, there will be no disappointment.

Though an indirect market price reaction will occur in both cases of zero-priced merit and public goods, in neither case will this price information be sufficient as a guide for public service planning. We shall discuss the index of land values as a guide to public services planning in the section on benefit-cost analysis, but it is clear that the 'demand' for facilities by the users will not have been satiated. Rents may ration access but not limit pressures to expand the quantity of services; the 'deserving poor' may have been forced away from the park or the better school but they want this free facility in their new location.[8]

A second and more obvious form of rationing is administrative criteria. Education may be limited to age groups, subjects, number of hours; hospital beds may be restricted to types of diseases; libraries may limit the number of books borrowed; police will be distributed by area or population or crime rate. If the services are free to the direct users, excess demand will exist, administrators will decide who is most 'deserving' of the service, and pressures will exist to expand them.[9] Since there need not be any private costs inhibiting pressures on extending the service, the amount of 'excess demand' or 'undersupply' will appear dramatic.

8. Land value effects are only one type of indirect market. Political corruption could be viewed as another. Legal costs to overcome crowding in courts and regulatory bodies would be still another. There is an abundance of scattered case material dealing with the consumers' adaptation to zero-priced public services, but there has been no systematic study of this process except in water resources and urban transportation.

9. 'The operating agencies can offer some evidence about the demand for their services, for example, the number of unprocessed applicants or the extent of unserviced areas. Unfortunately, the unmet demand for government service always falls short of the resources available to the public sector' Boyle (1966, p. 216).

The 'scientific' analysis of this source of excess demand would be the standards developed by professional associations. Librarians, recreationists, educators, almost every branch of the public services seek to expand their services to the rationed populations. The individualistic theory of merit goods finds its justification in the utility functions of the subsidizers, but the professional associations find their arguments in the capacity of their clients to consume their services. Since the associations do not try to estimate benefit, but only 'need' under conditions of zero pricing, their representation of demand for their services is limited only by the capacity of their clients to consume. It is not surprising that urban public services do not measure up to the standards and are therefore always painted as inadequate. Though the subsidizers are prepared to extend the supply of merit goods beyond the consumers' willingness to pay, they are often rightfully suspicious of the possible motives of the administrative agencies. If an individualistic basis for merit goods could be established, then rationing rules might be devised to reduce the apparent excess demand. A pricing scheme, if feasible, might still be more efficient but, unfortunately, it is not always feasible. A large part of the new work in public systems analysis is directed towards the rationalization of administrative rules.[10]

If administrative rationing were not adopted, then we are likely to find the most public form of seemingly inadequate supply – quality deterioration. Congestion imposes social costs which then become the rationing device. The government does not charge a price, but quality may deteriorate so that substitute products are chosen – e.g., private schools instead of public schools, private recreation and so on. But the excess demand, the desire on the part of the actual or rationed user for more of the service at the price he is charged, is great.

In the case of a public good, such as transportation, the social costs provide information, though no incentive, for the government to expand the services. In the case of a merit good, the social costs – quality deterioration – do not provide this information, since we do not know about the reduction in the utility of the externality beneficiaries.

10. For a useful analysis of rules and pricing in regard to a public good, see Kneese (1965).

Political processes

Rather casual assumptions are often made that political processes will reflect the preferences of consumers or that public decisions should reflect their preferences. However, systematic explorations of the likelihood that the urban political system does succeed in reflecting preferences, or of the conditions where the system could be successful, are extremely few. It would be hazardous to project the trend of these few studies, but I believe that the number of political studies by economists will increase greatly in the next decade. Hopefully, we will enlist the aid of political scientists.

A degenerate case of the political decision-making process is the Tieboutian model of individual choice of local governments (Tiebout, 1956). I classify it as 'degenerate' because there is no specification of a political process by which the government policies are formed; despite this failing, however, it has a virtue which other political models lack – individuals can move among government jurisdictions. Movement has the quality of resignation from the social contract. Mobility of population is an important factor in local political decisions. A substantial part of local decision-making is directed towards attracting activities from other areas or discouraging 'their' activities from moving elsewhere.

The Tieboutian scheme was an attempt to solve the public goods problem, but its main impact was to increase the awareness of economists of the value of a competitive model of governments. The model is one of an infinite variety of communities, each with a different package of public services and taxes. Assuming that all private goods are available, at the same price, the individual chooses a site so as to balance off his marginal site costs (housing costs including taxes) with his marginal evaluation of the set of public services. The model, as an argument that public goods will be optimally supplied, is not persuasive since it has no political mechanism to generate the optimal set of packages to be available to the itinerant households. However, the model did have a salutary effect of reminding the rationalizers of metropolitan government that differences among communities had social advantages, even if there were external diseconomies.

Migration among communities is interesting at several levels. It greatly expands the possibilities of individual choice of a preferred set of public services and style of living, as stressed by Tiebout. It also offers an interesting dimension to the analysis of demand for public services as seen through planning or political processes.

If individuals can be made aware that over their life-cycle they will choose to live in different types of communities, or at least in different neighborhoods within the city, they may be more likely to consider the merits of metropolitan proposals which may benefit areas other than where they live at the moment. If it is less costly to increase their utility by an improved set of options than by improving their neighborhood, then they may accept the more far-reaching solutions. This attempt to focus on the full set of options is part of the strategy of master planning. The record of success of the strategy is poor. Despite the stress on the distant future and the attempt to divert attention away from the immediate and particular, payoffs to specific areas dominate and master plans have not become operating documents.[11]

A third level of interest in intercity migration is the fact that movement is itself a form of 'voting'. It is this interaction between a market decision, the choice of a site and the political decision on public services that is particularly interesting.

One of the most common goals of community leaders, especially in suburban communities, is that of fiscal profitability. The criterion they use in evaluating a public act is the change in tax revenue and public costs associated with the act. Though these studies have been primarily concerned with land use policies like zoning and annexation, fiscal profitability considerations are implicit in many other decisions. For example, an improved water supply is more costly, but is this offset by more industry with its larger tax base? The popular base for this criterion is not 'profits' to the city treasury, but the assumption that a fiscally profitable decision will result in lower taxes to the remaining residents. Of course, if fiscal profitability is an operational criterion of city leaders, and if individuals make locational decisions on the basis of a value of services-tax cost differential then it might seem reasonable to hypothesize that we might find a confirmation of public decisions in the operations of the market. Land values should rise in the more 'fiscally profitable' cities. The 'profits' should be capitalized into gains for the current residents. Immigrants might still face a low tax rate, but higher property values would mean greater interest and tax payments so that in equilibrium the advantage will be lost.

11. For some case material on the problems of master planning, see Banfield and Wilson (1963, ch. 14).

If we tested the above hypothesis of market confirmation of fiscal profitability criteria, it is unlikely to be validated, but the mechanism of market verification of the political leaders' fiscal decisions is suggestive of further hypotheses. Fiscal profitability is generally too crude a criterion. There are interdependencies among land uses that are ignored, and it is silent on the problem of evaluation of the public services. It implicitly assumes a requirements approach. Individual decisions on location will be determined by the costs of the site, including taxes, and the benefits to the purchasers. The benefits would include the value to the individuals of the public services as well as the quality of private facilities available, as shopping districts, job possibilities, social groups and so on. A fiscally profitable decision need not be one where the sum of individual benefits minus costs calculations is positive. Let us consider the consequences of mobility based on fiscal benefits, gains and losses to the residents, rather than just fiscal profits.

Assume that the sum of individual benefits minus costs of the public expenditures were positive and individuals perceived this. In this case, if the residents were randomly drawn from the community at large, the outsiders would perceive the fiscal advantages in the community and land values would rise. Note that the residents first received a fiscal gain, and this was then converted to a capital gain to the asset they held. But the full story would not end at this point.

Not all residents would have received the same fiscal gain, but all of them would receive the same capital gain. The new land values would be the competitive market value, determined by the demand of many residents and outsiders and the supply of the many sites in the city and outside. Each site would receive the same increase in value. The fiscal gain to the residents would be unique to each resident – it would be based upon the utility to him of the public services. After market values adjusted, each resident would find that his housing costs, including imputed rent based upon new site values, would have increased but this increase in costs would be above or below their previously estimated fiscal gain. For those who never had a fiscal gain, continued residence in the community would not be advantageous. For these two groups, costs, including opportunity costs, would be greater than the benefits of the public decision. The composition of the residents would shift to include only those for whom the net fiscal gain was greater than the average. A desirable pattern of public services would result in gains to a majority of the residents and a reshuffling of the population to exclude those who least welcomed the pattern. The population would become more homogeneous relative to tastes for public services and the political leadership would be confirmed in their decisions.

'Voting with one's feet', as developed above, is an interesting model which stresses the importance of mobility and the market for assets which gives access to the fiscal package of government, but it is far from an adequate model of public choice. First of all, it should be pointed out that it is not an optimizing model. Further, it does not contain any discussion of voting by ballot or any other form of political influence.

Any set of public acts would generate a change in the ratio of residential costs to benefits of public services. Migration, according to the pattern outlined above, may take place, but this does not mean upgrading of community welfare but only a greater homogeneity among residents. A poorly designed package of public services would have led to capital losses, migration, a homogeneous community and a state of welfare well within the utility possibility frontier of the metropolitan area.

In the real world, heterogeneity and political conflict will persist. Some of the heterogeneity can be explained by the costs of moving and differences in economic base. Others may be accounted for by informal political actions which prevent the market from operating. For instance, older, childless couples would be forced out of a growing community because of the higher property taxes. But usually these couples live in older houses which are highly underassessed. The opportunity costs of living in the community have increased but not the cash costs. The 'inequitable' property tax administration reduces the political opposition and the speed at which the community becomes homogeneous.

It would be intriguing to explore the question whether voting both by ballot and by feet would solve the public goods problem and give rise to an optimal set of public services (ignoring merit goods, distributional criteria and externalities among communities). Unfortunately, this is not the place for such a digression. I raise it here because political influence on the provision of public services in a community is exercised both to affect the density of economic activity to achieve growth and capital gains, and also to achieve net fiscal benefits to the residents who are hostile to in-migrants and ignorant of, or indifferent to, capital gains effects. This sharp distinction between utility of services and asset enhancement is drawn too strongly. The protagonist of 'better' schools will vote for schools in any event, but his campaign literature stresses that better schools mean better neighborhoods and therefore, the preservation of property values. In turn, the chamber of commerce member who seeks to keep taxes down to encourage industry jobs, and growth concedes that good schools are useful to attract executives and technicians. Therefore, it would not be too amiss to assume an objective function for political leaders which evaluates public services in terms of benefit and asset position of the residents. But we shall not pursue this model at this point. Before turning to the more explicit political models I would like to amplify a bit the asset-enhancement goal.

A major goal of community leaders is growth of the city. Public services, taxes and land policies are frequently evaluated in terms of their effects on growth. The declining rate of growth of the central city is a signal of danger, a call to organize countermeasures. But growth in city A can only be earned at the expense of city B. Does it matter greatly to the resident in city A if his new job is located a mile south in the central business district of A or a mile north across the border in city B? For most purposes the resident would not care, and few residents feel strongly about services to attract the firm. But those with large property holdings who stand to gain with increased density feel quite differently. Growth is not only a synonym for progress but it is the source of capital gains. The large investors in land are not mobile, at least in terms of their planning horizons. They are very interested in mobility, but it is the mobility of the in-migrant. It is their heavy investment which makes their payoffs from public activities very different from those of the residents, and which will create difficulties in interpreting the political process as an instrument to evaluate the consumers' demand for urban public services. Goals for land enhancement are not the same as utility optimization.

Let us now turn to the more explicitly political models.

There are several political approaches to the positive or normative analysis of urban public services adopted by economists. The first is identified with the work of Downs and Buchanan-Tullock and is an extension of the classical literature of welfare economics.[12] Most of the research has been theoretical but there

12. See Downs (1957); Buchanan and Tullock (1963); Rothenberg (1965).

have been statistical studies which have sought to verify hypotheses suggested by this literature.[13] The studies substitute political institutions for market processes in linking individual preferences to public expenditures.

A second approach has been to concentrate on the behavior of the legislature, as a political body, and its relationship to the administrative bodies which represent the public services. The legislature is representative of the interests of the electorate, but the connection between the individual and his representative is developed in only a rudimentary way.[14] The substitute for the market would be bargaining among legislators and administrators.

A third approach is much more informal than the other two. There are many case studies of specific public services or cities which introduce political factors to explain decisions or which discuss revisions in government structure. Though politics are important inputs, the authors make no efforts to explore systematically the structure or behavioral characteristics of the political process.

In recent years political scientists have begun to study local political decision-making at a more analytical level.[15] At the moment, economics and political science literature exist side by side and there has been little cross-fertilization, but both sets of studies have short histories and few things travel slower than communications across departmental borders. Hopefully, this insulation will disappear.

The classic form of the political model is to assume that politicians present tax and expenditures options to voters so as to maximize the vote they receive. In this search for political support they will discover the preferences of consumers, innovations in services and tax alternatives, and they will be motivated to maximize the sum of the fiscal surpluses (benefits minus costs) going to the citizenry. There has been disagreement as to whether a fiscal program which emerges from such a model would result in too large or too small a government or whether it will be inequitable. Certainly, if we can substitute the politician-voter for the entrepreneur-consumer relationship and the election for the marketplace we would have established a very useful means to analyze the demand for public services.

13. See Barr and Davis (1966); Banfield and Wilson (1965).
14. Lindblom (1961); Wildavsky (1964).
15. See Polsby (1963); Banfield and Wilson (1963); Dahl (1961); Wood (1961).

There are many shortcomings to the political model of public finance, or economic model of political decision-making, which have yet to be overcome. A glaring limitation exists in the central role assigned to the voter. It will be difficult for economists to abandon this central role of the voter since it is the most direct means to associate fiscal outcomes with individual preferences. But if one feels there is any merit to Galbraithian strictures in regard to consumer sovereignty, then one should gag at accepting a model dependent upon voters' sovereignty.

A politician certainly wants to be elected and this does require a majority of the vote, but this is usually far less than the majority of eligible voters. The median percentage of adults voting in 461 city elections in 1961–2 was 33 per cent.[16] This is probably an overstatement of community interest. When city elections were held at the same time as state or national the median percentage was 50, and when it was held independently the median fell to 29. When the citizenry are asked to focus on the important local issues free of partisan debate they demonstrate great disinterest. The support of only a relatively small minority of voters is sufficient for the great majority of municipal candidates. This low turnout to vote is matched by ignorance about local affairs and inactivity in regard to campaigns.

The lack of voter interest may be distressing but it is not unreasonable. A single vote is to be cast for a man who is to take a position on a great many issues. An 'enlightened' vote would require a tremendous investment of study time. We should not expect any voter to make this investment, given the extremely low probability that his ballot will affect the outcome of the vote or that his candidate will be bound by his campaign promises. If voting were to provide a reasonable register of preferences it would be extremely costly. The ersatz polling which does take place bears little relationship to an 'optimal' choice. None of this is meant to disparage the critical role that elections may play in the creation of political stability and also for community improvement, but only that it is not a device by which to discover the demand for public service.

The slender popular base of support for the elected officials encourages the analyst to look for roles to be played by men other than voters and politicians. If there are such other roles, then the politician's function would have to be redefined. To be effective it would be insufficient for him to have gained a majority of votes

16. Lee (1963, p. 83).

cast; the support of others would be necessary. Clearly, the politician's objective function would be to maximize his utility, and the inputs to his utility function would be supplied by a variety of groups in the community. He may have to satisfy that small minority which ensures him a post, but beyond that he is free to respond to many informal pressures. The studies of the political scientists give very little space to the electorate and even the elected officials are usually merged together with a host of other wielders of influence: civic leaders, voluntary commission members, social elites and so on. Their studies deal with who makes decisions, how they are made, how influence is exercised. Their system, in contrast to the economists' model, is an extremely elaborate scheme. It does not defy formalization (Rothenberg, 1965), and it should be possible to link it to the economists concern with the payoffs to individuals of specific public acts and services.

The political scientist's finding of a pluralistic power group – specialized influentials who concentrate their attention on restricted areas, and a relatively small group of influence wielders – is consistent with the facts of urban government, which provides many different services for different groups. The concentration of political power is consistent with a concentration of economic power in the community. In New Haven the ten largest owners of real estate paid almost one fifth of the total taxes levied by the city, and their taxes financed one eighth of the city's total expenditures (Dahl, 1961). It is not surprising that with this type of disparity we have a disparity of influence in metropolitan public decision-making. Units with large capital investments in the city are likely to incur much greater political costs to safeguard and enhance their investments. Much of the payoff in public service finally rests in property values and this will mean a market in influence to supplement the electoral aggregation process.

A political model of public finance or an economic model of public decision-making should include the factor that larger property holding will lead to increased political participation and this, in turn, will make planning for space relatively more important than planning for persons. Peculiar competitive practices may develop among cities which may reduce the welfare of the aggregate of persons but increase property values of a subset. I suspect that a model can be constructed which would enable us to construct a demand for public services through political institutions, but it will reflect the distribution of wealth within the city. Of course, the normative properties of this 'political' demand curve are dubious.

The normative properties of the second approach of economists to political decision-making is equally uncertain. The bargaining adjustment models were developed for legislative and administrative haggling which made them most appropriate for the federal and national governments. At the local level the process of adjustment among groups is far less formal and uniform. Trade-offs in support on municipal issues are less manageable or explicit than legislative logrolling. On the whole, the political science studies have tended to be consistent with what could be roughly called bargaining models. These models focus on the decision, the forces affecting it, and the terms. Though insight into the decision process is of great value, it does not enable one to make an independent estimate of demand.

Our political models are not yet sufficiently advanced to tell us how to estimate demand, nor can we be sure that they ever will be successful in that role.

References

BANFIELD, E. C., and WILSON, J. Q. (1963), *City Politics*, Vintage Books.

BANFIELD, E. C., and WILSON, J. Q. (1965), 'Voting behavior on municipal public expenditures: a study in rationality and self-interest', in J. Margolis (ed.), *The Public Economy of Urban Communities*, Resources for the Future.

BARR, J., and DAVIS, O. A. (1966), 'An elementary political and economic theory of the expenditures of local governments', *Southern econ. J.*, vol. 33, October, pp. 149–65.

BATOR, F. (1957), 'The simple analytics of welfare economics', *Amer. econ. Rev.*, vol. 47, March, pp. 22–59.

BOYLE, G. J. (1966), 'The New York City budget process', in *Financing Government in New York City*, final research report of the Graduate School of Public Administration, University of New York.

BUCHANAN, J., and TULLOCK, G. (1962), *The Calculus of Consent*, University of Michigan Press.

DAHL, R. A. (1961), *Who Governs?*, Yale University Press.

DOWNS, A. (1957), *An Economic Theory of Democracy*, Harper.

HIRSCH, W. Z. (1966), 'Regional accounts for public schools', in W. Z. Hirsch (ed.), *Regional Accounts for Policy Decisions*, Johns Hopkins.

KNEESE, A. V. (1965), 'Rationalizing decision in the quality management of water supply in urban-industrial areas', in J. Margolis (ed.), *The Public Economy of Urban Communities*, Resources for the Future.

LECHT, L. A. (1966), *Goals, Priorities and Dollars*, Free Press.

LEE, E. C. (1963), 'City elections: a statistical profile', in *Municipal Yearbook: 1963*, International City Managers Association, Chicago.

LINDBLOM, C. E. (1961), 'Decision-Making in taxation and expenditures', in *Public Finances: Needs, Sources and Utilization*, Princeton University Press.

MARGLIN, S. (1963), 'The social rate of discount and the optimal rate of investment', *Q. J. of Econs.*, vol. 77, February, pp. 95–111.

MUSGRAVE, R. (1959), *Theory of Public Finance*, McGraw-Hill.

POLSBY, N. (1963), *Community Power and Political Theory*, Yale University Press.

ROTHENBERG, J. (1965), 'A model of economic and political decision-making', in J. Margolis (ed.), *The Public Economy of Urban Communities*, Resources for the Future.

SAMUELSON, P. A. (1958), 'Aspects of public expenditure theories', *Rev. of Econ. and Stats.*, vol. , 40, November, pp. 332–8.

TIEBOUT, C. M. (1956), 'A pure theory of local expenditures', *J. of Pol. Econ.*, vol. 64, October, pp. 416–24.

VICKREY, W. (1963), 'General and specific financing of urban services', in H. G. Schaller (ed.), *Public Expenditure Decisions in the Urban Community*, Resources for the Future.

WEISBROD, B. A. (1964), 'Collective consumption services of individual consumption goods', *Q. J. of Econs.*, vol. 68, August.

WEISBROD, B. A. (1964a), *External Benefits of Public Education*, Princeton University Press.

WILDAVSKY, A. (1964b), *Politics of the Budgetary Process*, Little, Brown.

WOOD, R. C. (1961), *Fourteen Hundred Governments*, Harvard University Press.

12 R. C. Wood

A Division of Powers in Metropolitan Areas

R. C. Wood, 'A division of powers in metropolitan areas', in A. Maas
(ed.), *Area and Power*, Free Press, 1959, ch. 3.

I

As a theoretical concept, the areal division of powers emerges
from the preceding discussions with two pre-eminent characteristics. First, it is designed to secure, through a particular
pattern of areal distribution, the values prevalent in a given time
and place. Second, it is designed to distribute political power in
such a way that governments can act decisively and effectively.

Mr Hoffmann's survey (1959, ch. 6) of the writings of certain
philosophers who have been concerned with the subject pays
special attention to the relations between the various territorial
patterns proposed for government and the different purposes for
which these arrangements are constructed. But it also concludes
that a valid areal division of powers must provide a government
equipped to act vigorously and purposefully for whatever ends
intended. Mr Ylvisaker (1959, ch. 2) writes in the same vein. He
establishes for our culture and our time, basic values of liberty,
equality and welfare and an array of instrumental values by
which an areal division of power may contribute to the fundamental objects of a modern democratic state. He singles out as a
major criterion the requirement that each government possess the
power to govern generally. From a common starting point – an
agreement that the basic aim of dividing power is to restrain its
arbitrary use and ensure legitimacy in the constitutional sense –
both add these important standards: answers to the normative
questions of 'power to whom?' and 'power for what?' are to be
modified continually in the light of contemporary values, and
effective power must continue to exist after the division is completed.

The analyses make an additional methodological contribution.
They clarify and distinguish among the genetic notion of a
division of powers and the closely related but subsidiary concepts

of separation of powers, federalism and areal division of powers, too often treated as interchangeable.

The basic definition is, of course, that of the division of powers in general, a governmental arrangement with the objective of distributing various segments of public authority in various ways for the purposes of assembling and restraining power for some given ends. The areal or territorial division of powers accomplishes this objective by assigning authority spatially. If the areal division takes the form of federalism, the different units are required to possess constitutional autonomy, and usually the emphasis is upon division by functions and upon the procedures by which federal systems begin and mature. But, as Mr Maass (1959) has demonstrated, there are other forms of territorial division, and other factors in evaluating any areal arrangement beyond its contribution to creating one from many, or devolving responsibilities in the opposite direction. Finally, the general concept of division of power may express itself in a capital division of powers, the most familiar form of which allocates executive, legislative, and judicial processes within a single government.

All these notions are commonplace, of course, but the distinctions are important and to be treated precisely when we turn to the job of applying the concept of *adp*. The assignment now is to test the doctrine, as defined and developed, in a concrete situation; specifically, to make an evaluation of the governmental pattern in the large metropolitan regions of the United States.

The choice of this example may seem bizarre or uninspired, but at least three good reasons can be offered for the selection. First, metropolitan areas today contain the largest and the fastest growing proportion of our population; they are vital centers of our economic system and they represent significant features of our social life. What happens in these areas is important in terms of our prosperity, our defense posture, and our patterns of living. Second, the governments of these areas are in trouble. Their quantitative and qualitative deficiencies are now so elaborately documented there is no doubt that a genuine crisis exists.[1] Finally, and happily, perhaps, there appears a readiness to experiment with new structures of government, which adds an aspect of

1. See, for example, the proceedings of the National Conference on Metropolitan Affairs, East Lansing, Michigan April 1955, and the Report of the Arden House Conference on Metropolitan Area problems, September 1957.

utility to proposals for innovation and substantial change in governmental arrangements for these regions. If a set of criteria for the territorial division of powers can help in evaluating these structures, present and proposed, more systematically and accurately, the contribution to American institutions may be substantial.

II

In the context of past inquiries into the metropolitan problem, a focus on areal division of powers may appear to have little to offer. A system of analysis, dedicated to emphasizing the instrumental values of countervailing power, friction, the maximum devolution of authority, seems inevitably to imply 'fractured governments' and 'fragmented authority', the continuation, if not the reinforcement, of our present situation of hundreds of local jurisdictions, rattling about ineffectively within a closely developed area. Our 170 odd metropolitan areas now have more than 16,000 separate units for each 10,000 citizens. At the extreme edge, eleven areas have more than 250 governments apiece and five areas more than 500 units.[2] Prevalent doctrine would argue that we have Mr Ylvisaker's values in abundance, and that other and, indeed, opposite objectives, have priority today.

Indeed, to most scholars, the entire objective of efforts toward metropolitan reform for the last twenty years is to consolidate and enlarge political jurisdictions 'to create a government contiguous to the boundaries of the metropolitan community'. The textbook – any textbook – solution is to somehow rid ourselves of 'ineffective, multiple local jurisdictions'. Luther Gulick (1955), one of the most eminent authorities at work in the field today, has provided a comprehensive statement of the problem, when after defining the metropolitan complex as composed of elements of large size, high population density, interdependence, fluidity of movement and fractionated governments, he concludes that metropolitan problems arise 'from a large congested population, living and working interdependently in a considerable territory, rushing to and fro, with governments which do not coincide with the patterns of life'. John C. Bollens (1956), in his exhaustive survey of existing metropolitan problems and solutions, concluded that the preferred solutions are likely to be the creation of the urban county, the multipurpose special district, or perhaps a

2. US Department of Commerce (1954).

federal structure, though he views this structural cousin to the division of powers as probably a stepping stone to a larger super-structure (Bollens, pp. 132–5). Quite obviously, most metropolitan reformers today are convinced that only a consolidation of power into some kind of new layer of government, in which governmental responsibilities are taken in increasing measure from existing jurisdictions, will solve our growing dilemma.

Without for the moment disputing the wisdom of such proposals, it is fair to ask whether the definition of 'fractured governments' is the same as that of an adequate areal division of powers. It is also fair to ask whether the recommendations for a single metropolitan government, for partial consolidation or for *ad hoc* schemes of co-operation and collaboration are built upon a full consideration of the different value connotations and patterns of power distribution involved. It may well be that a spatial division of powers, as understood here, is something quite different from preceding definitions, and the issue may not be between division or no division of power, but between desirable and undesirable, effective and ineffective divisions. It seems certain that unless the relationships between structure, powers and norms are made explicit, the analysis is purposeless and incomplete. It is here that our analytical model may be useful; that an analysis in terms of the areal division of power may show promise.

III

There is good reason to believe that contemporary analysis of metropolitan government neither began with a consideration of effective patterns for distributing power territorially nor investigated very exhaustively the value implications of patterns that resulted. By the time metropolitan communities came into existence – in Dr Reed's terms when the city was no longer a bastion of defense and the countryside was made accessible by the automobile – the European concept of the division of powers had been largely relegated to dusty library shelves. Generations of American political scientists had been busily at work in their efforts to overcome what seemed intolerable by-products of the national separation of powers and federalism. In the context of the service state, in which the virtues and institutions of strong government were well established, the overriding concern was not the establishment of power, or even its subjugation under law, but the assurance that the state could carry out its functions well.

There was little disposition to review concepts of dividing power, partly because their role in establishing constitutional nation-states seemed to have been completed, and partly because their operation seemed increasingly troublesome in the new environment of positive government.

The disenchantment was especially prevalent in urban government. Here the breakdown of the capital variant of the general concept of power division – the internal mechanism of *cdp* by process, or separation of powers – was most apparent. Almost all of our large cities, at the end of the nineteenth century and for at least the first third of the twentieth, displayed great stresses and strains in the functioning of their bicameral legislative systems and politically oriented executives. The hey-day of the bosses demonstrated the vulnerability of city institutions to corruption, mismanagement and private control and made the fusion of powers, represented by the town meeting and the board of supervisors in small communities, seem a superior alternative. Both territorially and internally, division of powers as a basis for organizing government did not appear to be a promising path for investigation.

Coincidentally, pressures generated by the emerging service role of government pushed objectives other than those associated with the restraint of power to the fore. The demand that governments not only perform but perform well affected every public institution in America, and nowhere was the overriding concern with the quality and quantity of public services so evident as in urban government. Our cities bore the brunt of the demand for new public activities which were the underpinnings of our industrial operations – streets, water, sewage, fire protection, welfare aid to the casualties of the business cycle. Efficiency of operations became important dollar-wise and service-wise and, with problems in political theory apparently far behind us, rose high in the value scale of objectives.

It is not surprising then that the premises on which the evaluation of urban governmental performance proceeded were more closely akin to those of public administration than to political theory. The great innovations in local institutions – the commission form of government, the strong executive, and finally the city manager with its accompanying non-partisanship and streamlined democracy – were predicated on the belief that efficiency in the 'bundle of services' which were thought to make up city government was of overriding concern. An acute awareness of the kind of abuse of governmental authority that can develop under a separation of powers system (rather than the more typical concern over abuse when authority is centralized) combined with a steady pressure to undertake really large-scale utility enterprises and growing financial burdens to accelerate the quest for efficiency. The conviction grew that Pope was right, that institutions serve administrators, not administrators, institutions.

The crosscurrents of these beliefs produced a body of thinking essentially committed in functional analysis, to the determination of what powers a local government needed according to the activities it had to carry out. The emphasis was not on a consideration of the capacity to govern, to provide orderly community existence, either in absolute power terms or in the legitimizing of that power. Rather, it was oriented toward need; that is, toward the way in which the capacity to act was exercised, the removing of deficiencies in all sorts of services, from police protection to planning.

Thus when the metropolitan problem was recognized, there developed a natural disposition to reshape the administrative patterns and institutions in terms of *functional requirements*. The increasing discrepancy between functional boundaries and general purpose governmental boundaries became obvious, and primary attention went to the functional areas. The observation of H. G. Wells that the matter of scale is a vital consideration in local administration became fashionable, although his other strictures did not catch on. Technical specialist after technical specialist moved from one city to another, engaging in painstaking examinations of the current conditions in his own narrow proficiency, and solemnly proclaiming that no public health department could work properly unless it had a clientele of at least 50,000 people; or that no zoning regulations made sense without reference to a master plan of land use for a region as an entity; or that no police force could support a qualified crime laboratory until x number of precinct stations were in being to refer a sufficient quantity of cases to keep the scientific technicians analyzing at optimum speed.

In short, when we recognized twenty-five years ago the existence of institutional inadequacies in our most important new communities, by training and instinct our answer was to apply functional criteria, in terms of size of area, amount of resources, number of people, optimum location of district offices, in determining the rearrangement of our governments. In theory, these criteria revealed themselves in the way we went about proposing the establishment of the urban county, the multi-purpose district and metropolitan federalism. We *called* them 'new divisions or amalgamations of power' but what we meant, quite clearly, were new divisions of functions. One has only to look at the grants of authority vested in the metropolitan authority of Toronto and the new metropolitan government of Miami, to recognize that the overriding criteria were administrative. Functions 'inherently requiring larger size' or 'clearly metropolitan in nature' – water, sewage, transportation and the like – went to the larger government; functions whose administrative requisites were capable of being fragmented, remained fragmented.

In practice, an even greater administrative flavor is evident, at least in the United States. Those few limited successes we have enjoyed in revamping the metropolis are almost all in the form of special districts, corporate authorities, or functional consolidations and transfers which studiously avoid any consideration of their impact on the capacity to govern of the body politic. Both in theory and practice, we have become more sophisticated in recognizing 'aspects' of functions capable of subdivision and in inventing countless patterns of possible combinations, but we have never strayed from the basic premises erected at the turn of the century (Gulick, 1955).

Throughout the long years of wrestling with metropolitan problems, then, the norm of efficiency came to predominate. Issues associated with liberty and equality dropped out of sight when metropolitan governments were studied; issues concerned with welfare, in its narrow service sense, became the almost exclusive concern. Little real attention was paid to the construction of meaningful political communities, or to the question of obtaining political responsibility, although these objectives were honored in passing. It is a division of functions – or the ways in which service needs are met – which claimed an almost universal attention.

IV

Historical forces explain, then, the foundations of contemporary analysis; they do not justify it. How has this reading of 'function' for 'power' hindered our efforts to develop satisfactory metropolitan governments, and how might an areal analysis of the division of powers help?

First, the administrative emphasis has resulted in a lack of balance in the values sought by an areal division of powers. The norms sought by reform and reorganization became inevitably lopsided, and the political values usually associated with self-government and popular control were muted. Arrayed against the Ylvisaker value scale, functional analysis was disposed to emphasize those values which are advantageous to the governmental process rather than to the individual; it concentrated on operating efficiency and effectiveness, and brushed aside the objectives of liberty and individual participation.

Second, the administrative emphasis has resulted in neglect of the central principle that the government in metropolitan areas possess sufficient power and competence of a generalized form to make meaningful decisions and to develop a vigorous political process. We saw clearly enough that the creation of special districts for lighting, schools, highways and parks and the establishment of authorities, unless carefully constructed, affected adversely the goal of efficiency. We recognized that the indiscriminate scrambling of functional and political jurisdictions, the continual reassignment of duties among county, village, town, township, borough and city offended administrative rationality. But not until very recently did we come to ask ourselves if the qualities of participation and responsiveness were surviving in the new metropolitan pattern of functional authorities. Nor did we inquire extensively as to the implication for effective popular action of a pattern of such fiscal and administrative confusion that only the professional politician could find his way through the forest of governmental boundaries.

Had the appraisal been conducted in Mr Ylvisaker's terms of the degree to which discussion and debate were encouraged, the metropolitan political process might have revealed itself as consisting of little more than clusters of concentrated power, in themselves impotent, and largely free from popular control. The present structure, in his context, would stand indicted not only as violating his injunctions respecting the number of levels of government, and the exclusive allocation of functions. Far more important, it would be condemned as flouting his basic prerequisite that governments possess a political process, that each be a vehicle for debate and decision, and each be so composed as to contain elements which yield debate and foster loyalties.

Lacking the proper framework of analysis, we have been able

to identify these problem areas of metropolitan government only tangentially. Students of political behavior have pointed out for some time the unhealthy political conditions in local governments, and particularly in surburban and metropolitan politics. They have stressed the low level of popular participation, the disintegration of party structures and the lack of discrimination by voters in their display of party allegiance in relation to the level of government and issues involved in a particular election. But nothing like a complete explanation of these deficiencies has appeared, for nothing like a complete understanding of the power vacuum, of the deficiencies in political process, is possible by functional analysis.

The extreme example of the incomplete theory of metropolitan government is found, of course, in the 'practical' reforms which occur piecemeal in metropolitan areas. The astounding renaissance of public corporate authorities strikes at both the concept of meaningful, responsible governments and the maintenance of individual values, all in the name of efficiency. Advocates of this metropolitan innovation openly call for the exclusion of politics *per se*, whether it be by the individual citizen or the professional political leader, and the consequent removal of public activities from public control. They make much of the authorities' 'accountability' to the public by pointing to the stacks of brochures, accounting records and the audit reports released annually for general consumption. They emphasize, as in the case of the New York Port Authority, that the governors of the state or states involved in capitals miles away from the areas concerned can veto the authorities' actions (although they never do). But by their very choice of weapons they reveal a lamentable misunderstanding of the notion of popular control. However impressive the physical accomplishments of these bodies, the conclusion is inescapable that their operations remove from popularly-constituted governments activities and decisions fundamental to the growth and well-being of the region, or at the very most, subject them to only an indirect type of informal pressure-politics control.

These limitations of the functional analysis go far to explain the difficulties which arise when reformers undertake to put grand designs for 'genuine' metropolitan government into effect. Because the new assignments of authority which they advocate do not correspond to political communities, basic and instrumental values of the areal division of powers are ignored. It is true that some reformers have come to emphasize the importance of popular participation and control. In the check-lists of 'reasons why metropolitan reform is necessary', 'political problems of popular control' appear alongside of 'service problems' and 'financial inequities' – although invariably after them. But just as invariably the structural reorganizations advocated are based primarily upon a division of functions determined to be 'area-wide' or 'local' according to their substantive characteristics, and almost invariably, the problem of political participation and debate are tacked on as an afterthought.

By ignoring the effects of their proposals on existing power structures, by failing to set an alternative and better political process as a goal, and most of all by slighting individual values, advocates of annexation, consolidation, or even federation thus raise insuperable problems of representation and shifts in political influence. In effect, they demand sizeable surrenders of local privileges and prerogatives in return for promises of administrative benefits. There is small assurance that the new political process, designed usually to provide for indirect representation or to refurbish a county government long in disrepute, will protect the individual's interest in customary ways or enhance his capacity to participate in the vital decisions of the region. All that is clear is that functions are moving upstairs to a 'greater government', undefined and unknown in its political balance, while the localities are to be left such challenging tasks as the erection of street signs and traffic lights, tree care and the celebration of holidays. Questions of procedure and process, of how local communities might influence the policies of the larger government, of how they might retain options with respect to the conduct of activities in their areas, of how flexible administration was to be assured, were largely ignored. Elegant skeletons of government spring forth, but the capacity to govern subject to regularized restraints is missing.

As a consequence, when we turn to the problems of political acceptability for proposed changes in metropolitan governmental structures today, the most usual approach is to appeal for leadership and popular enlightenment. Leadership is an admirable and necessary requirement for effective democratic government, and no one discounts its value in this area. But leadership unequipped with institutions and unbridled by legal strictures, of course, may partake of qualities unattractive to our value scheme. At best, it places a burden on our party organizations which is unrealistic in the metropolitan context, if for no other reason than the present deployment of Republicans and Democrats within the boundaries of these regions.[3]

V

If the reasoning employed so far makes any sense, then in effect political scientists generally have not been engaged in political analysis when they investigated metropolitan government. The obvious corollary is that if political analysis is undertaken in earnest, proceeding in a conceptual framework, we can make progress in devising institutional arrangements to meet metropolitan problems.

The line of departure for such an analysis is the recognition of a basic fact of metropolitan life: that while the existence of hundreds of general purpose and functional governments within an area may constitute a division of power, it does not, in and of itself, constitute a *valid* areal division of power. On the contrary, such a division violates the two main requirements which Mr Hoffman identifies. It fails to provide adequate popular controls, so that the pattern, in Burdeau's words, is best described as a 'juxtaposition of monocracies'. At the same time it fails to ensure a capacity to act purposefully on the major problems affecting larger parts of the area. On the one hand, the local jurisdictions have the legal weapons to perpetuate themselves; on the other, they lack the resources and heterogeneity of interests to make the decisions they must make. The present arrangements produce then, an aggregate of power at once unrestrained and inadequate, and only faintly attuned to the realization of the values we seek. As it stands now, the 'fractured government' of metropolitan areas is undesirable not because it is divided but because it is divided for purposes unacceptable for a democratic state.

This is not to say that the general purpose governments in the present system do not have reasons for existence. They do, although functional analysis has exposed them only obliquely and remains apparently bewildered by the intransigence of the citizens of certain of these units toward any changes. The present quiltwork of local units often fulfills the objectives of particular

3. In this setting, the widely hailed Toronto Plan appears as one of those extraordinary coincidences in which strong political institutions separate from the community involved, specifically the Ontario Municipal Board and party organization in the provincial legislature fortuitously combined with a functional proposal to see it through.

groups and classes who seek to promote social and cultural homogeneity by maintaining jurisdictional boundaries which protect them from those whose standards they do not share. Furthermore, it provides opportunity to rule for those pitiful elites who inhabit the court house rings, the county party organizations, the city halls, content with the personal power which politics may bring though their ambitions must of necessity be small, and oblivious to the issues which attract larger men.

These are the realities of the situation which new designs must take into account if a new allocation is to be constructed. The task of organizing metropolitan government thus becomes not a wholesale integration of jurisdictions as soon as possible (although this is not necessarily excluded) and certainly not an integration according to functional requirements, but the creation of an areal pattern of divided powers in which systematic restraints truly operate and the decision-making process partakes of qualities of debate and compromise.

How do we proceed to outline and secure such an areal division of power? The ground rules of my colleagues give students of metropolitan government much needed elbow room. They do not saddle us with any precise forms but leave us free to devise institutions suitable to the times as long as the institutions are built on these foundations: the capacity to act effectively in a political sense; the fostering of debate and compromise; the establishment of systematic and purposeful restraints; a realization that all of the values sought today must be tempered, none maximized. Therefore, mechanisms which enhance political capacity to act are welcomed even if they do not replace existing units immediately.

In this connection Mr Ylvisaker's requirement that the power to govern be a general one does not mean necessarily and at once a power to govern generally (i.e., with respect to all matters) for the entire metropolitan region, although it certainly can and probably does mean this for the long run. A single metropolitan government, in the context of our federal system, may constitute the best areal division of powers and in a mature and cohesive area the desirable allocation of powers may be a general one. But in the less than mature system, a transitional device may be to select one or a group of powers, institutionalize them, and nurse them along in such a way that they lead to greater cohesion for the region, and as a consequence, to a more general power to govern. The essential point is that the powers granted should be stated in terms of the community and constituency affected and the political process involved, and that they should be powers – not functions. As communities coalesce, so may the instruments and institutions of government; but the focus remains upon the capacity to make meaningful decisions, provide the benefits sought, and insure popular control.

Thus, as the immediate necessity for grand designs or general systems diminishes, attention can be focused on adjustments in the responsibilities of existing governments, a host of co-operative arrangements, and a tradition of intergovernmental collaboration insofar as these can be used to break down the isolation of surburban repositories of Rousseau's general will and that of functional single purpose units. The solutions most scorned by some experts, the 'stop gap', *ad hoc* improvisations of co-operation, contractual services among local units, states' grants-in-aid, shared taxes and joint planning efforts, take on new meaning If these arrangements can bring together different groups of participants to debate and compromise for pluralistic action, they will provide at least a basis for the exercise of power under democratic control. Also, these arrangements serve to refute the classic assumption, which my colleagues have exposed, that all government activities, of whatever state in whatever time, can be neatly divided into 'matters requiring local knowledge and local adjustment' and 'matters requiring expert knowledge and uniform treatment'.

VI

Such arrangements may not be adequate in the long run, however, and we can go beyond them, and suggest a specific model for an acceptable areal division. It is based on the hypothesis that the only identifiable metropolitan political community at present is likely to be found, in H. G. Wells' happy phrase, among the delocalized inhabitants, popularly known today as the commuters. These are, perhaps, the only citizens who, through their daily journey to work, are constantly aware of what it means to live in the larger area, who are unfranchised in their places of work, and usually outmaneuvered politically in their places of residence. All other more static notions of community, it seems, fragment as rapidly as the present governments themselves.

Rapid transit is indeed the fundamental reality of the so-called metropolitan community, the thing in common. As such, its present day frustrations and inadequacies command the citizen's attention and excite, as no other issue except possibly public education, the political animal in him. Further, this is public function crying for political process not only because it is clothed more and more in the non-political garb of the corporate authority, but because public issues of the gravest nature are represented here. These are not just questions of the relative priorities and subsidies to be given to the private automobile, the subway, the bus, or the railroad, though these are important enough. They are also the issues of equity between the various classes of citizens, and the relative appropriateness of public and private action. In a very real sense twentieth century socialism, American-municipal style, is on the verge of unconscious adoption here.

Moreover, the recognition of these problems and this community might generate political forces sufficient to batter down the opposition within existing jurisdictions. The opportunity to develop a system of direct representation and participation – to be extreme and perhaps facetious, a user's association – which includes the different political components of the commuter world could well be appealing.

The precise forms which the institutionalization of the power to manage transportation affairs can take are several. It would be possible either to devise a co-operative arrangement among the metropolitan jurisdictions involved, or assign the authority to a state agency within the established framework of that government, or create a special district with direct citizen participation and control for the area. The choice would be dictated by the possibilities of effective political action and of systematic restraints.

It may be objected that this proposal is deficient on two grounds. First, it involves essentially a single function and consequently is little more than a backdoor into the same old functional construction, a bit more grandiose but with the same ultimate end. Second, therefore, it does little to eliminate the deficiencies of existing jurisdictions, their inadequate capacity to act and their uncontrolled authority to interfere.

The answer to the first criticism is that this arrangement *comprehends* a function, but that its structure is based on the community involved, on the possibilities of diversity and debate and not on the engineering requirements for the most effective transit system. As to the second point, the reply is that there does not appear to be any metropolitan community, politically speaking, other than that made by a common concern for transportation. We can view with sorrow and alarm the current political practices in our central cities and our suburbs, and we should continue to search for issues and activities which contain the common denominators of political consciousness from which an institution can be built. Perhaps, education and recreation will soon be likely candidates, and at least partial integration into larger units made possible. Sewers, fire or police, however, are unlikely to be effective catalysts for a long time to come. In any event, it would be a serious mistake to undertake to create a government before the political consciousness exists.[4] This was, of course, the error of functional analysis when, weighting the value scales heavily on the side of efficiency, it chose to ignore the political values involved. It is natural for the engineer or the substantive specialist to make this error. It is a pity when the political scientist aids and abets them.

4. There is, of course, room for debate on which metropolitan function is most likely to come equipped with an effective political process. Mr Ylvisaker has high hopes for regional planning. I can agree that the *need* for planning is substantial, but I fail to see the coincidence of interests among a large section of the public necessary to support its activation. The distinction between function and power remains critical.

References

BOLLENS, J. C. (1956), *The States and the Metropolitan Problem*, Council of State Governments.

GULICK, L. (1955), *Address*, National Conference on Metropolitan Affairs, 30 April.

HOFFMANN, S. (1959), 'The areal division of powers in the writings of French political thinkers', in A. Maass (ed.) *Area and Power*, Free Press.

MAASS, A. (ed.) (1959), *Area and Power*, Free Press.

US DEPARTMENT OF COMMERCE (1954), *Local Government in Metropolitan Areas*, no. 36, Bureau of the Census.

YLVISAKER, P. (1959), Chapter 2 in A. Maass (ed.), *Area and Power*, Free Press.

13 W. H. Form

The Place of Social Structure in the Determination of Land Use

W. H. Form, 'The place of social structure in the determination of land use', *Social Forces*, vol. 32, 1954, pp. 317–23.

Deriving a satisfactory theory of land-use change is a pressing problem for both ecologists and urban sociologists.[1] Most of the current thinking on this subject revolves around the so-called ecological processes. A brief inspection of the literature reveals, however, a lamentable lack of agreement on the definition, number, and importance of the ecological processes.[2] It is apparent that the economic model of classical economists from which these processes are derived must be discarded in favor of models which consider social realities.

In studying land-use change, this paper proposes that ecology abandon its sub-social non-organization orientations and use the frame of reference of general sociology. Even though the focus of attention of ecology may remain in the economic realm, a sociological analysis of economic behavior is called for. This means that most of the current ecological premises must be converted into research questions capable of sociological verification.

The first step is to analyze the social forces operating in the land market. Obviously the image of a free and unorganized market in which individuals compete impersonally for land must be abandoned. The reason for this is that the land market is highly organized and dominated by a number of interacting organizations. Most of the latter are formally organized, highly self-

1. For purposes of simplification this paper will limit itself to a consideration of land-use change in middle-size, growing, industrial cities of the United States. Historical analysis of land-use change is not within the province of this paper because of the methodological difficulties in reconstructing the ecological processes.

2. One reason for this confusion centers on the controversy whether human ecology should be related to or divorced from biological ecology. Amos H. Hawley claims that the difficulties of human ecology arise from its isolation from the mainstream of ecological thought in biology; see Hawley (1944, pp. 399–405). Warner E. Gettys is of the opinion that human ecology should free itself from its primary dependence on organic ecology; see Gettys (1940, pp. 469–76).

conscious, and purposeful in character. Although at times their values and interests are conflicting, they are often overlapping and harmonious. That is, their relationships tend to become structured over a period of time. From a study of this emerging structure one obtains a picture of the parameters of ecological behavior, the patterns of land-use change, and the institutional pressures which maintain the ecological order.

Four organizational congeries in the land market

The interacting groups, associations, and relationships which comprise this emerging structure may be identified by asking such questions as: (a) Who are the largest consumers of land? (b) Which organizations specialize in dealing with land? and (c) Which associations mediate the conflicts of land use? Preliminary research suggests that, among the many associations and interests in American society, four types of social congeries or organizational complexes dominate the land market and determine indirectly the use to which land is put.

The first and perhaps most important of these congeries is the real estate and building business.[3] Since they know more about the land market of the city than comparable groups, it is suggested that the study of the real estate building groups (along the lines of occupational-industrial sociology) would provide more insight into the dynamics of land-use change than present studies which are based on the sub-social ecological processes. The analysis of real estate organizations is an especially good starting point to build a sociological ecology because these organizations interact with all of the other urban interests which are concerned with land use.[4]

The second social congeries which functions in the land market are the larger industries, businesses and utilities. While they may not consume the greatest quantities of land, they do purchase the largest and most strategic parcels. Unknowingly their locational decisions tend to set the pattern of land use for other economic and non-economic organizations. Most of the land-use decisions of these central industries and businesses are a response to peculiar historic circumstances in the community. Therefore it

3. It appears that an interpenetration of organization and interests of these two groups is increasing so rapidly in American cities that for many purposes they may be conceived as one interest group.
4. This is strongly suggested by strikingly parallel studies in two different types of cities. Cf. Hughes (1928); Bouma (1952).

would seem fruitless to describe *a priori* the geometric shape of the city as a series of rings, sectors or diamonds.

The third social constellation in the land market is composed of individual home owners and other small consumers of land. In a sense their position is tangential to the structure or important only under rather unusual circumstances. Most of their decisions on where to buy, when to buy, and what land to buy are fitted into an administered land market and are not, as many would assume, individual, discrete, free and unrelated. The social characteristics of the consumers, their economic power, degree of organization and relations to other segments of the community help explain the role they play in the market of land decisions.

The fourth organizational complex is comprised of the many local governmental agencies which deal with land, such as the zoning boards, planning commissions, school boards, traffic commissions and other agencies. This organizational complex is loosely knit internally, for its segments often function at cross purposes. Their relations to other groups in the community vary with political currents. Unlike other organizations, these governmental agencies are both consumers of land and mediators of conflicting land-use interests. Thus political agencies not only require land to placate private and public pressures, they are also called upon to resolve conflicts between different types of land consumers. Moreover, some of these governmental agencies try to fulfill a city plan which sets the expected pattern of the ecological development of the city.

These four organizational complexes[5] – real estate, big business, residents and government – do not comprise all of the organizational entities which participate in land-use decisions. However, they are the main ones. Once identified, the problem is to find the nature of the social relationships among these organizational complexes. Is a stable pattern discernible? How does the pattern manifest itself in physical space? In what direction is the pattern emerging as a response to inter-institutional trends in the broader society? To answer these questions, an analytical model is needed to appraise the social relations among the four organizational congeries identified above.

5. Each organizational complex is comprised of groups, associations, aggregations, social categories and other types of social nucleations. To facilitate communication, the term 'grouping' will be used to refer to this organizational complex. I am indebted to Professor Read Bain for pointing to the need for terminological clarification in matters dealing with interaction of different types of social nucleations.

Elements in the analytical model

Sociologists have not yet derived completely satisfactory scheme to analyze inter-organizational relations, either in their structural or dynamic dimensions. However, ecologists are dependent on such general schema as have already been worked out. Some of the basic elements in the analytical scheme to appraise the relations among the four land consuming groups are described below.

1. The first element in the model is the amount and types of economic resources which each 'grouping' has to buttress its land-use decisions. Obviously the resources of the four 'groupings' differ considerably. Thus, industry has property and capital which are somewhat greater and more mobile than those of the real estate industry. In addition to their tax resources, governmental agencies have the power to expropriate land in their own name or in the name of any interest which can control them. The individual home owner and the small businessman, on the other hand, not only have the smallest but the least organized economic resources. The economic resources of each group must be carefully gauged in each community where there is a contest to control particular parcels of land. However, economic resources comprise only one cell in the paradigm needed to analyze the structural setting of land-use changes.

2. The second factors which merit consideration are the manifest and latent functions of each 'grouping' in the land market. Thus, the functions of the real estate industry include, in addition to maximizing its earnings, bringing knowledge of available land to different segments of the community. Moreover it tries to organize the land market and control land values to assure itself stability and continuity of income.[6] In the process of so doing, the realtors come into contact with political, citizen, and business agencies.[7] The land interests of big business, on the other hand, are much more specific and spasmodic than those of the real estate business. The desire of businessmen to have large stretches of land under one title, to obtain land additions close to present plant operations, and to dominate the landscape of the community, often leads them to make diseconomic decisions which are in conflict with those of other groups.

6. See Hughes (1929, pp. 91–4).
7. Hughes indicates that the real estate industry is a loose federation of different types of businessmen. Each type plays a different role to correspond to its clientele and market.

Government agencies have quite different and sometimes conflicting functions to perform. Among these are: protecting present tax values, acquiring parcels of land for specific public or quasi-public uses, altering certain land-use patterns to conform to the plan of the 'city beautiful', acting as a clearing house and communication channel for those who need land-use data. Most important, they mediate conflicts in land use and exercise their legitimate authority for groups which curry their favor.

Individual residents and small businessmen are mostly concerned with preventing changes in land use. They tend to be defensive-minded and sentimentally attached to their neighborhoods and to fight to prevent the encroachment of usages which would threaten present economic and social investments. In general, resident groupings do not play dynamic roles in changing urban land usages.

3. The internal organization of these four groupings differs considerably. Knowledge of this factor is important to assess the degree to which they may be mobilized to fight for control over desired lands. Often small, unified and organized groups with meagre economic resources can dominate larger, richer and more loosely knit groups in a land struggle. These four 'groupings' differ in their internal structure and external relations. There is an urgent need for research to study the cleavages, cliques, alliances and arrangements found within and among these groupings. However, certain trends may now be noted.

The real estate industry is slowly emerging from a haphazard aggregation of local agents to a tightly organized professional or fraternal society which seeks to establish control over the land market (Hughes, 1929). Big business and industry, on the other hand, have typically bureaucratic structures capable of marshalling tremendous resources in the community for or against other land-interested groups. Municipal agencies, though individually powerful, are often unaware of each other's activities. Therefore they tend to comprise a loosely knit set of bureaus which often function at cross purposes. Since many governmental agencies are tied into the fabric of private associations, they are united to common action only under unusual external pressures. Individual residents and small businesses are the most loosely organized.[8] In

8. Higher status areas of the city are usually more formally organized to protect land uses than are lower status areas. The formation of neighborhood 'improvement and betterment' associations stabilizes land use and resists the invasion of other land uses.

fact, they tend to remain unorganized except under 'crisis' conditions.

4. Each grouping has an accountability pattern differing in its consequences for action. Each has different kinds of pressures and influences to which it must respond. For example, the real estate organizations are primarily accountable to themselves and sometimes to their largest customers, the building industry and the utilities. On the other hand, the local managers of larger corporations tend to be accountable to other managers, stockholders and board members who may not reside in the community. Thus, local managers may have to respond in their land decisions to pressures generated outside of the community. Municipal agencies are formally accountable to the local citizens who are, *according to the issues*, realtors, individual landlords, businessmen, educational, political or any other organized interest.

Each of the four social congeries being considered is organized differently as a pressure group interested in land-use policies. Each, in a sense, lives in a power situation which consists of its relation to the other three. Different kinds of alliances are made among them and among their segments, depending on the issues. The types of collective bargaining situations which arise among them must be studied in a larger context in order to understand the sociology of land-use decisions. For example, businessmen who are sometimes appointed as members of city planning commissions may be constrained to play roles incongruous with their business roles. As members of residential and recreational organizations they may be forced to make decisions which may seem contradictory to their economic interests.

5. In land decisions involving the whole city, the image which each grouping has of the city must be appraised. The realtors are usually the most enthusiastic boosters of the city. They envision an expanding city with an ever-growing land market, for this assures them income and security. Consequently, they exert pressure on the municipal agencies to join them in their plans for the 'expansive city'.

However, municipal officials do not conceive of the city primarily as a market. They see it as the downtown civic center, the city beautiful and the planned community. Although desiring an expanding city, they are equally concerned with the politics and aesthetics of locating parks, avenues, schools and other services. At times their aesthetic-political plans conflict with the boom ideology of the realtors and the industry-oriented plans of businessmen. Indeed this is almost inevitable in some situations, for politicians must secure votes to remain in office. Plans for different areas of the city must be weighed in terms of how they affect votes.[9]

The industrialists conception of the community tends to be more partial than that of any other group. Since industries often have allegiances to non-community enterprises, they are not necessarily enamoured by the vision of the expansive city or the city beautiful. They are inclined to view the city primarily as their work plant and residence. They usually regard the existence of their enterprises as economic 'contributions' to the city. Therefore they feel that any land decisions they desire as businessmen, golfers or residents are 'reasonable and proper' in view of their 'contribution' to the locality. When their demands are not met, they can threaten to remove the industry to more favorable communities.

The citizen's view of the city is also segmental. He tends to envision it as his neighborhood, his work plant, and 'downtown'. These are the areas he wants to see protected, beautified and serviced. Since residents do not comprise a homogeneous group, obviously their community images differ. The nature of the intersection of the segmentalized city images of these four social congeries provides one of the parameters for studying their interaction. Needless to say, other non-ecological images that these groups have of themselves and of each other have a bearing on their relations. However, since the problems of this paper are more structural than social psychological, this area will not be expanded.

6. Other factors in the analytical scheme may be derived which point to the different orientations and relationships existing among these groups. For example, their primary value orientations differ. For government, community 'service' is ostensibly the chief value; for real estate, it is an assured land market; for business, it is profitable operations; for the resident, it is protection. Another distinction may be in terms of the amount and type of land interests of the groups. Whereas real estate is interested in all of the city's land, municipal agencies are more interested in communal lands and industry is concerned with its private land use. The future task of sociologists will be to select

9. For an illuminating case history of this, see Whyte (1947, pp. 245–52).

the most important interactional areas of these groups to locate the forces responsible for land-use patterns and changes.

Land-use changes in a zoning context

Following the selection of some of the important dimensions in the paradigm, the task is to characterize briefly the pattern of the relationships among the four 'groupings'. In the broadest sense, the model to be followed is that used in analyzing the collective bargaining structure and process.[10] An excellent place to begin observing the 'collective bargaining' relations among these groupings is in the zoning process of cities. Zoning is recommended because the methodological problems of studying it are minimal, and yet the kinds of intergroup relations found there are not unlike those in non-zoning relations.

Since almost every city of any consequence in the United States is zoned, any significant deviation in a pattern of land use necessarily involves a change in zoning. It would appear then that sociologists and ecologists should study the relations of land-interested agencies to municipal agencies.[11] Most zoning commissions tend to freeze an already existing pattern of land use. If they formulate plans for city growth, these plans tend to correspond to a sector image of expanding areas of ongoing land use. This results in a rather rigid ecological structure which inevitably generates pressures for changes. Since such changes involve obtaining the consent of municipal agencies, a political dimension inserts itself in the study of ecological processes.

Traditional ecologists may object to this social structural and political approach to problems of land-use change. They may suggest that the ecological concept of 'dominance' provides the answer to the question of which group will determine land use or land-use change. An examination of this concept in the ecological literature reveals a basic shortcoming. Ecological dominance refers to economic control in the symbiotic sense; it provides no analytical cues to appraise the relations among organizations which comprise the structure dealing with land-use changes.[12]

Traditional ecologists may object that the proposal to study the relations of the four land 'groupings' in a political context is merely a methodological innovation, in that the *results* of such a

10. See Blumer (1947, pp. 271–8). See also the articles in Lester and Shister (1948); Whyte (1951); Lasswell (1936).
11. See Dewey (1950, p. 502–507).
12. See McKenzie (1933, pp. 81–131); Bogue (1949, pp. 10–13).

study would point to the same pattern of land-use change available by recourse to the traditional ecological processes. They may reason that determination of land use after all is an economic struggle or process, in which the most powerful economic interests determine to what use land will be put. While it is true, they may agree, that this process is not as simple and as impersonal as hitherto believed, the end result is very much the same.[13]

The writer has recently been gathering cases of zoning changes that have occurred in Lansing, its fringe and in the outlying areas. In addition, cases have been observed where attempts to institute zoning changes have failed. In both types of changes the questions were asked: (a) Did naked economic power dictate the decision to change or not to change the zoning? (b) Could the outcome of these cases be predicted by using a cultural ecology frame of reference? A brief analysis of the cases revealed that no simple economic or cultural analysis could account for success or failure of zoning changes. The actual outcome could be better analyzed on the basis of the paradigm suggested above. Four cases will be briefly summarized to suggest typical kinds of alliances found in attempts to change land use.

In Lansing, the zoning commission may recommend changes in zoning but the City Council must approve of them. This means that all changes in land use must occur in a political context. In 1951, a local metal fabricating plant asked the Council to rezone some of its property from a residential to a commercial classification so that an office building could be erected on it. The residents of the area, who are mostly Negroes, appeared before the Council urging it to refuse the request on the ground that the company had not lived up to legal responsibilities to control obnoxious smoke, fly-ash, traffic and so on. In addition, they contended that space for Negro housing was limited and rezoning would deprive them of needed space. Moreover, they hinted that the company's request came indirectly from a large corporation which would eventually obtain the property. In short, they urged rejection of the request not on its own merits but on the basis that the company had not lived up to its community responsibilities. Company spokesmen denied any deals, promised to control air

13. In this respect the position of ecologists is not significantly different from the Marxist analysis of land-use changes. This may explain the appeal of the ecological approach to some otherwise sophisticated sociologists. I am indebted to G. P. Stone for the elaboration of this idea.

pollution, and got labor union spokesmen to urge rezoning. The Council complied. Four months later all of the properties of the company, including the rezoned areas, were sold to the large corporation in question.

Here is a clear case of economically powerful interests consciously manipulating land uses for their purposes. The question arises: why did not the large corporation itself ask for rezoning? Apparently, it realized that greater resistance would have been met. The local company is a medium-sized, old, home-owned enterprise which has had rather warm relations with its employees. The large corporation, on the other hand, is a large impersonal, absentee-owned corporation that has at times alienated local people.[14] Therefore, its chances of getting this property without fanfare were increased by the use of an intermediary.

Yet business does not always win. In another case, a respectable undertaker established a funeral parlor in a low income residential area. The local residents objected strenuously to the presence of the business. The legal aspects of the case remained obscure for a time because the undertaker insisted he did not embalm bodies in the establishment. In a preliminary hearing he appeared to have won a victory. The aroused residents called upon the Republican ward leader who promised to talk to the 'authorities'. Just before a rehearing of the case, the undertaker decided to leave the area for he was reliably informed that the decision would go against him.

Struggles between businessmen and government do not always work out in favor of the former. Currently, the organized businessmen of East Lansing are fighting an order of the State Highway Commission which has passed a no parking ordinance to apply to the town's main thoroughfare. The retailers are fearful that they will lose business if the order holds. Since business will not be able to expand in the same direction if the order holds, pressure to rezone residential areas in the community for commercial and parking purposes will be forthcoming. In a community where residents are a strong, vocal, upper middle status group majority, such pressure may be resisted strongly. Clearly a power struggle involving the State, local businessmen, local government and the residents will determine the ecological pat-

14. For example, workers insist that during the depression the company recruited Southerners rather than local labor.

tern of the city.[15] A knowledge of their relationships is needed to predict the outcome of the struggle and the future ecological changes in the community.

S. T. Kimball (1946) has documented a case where the failure to inaugurate zoning involved the same kind of social structural analysis of group relations as suggested above. Kimball studied a suburban rural township where the upper middle status groups failed in a referendum to obtain zoning in the face of an industrial invasion of the area. An analysis of the case showed that the issue would be misunderstood if studied as a struggle of economic interests. In fact, the industrial interests were not an important variable in the case. The failure of the referendum was accounted for by analysis of five types of relationships: (a) those among the suburbanites, (b) those within the township board, (c) those between the supervisor and his constituents, (d) those between the farmers and suburbanites, and (e) those between the supervisor and the informal 'leaders' in the community (Kimball, p. 4).

This paper has proposed the need to consider social structure in addition to ecological and cultural factors in the study of changes in land use. The traditional ecological processes are no longer adequate to analyze changes in land use. These processes, like most ecological concepts, are based on models of eighteenth century free enterprise economics. Yet fundamental changes in the structure of the economy call for new economic models which in turn call for a recasting of general ecological theory. The new vital trend of cultural ecology does not do this adequately, for it considers the structural realities of urban society only indirectly.

This paper proposes that ecological change be studied by first isolating the important and powerful land-interested groupings in the city. Certain elements in an analytical scheme have been proposed to study the collective bargaining relationships among these groupings. The *forces* that operate in land-use change may well be studied in the socio-political struggles that are presently occurring in the area of zoning. A brief survey of some changes in urban zoning points to the greater adequacy of the sociological over the traditional ecological analysis for understanding and predicting land-use changes.

15. My colleague, G. P. Stone, suggests that it begins to appear that the State's position will force a very unusual ecological phenomenon: a business district turning its back to the main highway and reorienting itself to the 'back-yards', as it were.

References

BLUMER, H. (1947), 'Sociological theory in industrial relations', *Amer. Sociol. Rev.*, vol. 12, pp. 271–8.

BOGUE, D. J. (1949), *The Structure of the Metropolitan Community*, University of Michigan.

BOUMA, D. H. (1952), *An Analysis of the Social Power Position of the Real Estate Board in Grand Rapids, Michigan*, unpublished Ph.D. dissertation, Michigan State College.

DEWEY, R. (1950), 'The neighborhood, urban ecology and city planners', *Amer. Sociol. Rev.*, vol. 15, pp. 502–7.

GETTYS, W. E. (1940), 'Human ecology and social theory', *Social Forces*, vol. 18, pp. 469–76.

HAWLEY, A. H. (1944), 'Ecology and human ecology', *Social Forces*, vol. 22, pp. 399–405.

HUGHES, E. C. (1928), *A Study of a Secular Institution: the Chicago Real Estate Board*, unpublished Ph.D. dissertation, University of Chicago.

HUGHES, E. C. (1929), 'Personality types and the division of labor', in E. W. Burgess (ed.), *Personality and the Social Group*, University of Chicago Press.

KIMBALL, S. T. (1946), 'A case study of township zoning', *Michigan Agricultural Exper. Station Q. Bull.*, vol. 28, p. 4.

LASSWELL, H. D. (1936), *Politics*, McGraw-Hill.

LESTER, R. A., and SHISTER, J. (eds) (1948), *Insights into Labor Issues*, Macmillan.

MCKENZIE, R. D. (1933), *The Metropolitan Community*, McGraw-Hill.

WHYTE, W. F. (1947), *Street Corner Society*, University of Chicago Press.

WHYTE, W. F. (1951), *Pattern for Industrial Peace*, Harper.

14 D. R. Mandelker

A Rationale for the Zoning Process

D. R. Mandelker, 'A rationale for the zoning process', *Land-Use Controls Quarterly*, vol. 4, 1970, pp. 1–7.

We face a deepening crisis in zoning, in zoning administration and in zoning law. National commissions report that exclusionary local zoning is an obstacle to the fulfillment of national housing policies, the national administration contemplates federal legislation pre-empting local zoning ordinances that stand in the way of housing programs, and lawsuits are brought nationwide challenging local zoning policies on the grounds that they are constitutionally discriminatory. In the face of these attacks, lawyers and planners have serious questions to ask about the basis of zoning law, and about the criteria for its implementation to which we have given legal sanction. If zoning is both racially and economically discriminatory, what is the origin of that discrimination? If zoning presents obstacles to social and economic equality, in what policies and practices do these obstacles lie?

This brief essay seeks tentative answers to these questions, not in the more dramatic issues of racial and economic discrimination, but in the more mundane issues of zoning policy which we have conveniently managed to sweep under the table. The focus here is on those zoning controversies in which marginal changes are requested in uses and densities and, even more narrowly, on the criteria which guide these changes in our partly-urbanized suburban areas. Viewed against the totality of our urban crisis, these issues may seem peripheral, even unimportant. But zoning changes in suburbia provide an important testing ground for the concepts and ideas which underlie our attempt to intervene, in the name of the public interest, in the private market of land development. They present a good opportunity to evaluate the rationale for the zoning process.

Krause vs City of Royal Oak,[1] decided by the Michigan Court of Appeals, is a representative case in which the dominant issue was marginal change in land uses and densities. In a suburban

1. 11 Michigan Appeals Court 183, 160 N W 2d 769, 1968.

area which had for some time been zoned single-family residential, a developer attempted to get a zoning change that would permit him to develop a tract of 3·5 acres for garden apartments. After several years of unsuccessful effort, he undertook a direct attack on the zoning ordinance. He presented the court with a rich matrix of environmental fact: the nearby presence of a railroad; a busy highway; a mixed pattern of residential development; and a comparative evaluation of the neighborhood impact of his proposed development and of the development permitted by the zoning regulation.

The *Royal Oak* case is typical of the elaborate factual settings in which zoning controversies are presented to the courts. The courts, however, react to these complex factual patterns by utilizing a series of generic concepts and presumptions which have their roots in the constitutional requirement of due process of law. Generally, a zoning ordinance is presumed constitutional. Generally, a zoning ordinance is held constitutional if the basis for its allocations is reasonably debatable. What is lacking is a middle level of concept and idea which can tie the generic nouns and presumptions of constitutional doctrine to the evidentiary facts that produce the zoning dispute. Cases veer backward and forward in similar factual situations. On one occasion, the presumption of constitutionality will save the day. On another, it will not. But we are never quite told why the court chose as it did. What conceptual basis should we seek in arriving at a solution to these controversies? To answer this question, we must first look at some history. We will then return to the Michigan court's decision in the *Royal Oak* zoning controversy.

The nuisance basis of zoning law

I have dealt elsewhere with the nuisance basis of zoning law,[2] but I think it may be helpful to review this background here. An economist looking at the law of nuisance would tell us that it deals with the problem of externalities, with the problem of land-use activities which detrimentally affect the use of land held by others. Courts handled the externalities problem by modifying or prohibiting those uses which were so offensive that they could be called nuisances. Some of these nuisances were offensive in and of themselves, regardless of location. With increasing urbanization, however, a nuisance had to be evaluated in terms of its environment. A noisy and dusty stone quarry might be acceptable in an

2. See Mandelker (1965).

area that was entirely rural. It was not acceptable in a built-up residential neighborhood. And nuisance law was ruthless. If the use was offensive, it was usually forced to discontinue, even with considerable loss to the owner. No compensation was payable under the nuisance decree.

Some important judgmental issues were hidden by the nuisance cases, however. Perhaps the most important was the selection of the environmental standard against which the nuisance was to be evaluated. Courts tended to handle this issue by looking to the state of development in the area immediately surrounding the nuisance. If the area was fully developed, the character of that development determined whether the nuisance was or was not offensive. Thus, a slaughterhouse would be prohibited in a residential neighborhood. If the area was partly developed, the court might hesitate; and if the development pattern was yet unformed, the court might not prohibit the nuisance at all.

Zoning, as the leading United States Supreme Court case of *Euclid vs Ambler Realty Co.*[3] told us, borrowed heavily from nuisance doctrine. But there were important differences. Instead of an *ad hoc* judicial determination of the character of the neighborhood as the basis for the judgment against the offending use, the zoning ordinance prescribed, in advance and by district, the uses that were permissible throughout the municipality. For lawsuits against existing uses carried out in existing structures, the zoning ordinance substituted regulations for vacant land. True, the zoning ordinance applies to uses in existence at the time of its enactment, but these uses cannot immediately be eliminated if they are nonconforming to the ordinance. Court-made nuisance law worked from opposite assumptions. Because the nuisance had to be evaluated in the context of its surroundings, and because the character of that use could not be determined in advance, courts were reluctant to prohibit on nuisance grounds the commencement of a new use on vacant land.

These differences in the assumptions underlying the application of the zoning ordinance create an entirely different setting for zoning litigation. In nuisance cases, the courts balance the equities to determine whether they can justifiably deprive the landowner of the value which his existing development represents. In zoning cases, the issue is more subtle. Vacant land has a value for the uses permitted by the zoning ordinance, but this is not the point. The zoning challenger alleges that, were it not for the

3. 272 US 365 (1926).

zoning ordinance, he could commit his land to a different use which would increase the value of his land.[4] He argues, in other words, that the deprivation of development value which he suffers under the zoning ordinance is an unconstitutional deprivation of property without due process of law. Unlike the property owner in a nuisance case, the property owner in a zoning case argues that he has been unconstitutionally deprived of a legally protected expectancy. In *Euclid*, for example, the value of the land for the prohibited use was four times its value for the permitted use.

Value disparity is recognized by the cases, but they have not known how to deal with it. To decide whether the deprivation of value can be constitutionally imposed, courts are usually forced to fall back on an appraisal of the environment in which the undeveloped land is located. This evaluation parallels the similar though *ad hoc* evaluation of the neighborhood which is typical of the nuisance cases, except that in the zoning cases the courts review a legislative judgment which is handed to them in the form of a zoning ordinance.

The planning input to zoning

But the zoning process adds yet another conceptual ingredient to land-use decisions, for zoning, in the language of most enabling acts, must be 'in accordance with a comprehensive plan'. The statutory planning command has been given a restrictive definition by most court decisions. Nevertheless, as planning provides the justification for collective decisions about land-use allocations, and as these allocations are implemented through the zoning process, we are entitled to ask what justification planning provides. Just what is the planner to do? What guides him in producing the community comprehensive plan to which the zoning process is to conform?

These questions are not easy to answer, but we can at least offer conventional wisdom. Apparently, within the limits of his political jurisdiction, the planner is charged to plan comprehensively to co-ordinate both public and private development to achieve the most efficient use of land. We need only look at the language of the Standard Planning Enabling Act. The plan shall be made with the purpose of 'guiding and accomplishing a co-ordinated,

4. We put aside for purposes of this discussion the case in which existing zoning is tightened, thereby depreciating the value of the land by denying the property owner a use to which he was previously entitled.

adjusted and harmonious development of the community that will best promote health, safety, morals, order, convenience, prosperity and the general welfare' (§7).

Just what meaning 'efficiency' is to be given in the statutory context is not made clear, though it would seem to connote avoidance of waste in the use of resources, rather than some economically-defined optimal state in the employment of those resources. Thus planning (and presumably zoning) would be efficient in our *Royal Oak* example if the allocation for higher-density development such as apartments were 'co-ordinated' with the provision of the necessary public facilities so that the provision of each would be 'efficient'. This is not the only meaning to be put on the word, but it is the one we will accept for purposes of our analysis here.

To the extent that planning and zoning take co-ordination as their guiding purpose, and to the extent that co-ordination implies efficiency in land use, then public control of land use, like nuisance law, is based on the need to deal with externalities. The difference, of course, is that we have given the efficiency objective in planning and zoning a broader definition than the prevention of unsupportable external costs, which is the purpose of nuisance litigation. These comments also suggest that finding a rationale for the zoning process will be complicated by differences in perspective between the planner, whose plan the zoning ordinance implements, and the lawyer, who must secure judicial acceptance for both plan and ordinance. In particular, the planner does not address himself explicitly to the due process problem. He plans without an immediate concern that what he decides may be regarded as an unconstitutional deprivation of development value. Nevertheless, his planning decisions affect and redistribute development values throughout his jurisdiction.

These differences in outlook would not necessarily cause difficulty were it not for the fact that the efficiency predicate for planning is itself suspect. Planners themselves are anxious to abandon it for a more satisfactory foundation. But what shall they substitute? Professor Altshuler (1965), in his classic study of the planning process, has noted the inadequacies of co-ordination as a goal for planning. 'In the end, no act of co-ordination is without its effect on other values than efficiency' (1965, p. 332). Professor Altshuler is referring, of course, to normative or judgmental values, not to land values. But 'acts' of co-ordination have their effect on land values as well. Where does the planner find the normative values that will guide his professional judgment? In the words of Professor Seeley (1962), is he a 'trustee' for utopia, or does he simply reconcile the interests of others? Is he a 'protagonist' for a scheme which is more or less ideal, or is he passive, an 'honest broker' in the interplay and conflict of interest? (1962, p. 91). These questions have not been answered. Nor are the answers easy to find. The Standard Planning Act attempted to differentiate the making of the land-use plan from the making of community policy. 'The making of a plan . . . is an entirely different kind of work' (§2, n. 10). But is it?

Land-use decisions in suburbia

Let us return once more to our Michigan case. We deal here with a marginal change in land use in an area that is almost entirely, but not quite, urbanized. These cases have been difficult to handle because development patterns in the neighborhood are often mixed and point in more than one direction. In the *Royal Oak* case, the planning director was concerned about the kind of externalities that are usually considered in nuisance litigation, and both sides attempted to derive significant clues from the character of the surrounding environment. In testimony quoted in the court's opinion, the planning director argued that the construction of garden apartments on the disputed site would bring noise, congestion and confusion to residents in the adjacent single-family area – would visit unjustified externalities on them. The developer emphasized the nearby presence of a railroad, which he advanced as a reason why residential development for single-family homes was not desirable. Brief reference was also made to the impact of the proposed apartment development on highway congestion, but since the apartment development was small, the added impact was not that substantial. In other words, it could be argued that apartment development at the site would be efficient in our sense because it could make use of existing facilities without added investment.

But the court in the *Royal Oak* case did more than discuss the assumed incompatibilities in land use that the apartment development would create, and it did this by way of an interesting detour to discuss the constitutional basis of the developer's lawsuit. We should first note that the court was sensitive to the fact that the developer in this case had not been deprived by the ordinance of any existing value in his land. We do not have what is sometimes called an upzoning, an attempt to tighten or raise restrictions on development with a consequent loss in value to the affected owner. Rather, as the court noted, the developer had attempted to set aside the zoning regulation in order to realize additional development value from his tract. The court was willing to discount this kind of disparity in value when it considered the constitutionality of the zoning regulation. As the court pointed out, a zoning ordinance often takes value out of land. Especially because the value disparity urged by the landowner arose from a denial by the zoning ordinance of an increment in the development value of his land, the court was encouraged to apply a presumption of constitutionality.

But the court did note that value disparity had led to invalidation of the zoning ordinance when 'other factors' were present 'which clearly affect the public health, safety or general welfare of the people.'[5] The court's typical reliance on the conventional police power nouns to solve a complicated regulatory problem in a multi-faceted controversy simply reflects the usual judicial tendency to avoid facing the difficult problems in zoning disputes. But the court did not stop even here, for it offered its own observations on the desirable mode in land development patterns, reinforcing Altshuler's comment that values other than co-ordination are implicit in land-use decisions. Falling back on and quoting from the landmark *Euclid* case,[6] which also considered an ordinance excluding apartments from single-family neighborhoods, the Michigan court adopted the rationale of *Euclid* that apartments in residential neighborhoods are parasitic. Though the technology of apartment building has changed radically since *Euclid*, the Michigan court was nevertheless willing to accept the judgment values implicit in that decision. Under the *Euclid* value system single-family residences stand highest in a pyramid of land uses. The job of zoning is to preserve the pyramid. Upward pressures of 'lower' uses, such as apartments, into zones reserved for 'higher' uses, such as single-family homes, may constitutionally be prohibited.[7] Nor was the developer in the Michigan case a protagonist of a more radical social order. His argument for apartment development was based largely on his assumption that the proximity of the railroad made his tract unsuitable for single-family residential use. He did not attack

5. 11 Mich. App. at 191, 160 N W 2d at 772.
6. 11 Mich. App. p. 193, 194, 160 N W 2d at 774.
7. This explanation of the zoning power has been accepted by Professor Dunham (1958), as the rationale for the application of land-use controls.

the *Euclid* pyramid. He merely urged that the assumptions underlying the construction of the pyramid pointed to a different result in his case.

Some comments on a rationale for zoning

These comments have focused on the problem of marginal changes in land-use patterns because they should present a comparatively simple developmental context in which to search for a rationale in the zoning process. Decisions about marginal changes in land use should be easier to handle than more wide-sweeping proposals, such as new towns or massive urban reconstruction. Much of the development pattern is fixed, and we ought to have ready-made principles to decide how the physical environment should move toward completion.

We find no such guidelines. If the lawyer falls back on his nuisance background, he may find himself consulting the character of the existing environment, which often points in many directions. Planners attempting to apply a test of efficiency and co-ordination may only have a limited contribution to make. Because the development is itself marginal to the existing land-use pattern, and is often small-scale, its impact even on community facilities may be insubstantial. More likely than not, the judgmental basis of the decision will be exposed, as the court falls back on crude notions of social order that have a judgmental character. This is how the Michigan case we have been discussing was decided.

Now we can understand why the zoning system might appear as an obstacle to the accomplishment of housing programs. Sites like those in contention in the Michigan case are ideal locations for vest-pocket public housing, or private, low-income housing projects financed under recently-enacted federal housing legislation. Indeed, as the search for low-income housing sites in metropolitan areas grows increasingly more difficult, even vacant tracts of moderate size become attractive to would-be developers. We may find that our marginal land-use changes in suburbia are more important than we thought.

But recognizing the obstacles that zoning can present to the achievement of social and economic equality in housing does not necessitate destroying the entire zoning system. At the same time, justifying planning and zoning judgments in the name of efficiency and co-ordination is no longer enough. What we desperately need is to investigate that missing middle level of concept which provides the bridge in zoning law between the detail of environmental fact, and the generic concepts that underlie constitutional protections. When we look closely at that middle level of concept we find embedded within it a model of land development which implies social and economic discrimination. If we are to redirect the planning and zoning process, we must take explicit account of these social judgments which so far have remained largely hidden in the decisions we make about the physical environment.

References

ALTSHULER, A. (1965), *The City Planning Process*, Cornell University Press.
DUNHAM, A. (1958), 'A legal and economic basis for city planning', *Columbia Law Rev.*, vol. 58, p. 650.
MANDELKER, D. R. (1965), 'The role of law in the planning process', *Law and Contemporary Problems*, vol. 30, pp.–37.
SEELEY, J. R. (1962), 'What is planning? definition and strategy', *J. of Amer. Inst. of Planners*, vol. 28, p. 91.

Part Four
Planning and the Social Sciences

Parts Two and Three outlined the nature of the urban process.
The readings in this part attempt to illustrate some of the points
at which intervention in the process can be most usefully made.
Mandelker's earlier article (Reading 14) demonstrated the role
that the law can play in strengthening or weakening established
power; Dunham's article (Reading 15), although primarily
related to the United States, raises, as its title suggests, a number
of fundamental, though general, questions about the nature of
planning and the way in which the law can and should seek to
impinge upon the expectations of individuals. Property rights and
zoning are only two of the many aspects of the urban process
discussed by Harvey (Reading 16) in his comprehensive analysis
of the relationship between social processes, spatial form and the
redistribution of income. This reading represents more than any
other in this volume an attempt to integrate a considerable
volume of varied theoretical and empirical work into one
interdisciplinary essay. No excuse is necessary for including an
article almost twice as long as any other since it brings together
many of the issues already mentioned here – spatial structure,
slums, community, public goods, political organization and
others. Harvey suggests a broadly based, comprehensive
approach towards goals of equity and income distribution, but
he is fairly non-committal about the organization of government.
Nevertheless this is one variable in the urban system which is
likely to see change in the near future; in the UK following the
Government's reaction to the Redcliffe-Maud report, and less
certainly in the USA as the pressure for metropolitan government
builds up. Smallwood (Reading 17) analyses the reform of London
government, enacted in 1963, with the final chapter of his book
summarizing a number of the political issues of governmental
reform within a theoretical framework which bears a close
relationship to that presented by Wood (Reading 12). Finally

Gans' article (Reading 18) provides a focus for much of the philosophy of this reader. His article on 'Planning for People, Not Buildings' was not one of the essays reviewed by Pahl (Reading 3) but the theme is similar and Gans discusses in turn the physical bias of planning, his belief that in fact physical planning has little effect, and his conviction that planning has to be more consumer oriented – 'for people' in his own words. In short he takes the (fairly extreme) position that the planner should concern himself more with social and economic policies and less with spatial form, as well as playing down the relationship between spatial and non-spatial policies.

15 A. Dunham

Property, City Planning and Liberty

A. Dunham, 'Property, city planning and liberty', in C. M. Haar (ed.), *Law and Land*, Harvard University Press and MIT, 1964, pp. 28–43.

Planning literature in the United States has, on the whole, been unconcerned with the relationship of city planning to private property and to liberty.[1] Aside from the professional articles about how to plan, about needed factual research and about the use by planners of the techniques of economic analysis used by private owners in making their own land-use decisions, the planning literature shows three phases of intellectual thought: there is, first, the phase, heavy in the first twenty-five years of planning but still an undercurrent in the literature, of trying to demonstrate the need for planning controls from the picture of chaos and squalor with which our nineteenth century cities leave us in the twentieth century;[2] there is, second, a great deal of theorizing about the place of the city planner in the power structure of urban government (is he, for example, to make governmental decisions himself, or is he only to make advisory plans on the basis of which action may or may not be taken by municipal officials as they choose?)[3]; third, there is something in the literature from time to time about the need to permit the people to participate in planning in order that plans may be democratically arrived at.[4] Thus the planner has not been con-

1. If the 1950 issues of the *Journal of the American Institute of Planners* can be taken as a fair sample, the following is revealed: out of seventeen main articles two dealt with general principles none of which concern the subject at hand, eight with specific planning, three with the need for research, one with the problem of putting plans into effect, that is, with governmental machinery and the balance were general articles. The editorials consisted of exhortations on the need for planners to formulate agreed objectives, on how to get citizens to participate in planning and on the danger of rigidity and the like.

2. Illustrative of this approach is Mumford (1943).

3. The best general treatment of this problem may be found in Walker (1950). For the analysis of the place of a particular city planning commission in the power structure of government, see Sayre and Kaufman (1960).

4. See generally Woodbury (1953a and 1953b). See also Duggar (1957).

cerned about what should constitute the respective spheres of private decisions concerning land use and of decisions centrally arrived at, but rather has proceeded with theoretical discussion on the assumption that centrally arrived-at decisions are made, and the problem from the planning point of view is to have the planner participate and yet to have the people participate as well through governmental machinery. About the turn of the century a satirical German weekly said that an economist should be defined as a person who went around with a ruler measuring workers cottages, finding them all too small. A modern paraphrase of this might be that a city planner in the United States is a person who goes around taking pictures of all of the chaos in our cities and of all of the good things in our cities, finding the chaos due to private decisions and the good things due to centrally arrived-at decisions, at least if the planner and the people participated in the decision-making.

My topic is more or less virgin territory for American planning. It is my impression as well that not until the catastrophe of the Town and Country Planning Act of 1947 did British planners exhibit any real interest in the delimitation of a sphere for private decision-making.

In fairness to professional planners it must be admitted that until recently economists[5] and lawyers[6] gave regrettably little attention to the different aspects of urbanism. Theoretical economists on the whole followed Adam Smith's view that the problems of municipal government, 'to wit, the proper method of carrying dirt from the streets and the execution of justice (in city regulation) . . . though useful, are too mean to be considered in a (theoretical) discourse of this kind' (Smith, 1896, p. 154). Lawyers, too, are to blame. We have recognized the untruth of Blackstone's statement that the right of property is 'that sole and despotic dominion which one man claims and exercises over the

5. While we have in the United States a school of 'land economists', Professor Anthony Scott of the University of Toronto has pointed out that this whole school largely traces back to the concern of America for particular land problems such as conservation. See Scott (1955).

6. While it is true that much of the land planning in the United States can be said to be the product of lawyers such as E. M. Bassett, Alfred Bettman, Philip Nichols and Frank B. Williams, the legal profession as a whole did not become interested in the theoretical aspects of the relation of law to city planning until much more recently. The earliest theoretical discussion may be found in Freund (1904). More recently see the articles by Haar referred to in note 9 and 13 and my own articles, Dunham (1958a, 1958b and 1959).

external things of the world, in total exclusion of the right of any other individual in the universe' (Blackstone, 1809); from time immemorial the common law and statute law in England and the United States have regulated land use.[7] It was a true statement only in the sense that all of the great legal texts on property concentrated on the transfer of rights and the creation of estates and left to others, primarily to writers in torts, the task of dealing scantily with land use,[8] which the property writers treated as analogous to assault and battery and other personal injuries.

In constructing a theory about the relation of property law to planning, we are not interested in the formal shape of property law – in such matters as estates, future interests and formalities of transfer. Bentham tells us that property is nothing more than the expectation of deriving a certain advantage from a thing which the law allows us (Bentham, 1864, pp. 111–13). We cannot be interested in the technical legal aspects of property, for, under Bentham's definition, private property today includes whatever limits on expectations planning law has imposed, rightly or wrongly, during the past fifty years. We must be concerned with a deeper question: what expectations should the law allow a private citizen? To answer this question, in relation to planning, we must think a bit about economics and the philosophy of liberty.

A first point is this: if property is the established expectations which the law gives an owner, then as long as the owner is not commanded to use his property in a particular way and is secured some freedom of choice as to its use, it cannot be said that government restriction on land use has in it any denial of private property. Prohibition on the use of a person as a slave, on the private use of land as a fort, military establishment, brewery, or as a factory in a residential district, may or may not be wise economically, may or may not be a serious interference with personal liberty, but such prohibition merely subtracts from an owner's expectations of enjoying a thing. Any particular use an

7. For examples of early legislation, see An Act for Rebuilding the City of London, 19 Car. 2, c. 3 (1679): An Act for Prevention of Common Nuisances arising by Slaughterhouses, etc., Acts and Resolves of the Province of Massachusetts Bay (1692).

8. More recently property books deal to some extent at least with the problem of land-use control. See, for example, Cheshire (1958); Megarry (1955); Powell (1949), particularly vol. 6 (1958). It should be noted, however, that a standard treatise on real property published in 1952 treated land-use problems as an afterthought in a separate volume published in 1954, and even then had no material on city planning.

owner can or cannot make of his property is not of importance to the existence of private property. This does not mean that a governmental decision to remove some one or more expectations from those which an owner previously had may not be costly to the individual or to society. We shall have more to say on this later.

A second point is this: society's objective in imposing a restriction of land use would likewise seem irrelevant to the system of private property. However wise or unwise for reasons of liberty and economic well-being it may be for a government planner to impose the ideas of a Geddes, Mumford, Stein or Howard on the physical and social organization of a city, it is of little concern to the system of private property. That there is such a restriction is not important, but, and this is my main thesis, how that restriction is imposed is important for a system of property, and, as we shall see, how it is imposed, what the restriction is, and for what reason it is imposed may be important for liberty as well.

Private property and planning

Prior to the advent of planning legislation about fifty years ago there was in the United States a great deal of land-use regulation (much more than many of us are inclined to credit), which on the whole presented no serious problems for private property as an institution. The regulation was stated abstractly, providing that in certain circumstances the actions of individuals must satisfy certain conditions. Thus a fire district would prohibit wooden buildings beyond a well-defined line in a municipality; or the regulations specified that a saloon could not be located within a given distance of a church or school. So far as private property was concerned, these regulations merely subtracted from the owner's possible expectations one or more methods of land use. So far as the owner was concerned, they became part of the data upon which he could base his decisions. So far as the lawmaker was concerned, he did not try to foresee the effect of these laws on particular people or for what purposes he would use them. The law prohibited wooden houses; it did not prohibit them unless the owner was building a house for his widowed mother or low-cost housing or a house of religion. Neither did the application of the law turn on the lawgiver's ends. It prohibited saloons near a church even if the operator of the saloon was determined by all observable standards to be a good churchgoer, even a member of the adjacent church. The owners built brick houses or buildings because they, not the lawgiver, wanted brick houses. These laws provided fixed features in the owner's environment, and although they eliminated certain expectations previously open to him they did not, as a rule, limit the choice to some specific action that somebody else wanted him to take.

The other type of restriction on private land use was judge-imposed through such common-law rules as nuisance. While these restrictions were admittedly less certain than the legislation previously referred to, the ideal was the same predictability and objectivity. Witness the requirement of written opinions containing reasons applicable to other situations, the principle of *stare decisis*, the assertion that judges were not making law but following previously established general principles and, most importantly, the principle that the judge had no purpose in mind when he imposed a restriction.

In its origin in the United States about fifty years ago planning law also was in the tradition of this legislation. The municipality was divided into districts, with the permitted and prohibited uses and structures fairly clearly set forth. While the ordinance might delete one or more expectations of an owner, thereafter within the bounds set by the zoning law the owner's choice was unlimited, not subject to the will or objective of any other person. Thus one of the fathers of planning in the United States, Edward M. Bassett, could object to a zoning ordinance which authorized an administrator to adjust the regulations at district boundary lines, on the ground that 'every owner is entitled to know the exact boundary line. In building he can take into account the likelihood of the boundary being altered at some future day' (1940, p. 51). This principle of certainty and limited administrative discretion was also found in the official map acts and the early subdivision regulations. This attitude toward the form of the zoning regulation may also explain the unwillingness of our courts to be concerned with the requirement in almost all enabling acts that zoning be done in accordance with a 'comprehensive plan'. While such a plan might be useful in a constitutional argument as to reasonableness, it had no other value, for the governing law was the zoning ordinance passed by the legislative body[9] and not the asserted objectives or policies on which the planning officials had based the ordinance.

This general attitude toward law was also shown in the original

9. See Haar (1955a).

legislation authorizing creation of master or comprehensive plans. Bassett objected very strongly to the adoption of the plan or policy by the legislature, and thought it proper that it should be adopted, if at all, by the planning commission. To him, the plan was policy on which law *could* be based, but it was not law because it was policy of the moment.[10]

More recently there has been a shift in attitude. Two instances may set the problem: the rise of a list of special uses for which development permission is needed,[11] and the increase in clauses in subdivision regulations which permit the administrator, usually the planning commission, to refuse permission on the ground that the proposed development does not conform to its master plan or policy.[12]

This raises serious implications for a system of private property. While private property does not presuppose freedom to engage in any particular action, it does presuppose an area of activity within which the private volition of an owner is free of arbitrary decision by others, that is, free of a decision based on another's policy.

This is one important aspect of the discussion initiated by Professor Haar (1955b) of the master plan as an 'impermanent constitution'.[13] Although it moves quickly into another important question concerning democratic ideals such as the propriety of a plan having coercive effect if not adopted by the legislature, much of Professor Haar's discussion concerns the need for a rule of law by which to judge action.

He seems to recognize that a plan should be more than advisory so that it may become part of the owner's arsenal of facts on which to exercise choices concerning land use and, more importantly, part of the material which a court may use to determine whether the administrator is acting in accordance with law. This can mean only that it is more important for private property that an owner have a set of expectations on which he can act than that he be permitted to do any particular thing. I might add that

10. See Bassett (1938); Bassett, Williams, Bettman and Whitten (1934).

11. See Blucher (1955); Babcock (1959); For a judicial discussion of the matter, see Ward vs Scott, 11 NJ 117, 93 A 2d 385 (1952).

12. See Lautner (1941); see also Washington Revised Code (1951), § 58.16.060, which authorizes the planning commission in approving or rejecting a subdivision to 'consider all other facts deemed by it relevant and designed to indicate whether or not the public interest will be served by the plotting, subdividing or dedication'.

13. Haar (1955b, p. 353).

as far as private property is concerned it is not material whether the master plan be adopted by a legislature or a planning commission; the important thing is that it be adopted without knowledge of any particular case of land use; that it be definite enough so that it can be objectively determined whether administrative action conforms to it or not; and that it be adhered to when government action is taken.

We have developed various constitutional rules about unauthorized delegation of power – that there must be standards imposed on an administrator, and the like. While many cases have been decided on the basis of the ordinance giving the administrator standards by which to judge an application for a special exception or use, the important point of policy is that there must be some standards in order to give private property any meaning.

So far I have not been concerned with the merits of any planning scheme because the merits are not particularly relevant to the institution of property. That the town planning schemes of an Olmstead or Geddes are part of an anti-economic movement or present serious implications for personal liberty does not necessarily mean that the system of private property is endangered if the scheme is adopted by some government authority.

Economic policy and land-use restrictions

If we shift from thinking about the nature of private property to thinking about the relationship between land-use restrictions and economic policy, then the character of the governmental restriction rather than its extensiveness or form becomes important. The institution of private property can survive if Lewis Mumford's conception of land use is adopted with certainty and inflexibility, but if we consider economic policy we must pass judgment on the merits of his plan (1943). Judgment must be passed not only from an economic point of view, but also from the point of view of liberty.

Planning legislation in the United States, as distinguished from its administration, has made no frontal attack on the historic method of obtaining the optimum social welfare; it has accepted the principle that market prices are on the whole the best signals toward optimum welfare. This is not to say that the market pricing system, utilizing a host of individual decisions made for one's own ends, always operates at its optimum; price signals for example may not be received by those who make the decisions.

Urban living is a case in point. The enormous increase in productivity made possible by urban industry has been obtained at great costs which are to a large extent communal: they do not always fall on those who cause them and may have to be borne by all. A level of poverty perhaps tolerable in a rural atmosphere produces outward signs of squalor which are shocking to fellow men; the squalor and lack of amenities in urban living may make demands on community services beyond those for which the community is paid. Thus in many respects the contiguity of city life invalidates the assumptions underlying the market-pricing system. We have a proposition then which fits into the assumptions of the market system: the completely unrestricted use of urban land by its owners according to what each deems to be in his own interest leads to results injurious to all owners and consumers as a group. For the market to bring about an efficient co-ordination of individual endeavors, both private owners and the authorities controlling communal property must be compelled to take into account the effects of their action on other property. Insofar as planning legislation is negative and denies an owner a particular use in a particular location because of the cost which it imposes on others, it is operating within market principles by making the restricted activity settle in a more costly location and thus bear the costs formerly thrown on others.

The main theoretical difficulty comes in distinguishing restrictions imposed for this purpose from those imposed in order to secure a desired development, such as a Mumford plan. Are planning restrictions imposed on residential construction in industrial districts designed to relieve industry of the adverse effect of proximity to residences, or are they designed to obtain the advantages of reserving land for future industrial growth? Are the requirements in a subdivision development for long curving blocks with lots of greenery imposed because any other layout will cause harm to persons and property in the community who do not choose to live in the subdivision, or are they imposed because the planning authority desires that kind of layout for its own sake, or because it will enhance the value of neighboring properties?

The practical problem in the United States comes from the fact that under our written constitutions, as interpreted, we have not as yet been able to subject planning decisions by government authority to the tests of the market place. Most planning measures will enhance the value of some individual properties and reduce that of others. If the measure is to be beneficial to society the sum of the gains must exceed the sum of the losses, and to assure ourselves that this calculation is made as accurately as possible, the gains and losses must accrue to the planning authority. Why not impose a Mumford plan on private landowners if the governmental decider has no costs to bear? And if a Mumford plan is indeed beneficial to neighboring land why not coerce an owner to use the plan so as to benefit persons who happen to own the neighboring land?

An effective system would require that the government authority have the power and responsibility to charge the individual owner for the increase in value of his property due to a planning scheme (even if the benefit accrues against the will of some of the owners) and the power and duty to compensate those whose property has suffered. That we do not as yet have an effective way of achieving this balance is in part due to our constitutional history.

Although our colonial and postrevolutionary legal system offered many devices to offset these gains and costs, sometime in the early 1800s our courts adopted a set of rules which made this all but impossible.[14] In the first place, the courts tried to prevent government from expropriating property even though government was willing to pay a fair market price. They did this by adopting a rule of constitutional law that property could not be taken unless the end result was public enjoyment of the property taken in the same physical sense that a public highway or public building results in enjoyment by the public at large (Nichols, 1950). The effect of this requirement of 'public use' was to prevent government from charging an individual owner for the benefit of a planning measure by expropriating his property at market price, then imposing the planning measure, and finally reselling the property to him or others at a price which reflected the benefit conferred. True, some of this could be accomplished through use of special improvement districts, but these operate only where a physical improvement is made.

The second legal difficulty imposed by the courts was a narrow interpretation of the government's duty of compensating those whose property had suffered from governmental action. Unless land was taken in a physical sense, many of our courts said, there was no constitutional requirement of compensation for damage which was called 'consequential' (Freund, 1904).

14. See Nichols (1950).

The first of these two legal difficulties is the more serious because it imposes a real limitation on governmental power, but we are beginning to extricate ourselves by interpreting 'public use' to be equivalent to public purpose. Thus, the United States Supreme Court recently permitted the federal government in the District of Columbia to condemn land near the capitol for the purpose of resale to a developer who would, by providing newer buildings and better arrangement, improve the amenities of the capitol.[15] Presumably because of other doctrines now worked out, the government in this case could have purchased the neighboring area not to be redeveloped and sold it back to the present or other owners at the increased value caused by the first redevelopment project.

The second of the legal difficulties is less serious because even if there is no duty to pay for consequential damage, there is no serious limitation on the power of government to choose to compensate those who suffer loss from a planning decision.[16] Government could, if it wished, establish a procedure similar to some provisions in English planning acts providing for a reverse expropriation – in certain circumstances a private citizen injured by a planning decision could compel government to buy his land.

The need to have gains and losses accrue to the same deciders is all that is necessary to have a proper accounting. Nothing is needed as complicated as the British Town and Country Planning Act of 1947, which attempted to secure for government not only the increase in value attributable to a planning decision but any increase in value, while at the same time putting all risk of loss on the owners, nor as monopolistic as that same act which gave government sole power to decide new uses of land in England.

The danger to economic policy and probably to private property and certainly to liberty comes in our system from not co-ordinating gains and losses, and also from the desire of many planners to be released from the necessity of counting all the costs of the scheme. We do not have anything comparable to the British planning acts, which compel the planning authority to buy land from a private owner if planning permission is refused. If I read the British planning literature correctly, this provision has had a salutary effect on planning decisions because of the

15. See Berman vs Parker, 348 US 26 (1954).

16. Many states have amended their constitutions (for example, Illinois Constitution, article 2, § 13) or have by statute given a right to damages for injury in some cases.

necessity of counting costs; but I also read it as reflecting the same desire to be relieved of this necessity.

This desire, current in the planning literature of both countries, to be released from the necessity of counting all costs of a scheme ought, in my opinion, to be treated with great suspicion. If it is democracy we seek, nothing can be better calculated to induce voters to make rational choices than to compel them to ask: Do I really want this kind of development, considering its costs? If it is equality we seek, the necessity of government's counting costs assures that the costs will be borne equally throughout society. Although it is generally made to appear that reducing the costs which government must bear effects an absolute reduction of costs, in reality such a scheme merely transfers the costs to the shoulders of some private owner and then disregards them. The problem here, although often couched in the language of law, is in reality an ethical one of determining whether government should pay for the external costs which its decisions impose on others to the same extent that other planning legislation seeks to compel private decision-makers to pay for the diseconomies which their decisions, made in the market, impose on others.

Freedom and land-use restrictions

While the planning literature has expressed little interest in the economic, humanitarian and private-property implications of planning decisions, it does abound with the terminology and criteria of private property – albeit used in another context. The literature of private property and of economic policy at times judges the merits or demerits of a proposal in terms of the security, protection and predictability which it brings, and at other times in terms of its flexibility and adaptability. Thus it is said that the security and protection of private property in a market economy gives the economic system its flexibility and adaptability. Planning literature, too, talks about the need for flexibility and adaptability of plans, and about measures to secure and protect plans against inroads. The problem is that the more flexible and adaptable the planning scheme the greater may be the restriction on liberty; or to state it conversely, the more coercive the system may become.

I am not at this point using liberty or freedom as a function of the number of courses of action open after a planning decision has been made; rather I am using it to indicate the extent to which the pattern of conduct is of a man's own design and directed toward his own ends rather than toward positions created by others in order that he do what they want. In this sense, whether a man is free depends not on the range of his choice but on whether he can expect to shape his course of action in accordance with his own intentions. The range of physical possibilities from which a person can make an effective choice at a given moment thus has no relation to the freedom we are discussing. The driver of an automobile faced with impending danger who sees only one way to save his life is unquestionably free, though he may have no effective choice.

It should likewise be clear that liberty in this sense is not political liberty. I may enjoy the political liberty to turn the rascals out who have prevented me from building a gasoline station because they do not like gasoline stations, but I would not have freedom or liberty in the sense used here if I nonetheless need the consent of some government official. Nor is liberty used in John Dewey's sense as power to do specific things. In this sense a modern planner, at least quite frequently, has liberty, since he may under a subdivision regulation have power to effect his desire that all subdivisions resemble Radburn.

The problem of liberty or freedom in relation to planning is the inability of a property owner to anticipate the restraints which are to be placed upon him. As Maitland, the great legal historian, said, 'Known general laws, however bad, interfere less with freedom than decisions based on no previously known rule' (1911, p. 80).

As suggested earlier, it is in relation to liberty that we see the real importance of the debate initiated by Professor Haar with our planners concerning the master plan as an impermanent constitution (1955b). Whether restrictions on administrative action should be laid down by the general legislature or whether this function may be delegated bears on the question of democratic control of government but not on the question of freedom. The important point is that there be known rules announced prior to application to which the administrator must adhere. This, I take it, is what Professor Haar is asking for in matters where administrators can approve or reject private decisions concerning land use.

The problem of freedom is also involved in Bassett's very limited conception of city planning, which, as evidenced by his writings and the model city planning enabling act drafted by him,[17] emphasizes the location of public improvements and

17. See US Department of Commerce (1928); see also Bassett (1938).

minimizes the regulation of private land-use decisions. In the one case where the plan deals with major private decisions, the master plan is to be only the basis of the zoning ordinance. This conception reflects the differences in areas of permissible discretion in relation to freedom. Where government is directing and allocating resources put at its disposal, the professional administrator properly enjoys unlimited discretion in deciding what tasks to undertake and the means to be used in undertaking them. Here policy, meaning the aims of the government of the day, is important. Decisions as to upkeep, design and location of roads and public building are necessarily of this kind and may be as flexible as the public administrator wants. Here government has little coercive power over the acts of private citizens and their own decisions concerning land use. Where this type of administrative decision impinges on the private sphere, the principle of no expropriation without just compensation serves as an important restraint on infringements on liberty. This is the case not because the landowner is paid, which justice may require, but because compensation tends to restrict the administrator's interference with the private sphere to cases where the public gain is clearly greater than the harm done by the disappointment of normal individual expectations.

The recent hassle in Illinois, where a community park board decided to condemn land for park purposes after the private developer had decided to build racially integrated housing, is illustrative of the difference. Assume that the purpose of the board's action was the dubious, if not illegal, policy of coercing the owner into adopting the community aims rather than his own. How much greater is the potential restraint on liberty if the community could deny permission to develop on the ground that 'public welfare' would not be served or that the development is 'not in accordance with community plans for development' than if, when it entertains these views, it must compensate the disappointed developer for loss of his development rights!

The difference in the two situations is illustrated also by the difference of the ideal in the two types of community action. The ideal where the administrator can deny permission to develop has been that his action is reviewable by a court in order to determine whether the action is in accordance with a rule of law; but in the case of expropriation the power of a court to control the decision to expropriate is ideally much less, actually not much more than a concept of *ultra vires*.

From the standpoint of freedom an administrator's decision need not be reviewable by a court if it is reviewable by someone as to its conformance with a previously announced rule. We do not have in the United States any procedure for a review of local planning regulations and decisions under those regulations, by another administrator. The fact of review is not enough, however; the scope of the review is important. We do have in our subdivision control decisions in many states (and even in zoning decisions) a procedure whereby the decision of the administrator may be reversed by the local legislative body. But if the reviewing body, be it another administrator or a legislative body, merely substitutes its aim for another, our private citizen is still coerced into doing something because some other person wants it; only if he is reasonably free to do what he wants within the confines of a known rule of law can he be said to be free.

The tendency in American, as in English, planning has been away from these relatively simple concepts of Bassett. From the idea that law, be it legislation or previously announced regulation, should coerce private persons to do or not to do something, we have moved toward wider and wider administrative discretion. Thus many subdivision regulations are so indefinite that the administrator can reject a subdivision unless the private citizen agrees to the administrator's conception of amenities, appropriate layout, or even timing of development. This development parallels the 'special exception' or 'special use' development in the zoning ordinance to which I have referred.

From the standpoint of freedom or liberty it is no defense of this development to require that the administrative discretion be exercised only on the basis of the official's estimate of community sentiment, desires, or aims. Liberty in this sense requires that there be some sphere where a private citizen may serve his own ends and not the ends of state.

Another aspect of freedom or liberty is not as yet involved with planning in the United States, for we have no planning worthy of the name governing areas larger than counties.[18] True, the statute books authorize various forms of regional planning; these almost without exception permit, but do not require, the smaller units of government to participate in such planning if they wish. Insofar as the decision of a small unit of government to restrict certain kinds of private activity within its borders imposes external costs on neighboring areas, a case can be made for

18. See Haar (1957).

planning by some larger unit in order to minimize or equalize the costs. Insofar as the small unit of government provides services of lesser quality than neighboring units, this may increase demands for the services of the neighboring unit and accentuate its governmental problems. It is not uncommon in the United States for prospective home purchasers to shop for schools and other services in deciding the suburb in which to live. This factor would not seem to justify a larger unit of government compelling a community with lesser services to increase the quality or quantity of its services, nor compelling one more attuned to consumer demands to reduce its quality and quantity. Insofar as there is economy in providing services such as water and sewerage for a larger group there is an argument for provision of these services by a larger unit. The question is whether economic forces can be allowed to induce the needed centralization or whether the smaller units should be compelled to join together. Undoubtedly there may be situations where circumstances require such coercion, but they would seem to be very few. Popular literature for regional planning of a coercive variety presents anew the question of individual liberty which we have been discussing, and perhaps another important liberty: freedom to associate with individuals of one's own choosing. The small unit of government serves as an effective check on tendencies to interfere with private choices, just as does the requirement for compensation on expropriation. For if the local unit plans or fails to plan itself so that it discourages economic development or community stability, economic pressures are likely to be a check on its extravagances.

In this paper I have not discussed one topic that interests many American planners, that of the relation of planning to democracy, although I think it could more accurately be termed the relation of planning to the principle that all men should have the same share in making governmental decisions. I have done this because it seems necessary to distinguish political liberty from the ideal of freedom and of private property. It provides no answer to what ought to be the relation of planning to private property and freedom to assert that the coercive decisions are democratically arrived at. We can agree that whenever coercive rules have to be laid down the decision ought to be made by the majority. We can also agree that where there is administrative discretion as to the use of resources subject to governmental control, democratic majorities are a useful method of allocation. When it comes to decisions about how private land ought to be used, democratic procedure is a useful and perhaps the only method available for determining whether a particular decision affects persons other than the deciders. But when it comes to such questions as whether development in a particular area should be sparse, as in a green-belt (as distinguished from a park or public recreation area), or whether industry which has no external effects should be located in an area already heavily developed, we have a question of which procedure best records the wishes of the consumer of the service – a Gallup poll by an administrator, a vote by a representative assembly or the price signals in the market.

Planning in the United States does not yet seem too conscious of the possibility that the price mechanism is a more adaptable and flexible method of land-use allocation than a flexible plan administered by an inflexible administrator. Publicity of bureaucratic decisions is not enough; some philosophy about the relation of planning to liberty and to private property seems in order.[19]

19. The best attempt at presenting the problems of liberty, democracy and property is the imaginary dialogue by Professor Haar (1959, pp. 730 ff.).

References

BABCOCK, R. F. (1959), 'The unhappy state of zoning administration in Illinois', *Univ. of Chicago Law Rev.*, vol. 26, p. 509.

BASSETT, E. M. (1938), *The Master Plan*, Russell Sage Foundation.

BASSETT, E. M. (1940), *Zoning*, Russell Sage Foundation.

BASSETT, E. M., WILLIAMS, F. B., BETTMAN, A., and WHITTEN, R. (1934), *Model Laws for Planning Cities, Countries and States*.

BENTHAM, J. (1862), Theory of Legislation, (ed.) E. Dumont.

BLACKSTONE, X. (1809), Commentaries, vol. 2, 15th edition.

BLUCHER, W. H. (1955), 'Is zoning wagging the dog?', *J. of Planning*, p. 96.

CHESHIRE, G. C. (1958), The Modern Law of Real Property, 8th edn, Butterworth.

DUGGAR, G. (1957), 'Urban renewal re-examined', *J. of Planning*, p. 209.

DUNHAM, A. (1958a), 'Legal and economic bases for city planning', *Columbia Law Rev.*, vol. 58, p. 650.

DUNHAM, A. (1958b), 'City planning: an analysis of the content of the master plan', *J. of Law and Econ.*, vol. 1, p. 170.

DUNHAM, A. (1959), 'Flood control via the police power', *Univ. of Penn. Law Rev.*, vol. 107, p. 1098.

FREUND, E. (1904), *The Police Power*, Callaghan.

HAAR, C. M. (1955a), 'In accordance with a comprehensive plan', *Harvard Law Rev.*, vol. 68, p. 1154.

HAAR, C. M. (1955b), 'The master plan: an impermanent constitution', *Law and Contemp. Probs.*, vol. 20, p. 353.

HAAR, C. M. (1957), 'Regionalism and realism in land-use planning', *University of Pennsylvania Law Rev.*, vol. 105, p. 515.

HAAR, C. M. (1959), *Land-Use Planning*, Little, Brown.

LAUTNER, H. W. (1941), *Subdivision Regulations*, Public Administration Service, Chicago.

MAITLAND, E. W. (1911), *Collected Papers*, Cambridge University Press.

MEGARRY, R. E. (1955), *A Manual of the Law of Real Property*, 2nd edn, Stevens.

MUMFORD, L. (1943), *The Social Foundations of Post-War Building*, Faber & Faber.

NICHOLLS, P. (1950), *Eminent Domain*, 3rd edn, J. L. Sackman and R. D. van Brundt (eds), Bender.

POWELL, R. R. B. (1949), *Real Property*, Bender.

SAYRE, W. S., and KAUFMAN, H. (1960), *Governing New York City*, Russell Sage Foundation.

SCOTT, A. (1955), *Natural Resources: Economics of Conservation*, University of Toronto Press.

SMITH, A. (1896), *Lectures on Justice, Police, Revenue and Arms*, edited by J. C. Cannan, Oxford University Press.

US DEPARTMENT OF COMMERCE (1928), *A Standard City Planning Enabling Act*, Washington, D.C.

WALKER, R. A. (1950), *The Planning Function in Urban Government*, 2nd edn, University of Chicago Press.

WOODBURY, C. (1953a), *The Future of Cities and Urban Redevelopment*, University of Chicago Press.

WOODBURY, C. (1953b), *Urban Redevelopment, Problems and Practices*, University of Chicago Press.

A. Dunham 295

16 D. Harvey

Social Processes, Spatial Form and the Redistribution of Real Income in an Urban System

Extract from D. Harvey, 'Social processes, spatial form and the redistribution of real income in an urban system', in M. Chisholm *et al.*, *Regional Forecasting*, Butterworth, 1971, pp. 270–300.

Some features governing the redistribution of income

[. . .] It is perhaps invidious to isolate out any particular features which account for the redistribution of income. Nothing less than complete understanding of how an urban system works is really required. But there is a number of recurrent themes in what follows and it is useful to isolate these before proceeding, since by so doing we can avoid repetitious discussion.

The speed of change and the rate of adjustment in an urban system

Much of our analytic understanding of the urban system comes from equilibrium analysis. Most of these equilibrium analyses seek to define an optimal allocation of resources (e.g. land resources) under conditions where the *distribution of income is given*. Most of the analyses of the urban housing market, for example, indicate the structure and form of equilibrium assuming a given distribution of income. Only under this assumption is it possible to determine what is usually termed a 'Pareto optimum' (a situation in which nobody can become better off from moving without making somebody else worse off). These models provide us with important insights into the allocation mechanisms which underlie the formation of an urban structure, but they tell us little about how a given distribution of income comes about. Even if we accept the assumption of a given distribution of income, however, we still have to consider the speed with which equilibrium is achieved.

It has been an underlying assumption of much of the work on urban modelling that some kind of natural equilibrium can be identified in an urban system. This is true of both the deterministic models of urban structure developed by writers such as Alonso (1964) and Mills (1969) and the statistical models of equilibrium assumed in gravity type and entropy maximizing models (Wilson, 1970). These equilibrium analyses have undoubtedly provided us with some important insights into the urban systems, but I believe such equilibrium models can be misleading if they are applied without considerable qualification. The main question here, of course, is the speed with which different parts of an urban system can adjust to the changes occurring within it. The changes have been rapid in recent decades but there is considerable evidence that the adjustment process takes a relatively long time to work itself out. Furthermore, different parts of the urban system have different capacities for adjustment. Some aspects of urban organization respond immediately whereas others respond very sluggishly. It is therefore misleading to think of adjustment in the urban system as a homogenous process proceeding at a unified rate. This varying speed of adjustment means that there are substantial differentials in the disequilibrium in the urban system at any one point in time. To give a simple-minded example: it is clear that there has not been an equal response in the urban population to the potential of mobility associated with the auto-mobile. The time lag is anything from twenty to forty years between different groups in the population. It would be very surprising indeed if the better educated and more affluent groups had not taken advantage of this time lag to further their own interests and enhance their own income. The allocation of resources then takes place as an adjustment to this new income distribution and a cumulative process of increasing inequality of income distribution gets under way. This is a crude example, but I think it is very general. Certain groups, particularly those with financial resources and education, are able to adapt far more rapidly to a change in the urban system and these differential abilities to respond to change are a major source in generating inequalities. For this reason I believe that it is very important to accept the notion that any urban system is in a permanent state of differential disequilibrium (by which I mean that different parts of it are approaching equilibrium at different rates). The speed of change and the relative capacities of elements in the urban system to adapt are very important features in the analysis which follows. This implies that we cannot analyse our problem via some general equilibrium framework, although this does not prevent us in any way from making use of some of the theoretical and empirical insights generated from equilibrium analyses.

It is generally agreed that accessibility and proximity are important features of any urban system. I shall briefly examine both from the point of view of households acting as consumers.

Accessibility to employment opportunities, resources, welfare services, can be obtained only at a price and this price is generally equated with the cost of overcoming distance, of using time, and the like. But it is by no means easy to measure the price which people pay. Consider, for example, the difficulty of putting some value upon time in transport studies. But there are other even more complicated problems involved here, for the social price which people are forced to pay for access to certain facilities is a very complicated thing which can vary from the simple direct cost involved in transport to the emotional and psychological price imposed upon an individual who has an intense resistance to doing something (the kind of price which may be extorted, for example, from someone who has to take a means test to qualify for welfare). These social and psychological barriers are important. Any discussion of accessibility, therefore, requires that we answer a fundamental question regarding the meaning of 'distance' and 'space' in an urban system – a problem which I have examined in detail elsewhere (Harvey, 1970; see also the excellent review by Buttimer, 1969). In this essay I am going to use the term 'proximity' to refer to a rather different phenomenon than accessibility. By proximity, I mean the effects of being close to something which people do not make any direct use of. A household may thus find itself proximate to a source of pollution, to a source of noise, or to a run-down environment. This proximity tends to impose certain costs upon the household (e.g. cleaning and laundry bills, sound-proofing etc.).

It should be self-evident that as we change the spatial form of city (by relocating housing, transport routes, employment opportunities, sources of pollution etc.) so we change the price of accessibility and the cost of proximity for any one household. We will likewise find that these prices and costs are a function of the social attitudes of the population at large insofar as psychological factors play a part. The balance of these changes clearly has the potential for bringing about quite substantial redistributions of income.

Externality effects

The activity of any one element in an urban system may generate certain unpriced and perhaps non-monetary effects upon other elements in the system. These effects are usually termed 'externalities', 'spill-over effects', or 'third-party effects'. Mishan (1969, p. 184) states:

External effects may be said to arise when relevant effects on production and welfare go wholly or partially unpriced. Being outside the price system such external effects are sometimes looked upon as the by-products, wanted or unwanted, of other people's activities that immediately or indirectly affect the welfare of individuals.

Such external effects can arise from both private and public activity. Some of the simplest examples can be found in the pollution field, for waste discharge into water and into the air are classic examples of by-product effects which, until recently, have benefits according to whether the producer or the consumer is affected and according to the nature of the effect. A hydroelectric power operation, for example, may create positive benefits in the way of flood control and recreational opportunities. Waste discharge may create external losses through environmental degradation. Casual observation of urban problems indicates that there is a whole host of externality effects which have to be taken account of – a fact which is implicitly recognized in Lowry's (1965, p. 158) comment that 'in the city everything affects everything else'. Many of these relationships are transmitted as third-party effects. Until recently, however, the role of externalities in an urban system has largely been ignored. But recent statements have drawn attention to the fact that 'external economies and diseconomies are a pervasive and important feature in the urban scene' (Hoch, 1969, p. 91; see also Perloff, 1969, p. 9; Margolis, 1965; 1968; Mishan, 1967, pp. 74-99; Rothenberg, 1967). I think it is a reasonable working hypothesis that 'as societies grow in material wealth the incidence of these effects grows rapidly' (Mishan, 1969, p. 184). In urban systems it seems reasonable to suppose that the larger and more complex they are the greater is the significance of externality effects. In what follows I shall tend to the view that much of what goes on in a city (particularly in the political arena) can be interpreted as an attempt to organize the distribution of externality effects to gain income advantages. Insofar as these attempts are successful, they are a source of income inequality. Even if this interpretation be not accepted, however, there are still some vast unanswered questions concerning the redistributive effects of decisions made in the public sector of an urban system (Thompson, 1965, p. 118; Margolis, 1965).

The significance of these externality effects for an economic analysis of urban structure cannot be underrated. The larger these externality effects are 'in range and magnitude the smaller is the faith that can be reposed in the allocative virtues of the market mechanism even when working under ideal conditions' (Mishan, 1969, p. 181). The inability of the market mechanism to allocate resources efficiently when externalities are present has posed a major problem for economic theory. From a policy view-point, it has also provided a rationale for public interference with the market mechanism and it has also led into the thorny question of who should be responsible (and how) for the production of public goods. The externality problem has therefore received considerable attention from economists in the past decade (see the review by Mishan, 1969, chapter 7; and the work of Buchanan, 1968a). Almost all of this extensive literature has focused on the allocation problems posed by externalities and very little attention has been paid to the distributional effects mainly because any theory of the distribution of external costs and benefits involves those ethical and political judgements about the 'best' distribution of income which most of us prefer to avoid. The economic theory of external effects does not tell us all we want to know when it comes to distribution. But it does provide us with some insights into the problem of how externalities arise and how arguments over their allocation can be resolved by resorting to a game-theoretic framework for decision-making (Davis and Whinston, 1962).

It is useful to begin by dividing goods into purely private goods (which can be produced and consumed without any third-party effects being present) and purely public goods (which, once pro-duced, are freely available to everyone). As Buchanan (1968a, pp. 56–7) points out, however, most of the interesting cases lie between these two extremes – i.e., goods which are partly private and partly public. It is of interest to note that one example of an 'impure' public good used by Buchanan is a locational one. The very fact of location of a public facility such as a fire station (or for that matter any public service) means that the population does not enjoy exactly homogenous quality and quantity of fire pro-tection as far as consumption is concerned, even though they have the same quantity and quality of fire protection available to them in terms of production. From the point of view of distri-bution and consumption, therefore, location is an absolutely vital factor to be considered when we seek to understand the impact of externality effects in a city system. From the point of view of the production of public goods, location may be irrelevant. The recent shift towards decentralization of city services may thus be seen as a shift from a policy based on the production of public goods to a policy based on the consumption of public goods. To understand the distributional impact it is important to combine the notions of accessibility and proximity developed earlier with the notion of an impure public good. All localized public goods are impure and the externality exists as a 'spatial field' of effects. We might generalize these spatial fields by distance-decay functions or by diffusion equations (such as those which describe the general field of external costs imposed by a source of atmospheric pollution). These spatial fields of externality effects will vary in intensity and extent, varying from the influence of a derelict property on the values of the adjacent properties to the extensive field of influence of airport noise. These externality fields can be positive or negative or, as in the case of an airport, both (since an airport is a nuisance from the point of view of pollution and noise close by but has important benefits for employment and movement). We know very little about the shape and form of these externality fields in an urban environment. But there can be no doubt that their location has a very powerful effect upon the real income of the individual. Changes in these externality fields can be a factor in the redistribution of income and, hence, a potential source of income inequality. The political process has a profound influence over the location of external benefits and costs. Indeed, a case can be made for regarding local political activity as the basic mechanism for allocating the spatial externality fields in such a way as to reap indirect income advantages.

The redistributive effects of the changing location of jobs and housing

Cities have grown very rapidly in the past twenty years or so and this growth has resulted in some very significant changes in the spatial form of the city. There has thus been (and always presumably will be) a significant reorganization in the location and distribution of various activities in the city system. It is very easy to regard these changes as somehow 'natural' and 'right' and simply a manifestation of adjustment in the urban system to changing technology, changing demand patterns, and the like. From the policy point of view, however, it should be clear that these adjustments in the spatial form of the city are likely to bring about a redistribution of income in a variety of ways. It will not be possible in this essay to discuss all the ways in which this might occur. I shall, therefore, proceed largely by way of examples.

The changing location of economic activity in a city means a changing location of job opportunities. The changing location of residential activity means a changing location of housing opportunities. Both of these changes are likely to be associated with changing expenditures on transport. Changes in transport availability certainly affect the cost of obtaining access to job opportunities from housing locations. These changes are fairly well understood (indeed they are invariably built into any model of urban growth) but their implications for the redistribution of income are not always so well understood. Consider, for example, the typical situation in many American cities in which there has been a very rapid suburbanization in both the location of residences and the location of employment opportunities (Kain, 1968; Kerner Commission Reports, 1968). If we consider the way in which the location of jobs (by category) and housing (by type) has changed, together with the typical adjustments in transport facilities, it will be clear that a redistribution of wealth has occurred. There is considerable evidence that the supply of low income housing is less than elastic (Muth, 1969, p. 128) and that it is locationally fixed partly by the characteristic pattern of the housing stock available in any city and partly by the existence of a strong social contiguity constraint. For these reasons, we can expect that the main source of supply of low-income housing will be in central city areas. The urban system seems to have reacted very sluggishly indeed to the demand for low-income housing in suburban areas. The difficulty of expanding the supply in the inner city (partly due to institutional constraints such as zoning regulations) means that poor quality, low-income housing is relatively high priced and frequently more profitable for property owners than we would expect under true equilibrium conditions (Muth, 1969, p. 126). Low income families therefore have little option but to locate in the relatively high priced inner city. In most American cities, of course, this condition has been exacerbated by the lack of an open housing market for the negroes who, of course, just happen to constitute a large segment of the poor. Meanwhile most of the growth in new employment has been in the suburban ring and hence the low-income groups have gradually been cut off from new sources of employment. They have had to resort to the local employment opportunities in the fairly stagnant industrial areas of the inner city or in the CBD, which in any case only offers a small proportion of its employment in the unskilled, low-income category. By contrast, residents in the suburban communities have a far wider range of options open to them. They can make use of rapid transit facilities into the CBD, they can seek employment locally in growing suburban employment centres, or they can make use of the pattern of ring-roads and beltways to move around the suburban ring in search of employment opportunities.

The process of relocation within the urban system has thus served to improve the options for the affluent suburbanite and cut down the possibilities for the low-income family in the inner city. This situation could be partly counteracted by transport policy but by and large that policy has facilitated the existing trend rather than counteracted it. Meyer (1968, p. 68) thus comments on the implications of developing different kinds of urban transport system:

It should be quite clear that since the groups served by these . . . different basic urban transportation systems are rather different, the incidence of benefits derived from improvements in these systems will vary considerably. For example, improvement in the long distance, high performance suburb to downtown system will tend primarily to benefit higher income groups. To the extent that development of these systems is subsidized from public funds, the implicit income transfer probably would be regressive. By contrast, expenditures aimed at improving conventional short-haul central city transit will almost certainly benefit mostly low- to middle-income groups.

Meyer goes on to comment that the one kind of system which has been very weakly developed (and in most cases totally neglected) is the *inside-out system* for conveying people from central city areas to job opportunities in the suburbs:

The Negro female domestic working in a suburban home and living in a centrally located ghetto is the archetype: today, however, she is increasingly joined by male Negroes because employment opportunities in manufacturing, inter-city transportation and even wholesaling and retailing are increasingly found at suburban locations whereas housing opportunities remain restricted to the central ghetto (p. 68).

In general, the adjustments to transport systems have favoured suburban areas and neglected the needs of inner city areas as far as access to employment opportunities is concerned. But even if transport policy reversed this trend, there is something paradoxical about expecting low-income households, whose rationale for locating in the inner city in the first place (we are told) depended upon minimizing their outlays on transport cost, to lay out the expenditure necessary to reach suburban employment

D. Harvey 303

centres simply because the housing market cannot adjust (in terms of quantity or location) to the changing location of employment. This seems a classic case of the inflexibility of a city's spatial form generating almost permanent disequilibrium in the city social system. From the policy point of view, this indicates the need for public interference in the housing market (by, for example, constructing low-income housing close to suburban employment opportunities). Otherwise, there seems little hope of achieving the so-called 'natural equilibrium solution' in any reasonable time period, even if we concede that this natural equilibrium is one which is socially acceptable.

The general picture which emerges from this brief survey of the mechanisms governing redistribution of income by way of locational shifts can be summarized as follows:

1. The predominantly low-income inner city area has a decreased opportunity to tap new sources of employment since these are mainly located in suburban areas. As a result there is a trend towards a high and growing incidence of unemployment in inner city areas.

2. Because of inelasticity and locational inflexibility in the supply of low-income housing, the low-income household has little opportunity to migrate into suburban areas, and faces rising housing prices in the inner city area.

3. If the low-income household of the inner city does obtain employment in the suburbs, it is faced with greater outlays on transport costs than it should theoretically be able to withstand (a situation which has not been helped by the lack of attention paid to *inside-out* transit systems).

Differential disequilibrium in the spatial form of the city can thus redistribute income. In general, the rich and relatively resourceful can reap great benefits while the poor and necessarily immobile have only restricted opportunities. This can mean a quite substantial regressive redistribution of income in a rapidly changing urban system.

Redistribution and the changing value of property rights

I do not want to examine all aspects of the changing value of property rights and so for illustrative purposes I shall consider that particular property right which remains embedded in the spatial form of the city – land parcels and the buildings thereon. The value of such property rights can change differentially in a city quite markedly over fairly short periods of time. These changes are often thought of as the result of demographic movements, changes in local facilities, swings in fashion, changing investment policies and so on. It is also clearly evident that the value of any one property right is very much affected by the values of neighbouring property rights (Mishan, 1967, pp. 60–63; Muth, 1969, pp. 118–119). The actions of individuals and organizations other than the owner can therefore affect property values. These external effects on the value of a property holder's rights are not under the property holder's control nor are they adequately catered for in the pricing system operating in a supposedly free market. In reality, of course, there is never a free and open housing market nor do all operators in it have perfect information. Also, as we have already seen, there are different elasticities of supply for different types of housing (low-income housing being in general far less responsive to changes in demand than middle- or high-income housing). But even if we assume away these complications, we still have to deal with the theoretically thorny problem of externalities in the housing market. These externalities can arise from many different sources – they are, so to speak, constantly hovering over the land and property market. Insofar as the property market is sensitive to them, we can expect them to influence land values (e.g. a new source of pollution will lead to a decline in land values, a new park facility may lead to a rise in land values). I shall examine these kinds of externality from rather a different point of view in the next section. In this section, I shall concentrate upon the impact these externalities have upon the land market itself. Davis and Whinston (1964, p. 443) put the theoretical problem in these terms:

If independence is present, then individual action is sufficient for the market mechanism to produce prices with sufficient information content to lead the system to Pareto optimality. On the other hand if independence is not present, then purely individual action alone cannot be expected to achieve Pareto-optimality via the unrestricted pricing mechanism.

The meaning given here to independence is that the 'utility payoffs to any person are not affected by the choice of sites made by any other person'. This condition is clearly violated in the housing market since the utility payoffs of one person are very sensitive indeed to the choice of sites made by other people and to the investment decisions of other land and property owners. The problem then arises of how a Pareto-optimum can be achieved.

Government intervention could suffice, provided the central government possessed enough information regarding the varying utility which individuals attach to different sites. Such a situation seems very unlikely (which is not a sufficient reason for dismissing ultimate government intervention in the housing market). But one way of attaining a Pareto-optimum is by group action in the housing market. Thus:

if group action is allowed and if properly defined boundary constraints result in group independence, then prices have sufficient information content to lead to a two-step or multi-step solution. (Davis and Whinston, 1964, p. 433.)

These groups must be organized into a spatial structure of zones and conditions in each zone must have a negligible effect upon conditions in other zones. This independence between zones is, of course, unlikely to hold in practice, but the Davis and Whinston model is interesting in that it illustrates how group action in a housing market can serve to counter the difficult problems posed by the existence of externalities and thereby enhance the value of property rights. Different kinds of coalition can form:

First, consumers who mutually impose interaction costs upon each other might co-ordinate their strategies by selecting sites which are separated by some specific distance, thus reducing interaction costs and raising their security levels. This kind of coalition is called a non-homogenous group. Second, consumers may co-ordinate their strategies by selecting sites which are adjoining and thus excluding from the specified sub-area uses which impose interaction costs upon them. This latter type of coalition is called a homogenous group.

The logical outcome of this is a territorial organization of the city in which each territory contains a group with relatively homogenous values and utility functions and behaviours (insofar as these relate to property). This amounts to a spatial organization designed in such a way as to share out externalities (and create externalities for others). At this juncture, it is interesting to employ that shadowy form of inference (beloved of economists) called by Buchanan (1968a, p. 3) 'inferential prediction' to derive some kind of institutional order which would facilitate sharing externalities in the housing market. Zoning obviously fulfils this role and Davis and Whinston use their model primarily as a justification for zoning operations. Even without this institution, however, it would be tempting to hypothesize that the social organization of a city gains much of its efficiency and stability

through a spatial organization designed to protect external benefits and eliminate external costs as they arise within each community or neighbourhood. Some externalities can effectively be
dealt with in this way (e.g. those associated with the tone of a
neighbourhood). There appears, therefore, to be some theoretical
justification for the existence of territorial social organization in a
city. If we accept this proposition for the moment, it is interesting
to go on and ask how the city can be partitioned up in some
rational manner. Should the communities be large and face the
costs and difficulties of devising a co-operative strategy for a
large number of people or should they be small (and be unable
to control the externalities imposed by other small groups)?
Implicit, therefore, in this whole approach to a rational sharing
of external costs and benefits in the housing market is the awkward question of defining an appropriate regional or territorial
organization. An infinite number of regionalizations could be
devised, but presumably we need to identify that particular
regionalization which maximizes the sum of individual utilities
(Davis and Whinston, 1964, p. 442). But problems of this sort
have no easy or obvious answer.

There are a number of criticisms and qualifications to be made
of the preceding analysis. First, the rationality of the coalition
procedure assumes an equal ability and willingness on the part
of individuals to negotiate. The history of zoning indicates, however, that such a condition is unlikely to hold, particularly in
situations where there is considerable imbalance in the distribution of economic and political power (Makielski, 1966).
Second, we are forced to assume no externality effects between
zones and this condition is usually violated. It is possible to devise
stratagems for 'between-community' conflict resolution and it
should, theoretically, be possible to resolve such conflicts provided an adequate negotiating machinery exists. This raises some
awkward problems about inter-community bargaining processes,
however, and I shall therefore leave this issue for detailed
examination in a later section. It is sufficient to note here that
interdependencies of this sort destroy the conditions for a Pareto
optimum. Third, we have to consider the problem posed by the
assumed simultaneity of site selection. Site selection proceeds
sequentially and this implies that late arrivals in the market 'have
the advantage of additional information since they can observe
what had taken place' (Davis and Whinston, 1964, p. 433). The
pattern of externalities in the housing market is, therefore,

changing sequentially as the occupation of new sites will invariably impose new costs and benefits on sites already developed. If there were no costs or resistance to moving, no problems would arise; but since there are, we cannot expect the market to operate in an optimal fashion. Early-comers to the market will presumably either try to bribe or coerce the late-comers in order to maintain the pattern of externalities to their own benefit. Since the ability to do either of these things depends entirely upon the economic and political power of the groups concerned, we are likely to find a spatial evolution in the housing market and a pricing system which will tend to yield external benefits to the rich and impose external costs upon the poor and politically weak.

What this analysis of the housing market shows us is that a free market cannot give rise to prices conducive to a Pareto optimum and that the housing market, for reasons of its own spatial internal logic, must contain group action if it is to function coherently. This explains, in turn, why the housing market is so peculiarly susceptible to economic and political pressures, since it is only by organizing and applying these pressures that individuals can defend or enhance the value of their property rights relative to those of other individuals. In this, as in most things, it is the economically and politically weak who probably suffer most, unless institutional controls exist to rectify a naturally arising but ethically unacceptable situation.

The real income of an individual can be changed by changing the resources available to him (Thompson, 1965, p. 90). This change can be brought about in a number of ways. The quantity of a free unpriced resource (such as fresh air and quiet) may be altered, the price of a resource may be changed, or the cost of access to a resource may be changed. There is, of course, a connection between the value of land and housing and the price of resources, since changes in the latter are supposedly capitalized by changes in the former. Given the inadequacies in the housing market, we have grounds for thinking that this capitalization is not necessarily rational. In any case, this capitalization only reflects and does not match actual differentials in those operating costs affected by the availability and price of resources. We are, therefore, forced to consider the direct impact upon income distribution of the changing availability and price of resources as an urban system grows and develops.

It is perhaps useful to begin by setting up a working definition for the term 'resource' in an urban system. The concept of a resource as a commodity which enters into production is no longer adequate and probably would have been abandoned long ago were it not for the fact that this concept is basic to conventional forms of economic analysis. Recently, the concept has been extended to things like amenities and open space, but there is still an unfortunate tendency to think of resources as 'natural'. I think it far more satisfactory to regard the city as a gigantic resource system, most of which is man-made. It is also an areally localized resource system in the sense that most of the resources we make use of in the city system are not ubiquitous and their availability, therefore, depends upon accessibility and proximity. The urban system thus contains an areally distributed set of resources of great economic, social, psychological and symbolic significance. Unfortunately, when we get away from the simple production-based definition of resources to a definition linked to consumption, we increase the appropriateness of the concept for examining income inequalities and distribution effects, but decrease our ability to define quantitative measures for resource availability. The reason for this is easy to state. We must first of all take account of the externality effects inherent in the exploitation of any resource. Secondly, we have to face up to the fact that resources are also technological and cultural appraisals – in other words, their quantity is dependent upon the individual preferences existing in the population and the cognitive skills which people possess to help them exploit the resource system.

Natural and man-made resources are usually localized in their distribution. Location decisions, in turn, lead to the further evolution of the spatial availability of man-made resources. A general tenet of location theory and spatial interaction theory is that the local price of a resource is a function of its accessibility and proximity to the user. If accessibility or proximity changes (as it must do every time there is a locational shift) then the local price changes and, by extension, there is an implied change in the real income of the individual. Command over resources, which is our general definition of real income, is, therefore, a function of locational accessibility and proximity. Therefore, the changing spatial form of the city and the continuous process of run-down, renewal and creation of resources within it, will affect the distribution of incomes and it may form a major mechanism for the redistribution of real income. Consider, as an example, the resource of open space.

Let us assume that each person throughout a city system has an identical need for open space. The price of that open space is low if it is accessible and high if it is not. Assume also a complete inelasticity in the demand for open space and we can then treat the variation in access price within the city as a direct effect on income. The allocation of open space in and around the city will thus affect the distribution of income. Clawson (1969, p. 170) writes:

Any use of rural open space, relatively close to the city, as a substitute for or supplement to open space within the city has unfortunate effects in terms of income class participation. Truly poor people have no chance to live in the country and commute to work, nor to play golf in the country. These uses of rural open space are limited to middle and upper income levels. Moreover, if the more articulate and politically most active parts of the total population see such use of rural open space as one major solution to the open space problem, they may neglect or oppose costly programs which would provide at least some open space in the city centres where it is most lacking and most urgently needed.

Obviously, we could write much the same thing about the provision of any facility in an urban system – health and educational services, sanitation services, police and fire services, shopping opportunities, entertainment and other recreational facilities, transport facilities, to say nothing of the intangible features usually subsumed under the catch-all phrase 'quality of urban environment'. Many of these resources are located by public action and it is, therefore, important to recognize that 'the redistributive aspect of general governmental functions is far from trivial and increases with city size' (Thompson, 1965, p. 117). But others result from the decision of private entrepreneurs. No matter who the decision-maker, however, the very act of locational choice has distributional significance. In other words, public goods are involved. From the consumer's point of view, these are really impure public goods since they do not allow the consumer a homogenous quantity and quality of the good in question. At this point, therefore, we have to remind ourselves that a maximum-profit or maximum-efficiency solution for producers is not necessarily the same as a maximum social-benefit solution for consumers. Thus, in location theory we know that the forces governing location from the producer's point of view are not necessarily beneficial when analysed from the consumer's point of view – as Hotelling's classic example of the case of two ice-cream sellers on a beach demonstrates. We know, therefore, that in any situation of monopoly, duopoly, or oligopoly, the market process is unlikely to produce a location pattern which is the most beneficial for the consumer. Similarly, we also know that the very fact of externalities in the decision process can wreck our confidence in the market mechanism. There are plenty of theoretical reasons, therefore, for expecting considerable imbalance in the availability and accessibility of resources in an urban system. There are also good theoretical reasons (which will be examined later) for anticipating that this imbalance will usually operate to the advantage of the rich and to the detriment of the poor. The fact that this occurs is not hard to document from most American cities as a casual reading of the Kerner Commission (1968) report will show. Some of the local costs imposed upon a community by the differential availability and accessibility of resources are quantifiable (such as the real extent of overcharging for consumer goods) but there are many other costs (such as high infant mortality rate, mental disturbance and nervous tension) which are real enough but extraordinarily difficult to measure.

This style of analysis can be used to deal with differential costs imposed by proximity to those features in the urban environment which generate external costs. I am thinking here of such things as air and water pollution, noise, congestion, criminal activity and the like. The cost to the individual in each case will be a function of his location with respect to the generating source. The intensity of air pollution, for example, will vary according to the diffusion and dispersal rates from the source and the cost to the individual will depend on his location with respect to a spatial field of effects. The costs imposed in the air pollution case are difficult to total up. We can get reasonable estimates of the cleaning and maintenance costs (Yocum and McCaldin, 1968, pp. 646–9; Ridker, 1967) but the indirect costs to mental and physical health are extraordinarily difficult to estimate. We can likewise get some estimate of the impact of criminal activity in terms of the value of goods lost or damage inflicted, but the indirect costs of being cut off from normal physical and social activity on account of fear are incalculable (it may mean that an elderly person is cut off from an amenity resource such as a park, for example). The pattern of these costs clearly varies quite substantially throughout the urban system, so that some groups go fairly cost free while others suffer very considerable cost burdens.

We have briefly examined some of the ways in which the real income of an individual may be affected by the accessibility, availability and price of resources and by the costs imposed by the external effects of various activities contained in the city system. If we could measure these and somehow or other total them all up, what would the total effect be? This may appear an unanswerable question (since so few of the costs can be quantified), but it is nevertheless useful to ask it for doing so directs our attention to an important set of mechanisms generating inequalities in income. It is quite possible, of course, for diverse effects upon real income to cancel each other out – a cost of air pollution here may be balanced by a cost of criminal activity there, etc. Obtaining such a balance over all impure public goods and services over all time periods is essential if there is to be any logic to the provision and financing of such goods (Buchanan, 1968a, p. 162). It is difficult to resist the conclusion, however, that in general the rich and privileged obtain more benefits and incur lower costs than do the poor and politically weak. In part, this conclusion is an intuitive assessment. But it becomes more acceptable since it can be given some theoretical justification and this I now hope to do, albeit in a very sketchy fashion.

We are essentially concerned in this discussion with the distributive effects of activities arranged in a given spatial form and the redistributive effects of changes in that spatial form. Locational changes bring about redistribution mainly through the externalities associated with them. Locational decisions may be made by individual households, entrepreneurs, organizations, public agencies and so on. Most of these decision-makers (except, in theory at least, the last) locate for their own benefit and do not take account (unless legally obliged to) of the third-party effects of their decision. The real income of any one individual in an urban system is thus susceptible to change through the decisions of others. Since these decisions rarely take his welfare into account, there is little or nothing he can do about them except:

1. Change his own location (which will cost him something) to maintain or improve his real income

2. By joining together with others and exercising group or collective pressure to seek to prevent locational decisions which diminish his real income and to encourage locational decisions which enhance his real income.

The way in which the spatial form of an urban system changes, therefore, will partly be a function of the way in which groups form, bargain with each other and take collective action over the positioning of the various externality fields which will affect their real income. It is in this sense that the political processes in the urban system may be viewed as a way of sharing out external benefits and allocating external costs. In this manner one powerful group may be able to obtain real income advantages over another. The realities of political power being what they are, the rich groups will probably thereby grow richer and the poor groups will thereby be deprived. It seems, therefore, that the current real income distribution in a city system must be viewed as 'the predictable outcome of the political process' (Buchanan, 1968b, p. 185). Any attempt to understand the mechanisms generating inequalities in income must, therefore, involve an understanding of the political processes which operate in a city. This is such an important issue that I shall devote a separate section to it.

Political processes and the redistribution of real income

It is very difficult to devise an adequate framework for grappling with the complexities of the political process as they are manifest in an urban system. All I shall try to demonstrate in this section, therefore, is the rather obvious relationship which exists between the redistribution of real income and political decisions. I shall, however, seek to interpret much of the political activity of the city as a matter of jostling for and bargaining over the use and control of the 'hidden mechanisms' for redistribution (Wood, 1963). I shall also draw attention to certain aspects of this bargaining process and thereby provide some kind of theoretical basis for the assertion that redistribution of real income via these hidden mechanisms naturally tends to benefit the rich and disadvantage the poor.

Consider a simple case in which there are two communities (each forming a homogenous group) located close enough to each other so that the actions of one community impose external benefits or costs on the other community. Such interdependence between communities poses considerable theoretical problems – it will destroy one of the conditions necessary to achieve a Pareto optimum in the housing market, for example. How can these two communities resolve a conflict generated from such a situation? If community *A* invests heavily in a facility which also benefits community *B*, should community *B* be allowed in as a 'free rider' or should community *B* contribute to the investment, and if so, by how much? Similarly, if community A contemplates an action which is detrimental to B, how would B negotiate with A and what should A pay to B in the way of compensation? This problem can be formulated as a two-person non-zero sum game. It is then possible (provided certain conditions are met) to identify rational or 'optimal' solutions. Davis and Whinston (1964) for example, use this approach to allocate costs and benefits between two firms whose activities are interdependent through the existence of externalities. The definition of an optimal solution depends upon the way in which the game is structured and the behavioural characteristics of the participants. The outcome will thus depend upon the amount of information available to the participants, their willingness to co-operate, their pessimism or optimism, and so on. Isard *et al.* (1969, chapters 6 and 7) have reviewed these variations on the two-person non-zero sum game in depth. They also indicate how the problem of external effects between communities can be resolved through the extension of game theory to what are called *location games*. These games vary from the joint development and exploitation of a resource by two or three participants, through the allocation of funds across a system of regions, to the location and financing of a public facility (such as an airport or a high school). In all of these cases, it is possible to identify optimal solutions and thus provide a rational basis for resolving a conflict between communities over external benefits and costs. In general, of course, something as complicated as a city system requires a more extensive analytic framework – such as that provided by n-person, non-zero sum games in which side-payments are allowed (the latter condition is essential for the analysis of coalition formation; in the city political system, coalitions are extremely important). But these games are difficult to analyse and apply (Isard *et al.*, 1969). Nevertheless, we may conclude that it is theoretically possible to harness, by political activity and bargaining, the 'hidden mechanisms' of income redistribution so as to achieve a balanced allocation of all impure goods and services over a spatially distributed population. But we can also conclude that this will only happen if the political process is so organized that it facilitates 'equality in bargaining' between different but internally homogenous interest groups. This condition is unlikely to exist and an analysis of the reasons why will provide a justification for the expectation that the rich will generally benefit to the detriment of the poor.

In game theory, we usually assume that the participants are

equal in their command over resources. In coalition analysis, however, we can drop this assumption and consider a 'weighted decision game' (Isard *et al.*, 1969, pp. 400–402). In this type of game, each person brings to a coalition a certain 'resource' which can then be used in the bargaining process. This resource may be a vote, it may be money (e.g. for side-payments, both legal and illegal), it may be influence (e.g. contacts with members of another group), or it may be information (e.g. about competitors or about appropriate strategies). It is interesting to note that a vote is probably the least important of these resources to most aspects of political activity and this is the only resource which is divided equally among all members of the coalition. In a weighted decision game, the outcome depends on the emergence of a coalition which has enough resources to 'win'. In games of this kind, the payoffs are usually positive for the winning coalition and zero to the losers. This sort of situation is quite common in urban politics and this explains our expectation that the more powerful community (in financial, educational or influence terms) may be able to dominate locational decisions to its own advantage. Inequality of resources available for the political bargaining process thus creates a condition for the further disposition of resources so as to reinforce that inequality.

I have assumed so far that there is such a thing as an homogenous 'community' or 'group' which can function effectively within the bargaining process. This condition is rarely approximated. Therefore, we need some understanding of how and why groups form and how, once formed, they operate as a force in the political arena. This is an extremely complex question. I am primarily concerned, however, with the likelihood that a group will form, that it will act coherently, that it will exercise power in the political bargaining process, and that it will succeed in providing itself with collective goods. Here it seems that a major distinction is to be made between 'small groups' and 'large groups'. This distinction is brought out most clearly in the analysis of group choice provided by Olson (1965). The analysis proceeds on the assumption of self-interested behaviour on the part of individuals and then goes on to show that 'the larger the group, the farther it will fall short of providing an optimal amount of the collective good'. The proof of this conclusion need not detain us. The important point is that small groups may well be effective in providing themselves with collective goods particularly when one person in the group has an overwhelming interest in the production of the good. But larger more balanced groups are likely to fall short in this respect. This conclusion is similar to that developed by several analysts of group choice and collective behaviour (Buchanan, 1968a). It is not difficult to extend it to the political bargaining process and predict that:

The smaller groups – the privileged and intermediate groups – can often defeat the large groups – the latent groups – which are normally supposed to prevail in democracy. The privileged and intermediate groups often triumph over the numerically superior forces in the latent or large groups because the former are generally organized and active while the latter are normally unorganized and inactive. (Olson, 1965, p. 128)

That this condition can be predicted from an assumption of self-interest on the part of all individuals may seem surprising, even though bitter experience teaches us that small, resourceful, well-organized groups can usually defeat the wishes of a wide-spread mass of unorganized people. Olson points out that large masses of people motivated by self-interest can be organized for their own collective good only through inducements (such as retirement and insurance benefits) or through coercion (such as that imposed by a trade union closed shop policy).

These general conclusions have important implications for our understanding of the political system as it operates in the urban context. We can directly predict from it, for example, that:

neighbouring local governments in metropolitan areas that provide collective goods (like commuter roads and education) that benefit individuals in two or more local government jurisdictions would tend to provide inadequate amounts of these services, and that the largest local government (e.g. the one representing the central city) would bear disproportionate shares of the burdens of providing them (Olson, 1965, p. 36)

Any activity which generates strong external benefits throughout the political system will naturally tend to be underprovided and it is tempting to hypothesize that any activity that generates strong external costs will be undercontrolled or undercompensated for. Since small groups are likely to be more influential in the political decision-making process, we can also infer that most of the decisions (both allocational and locational) will disproportionately reflect the desires of small pressure groups as opposed to the mass of the population. Since these groups rarely act from altruism, we can expect these decisions to provide direct and indirect benefits to the members of the group rather than to members of other groups. There are two other predictable consequences of Olson's analysis. First, it is unlikely that a member of a large group will give up voluntarily a very small quantity of his resources in order to achieve a collective aim even when the achievement of that aim will make each individual in the community better off. It is not hard to find examples of this kind of behaviour (the study by Keene and Strong (1970) of reactions to the Brandywine plan is a good case in point). Second, it is unlikely that a large group will be able to retain voluntarily coherent policies and objectives since, if it is to do so effectively, it must by consensus or apathy allow a small group to negotiate and implement policy on its behalf. As there is always the possibility that the small group will, in the large group's name, achieve policies most appropriate for the small group, we must anticipate considerable within-group rivalry for executive power which will weaken the group's negotiating position. Again, this is a familiar event in the urban context and its frequency is a very influential force governing the outcome of a 'land-use planning game' (Keyes, 1969).

We may conclude that it is unlikely for self-interested individuals to come together to form a large group which will then act voluntarily for the collective good of everyone in the group. Large-group action is only likely when external inducements can be provided, when sanctions can be applied, or when institutional arrangements are created which formalize the 'rules of the game' for large-group decision making and within- and between-group negotiation. This conclusion is obviously not universally true and exceptions will undoubtedly be found (usually depending on the importance of the issue, the homogeneity of attitudes towards them, the subtlety and altruism of the executive group operating on behalf of the large group, and so on). This conclusion directs our attention to the institutional framework which exists for reaching collective decisions and arbitrating between the competing needs and desires of different pressure groups within the population. I do not intend any detailed account of how these institutions operate in bringing about a redistribution of income. But it is worth noting two things about them. In the first place, they partly reflect existing group activities and they are, therefore, far more able to take account of small-group pressures (special lobbies and special interests) than they are able to react to the needs and wishes of large groups – hence the recent rhetoric in many American cities about making city administration more responsive to the needs of the people. In the second place, an institutional structure, once it is created, may well become closed or partially closed. In a recent study of anti-poverty policy in Baltimore for example, Bachrach (1969) found that low-income groups experienced great difficulty in actually getting into a negotiating position. In other words, groups can effectively be excluded from the negotiating and bargaining game by institutional barriers or by the manoeuvres of other groups. Only a strong and cohesive group will be able to overcome such barriers and get around the problem of what is called 'nondecision-making'. This explains why the urban planning game often bears more resemblance to solitaire than to an n-person non-zero sum game.

The import of the preceding paragraphs is that we can expect considerable imbalance in the outcome of within- and between-group bargaining over external benefits and costs and collective goods because

1. Different groups have different resources with which to bargain

2. Large groups in the population are generally weaker and more incoherent than small groups and

3. Some groups are kept away from negotiation altogether.

If income redistribution is a 'predictable outcome of the political process' it is not hard to predict the general flow of that redistribution. In the first place, we can expect a 'central business district imperialism' in which the well-organized business interests of the central city (with their small-group oligopolistic structure) effectively dominate the looser and weaker coalitions found in the rest of the city. This thesis has recently been powerfully argued by Kotler (1969). In the second place, we can also anticipate a 'suburban exploitation of the central city' hypothesis (Netzer, 1968, pp. 438–448; Thompson, 1965, chapter 7). In other words, we can expect a 'pecking order' among various groups in the population for the exploitation of the various resources which the city has to offer. Those at the bottom of this pecking order are the losers:

The slum is the catch-all for the losers, and in the competitive struggle for the cities goods the slum areas are also the losers in terms of schools, jobs, garbage collection, street lighting, libraries, social services, and whatever else is communally available but always in short supply. The slum, then, is an area where the population lacks resources to compete successfully and where collectively it lacks control over the channels through which such resources are distributed or maintained. This may suggest some new approaches to metropolitan planning – recognizing the necessity for redistribution of power, broader access to resources, and expansion of individual choice to those who have been consistently denied. (Sharrard, 1968, p. 10)

The prospects for equity or for a just redistribution of income in an urban system through a naturally arising political process (particularly one based on a philosophy of individual self-interest) are bleak indeed. The extent to which a social system has recognized this fact and adjusted itself to counteract this natural tendency is, I believe, correlated with the degree to which that social system has succeeded in avoiding the structural problems and deepening social tensions consequent upon the process of massive urbanization.

Social values and the cultural dynamics of the urban system

The notion of 'real income' presupposes that values can be attached to individual property rights and to command over resources. The measurement of external costs and benefits also presupposes the existence of some value system against which we can measure (and thereby compare) the impact of an environmental change upon one individual or a social group. Casual observation teaches us that people value different things in different ways. This elementary fact of life has bedevilled economic and political theory ever since the abandonment of the neoclassical cardinal utility principle which assumed the existence of some common, identically calibrated measuring rod for measuring the 'intensity of preference' of individuals. The replacement of cardinal by ordinal utility provided more realism in measurement but posed problems of its own – in particular, it led to the impasse described by Arrow (1963) in which it is impossible to derive a social preference or welfare function from a set of individual ordinal utility functions. There are two ways out of this impasse. The first is to try to get some measure of intensity of preference without necessarily assuming complete cardinality. If an individual's preferences can be weighted to reflect his intensity of feeling, then it is possible to derive some kind of social welfare function (Minas and Ackoff, 1964). A good deal of attention has been paid in psychology and psychophysics to this whole question of measuring subjective values and the work accomplished indicates that information can be gained on preferences and weightings and techniques exist for manipulating, for example, ordinal data to obtain metric information (Shepard, 1966). This work (summarized by Coombs, 1964 and Nunnaly, 1967) has not been integrated as well as it might into the main body of the theory of consumer choice even though good statements do exist (e.g. Fishburn, 1964). The second way out of the Arrow paradox, and one which is usually taken by theoretical economists, is to assume the problems away by stating a 'unanimity rule' which conveniently assumes that everyone in the population has the same ranking of preferences over a set of alternatives (Buchanan, 1968a). Only under this assumption is it possible to derive a Pareto optimum. When the unanimity rule applies, the alternatives are said to be 'Pareto-comparable' and when it does not they are 'Pareto-noncomparable' (Quirk and Saposnik, 1968, p. 117). The usual economic theories of urban structure (such as the Davis and Whinston model examined above) and theories of location require that alternatives are Pareto-comparable. The question then arises as to what happens when they are not.

The implications for a theory of the allocation of public goods are serious. The existence of interpersonal utility functions 'plays havoc' with game theoretic formulations (Luce and Raiffa, 1957, p. 34). Bargaining between two communities which have completely different utility functions cannot be handled in any rational fashion and voting procedures can lead us to a position which is far from optimal. Likewise, the whole question of compensation between parties takes on a new dimension. A transfer payment of £1 may be very significant to a poor man and almost irrelevant to a rich man. By the same argument, the poor can less afford to lose an external benefit or incur an external cost. This leads us to an intriguing paradox in which the poor are willing to incur external losses for a far lower transfer payment than are the rich. In other words, the rich are unlikely to give up an amenity 'at any price' whereas the poor who are least able to sustain the loss are likely to sacrifice it for a trifling sum: a prediction for which there is some empirical support. In this case, however, we are dealing with the simple problem which arises when different parties express different orders of preference over a given set of outcomes. There are far more serious difficulties. What happens, for example, when groups do not perceive the same alternative choices or potential outcomes? In this case, each group has its own perceived action space and conflict may arise because neither can see or understand the action space as perceived by the other. A similar difficulty arises when groups cannot agree on the 'rules of the game' and since the establishment of these rules largely predetermines the outcome there is likely to be as much conflict over the rules as there is in negotiation itself. What this means is that inhomogeneity in social and cultural values may make it impossible for groups to get into a 'valid' negotiating position such as that which is specified in one of Isard's location games. From this it follows that an urban system will be unable to function smoothly (in the sense that conflicts between individuals and groups will not easily be resolved) if there is widespread inhomogeneity in the social and cultural values of the population. It seems that the 'natural' way for this sort of difficulty to be minimized is to seek out a pattern of territorial organization which minimizes both social contact between individuals holding different social and cultural values and the probability of quarrels over externalities. Territorial and 'neighbourhood' organization on ethnic, class, social status, religious and other lines thus has an important role to play in minimizing conflict in the urban system.

Inhomogeneity in social cultural values also plays havoc with any simplistic theory of the redistribution of income in an urban system. This can perhaps best be demonstrated by returning to an issue raised but not discussed in the section on the availability and price of resources, i.e., that resources should be considered as technological and cultural appraisals. Since the definition adopted of real income contains the phrase 'command over resources', cultural and technical variations in a population automatically affect the measurement of real income. Two individuals can command exactly the same resource but if they value it differently they have different real incomes. It is useful to ask, therefore, what the impact of this fact is for a theory of income redistribution.

Let me first define some terms. By a technological appraisal, I mean that an individual must possess the various cognitive skills and technological equipment to be able to make use of the resource system that is the city. By a cultural appraisal, I mean that the individual must possess a value system which motivates him to want to make use of these resources. The technology is partly comprised of the relevant 'hardware' such as machinery, tools, etc., and partly made up of the cognitive skills necessary for the use of that hardware. People raised in rural areas often lack the necessary cognitive skills to handle the city or the suburbs; the suburbanite might likewise lack those skills necessary for the country and the inner city; while the inner-city person may well not be able to handle the country or the suburbs. Cognitive skills are learned and it is possible to learn how to handle a great diversity of environments. But the skills are unlikely to be equally distributed throughout a population and since learning is affected by successful experience (or reinforcement), individuals will become most practised in the art of dealing with their own environment insofar as it impinges upon them. Environmental learning is not, therefore, independent of environment. The kind of environment created in an urban system affects which cognitive skills become developed. Under conditions of relative isolation, we may expect to find specialized sub-populations with particular cognitive skills relevant to a particular kind of urban environment – the slum dweller indeed possesses quite different skills from the rural dweller. Cognitive skills are not, of course, simply a function of environment. Innate intelligence and education obviously play a part. Consider, for example, the ability to think abstractly about and to schematize spatial relationships – a skill which is closely correlated with other aspects of intelligence (Smith, 1964). Such a schematic skill allows the individual to transcend space and command it as a resource. Those who lack such a skill are likely to be trapped by space. This kind of difference has significance for our understanding of income redistribution since it directly affects mobility and accessibility. Thus Pahl (1965) suggests that the higher income and better educated groups tend to make an active use of space whereas lower income groups tend to be trapped by it. Duhl (1963, p. 137) similarly remarks that higher income groups 'use the physical environment as a resource in contrast with the lower socio-economic groups who incorporate the environment into the self'. Webber (1963) also hypothesizes that all but the lowest income groups have now freed themselves from restrictions of 'territoriality'. Whatever the truth of the contentions, it seems reasonable to assume that cognitive skills are dependent upon education, intelligence and *experience with respect to environment*, and these cognitive skills in turn affect the value of a resource to a given individual.

In like manner, we may assume that cultural values are affected by (among other things) the opportunities created in the city environment. Cultures evolve in part through 'a specialized patterning of the individual stimulus situation, and a special patterning of the response that could be made to it'. (Smith *et al.*, 1956, p. 25; see also Kluckhohn, 1954.) So we may anticipate cultural evolution within the city system partly through the re-organization of the physical and social stimuli which exist within it. Thus, environment designers (e.g. Sommer, 1969) would point to the importance of physical stimuli in determining behaviour patterns – which is not to say that these are the *only* stimuli for culture change, as naïve environmental determinists would suggest. Let us now consider the import of this fact for the cultural dynamics of the urban system. Most of the decisions made on the physical planning of the urban system are likely to be made or strongly influenced by small and powerful oligopolistic groups. These groups are in effect rearranging the physical stimuli (a highway here, a power plant there) for large masses of poorly organized people. In other words a few small influential subcultures within the urban culture are patterning stimuli situations for the other subcultures. Most of the subcultures in the urban system have very little control over the different configurations of stimuli (visual, kinesthetic, social, etc.) in different parts of the urban systems which are likely to generate quite strong cultural divergence. The sort of thing that can happen is demonstrated by a survey of attitudes to air pollution in St Louis. In suburban areas, there was an acute awareness of air pollution whereas in the central city area, where the problem was at its worst, attitudes were only weakly formed. There were so many other problems in the inner city (jobs, housing, recreational facilities, etc.) that the negative stimuli from air pollution passed virtually unnoticed. The formation of attitudes is thus dependent upon the particular configuration of stimuli existing in a particular urban context. Once cultural inhomogeneity develops and social barriers to movement are imposed, cultural divergence may proceed apace within the city system (Thompson, 1965, p. 106). The cultural attitudes of the inner city have always been different from those of the suburbs and it does not seem that these differences are decreasing. Therefore, I find it hard to accept either Marcuse's (1964) thesis that there is a growing homogeneity in cultural values (and, therefore, no force for change in society) or the spatial form equivalent of it in which a 'one dimensional man' dwells in what Melvin Webber (1964) calls 'an urban non-place realm'. There are strong forces working towards cultural inhomogeneity and territorial differentiation in the urban system.

The implications of this conclusion are of interest. First, any theory of real income distribution must involve cross-cultural comparisons. Second, the decisions made about the location and allocation of goods and services in the urban system are 'Pareto noncomparable'. Thus, it is very difficult to compare the value of, say, open space from one part of a city system to another. Different groups will exhibit different elasticities with respect to their use of it and some groups may have no use for it at all. Consequently, the provision of large parks for inner city dwellers who may not (perhaps) be technically equipped or culturally motivated to make use of them will do absolutely nothing for them from the point of view of income redistribution – it may in fact be equivalent to giving ice cream mixers to the Boro Indians of Brazil.

If resources mean different things to different people, how can we measure their impact upon the real income of individuals and develop location policies with respect to them that achieve a given redistribution goal? This problem could partly be overcome if we could separate out those resources which everyone agreed upon as important from those which only part of the population valued. At least the first kind could be treated as if the unanimity rule held good. Whether or not we could identify such groupings is an empirical question to which there is no easy answer. It is reasonable to assume, for example, that housing opportunities and health services are in the former category. Yet even in these categories there are subtle but important differences in cultural values. Low-income groups, for example, often identify very closely with their housing environment and the psychological cost of moving is to them far greater than it is to the mobile upper middle class. Well-meaning but culturally insensitive middle class planners can consequently (through rehousing projects and the like) inflict heavy costs upon lower socio-economic groups (Duhl, 1963, p. 139). The story of the provision of mental health services to the poor similarly shows how inappropriate services can result from a failure of the predominantly middle class group providing the service to appreciate the specialized subculture of a different socio-economic group (Riessman *et al.*, 1964).

Equating real income with command over resources thus leads us into an impasse because cultural inhomogeneities in the population make it difficult to measure real income. It is very tempting at this juncture to return to the simplest concept of income as monetary income. This I refuse to do because the problems inherent in the impasse are real enough and extremely relevant to our understanding of the urban system. If we fail to investigate them, we abandon all hope of arriving at a firm basis for making socially meaningful decisions. But there are even deeper long-range questions to which this style of analysis directs our attention. By the constant rearrangement of stimuli in the urban system we are provoking a gradual process of cultural evolution. Evolution towards what? One way of making sure that a subculture places no value upon open space is to deny it all experience of it. The evolution of the urban system, whether we like it or not, can lead to large scale sensory deprivation with respect to certain phenomena (such as clean air, wilderness, etc.) and overexposure to others (such as suburban vistas, air pollution, etc.). In the long run, therefore, we must evaluate decisions about the growth of the city against a set of overriding cultural values which we wish to preserve or augment. If we do not do this, we may see the emergence of new sets of cultural values and, if present trends are anything to go by, these may lead to violent conflict and, perhaps, to an ultimate social self-destruction. The sensibilities of mankind cannot remain permanently immune from the environmental changes man is bringing about through his own actions. It is, therefore, salutary to remind ourselves occasionally that 'the long-range question is not so much what sort of environment we want, but what sort of man we want'. (Sommer, 1969, p. 173.)

Spatial organization and political, social and economic processes

The redistribution of income can be brought about by changes in 1. the location of jobs and housing, 2. the value of property rights and 3. the price of resources to the consumer. These changes are themselves affected by the allocations of external costs and benefits to different regions in the urban system and by changes in accessibility and proximity. Populations seek to control these hidden mechanisms governing redistribution through exercising political power. It is in the box marked 'social and cultural values' that the whole process feeds back into itself, for these values are both a cause and an effect – any theory of income distribution must be based upon them and yet they are themselves susceptible to change through the allocation of opportunities throughout the urban system. But also inherent in these social processes lies the question of spatial organization. Externality effects are localized, so are job and housing opportunities, resource benefits, communication links and so on. Political power is partly areally based. Many of the hidden mechanisms for redistributing income come to fruition in the act of location. This leads us to the last fundamental question I wish to pose in this paper. Is there some spatial structure or set of structures which will maximize equity and efficiency in the urban system or, at least, maximize our ability to control the powerful hidden mechanisms which bring about redistribution? This is both a normative and a positive question for it suggests that we can both explain current distributional effects by looking at existing spatial structures and devise spatial structures to achieve a given distributional goal. I will not try to separate these aspects of the problem in the analysis that follows.

The physical spatial form of a city system is a construction in three-dimensional Euclidean geometry. The phenomena within it can be conceptualized as points (retail stores, schools, hospitals), lines (transport links), areas (constituencies, territories) and volumes (buildings). This form should presumably facilitate the coherent functioning of social processes. The spatial form is not, however, infinitely adaptable nor are the social demands on it easily reconciled with each other. The actual physical form is necessarily a compromise between a whole set of conflicting demands. When we make decisions about spatial form we are presumably trying to reach an efficient compromise. This is not easy to do. It is the kind of problem which gives rise to lengthy Royal Commission deliberations (such as the Redcliffe-Maud Commission in Britain) and interminable arguments over the relative merits of community control or metropolitan government in the United States. I cannot consider all of these problems here and so I shall proceed by example.

The provision and control of impure public goods in an urban system

Impure public goods, once produced, are freely but not equally available (in terms of quantity or quality) to all individuals in the city system. Many goods are of this sort. In particular, all goods and facilities freely available but provided through some locational mechanism fall into this category – hence the interest in spatial form policies in an urban setting. Indeed, it is not unreasonable to treat much of location theory as a specific form of the theory governing the provision of impure public goods (Tiebout, 1961, pp. 80–81).

It is useful to distinguish between three different policy

situations. The first concerns goods which confer benefits upon all individuals. Here the policy issue is to ensure that the good is provided (by private or public action) in sufficient quantity and quality at the right locations to achieve a particular distributive objective. The second case is that of impure public goods (such as air pollutants) which impose costs through 'involuntary' consumption. Here the policy problem is to regulate location patterns so as to minimize the incidence of these costs and control their distributional effects. The third case (and this is probably the commonest) concerns a mixed situation in which a good provides both benefits and losses.

The provision of beneficial impure public goods can be accomplished through private or public action. In the former case, we rely upon some natural market mechanism to achieve a 'reasonable' location pattern (e.g., in retail opportunities and entertainment facilities) and, hence, to minimize (as far as production technology will allow) the differential income effect. Prices thus act to resolve the conflict between the technological necessity for a few productive points and the physical necessity for a large number of spatially distributed consumption points. Lösch's (1954) analysis provides us with some of the necessary equipment for discussing the general form of spatial equilibrium which will result. He indicates an hierarchical solution is inevitable since production functions, consumption functions, and sets of elasticities (with respect to prices, incomes and the like) vary considerably from one good to another. It would be unrealistic to expect the spatial pattern of private provision of impure public goods to conform to Löschian expectation for a whole host of reasons (concerning the conditions for entry for the firm, stochastic fluctuations in demand and supply conditions, product differentiation, bounded areas, interpenetration of market areas and so on). There are, therefore, good theoretical reasons for expecting that the market mechanism will be no more efficient in guiding the location of privately supplied impure public goods to Pareto equilibrium than it is in the housing market. The empirical evidence also points in this direction. Consider, for example, the location of supermarket facilities. The supermarket is itself an impure public good (although it is selling wholly private goods) and its location is presumably a function of balancing the need for economies of scale in operation against the effects of rising transport costs to the consumer as the market area is extended. Yet the Kerner Commission (1968, p. 277) comments on the general lack of these facilities in ghetto areas. It is difficult to tell, of course, whether this is due to genuine market failure, time-lag in achieving equilibrium, or social and economic conditions in ghetto areas which make supermarket operations uneconomic. But even in those areas of the private economy providing impure public goods (such as opportunities for shopping, recreation and the like) there is no guarantee that, because a set of demand and supply curves can be determined, there will automatically result therefrom a locational pattern which is anywhere near Pareto optimality. There are sufficient imperfections (through product differentiation and the like) and interdependencies to call into question any assumption of 'natural' competitive efficiency even given an ethically acceptable income distribution in the first place. It is not unreasonable, for example, to expect entrepreneurs to locate initially in those areas where excess profits are maximized – hence the 'natural' tendency for the affluent areas to be serviced well before the low-income areas and this, as usual, generates an implicit redistribution of real income. Even in the private sector, therefore, there is some ground for public interference if only to encourage the speedier achievement of equilibrium. There is an even stronger justification for interference if the objective is to attain some progressive redistribution in kind.

Many impure public goods cannot be provided through the normal market mechanism because it is difficult to determine a set of market prices. These goods (educational services, fire and police protection and so on) are provided by public action. It is strange that there are so few criteria developed for determining the location of public activities. Public finance concepts have 'up to now been largely spaceless', (Thompson, 1965, p. 257) while location theorists, as Teitz (1968) points out, have by and large neglected the problem of public facility location. Given that no adequate location criteria have been developed, we can hardly be surprised if locational decisions on public activities are almost entirely the result of those unbalanced political pressures reviewed in a previous section. Since 'local public services bid fair to become the chief means of income redistribution in our economy', (Thompson, 1965, p. 118) we ought to pay far more attention to the policies which govern their location if we are to control the process of redistribution. It will not be easy to formulate a theory for the location of public activity. In principle, of course, the problem is exactly the same as it is in the private sector, i.e., to find a location pattern which is most efficient subject to a set of distributional constraints. Thus the Löschian framework has some utility (Berry, 1967; Teitz, 1968). But the problem of finding a solution is theoretically obscured by the quasi-monopolistic structure of public organization and the inability to find any realistic pricing mechanisms. In effect, public facility location requires the simultaneous solution of problems of (a) finance (b) production technology (c) quantity and quality of supply (d) location (e) demand estimation and (f) welfare impact. Clearly, it is difficult to define an optimal solution. As in the private sector, we can anticipate some kind of hierarchical arrangement in the location of, for example, medical facilities, yet it is very difficult to determine the best form of this arrangement or evaluate alternative forms of spatial organization (Schneider, 1967, 1968; Schultz, 1969). More generally, the state of the art in the theory of public facility location has not progressed very much beyond the point of relatively simple model articulation (Teitz, 1968; Revelle et al., 1970).

Much of the same conclusion can be reached with respect to the regulation of those impure public goods which generate costs. There has been very little investigation of the form and nature of the spatial field of influence of particular externalities. We know, however, that they vary greatly in scale, a fact which indicates the necessity for some kind of hierarchical regulation (small-scale effects being controlled at the community level while large-scale effects must be controlled at the metropolitan level). The investigation of externality field effects is a problem in pure spatial analysis. It requires that we be able to specify or generalize the extent and varying intensity of the spatial surface. The regulation problem is then partly a matter of shifting the locations of the sources of these external costs to achieve a desired spatial surface, or locating activity with respect to an existing surface in such a way that certain social objectives (such as freedom from certain levels of air pollution) are achieved. We possess scarcely a vestige of a theory to guide policy decisions of this sort at the present time.

Variations in cultural values and, hence, variations in demands and needs in the population, complicate policy decisions very substantially. We find the same general dilemma we encountered in the housing market case – if a central agency is to make a decision, it must presumably possess information concerning the utility scales of each individual in the population. Since the government obviously cannot possess this information, how should it proceed? One answer is to bend to voting pressure but we have seen how this was likely to lead to inequity. Tiebout (1956, p. 418) suggests instead a fragmented community structure in which:

The consumer voter may be viewed as picking that community which best satisfies preference patterns for public goods. . . . The greater the number of communities and the greater the variance among them, the closer the consumer will come to fully realizing his preference position.

In some respects, this is not an unattractive proposition, since theoretically it maximizes the consumer's range of choice through some community control system whereby communities of individuals with relatively homogenous values and utility functions express their desires in group choice. Again, we find there is a certain logic to territorial organization in the city and there can be no doubt that consumers do shift from one community to another to satisfy their preference for public goods. There are many specific reasons for doubting the efficacy of Tiebout's proposal (e.g. assumptions of perfect mobility and information) but there are also some very general questions concerning territorial organization in an urban system and it is perhaps appropriate to close by examining these general arguments.

Regional and territorial organization in an urban system

There are various natural forces making for territorial organization in an urban system: kinship and ethnic groupings, communities with shared value systems, individuals with similar ideas about quality of urban environment, are good examples. These forces do not remain static. Ethnic and kinship groupings are breaking down (Webber, 1963) and traditional notions of 'community' and 'neighbourhood' are being replaced by something rather different – a neighbourhood concept which is implicit rather than explicit with respect to social organization (Keller, 1969). There are also good logical reasons for arguing in favour of territorial organization. An 'appropriate' organization can do much to minimize conflict and maximize group coherence and efficiency. Whether or not we can achieve such an organization of space and thereby facilitate the achievement of social objectives depends very much upon whether we can find out what is meant by 'appropriate'.

Territorial organization has many functions to perform within the city system. The classical problem of regionalization is to find a hierarchy of regions which will perform all of these functions reasonably well (see e.g. Boudeville, 1966). Some functions must be performed at the metropolitan level (e.g. the planning of transport systems, parkland facilities) while others can best be operated at the local level (e.g. play areas, child care centres). The first problem, therefore, is to find a form of organization capable of dealing with the obvious fact that different facilities have to be provided at different spatial scales. The second problem is to identify a form of organization which is flexible enough to deal with growth (social and economic), spatial overspill effects, changing spatial relationships and so on. If the organization is not flexible, it will act as an automatic constraint upon what Friedmann (1969) calls a general process of polarized development (Darwent, 1969). In other words, any territorial organization must be designed so as to be reactive to the dynamics of the urban system. This is perhaps the most difficult problem of all to resolve, and I shall therefore confine my attention to the static aspects of it.

Consider first the political, social and economic benefits to be had from a territorial organization based purely on local neighbourhood groups. According to Olson's (1965) analysis, the smaller the group the more willing it is likely to be to provide itself voluntarily with collective goods. The smaller the group, the more it is likely to achieve some collective aim. This has important economic implications, for it indicates the possibility of higher motivation in small community settings than in large – a quality which Liebenstein (1966) calls 'x-efficiency' as opposed to the usual economic measures of efficiency. Certainly, at election time, small communities usually show a higher percentage turn-out (other things being equal) than large communities. In part, this may be a function of the greater potential for individual participation in small communities – a quantity which Isard *et al.* (1969, chapter 3) have sought to measure as 'participation potential'. It may also be the result of what Thompson (1965, p. 263) calls the 'personalized styling and control which comes with small scale'. It has also been argued on more doctrinaire grounds that the only way to achieve a genuine democracy is through community control based on local neighbourhood units – only then, it is argued, will it be possible to ensure that everyone has a voice in decisions and presumably that voice is used to help control the mechanisms generating income inequalities. Thus Kotler

(1969, p. 71) argues that 'the poor need neighbourhood government to secure the liberty to achieve prosperity'. Before accepting this argument (and it is worth noting that Davis and Whinston's arguments on zoning and Tiebout's on the provision of public services point in this general direction), we must consider some of the disadvantages.

There is no doubt that some goods and services can be supplied and some operations effectively carried out at the local level. But what about those goods which must be supplied on a far broader scale? In these cases there are bound to be significant externalities involved. It has generally been shown by Olson (1965), Weisbrod (1965) and others that there is a tendency for public services to be underprovided when externalities exist (although Williams, 1966, dissents from this view and suggests that the problem is one of non-optimal provision rather than under-provision). One way to rectify this situation is to negotiate with neighbouring communities, but the problems of noncentralized information gathering and negotiation costs (including those to be imputed to a delay in decision-making) are likely to make this an inefficient way of rationalizing the provision of these services. An alternative solution is to internalize the externalities by forming a higher level territorial system which will be better able to provide the service in question. We have to be careful that we do not lose more in 'x-efficiency' than we gain in economic efficiency. It will not be possible to internalize the externalities completely, of course, and so the determination of an optimal regional organization will depend upon reducing externalities to an acceptable level rather than eliminating them entirely. It therefore becomes feasible to think of an upper level organization which will provide services such as transport, sewage disposal, large recreational facilities and the like. There is also the problem of financing to be considered. One of the more serious problems in American cities in the recent past has been the loss of a tax-base in many central areas (Netzer, 1968). Locally financed local government is clearly a disastrous proposition – it will simply result in the poor controlling their own poverty while the rich grow more affluent from the fruits of their riches. The redistributional implications are clearly regressive. Indeed, the existing territorial structure of local finance and public service provision in American cities must be regarded as one of the prime culprits in bringing about an inequitable allocation of fringe benefits to different parts of the urban system. Hence arises a very powerful argument for metropolitan-wide government. This argument is further reinforced by the existence of many regulatory problems which can only be solved on an urban or regional basis (e.g., regulating the general spatial form of the city and pollution levels).

There are powerful arguments for decentralization and neighbourhood government but there are just as powerful arguments for metropolitan-wide government. Doubtless we could make out arguments for intermediate-size units or even broader 'megalopolis-wide' government. These arguments are not irreconcilable, since it should be possible to devise a territorial organization which is hierarchical in nature and which allows maximum local participation while at the same time ensuring a closer to optimal provision of general urban services. In fact, this kind of hierarchical organization already exists in both Britain and the United States. The problem is to determine whether the existing organization is appropriate or whether it is in fact a hindrance – a question which the Redcliffe-Maud Report set out to solve. Unfortunately, there is no easy answer to this kind of question even though it has such important implications for the control of the mechanisms governing redistribution of real income. In effect, if we can provide a correct answer we will have solved the general question which this paper started out with posing – it is possible to harmonize the policies governing spatial form and social processes so as to ensure the achievement of some overall social objective?

A concluding comment

Forecasting the future of an urban system requires a thorough understanding of the processes generating change and a realistic evaluation of the direction in which the social system as a whole is being moved by those processes. I have concentrated my attention upon the mechanisms governing the redistribution of income and I have suggested that these seem to be moving us towards a state of greater inequality and greater injustice. Unless this present trend can be reversed, I feel that almost certainly we are also headed for a period of intense conflict (which may be violent) within the urban system. In the United States, there is enough evidence to indicate that open conflict is beginning. In Britain, the same processes are at work. I therefore conclude that it will be disastrous for the future of the social system to plan ahead to facilitate existing trends – this has been the crucial planning mistake of the 1960s. As Hoover (1968, p. 260) suggests, planning frequently makes an ideal out of the *status quo*, which is objectionable 'if we believe the *status* is nothing to *quo* about'. I therefore find the notion that we are moving in easy stages into an era of enormous affluence and electronic bliss unacceptable since it is at variance with my own analysis and the evidence of my own eyes. In part, the problem is an ecological one, for we may well be, as Mishan (1967) suggests, rolling out the carpet of opportunities in front of us while rolling it up even faster behind us. But in part it is a problem of exercising a wise control over social and spatial organization within the city system. Here an enormous task confronts us. We really do not have the kind of understanding of the total city system to be able to make wise policy decisions, even when motivated by the highest social objectives. It seems, therefore, that the formation of adequate policies and the forecasting of their implications is going to depend for their success upon some broad interdisciplinary attack upon the social process and spatial form aspects of the city system.

References

ALONSO, W. (1964), *Location and Land Use*, Harvard University Press.

ARROW, K. (1963), *Social Choice and Individual Values*, Wiley.

BACHRACH, P. (1969), 'A power analysis: the shaping of antipoverty policy in Baltimore', *Public Policy*, vol. 18, pp. 155–86.

BERRY, B. J. L. (1967), *The Geography of Market Centers and Retail Distribution*, Prentice-Hall.

BOUDEVILLE, J. R. (1966), *Problems of Regional Economic Planning*, Edinburgh University Press.

BUCHANAN, J. M. (1968a), *The Demand and Supply of Public Goods*, Rand McNally.

BUCHANAN, J. M. (1968b), 'What kind of redistribution do we want?', *Economica*, vol. 35, pp. 185–90.

BUTTIMER, A. (1969), 'Social space in interdisciplinary perspective', *Geographical Rev.*, vol. 59, pp. 417–26.

CLAWSON, M. (1969), 'Open (uncovered) space as a new urban resource', in H. S. Perloff (ed.), *The Quality of the Urban Environment*, Johns Hopkins.

COOMBS, C. H. (1964), *A Theory of Data*, Wiley.

DARWENT, D. F. (1969), 'Growth poles and growth centres in regional planning–a review', *Environment and Planning*, vol. 1, pp. 5–32.

DAVIS, O. A., and WHINSTON, A. (1964), 'The economics of complex systems: the case of municipal zoning', *Kyklos*, vol. 27, pp. 419–46.

DAVIS, O. A., and WHINSTON, A. (1969), 'Externalities, welfare, and the theory of games', *J. of Pol. Econ.*, vol. 70, pp. 241–62.

DUHL, L. J. (1963), 'The human measure: man and family in megalopolis', in L. Wingo (ed.), *Cities and Space: the Future Use of Urban Land*, Johns Hopkins University Press.

FISHBURN, P. C. (1964), *Decision and Value Theory*, Wiley.

FRIEDMANN, J. (1969), 'A general theory of polarized development', mimeo, School of Architecture and Urban Planning, University College of Los Angeles.

HARVEY, D. (1970), 'Social processes and spatial form: an analysis of the conceptual problems of urban planning', *Papers and Proceedings of the Regional Science Association*, vol. 25, pp. 47–69.

HOCH, I. (1969), 'The three-dimensional city: contained urban space', in H. Perloff (ed.), *The Quality of the Urban Environment*, Johns Hopkins.

HOOVER, E. M. (1968), 'The evolving form and organization of the metropolis', in H. S. Perloff and L. Wingo (eds.), *Issues in Urban Economics*, Johns Hopkins.

ISARD, W., SMITH, T. E., *et al.* (1969), *General Theory: Social, Political, Economic and Regional*, MIT Press.

KAIN, J. F. (1968), 'The distribution and movement of jobs and industry, in J. Q. Wilson (ed.), *The Metropolitan Enigma*, Harvard University Press.

KEENE, J. C., and STRONG, A. L. (1970), 'The Brandywine plan', *J. of the Amer. Inst. of Planners*, vol. 36, pp. 50–64.

KELLER, S. (1969), *The Urban Neighbourhood: a Sociological Perspective*, Random House.

KERNER COMMISSION (1968), *Report of the National Advisory Commission on Civil Disorders*, Bantam Books.

KEYES, L. C. (1969), *The Rehabilitation Planning Game*, MIT Press.

KLUCKHOHN, C. (1954), 'Culture and behavior', in G. Lindzey (ed.), *Handbook of Social Psychology*, vol. 2, Addison Wesley.

KOTLER, M. (1969), *Neighbourhood Government: the Local Foundations of Political Life*, Bobbs-Merill.

LIEBENSTEIN, H. (1966), 'Allocative efficiency versus x-efficiency', *Amer. Econ. Rev.*, vol. 61, pp. 392–415.

LÖSCH, A. (1954), *The Economics of Location*, English edn., Yale University Press.

LOWRY, I. (1965), 'A short course in model design', *J. of the Amer. Inst. of Planners*, vol. 31, pp. 158–66.

LUCE, R. D., and RAIFFA, H. (1957), *Games and Decisions*, Wiley.

MAKIELSKI, S. J. (1966), *The Politics of Zoning: the New York Experience*, Columbia University Press.

MARGOLIS, J. (ed.) (1965), *The Public Economy of Urban Communities*, Resources for the Future.

MARGOLIS, J. (1968), 'The demand for urban public services', in H. S. Perloff and L. Wingo (eds), *Issues in Urban Economics*, Johns Hopkins.

MARCUSE, H. (1964), *One Dimensional Man*, Routledge & Kegan Paul.

MEYER, J. R. (1968), 'Urban transportation', in J. Q. Wilson (ed.), *The Metropolitan Enigma*, Harvard University Press.

MILLS, E. S. (1969), 'The value of urban land', in H. S. Perloff (ed.), *The Quality of the Urban Environment*, Johns Hopkins.

MINAS, J. S., and ACKOFF, R. L. (1964), 'Individual and collective value judgments', in M. W. Shelly and G. L. Bryan (eds), *Human Judgments and Optimality*, Wiley.

MISHAN, E. J. (1967), *The Costs of Economic Growth*, Praeger.

MISHAN, E. J. (1969), *Welfare Economics: Ten Introductory Essays*, Random House.

MUTH, R. (1969), *Cities and Housing*, University of Chicago Press.

NETZER, D. (1968), 'Federal, state and local finance in a metropolitan context', in H. Perloff and L. Wingo (eds), *Issues in Urban Economics*, Johns Hopkins.

NUNNALY, J. C. (1967), *Psychometric Theory*, McGraw-Hill.

OLSON, M. (1965), *The Logic of Collective Action*, Harvard University Press.

PAHL, R. E. (1965), 'Urbs in rure', *London School of Economics Geographical Paper*, no. 2.

PERLOFF, H. S. (ed.) (1969), *The Quality of the Urban Environment*, Johns Hopkins University Press.

PERLOFF, H. S., and WINGO, L. (eds.) (1968), *Issues in Urban Economics*. Johns Hopkins University Press.

QUIRK, J., and SAPOSNIK, R. (1968), *Introduction to General Equilibrium Theory and Welfare Economics*, McGraw-Hill.

REVELLE, C., MARKS, D., and LIEBMAN, J. C. (1970), 'An analysis of private and public sector location models', *Management Science*.

RIDKER, R. G. (1967), *Economic Costs of Air Pollution–Studies in Measurement*, Praeger.

RIESSMAN, F., COHEN, J., and PEARL, A. (eds) (1964), *The Mental Health of the Poor*, Glencoe Free Press.

ROTHENBERG, J. (1967), *Economic Evaluation of Urban Renewal*, Brookings Institution.

SCHNEIDER, J. B. (1967), 'Measuring the locational efficiency of the urban hospital', *Health Service Research*, vol. 2, pp. 154–69.

SCHNEIDER, J. B. (1968), 'Measuring, evaluating and redesigning hospital–physician–patient spatial relationships in metropolitan areas', *Inquiry*, vol. 5, pp. 24–43.

SCHULTZ, G. P. (1969), 'Facility patterns for a regional health care system', *Discussion Paper* no. 34, Regional Science Research Institute, Philadelphia.

SHARRARD, T. D. (ed.) (1968), *Social Welfare and Urban Problems*, Columbia University Press.

SHEPARD, R. N. (1966), 'Metric structures in ordinal data', *J. of Mathematical Psychology*, vol. 3, pp. 287–315.

SMITH, I. D. M. (1964), *Spatial Ability*, Knapp.

SMITH, M. B. BRUNER, J. S., and WHITE, R. W. (1956), *Opinions and Personality*, Wiley.

SOMMER, R. (1969), *Personal Space: the Behavioural Basis of Design*, Prentice-Hall.

TIEBOUT, C. M. (1956), 'A pure theory of local expenditures', *J. of Pol. Econ.*, vol. 64, pp. 416–24.

TIEBOUT, C. M. (1961), 'An economic theory of fiscal decentralization', in Universities-National Bureau Committee for Economic Research, *Public Finances, Needs, Sources and Utilization*, Princeton University Press.

TEITZ, M. B. (1968), 'Toward a theory of urban public facility location', *Papers, Regional Science Association*, vol. 21, pp. 25–52.

THOMPSON, W. R. (1965), *A Preface to Urban Economics*, Johns Hopkins University Press.

WEBBER, M. L. (1963), 'Order in diversity: community without propinquity', in L. Wingo (ed.), *Cities and Space: the Future Use of Urban Land*, Johns Hopkins University Press.

WEBBER, M. L. (1964), 'Culture, territoriality and the elastic mile', *Papers, Regional Science Association*, vol. 11, pp. 59–69.

WEISBROD, B. A. (1965), 'Geographic spillover effects and the allocation of resources to education', in J. Margolis (ed.), *The Public Economy of Urban Communities*, Resources for the Future.

WILLIAMS, A. (1966), 'The optimal provision of public goods in a system of local government', *J. of Pol. Econ.*, vol. 74, pp. 18–33.

WILSON, A. G. (1970), 'Entropy in urban and regional modelling', *Monographs in Spatial and Environmental Systems Analysis*, no. 1, Lion.

WOOD, R. C. (1963), 'The contributions of political science to urban form', in W. Z. Hirsch (ed.), *Urban Life and Form*, Holt, Rinehart & Winston.

YOCUM, J. E., and McCALDIN, R. O. (1968), 'Effects of air pollution on materials and economy', in A. C. Stern (ed.), *Air Pollution*, vol. 2, 2nd edn, Academic Press.

17 F. Smallwood

Greater London: The Politics of Metropolitan Reform

F. Smallwood, 'Greater London: the politics of metropolitan reform', in *Greater London*, Bobbs-Merrill, 1965, ch. 13.

The vagaries of metropolitics are wondrous to behold.

With the adoption of the London Government Act of 1963, two central 'facts' had emerged with reasonable clarity. First, after seventy-five years, the death knell had finally sounded for the historic London County Council. Second, its successor – the new Greater London Council – faced a precarious future at best. After fighting the creation of this new council tooth and nail, the Labour Party had advanced the very ominous threat of recasting the entire London reform program if it captured control of the House of Commons in the next General Election.

In April of 1964, the Labourites swept the first Greater London Council elections, gaining sixty-four seats to thirty-six for the Conservatives. In May, Labour again captured clear majorities, on twenty of the thirty-two new London Borough councils. Far from destroying the London County Council, the Government's reform program had the practical effect of producing a new 'LCC Writ Large'.[1] And, far from facing a precarious future, this new 'LCC' appeared to rest on secure political ground indeed, no matter which party won the next General Election.

No more fitting conclusion could be found for the story of London's governmental reform, for, if this story indicates little else, it most certainly highlights our present lack of understanding of the intricacies of metropolitan politics in particular and of the local governmental process in general.

1. The phrase 'LCC Writ Large', from *The Times* (London) (11 April 1964), refers to the fact that half the newly elected GLC Labour councillors formerly served as members of the LCC, including all key committee chairmen and leaders with the exception of Sir Isaac Hayward and Mrs Freda Corbett, both of whom retired from the political arena. Hence, the elections had the practical effect of expanding substantially the geographical jurisdiction of the former LCC while leaving its former leadership patterns virtually intact. For a more detailed analysis of the surprising 1964 London election results, see Smallwood (1964).

The existing gaps in our knowledge are numerous. A major one involves the realm of theory. Despite centuries of reliance upon local governmental institutions, neither England nor the United States has ever really developed a coherent theoretical framework in which to evaluate the effectiveness of such institutions, especially in terms of their future relevance to the newer challenges of urbanization that have come to characterize modern society. This does not mean that local governmental mythologies do not exist, both overtly and subconsciously; yet these can hardly be classified as providing a meaningful theoretical framework upon which to build a viable local governmental system. Rather, such prevailing mythologies are more usually dusted off to champion a wild variety of divergent causes that bear little, if any, relationship to each other.

What has been lacking is an organized attempt to identify the central theoretical criteria that might help to expose past shibboleths and provide comprehensive conceptual guidelines that could clarify our future local governmental ideologies and development. With the exception of such occasional forays as Roscoe Martin's *Grass Roots* (1957), Arthur Maass's *Area and Power* (1959), Robert C. Wood's *Suburbia* (1959), and Luther Gulick's *The Metropolitan Problem and American Ideas* (1962), the American political scientist has avoided meaningful study of the more theoretical aspects of the local governmental process. The English response to this particular challenge has been equally sparse, especially during recent years, in which little of relevance has appeared beyond occasional papers by W. J. M. Mackenzie and Bryan Keith-Lucas.

In turn, America's failure to clarify its own local governmental theory has been compounded by a parochial avoidance of divergent theoretical approaches that fall outside the restricted confines of our native experience. A study such as L. G. Cowan's *Local Government in West Africa* (1958) represents a gold mine not only for what it tells about emerging developments in one of the world's most crucially important areas, but also because of its description of the theoretical dichotomy between a French 'assimilation' approach and a British Native Authority System. Cowan's analysis represents a relatively rare excursion into unfamiliar climes, however, at least for an American. In the field of comparative local government, the English most definitely can show us something of significance. Here the base for a future effort is to be found in the outlines of such studies as Ursula

Hicks's *Development From Below* (1961) and W. A. Robson's *Great Cities of the World* (1957).

A second aspect of the local governmental process that calls for the development of a more systematic body of knowledge involves the variety of stubborn practical problems that go into the making of any such project as the Greater London plan. Perhaps, as is indicated above, Professor Duncan (1951) is right in asserting that questions involving such considerations as the 'optimum' size of cities must inevitably originate in the 'realm of values', but certainly we can attempt to restrict somewhat the virtually limitless range of value choices that presently stymies our approach to these very questions. Once again, the subject has not been totally ignored. James Fesler's *Area and Administration* (1949), and more recently Paul Ylvisaker's attempt to suggest 'Criteria for the "Proper" Areal Division of Powers,' or the Advisory Commission on Intergovernmental Relations' efforts to analyse the *Performance of Urban Functions: Local and Area-wide*,[2] represent the types of studies that can provide both the insights and the hard data for a more sophisticated approach to these difficult problems in years ahead. Yet, our understanding of many of the most rudimentary functional aspects of the local governmental process is incredibly thin, a phenomenon that is all the more paradoxical in light of the tremendous amount of energy we have, in fact, poured into attempts to classify the more mundane organizational aspects of local governmental structure and procedure.

A third major knowledge gap has grown out of our past failure to develop a more systematic understanding of our metropolitan political systems. Here, however, more recent efforts provide a definite indication of very real progress. In addition to the expanding volume of metropolitan studies of such localities as Miami, St Louis, New York, Syracuse, Cleveland, Nashville, Toronto and a host of other cities,[3] we are finally beginning to see the subject of local politics take on the guise of a legitimate class-room concern. As Professors Banfield and Wilson note in one

2. See Ylvisaker (1959); Advisory Commission on Intergovernmental Relations (1963).

3. See, for example, Sofen (1963); Salisbury (1961); Sayre and Kaufman (1960); Martin and Munger (eds) (1961); Norton (1963); Watson and Romani (1961); Booth (1963); Smallwood (1963); Greer (1963); Martin (1963); Advisory Commission on Intergovernmental Relations (1962).

of the more recent texts, 'politics arises out of conflicts', and conflicts exist not solely or even primarily because of lack of information or lack of adequate organizational techniques, but 'rather because people have differing opinions and interests, and therefore opposing ideas about what should be done' (1963, p. 2).

The Greater London reform contest represents a classic example of such a collision between differing opinions and interests, and opposing ideas about what should be done. As such, its relevance stems in very large part from its political, rather than its organizational, connotations. Certainly the various administrative components of the Greater London plan do not constitute any elusive Rosetta stone that can be utilized to unravel automatically all America's metropolitan mysteries. Rather, the plan is of particular interest because it can tell us something about the divergent motivations, participants and strategies that went into the making of a bitter political clash over the specific issue of metropolitan reform – a clash which, when evaluated in light of our own growing body of literature on this same subject, may provide some fresh insights into our appreciation of the metropolitan reform process.

Motivations

Participants in the Greater London contest were activated by four basic motives:

1. Power drives
2. Professional concerns
3. Fears: real and imaginary
4. Ideological rationalizations.

Although there was a high degree of interplay and overlap between these four influences, each is worthy of individual summary analysis.

Power drives

The Greater London plan represented a predominantly self-contained, and highly reciprocal, exchange of powers, in that certain local 'actors' (i.e., the large borough councils, the London Conservatives, etc.) were originally designated to gain increased authority at the direct expense of other local 'actors' (i.e., the county councils, the London Labourites, etc.). As a result, power drives induced participants both to support and to oppose the reorganization program. The supporters were motivated by expectant power drives; the opponents, by defensive power drives.

The most apt example of expectant power drives was to be found in the attitudes of the frustrated second-tier councils, especially those of the larger Middlesex boroughs, which favored some system of reform from the outset. It is important to note that the primary thrust that originally led to the entire reorganization program was to be found among these local borough councils. Although surface appearances tended to indicate that the central Government took the lead in advocating reform, this was not actually the case. The underlying pressures first originated at the local level. The true nature of the origins of reform was later obscured by the fact that other local groups, motivated by defensive power drives, later decided to fight the reform program. As the objections of these defensive groups increased in intensity, the entire reorganization effort tended to take on the misleading guise of a dictatorial process, in which it appeared that an adamant higher governmental authority was grinding its heel upon its protesting local underlings. Actually, however, this higher authority did not provide the initial impetus for the reform program, nor did it really know how to handle the subsequent degeneration of this program.

This is not to imply that this higher authority failed to possess expectant power drives of its own. While the Conservative central Government authorities may not have provided the initial impetus for reform, they pressed ahead rapidly once the political implications of the Royal Commission's proposals became fully apparent. When the Labourite opposition accused these central Government authorities of 'indecent haste' in their attempts to use the reorganization program as a means of securing political control over London's government, the Conservatives flatly denied this charge. Yet, it is an obvious fact that the central Government did move extremely rapidly on this particular Royal Commission report, much more rapidly than is usually the case. It is difficult to assume that this same aggressive pace would have been forthcoming if the Royal Commission had somehow managed to recommend that a key Conservative local authority should have been abolished in favor of a potentially Labour-dominated council. The intensity of the central Government's expectations may have been somewhat less pronounced than was the case with the frustrated second-tier Middlesex boroughs, but it would be foolhardy to argue that expectant power drives played no part in shaping the Government's position on reform.

The London Labour Party represented a key illustration of a group that was motivated by defensive power drives. Since this Party was interested in protecting its existing power position, it tended to concentrate on an extremely short-range defense of the *status quo*. By and large, this same short-range approach toward reform was characteristic of all the defensive groupings. It was particularly obvious in the case of the London Labour Party because, as the reform program unfolded, it became increasingly more apparent that this program's potentially adverse impact on the LLP was not destined to be anywhere near as severe as the Party leaders professed. Each time the Government dropped additional Conservative authorities from the review area as part of its suburban fringe concessions, Labour's prospects of gaining control over the new Greater London Council increased significantly. Yet the local Labour leaders fought the plan bitterly to the very end. They were considerably more interested in protecting an immediate sure thing (i.e., their existing iron grip on the London County Council) than in gambling on potential long-range success with a larger, and more powerful, first-tier authority.[4]

In addition to the London Labour Party, other defensive power groupings were to be found in the first-tier county councils and county boroughs, and in the smaller second-tier authorities that were destined to lose status as a result of reform. Throughout the entire course of the reform contest, it was obvious that power drives, both expectant and defensive, played a crucial role in molding attitudes, pro and con, toward the reorganization plan. It is important to note, however, that these power drives did not

4. In fairness to the Labourite opponents of reform, it must be admitted that no one originally anticipated the massive Labour sweep that actually materialized during the first GLC elections in April–May 1964. In part, Labour was able to do so well because of the deletion of Conservative suburban fringe authorities noted above. However, the real key to the Labour success was to be found in the close relationship between the GLC voting and national electoral projections. By the spring of 1964, all the major electoral polls indicated a substantial national swing to the Labour Party, and in the GLC elections this swing was translated into a 7 per cent Labour gain in those marginal boroughs where direct comparisons could be made with the 1959 General Election voting. Thus, the Labour Party was able to capture every marginal borough in electing its sixty-four GLC councillors, before returning again in May to capture 1116 of the 1855 council seats at stake in the borough elections. While these results were obviously disheartening to the Conservatives, the Liberals actually made the most disastrous showing, being completely shut out in the April GLC election and capturing only sixteen of the 1855 borough seats in the May elections.

constitute the whole story. In many cases they were supplemented, and at times even supplanted, by other, more subtle, motivational influences.

Professional concerns

The major thrust of the professional concerns involved in the reform controversy was overwhelmingly negative in terms of its impact in activating opposition groups.

While, broadly conceived, professionally oriented arguments did provide some grist for the proponents of reform, such arguments were largely confined to abstractions. Supporters of reform, for example, attempted to justify the program in terms of vague claims regarding the increased efficiency to be realized through a rationalization of organizational structure, but these arguments were quite diffuse and carried little weight. The major impact of professional considerations was to be found in the influence that they exercised on a variety of important interest associations – the teachers, doctors, social workers and the like.

These groups were adamantly opposed to reform on the grounds that it would have an adverse effect on the discharge of their particular service specialties. Their protestations carried considerably more weight than the more nebulous 'efficiency' arguments advanced by the proponents of reform. Although the majority of these professional associations tended to take a narrow view of the situation (i.e., they were primarily concerned with potentially adverse impacts on their own particular service specialties), the combined weight of their protests eventually produced a very broad assault on the entire reform effort. The concerns of many of the groups ran very deep. The London Teachers' Association's interest in the comprehensive schools, for example, played a major role in shaping the position of this group, even though the reform proposals failed to take any direct stand, either pro or con, on the comprehensive school question.

While a variety of professional associations strongly opposed the projected reform program, there was little consensus on any alternative schemes. The alternatives that were advanced varied widely, and they were primarily dependent on preconceived value objectives. As a result of their inability to formulate viable alternatives, the professional dissidents preferred to remain with the *status quo*.

In their defense of this *status quo*, many of these associations relied upon the use of emotional symbols. Since these symbols grew out of the associations' own deep-seated anxieties, they tended to center upon the manipulation of one of the most powerful of all emotional weapons. With the passage of time, the manipulation of fear, both imaginary and real, played an increasingly more significant role in the proceedings.

Emotional fears

The Greater London contest was dominated by two basic fears – the fear of future uncertainty and the fear of loss of identity. Each of these fears tended to strengthen the opposition side tremendously while providing nothing in the way of support for the proponents of reform.

Fear of future uncertainty was a logical outgrowth of the professional associations' anxieties. In essence, these associations translated their own anxieties into increasingly more generalized fear symbols, by contrasting existing certitudes with future unknowns. Over time, these future unknowns took on ever more ominous overtones, until they finally hardened into sweeping prophecies of dire portent:

'Chaos or Progress?'
'A Leap Into The Dark.'
'The Education of the Children of London Will Suffer.'
'The Children of London Will Suffer.'
'The Patients of London Will Suffer.'
'The People of London Must Suffer.'[5]

These fears regarding future uncertainties were compounded by a second set of more immediately realistic anxieties – fears over the loss of identity. It was this second set of fears that dominated the attitudes of the inner county councils (i.e., London and Middlesex) and the smaller second-tier councils whose jurisdictions were scheduled to be amalgamated with those of their larger neighbors. This development was hardly surprising in light of the fact that both these groupings were, quite literally, fighting for their very lives.

The London experience indicates that the instinct for institutional self-preservation can run every bit as deep as the human

5. Quotations taken from 'The London County Council – Why Destroy It?' (pamphlet published by LCC, September 1962); press statement of child welfare agencies, 28 February, 1963; press statement of local medical committee for County of London, 22 January, 1963.

instinct for personal survival. Perhaps because the two are so deep-seated and intertwined, the struggle for institutional self-preservation often contains basic elements of dramatic heroics that can engender widespread public sympathy and support. This is especially true if the struggle centers upon smaller groups which are able to convey the impression that they are battling against superior odds.

The impact of this phenomenon was not confined to the London area alone. During the course of the Greater London reform, a series of complementary local government reviews was taking place throughout other portions of the country. One of these reviews centered upon the tiny county of Rutland in east-central England – a county which had 'prized its independence for more than 700 years' and was not about to give it up without a fight. Rutland contains some 25,000 loyal inhabitants, and when the Local Government Boundary Commission proposed that it should be abolished through a merger with its neighboring county, Leicestershire (having more than 400,000 population), the reaction of the local Rutlanders was violent in its intensity and Churchillian in its overtones. 'We'll fight on the beaches and in the ditches if necessary to keep Rutland free', asserted the house-master of one of the local Rutland schools. In time, the entire controversy began to take on a compelling David-versus-Goliath appeal. *The Sunday Times*, under the heading 'RUTLAND'S LAST STAND', advised its readers:

England's smallest county refuses to bow to the knee of the Whitehall legions who want to make it a mere rural district of its neighbor, Leicestershire (Parkinson, 1962, pp. 14–15).

Eventually, these Whitehall legions recanted, and Rutland was spared when the recommendations of the Boundary Commission were overruled. It was impossible for any such process of clemency to take place throughout the entire Greater London area, because the reform program would have collapsed if such a policy had been pursued. Yet, it is significant to note some of the major concessions that were made in London. The tiny City of London Corporation, for example, that unique local entity of 5000 resident souls, was allowed to retain its separate identity from the very beginning, and numerous suburban fringe authorities were permitted to escape from the rigors of reorganization with their skins intact. The instinct for institutional self-preservation was very much a part of the Greater London reform contest.

Ideological rationalizations

All three of the above basic motivations (i.e., power drives, professional concerns, real and imaginary fears) were reinforced by a variety of ideological abstractions that were designed to lend credence to the various participants' preconceived positions. Both the proponents and the opponents of reform employed ideological abstractions for such reinforcement purposes. Once again, however, the opposition side was able to make the most effective use of ideological symbols to strengthen its position.

This use of ideological rationalizations does not imply that either side failed to take such abstractions seriously. Many opponents of reform were quite honest in their ideological attacks on the reorganization program, while many supporters felt that the plan would restore the vitality of local government and halt the trend toward centralization of power. Thus, the Labour Party was able to justify its basic opposition to reform in terms of a functional approach to the local governmental process, while Conservative spokesmen were able to justify both support and opposition stances by drawing upon divergent streams of party ideology.

In very large part, however, this use of ideologies did represent a displacement process. Since many of the participants found it difficult to defend their stands on the basis of purely parochial power drives, they attempted to displace these drives with more attractive ideological rationalizations. There is, of course, nothing new or unique about this. Lasswell (1958) has described the political type as one who 'displaces private motives with public objects in the name of collective advantage' (p. 21). What is significant to note is that these ideological rationalizations played an important twofold role in the Greater London contest.

On the one hand, they produced a sense of comfort, and even of ethical well-being, for the various participants, with the result that the contest became continually more aggressive with the passage of time. Once the participants had converted their personal interests into ideological causes, they tended to defend their positions with increasing hostility.

In addition, ideologies were utilized to translate individual grievances into broad-based generalities. This permitted the formation of various coalitions that violated the prevailing norms of London politics. Ideological rationalizations, for example, justified the alignment of Surrey County's staid Conservative hierarchy with the Labour forces of central London County.

They also led to a natural grouping between the dissident professional associations and these same London County Labour forces.

In short, although their motive power was predominantly rationalizing rather than innovating, ideological abstractions played a very important role in the reform contest. Their major utility stemmed from their very vagueness, which permitted them to be used with a high degree of flexibility. In light of the fact that the nebulous nature of conflicting ideologies contributed to, rather than detracted from, their increased effectiveness throughout the reform contest, it is perhaps easier to understand our reluctance to develop any truly coherent and consistent theories of local government.

Other motives beyond those already identified also played a role in activating participants. Some groups, such as the Fulham Borough Council, appeared to indicate a genuine interest in the abstraction of 'good government'. Most participants, however, were stimulated by concerns that were considerably more practical than this. Financial considerations and status symbols, for example, were a factor in inducing both the outlying county councils and many second-tier fringe authorities to oppose the reform program. On the whole, however, these supplementary motives were not of crucial importance. The primary influences that shaped the Greater London conflict were the four identified above – power drives, professional concerns, real and imaginary fears, and ideological abstractions. These four constituted the quartet that called – if not, in fact, played – the tune in Greater London.

Participants

Participation in the Greater London contest was characterized by two highly distinctive attributes. The first involved the scope of participation; the second, the underlying nature of the participant groupings themselves.

Scope of participation

Despite all its sound and fury, the Greater London contest was, by and large, a private and restricted affair. At times this central fact tended to be obscured by the intensity and the bitterness of the struggle, yet the evidence that is available tends to indicate that the conflict was fought out against a backdrop of widespread public apathy. In their approach toward local government, the great mass of Londoners appeared to reflect the same apathetic attitudes that were to be found among their fellow countrymen throughout the British Isles.

An ambitious nationwide attempt to uncover information regarding the general public's attitudes toward England's local government was launched by the National and Local Government Officers Association in 1957. In all, some 10,000 NALGO members interviewed more than 180,000 people in an attempt to ascertain their concerns about, and their knowledge of, the local government process. This NALGO survey indicated that 'seventeen out of twenty householders in England and Wales consider local government to be important in their daily lives, but one in four has only the haziest idea of what it does'. When the 180,000 individuals were asked if they ever attended local council meetings, 6 per cent answered yes, and 94 per cent answered no. When they were asked if they belonged to local interest, or electoral, associations, 17 per cent said yes, and 83 per cent said no.[6]

The NALGO findings of widespread apathy are supported by occasional articles that appear in British scholarly journals. One recent study in the *British Journal of Sociology* (Bealey and Bartholomew, 1962) involved an evaluation of public knowledge regarding the 1958 local elections in Newcastle-Under-Lyme – an industrial community of some 75,000 people located about mid-way between Birmingham and Manchester. Based on a sample of 800 electors, the researchers found that 'there was widespread ignorance about the election and only limited interest in it'. The survey covered two rural wards and four urban wards, and, perhaps surprisingly, the lack of knowledge was most acute in the latter:

The ignorance of the urban voters about their candidates was astonishing. In all four borough wards, only 33 voters named both candidates correctly, and 419 could name neither. Out of 101 respondents in Ward 5, only 1 knew the names of both candidates, and 98 knew neither (Bealey and Bartholomew, pp. 273–83).

A good part of such widespread public apathy outside the central London area can undoubtedly be explained by the fact that there are so many uncontested local elections in England. According to the most recent statistics, the national average of uncontested seats in county elections is 65·6 per cent, while for rural district council elections this figure soars to 76·1 per cent.

6. *Public Service*, vol. 31, no. 5, May, 1957, pp. 146–148.

In other words, two-thirds of all the county councillors and three-quarters of all the rural district councillors seeking office in England are automatically assured of election because they are running unopposed.

In London County, on the other hand, every seat on the LCC was contested in every election between 1949 and 1961. Thus, the London County Council established the unique distinction of presenting the voters in each of its electoral divisions that key element of the democratic process – the opportunity of choice. When the Registrar General's official statistics are adjusted to reflect this fact, it can be seen that the LCC electorate exceeded the national average turnout by some 10 per cent to 20 per cent during the postwar era.[7]

Table 1 **Percentage of total qualified electorate voting: all council seats**

Year	LCC vote	England: average of all counties
	%	%
1946	24·9	23·3
1949	40·7	28·9
1952	43·4	23·5
1955	32·4	21·6
1958	31·5	20·0
1961	36·4	(n.a.)

As Table 1 indicates, however, the LCC turnouts actually were not overly impressive. The highest total in the postwar period (43·4 per cent) saw a little more than two of every five voters exercising their franchise, and the more typical turnout saw only one of every three voters exercising the franchise. Because of the fact that even the contested LCC elections did not light any great sparks, it should hardly be surprising that the general public failed to show any great interest in a rather complex reorganization plan that dealt with the structural reform of Greater London's government.

Indication that the general public did not, in fact, show such interest is to be found in the limited number of studies that have been made on the subject of electoral attitudes in the London

7. *The Registrar General's Statistical Review of England and Wales for the Years: 1946, 1949, 1952, 1955, 1958* (adjusted), part 2, Tables: Civil (London: HMSO); London County Council, Election Statistics, April 1961 election of County Councillors.

area itself. In a 1962 survey of the Clapham electoral division of the Metropolitan Borough of Wandsworth, L. J. Sharpe of the London School of Economics discovered a widespread lack of knowledge regarding the proposed Greater London plan. Only 37·2 per cent of his sample who had actually voted in the 1961 LCC elections were able to identify their Party's stand on this issue, while 30·6 per cent of the voting sample misinterpreted their Party's stand, and 42·2 per cent indicated that they did not know what the issue was all about. The corresponding figures for the nonvoters indicated an even more general lack of knowledge (Sharpe, pp. 84–6).

A similar lack of knowledge was uncovered in a study conducted by Ian Budge, a Yale University graduate student who has also engaged in opinion research in the London area. In 1962 Mr Budge interviewed a sample of Party leaders drawn from throughout the Greater London area and a sample of local voters in the Middlesex Borough of Brentford and Chiswick. He then attempted to compare the reaction of these two groups on a number of local issues, one of which was the proposed London reform program. Whereas 97 per cent of the Party leaders expressed a definite commitment, either pro or con, on this issue, only 47·6 per cent of the local Brentford and Chiswick voters expressed any definite preference. Of the 52·4 per cent of the local voters who had no preference, 31 per cent indicated they knew nothing about the issue.[8]

Further indications of the prevailing public disinterest which Messrs Sharpe and Budge discovered could be found throughout the Greater London area. Perhaps the most telling commentary of all was made by a local suburban newspaper in the northern portion of the review area. After making a survey of local reactions to the plan in the summer of 1962, this paper, *The Walthamstow Independent*, concluded, 'So Many People Just Couldn't Care Less'.[9] There is no doubt that all available evidence, as sketchy as it may be, points to a widespread lack of public concern over the reorganization of Greater London's government.[10]

8. Letters from Ian Budge to F. Smallwood dated 15 November, 1962, and December 1, 1962.

9. *The Walthamstow Independent*, 'The Truth About The Merger', 10 August, 1962.

10. One close observer of the London scene explains this widespread public apathy as follows:

As a result, the only time the issue did spill over into the public arena was when specific attempts were made to activate public opinion on a short-range basis. The London Teachers' Association's mass protest meetings with the parents of school children served as an apt illustration of this technique. On the whole, however, the Greater London contest was dominated by intensive infighting between a limited number of groups, which varied widely in terms of both their internal cohesiveness and their external commitments.

The nature of the participants

The Yale studies of community power structure have indicated the high degree of relevance that 'scope', or issue-area, has to the activation of different political actors.[11] In London, certain groups who reacted vigorously to the specific issue of metropolitan reform followed the Yale pattern very closely. These groups – the teachers, the doctors, the social workers, and so forth – could not be classified as part of any stable London political hierarchy or elite. Instead, they became involved in this particular reform controversy only because they felt that certain of their legitimate value objectives were being threatened in a very direct manner by the Government's reorganization proposals. In short, some of the key participants in the Greater London contest represented spontaneous pluralistic groupings of persons who responded aggressively to the specific issue of metropolitan reform but who presumably would have remained silent on other significant community conflicts.

In addition, however, there was a second class of participants who very definitely did indicate the traits of highly influential power elites. This second class of participants – the local political party leaders, the county council leaders, and the like – consti-

---

Part of the London problem is the rootlessness, the insecurity, especially in the central areas where almost nobody owns his own home and mobility is normal. . . . Many Londoners are not aware of their boroughs. They will tell you that they live in Kentish Town or Chalk Farm, rather than St Pancras; in Limehouse or Mile End, rather than Stepney; in St John's Wood, rather than Marylebone . . . Jeger (1962, p. 586).

Yet, while this sense of borough anonymity may have characterized the general public's approach toward reform, it did not hold true with respect to the various borough council leaders, many of whom were vitally concerned with the problem of institutional self-preservation noted earlier.

11. See, for example, Dahl (1961); Wolfinger (1960, pp. 636–44); Polsby (1963).

tuted the hard-core political hierarchy of Greater London. Presumably, they would have been activated by any major political conflict in the London area, regardless of the particular issue-area involved.

The two classes of participants differed quite widely in terms of their internal structural cohesion. Many of the hard-core 'power elites' were extremely tightly organized and controlled from the top, whereas the spontaneous groupings tended to be considerably more diffuse. A classic illustration of a tightly-structured elite grouping was the London County Council's Labour majority.

After the London Labour Party captured control of the London County Council in 1934, a series of organizational directives was issued to all Labour councillors. During more than a quarter of a century of unbroken rule, these directives hardened into a system of iron discipline. The kingpin of the LCC Labour hierarchy was the Leader of the Council, and his key lever of power was his authority to appoint all chairmen and vice-chairmen of the LCC committees. In turn, these committee leaders paid due homage to the Council Leader by re-electing him to his leadership post each year. By means of this automatic system of circular reciprocity, the LCC Labour hierarchy eventually took on the characteristics of a completely closed shop.

Over the course of time, the impact of this Labour Party's disciplinary pattern permeated every aspect of the Council's deliberations, primarily because of the major role the committees played in guiding the Council's program. Prior to each committee meeting, the Labour members of the various committees held a private caucus to determine precise lines of policy. Once established, these lines were to be followed by all Party members. As Section III of the LCC Labour Party's Directive on 'Organization' explained:

. . . Normally, of course, the [Committee] agenda will have been discussed in a group meeting held prior to the Committee, and decisions arrived at as to the line to be taken.

That is why it is most important to attend the group meetings. This is the member's opportunity to raise points of difference, and a member missing this meeting should not come into the Committee and raise difficulties for the Chairman. He or she can easily ascertain from a colleague the line that it has been decided to follow.

Once the Party's policy line had been duly ratified by the full Committee, there was little that individual Party members could do to modify it at a later date, even on the floor of the Council. As Section V of the Party's 'Organization' directive warned:

Every member is entitled to ask up to two questions at any Council meeting, but he or she should ascertain beforehand from the Chairman of the Committee concerned that the question will not cause the Party any embarrassment.[12]

The effects of this autocratic approach to Council deliberations were widespread. For one thing, it robbed these deliberations of any vitality, to a point where it was hardly surprising that general apathy marked the public's attitude toward Council affairs. Since every conceivable item of policy had been decided long beforehand, the LCC meetings took on all the spontaneity of an automatic computer grinding out myriads of precise statistics.

In addition to deadening the public's interest in Council affairs, the Labour Party's tightly structured leadership on the LCC was of considerable importance to the Greater London reform contest. On the surface it might appear that this tight structural hierarchy would help the Council majority to mount an effective opposition program, by permitting it to present a solid phalanx against the reform proposals. In actuality, however, the system hurt the Council. The fact was that this phalanx hardened into a monolithic mass that was unable to offer anything in the way of creative originality as an opposition force. The only significant response to the reform proposals that came from the LCC Labour majority was to be found in the testimony of an individual Party member, Mr Hugh Jenkins. Mr Jenkins, however, stood far from the top tier of the LCC leadership, and the fact that he dared to offer testimony at all represented an act of considerable political courage.

With this sole exception, the contributions of the LCC Labour majority toward the reform of London Government were totally negative and lacking in imagination. The significant opposition spokesmen were to be found outside, rather than inside, the ranks of the LCC hierarchy. It was Sir Cyril Black, a Conservative from Surrey County who demonstrated the initiative to formulate an alternative reform plan. It was Michael Stewart, a Labour member of Parliament, who presented the most articulate case for the opposition. It was a variety of professional associations that

12. London County Council Labour Party, 'Organization' (mimeographed), signed by I. J. Hayward, Leader of the Council, and W. G. Fiske, Chief Whip (undated).

attempted to modify the plan in a manner which they felt would make it more effective. In no case did the top leadership of the LCC majority step forward to provide the type of creative guidance that might have helped, rather than hindered, the future development of London's government.

This is not to imply that the London County Council represented an ineffective administrative organization that was racked by corruption or scandal. To the contrary, it was a highly efficient administrative body that had compiled a brilliant list of achievements in housing, education, the health services and a variety of other fields. The problem was, however, that years of tight party rule had robbed the Council of its political vitality to such a degree that its top leadership was unable to make any effective response during the Council's gravest hour of trial.

Whereas the LCC majority served as a classic example of the highly structured opposition force, the spokesmen for the various children's service groups represented a case of the more spontaneous opposition coalition. In the case of these groups there was no semblance of tight hierarchical organization in any sense comparable to the LCC Labour leadership. Instead, the children's service spokesmen consisted of a mixture of formal and informal groupings – members of the Association of Child Care Officers, chairmen of the Metropolitan Juvenile Courts, interested spokesmen from the academic community and the like. There is no doubt that such coalitions represented an illustration par excellence of the issue-area participant in action. Most, if not all, of the children's service groups had little sustained contact with the London political scene. They were activated on this particular issue-area by an altruistic belief that the reform plan represented a serious threat to the future administration of the particular service with which they were concerned. In light of this belief, they were willing to assume a political role in an attempt to preserve an existing value system which they found to be highly meaningful.

The same dichotomy between the informal and the highly structured groupings that characterized the opposition forces was also to be found among the proponents of reform. An apt illustration of an informal support grouping was the London School of Economics contingent. The central Government, on the other hand, represented the chief example of the tightly structured proponent group. It is interesting to note, however, that the central Government, like the London County Council hierarchy, also experienced its share of difficulties in responding to the reform program. The major problem here was not one of structural stultification, but rather a discontinuity in political leadership.

Throughout the course of the reform contest, the central Government received extremely able staff leadership, especially from Dame Evelyn Sharp, the Permanent Secretary of the Ministry of Housing and Local Government. The Government's major difficulty related to the fact that the implementation of the Greater London plan demanded a great number of political decisions that could not be made at the staff level. Because of a successive turnover of Ministers during the course of the reform contest, this top political leadership became unco-ordinated and inconsistent. It was not until Sir Keith Joseph was named Minister of Housing and Local Government in the summer of 1962 that the required leadership initiative was forthcoming. From this time forward, the Government consolidated its position and moved steadily ahead with the reform program.

Thus, in the final analysis, the structural divergencies between the various opposition and support groups were of somewhat limited significance. Obviously, effective action on either side was forthcoming only when the various groups had access to positions of community power. The key ingredient was not really ease of access, however, but the quality of the leadership itself. Some groups – such as the London Teachers' Association – were able to make highly effective use of relatively limited resources, while other groups – such as the London County Council Labour majority – were frozen into ineffectual positions despite their access to considerably more massive power resources.

The Greater London experience tends to indicate that, if metropolitan governmental reform is to be realized, it will not be totally dominated by any elite revolutions of formal community power leaders. Rather, it will be highly dependent upon a rich degree of political sophistication and sensitivity on the part of a wide variety of less formal groups who may decide to play this particular game. The tactics and strategies that were of most significance in Greater London were primarily a reflection of the innate leadership ability displayed by many informal groups, some of which were able to run circles around those who occupied positions on the topmost tier of the formal community power hierarchy.

Strategies

The opponents of reform were forced to carry the offensive throughout the Greater London contest. The proponents of reform attempted to neutralize these opposition attacks through a continuous series of concessions. The basic objectives of both sides followed closely the Schattschneider (1960) strategic concerns regarding the scale of the battle. When evaluated in light of American experience, however, the strategic roles adopted by the two sides presented something of a reverse twist. In London, the opponents of reform attempted to enlarge the scale of the battle, while the support forces attempted to restrict this battle.

This twist resulted from a basic procedural variation that distinguishes the English and American approaches toward local governmental reform. In the United States, the issue of metropolitan reorganization is generally decided by a public referendum. Under such circumstances, it is essential for those who favor reorganization to make a vigorous effort to enlist widespread public support for their program. They must take the initiative in selling their proposals to the public, since they can hope to realize their aspirations for success only by enlarging the scope of their support to secure a majority vote in the reform referendum.

In London, the issue of metropolitan reorganization was ultimately decided by a higher governmental authority, rather than by means of any direct public referendum. This higher authority – the central Government – favored the reorganization program from the very beginning. Since this central Government possessed the conclusive strategic advantage throughout the reform contest (i.e., its disciplined Parliamentary majority), it was anxious to limit, rather than enlarge, the size of the interested audience in the hope of restricting potential political conflict. The more controversial the reform plan became, the more difficult it would be to force Parliamentary action on this issue. In keeping with this all-important objective of limiting the size of the audience, the Government attempted to quiet down controversy as soon as it arose. The method it used was to buy off potential opposition through specific concessions to any group (e.g., the London teachers) that became overly vocal in its criticism of the plan.

The opposition forces, on the other hand, were continually trying to open up the scope of the battle. Since they were obviously in continuous danger of losing the contest (i.e., they did not enjoy the Government's ultimate strategic weapon of a disciplined Parliamentary majority), they could hope to reverse this losing trend only by making the plan so controversial that the Government would be forced to drop it. In attempting to pursue this objective, the opposition eventually turned to such direct pressure groups as the Committee for London Government. In turn, these groups employed increasingly more emotional symbols in an effort to induce new opponents to join the battle. In this manner, the Greater London contest followed the Coleman (1957) outline very closely. It was translated from the specific to the general, and it degenerated from disagreement into antagonism.

This opposition strategy very nearly succeeded. The supreme test for the Government came when it was no longer possible to grant further concessions without destroying the overarching unity of the entire reform effort. At this point, it became necessary for the Government to adopt a new strategy. It was forced to take off its gloves and engage in a direct power struggle with no holds barred. The Government accepted this challenge during the final Parliamentary phase of the battle when it employed the guillotine, and every other weapon at its disposal, to push the reform program through Parliament. It is extremely doubtful that the program would have been adopted if the Government had not been willing to adopt such drastic tactics. It is certainly highly debatable whether the program could ever have had any chance of success at all if it had been forced to undergo the same referendum procedure that is characteristic of the American approach toward the issue of metropolitan reform.

In terms of surface appearances, many of the motives, participants, and strategies in Greater London were quite different from those which are to be found in the typical American city. Underneath this surface, however, there were enough basic similarities to give pause for thought. One of the most significant findings to emerge from the Greater London story is the fact that all those who opposed the reform program were not necessarily misfits or dissatisfied fanatics. On the contrary, many groups found in the prevailing unstructured metropolitan system legitimate values – psychological, professional and otherwise – that they felt were well worth protecting and preserving.

This again begs the question as to the degree of knowledge which we presently possess on this crucially important issue of metropolitan government. More recent studies are beginning to indicate that there are, perhaps, many more meaningful values in our existing unstructured metropolitan systems than we had at first assumed to be the case. Thomas R. Dye, for example (1962), has pointed out that Philadelphia's existing 'decentralized political structure [is] functional to the metropolitan system' in a number of significant ways, many of which are very directly related to the psychological well-being of its inhabitants, especially minority groups (p. 11). In a similar manner, Vincent Ostrom, Charles Tiebout, and Robert Warren have indicated that, contrary to surface appearances, Los Angeles' highly unstructured metropolitan area possesses 'a very rich and intricate "framework" for negotiating, adjudicating and deciding questions that affect . . . diverse public interests' (1961, p. 842).

This is not to be interpreted as a plea against metropolitan government *per se*, but rather as a warning that we are dealing here with a highly turbulent issue that cannot be translated into effective action without a thorough knowledge of local conditions and a highly sophisticated expression of local leadership. Above all else, the Greater London experience indicates that metropolitan reform is not solely, or even primarily, an organizational issue; rather, it is a political question that involves the reconciliation of many opposing interests, opinions and ideas. From start to finish the London reform program was forced to wrestle with Almond's political 'input' functions, despite the fact that it was primarily concerned with modifying the administrative 'output' components of London's governmental system. In so doing, it most certainly added credence to Professor Hugh Whalen's observation that

a realistic reform program must temper the practicable in an administrative sense, with the practicable in a political sense. . . . In this, as in all other political questions, consensus must be worked for and won; and it is foolish to suppose that agreement is delivered by the stork, or miraculously worked by a hidden hand while men slumber (1960, p. 13).

As regards the magnitude of this political task, it is extremely significant that, in London's case, the great majority of motivational influences at work were 'negative' in that they tended to activate the opponents, rather than the supporters, of reform. Power drives were instrumental in activating both support and opposition groups, and ideological rationalizations were likewise used by both sides. The major thrust of professional considerations, however, was to stimulate strong opposition to the plan, and the fear and anxiety arguments were almost totally negative in activating opposition groups.

After full recognition of such political difficulties, however, we can hardly bury our heads in the sand and shy away completely from the massive environmental challenge we face today. At the present time, we are participating in an urban upheaval that is producing totally new residential patterns. If we are to believe Doxiadis' predictions, today's metropolis is already coalescing into tomorrow's cosmopolis, and we can hardly afford to sit on our hands indefinitely under such explosive circumstances. Certainly, the basic forces at work here show no signs of abating. As Scott Greer has noted, 'the metropolitan community is continuously improvised; its evolution is organic, not rational; change is crescive, not revolutionary; problems are solved by trial and error, rather than by fiat' (1962, p. 148).

It is in making our improvisations, and in subjecting ourselves to such tests of trial and error, that we cannot afford to lose sight of a second basic fact. The city has always been a human institution that has harbored deep human hopes and aspirations:

Visions of man's ultimate destiny on earth, and indeed, often in heaven, have usually taken shape around the image of the city. To build some kind of New Jerusalem or Celestial City has appeared to demand the most consummate artistry of which men are capable. . . . Prophetic revelation and Utopian gospel have, through the ages, presented visions of this imagined place. Though these visions have been blurred by the mists and disillusionments of history, yet the dream continues to recur in ever new forms.[13]

The unique significance of the Greater London plan was to be found in the Royal Commission's assertion that London's government was something more than an administrative mechanism; that it was not just 'a machine, or a piece of organization', but rather 'a living thing . . . in which . . . each part is integrally concerned with each other part'. As a result of this basic belief, the Commission developed a dualistic approach toward London's governmental needs, which encompassed both the functional requirements of the metropolis and the difficult value judgments that go into the making of a viable and healthy local governmental system.

Many, if they grasped this approach at all, tended to view the Commissioners as mystics at best. Most, however, failed to see such a humanistic, value-oriented approach as being of any relevance to the needs of the modern metropolis. 'What was

13. Carver (1962, p. 23).

appropriate to the Greek city-state of 500 BC is not therefore suitable to twentieth century London.'

Perhaps in an age which pays lofty tribute to the virtues of functional specialization, such displays of skepticism should not have been surprising. Yet, there still appears to be considerable merit in an observation Graham Wallas made little more than half a century ago:

Children will not learn to love London while getting figures by heart as to the millions of her inhabitants or the miles of her sewers. . . . Perhaps before we have a poet who loves London as Sophocles loved Athens, it may be necessary to make London itself somewhat more lovely (1962, p. 209).

The Royal Commission on Local Government in Greater London had its vision of a New Jerusalem which, with all its faults, represented no less than the vision of the old Jerusalem as it was praised in the Psalms – 'a city that is at unity in itself'.[14]

Whether or not this vision was an accurate one is a matter that will reveal itself in the course of time. It was the very existence of the vision in the first place, however, that made the bitter fight over its realization worth all the effort.

14. Psalm 122:3. The quotation is from *The Book of Common Prayer*. The King James Bible version is 'a city that is compact together'. I first noted this particularly apt quotation in Professor W. J. M. Mackenzie's 1952 Percival Lecture at Manchester University, entitled 'The Government of Great Cities'.

References

ADVISORY COMMISSION ON INTERGOVERNMENTAL RELATIONS (1962), *Factors Affecting Voter Reactions to Government Reorganization in Metropolitan Areas*, Washington.

ADVISORY COMMISSION ON INTERGOVERNMENTAL RELATIONS (1963), *Performance of Urban Functions: Local and Areawide*, Washington, September.

BANFIELD, E. C., and WILSON, J. Q. (1963), *City Politics*, Harvard University Press.

BEALEY, F., and BARTHOLOMEW, D. J. (1962), 'The local elections in Newcastle-under-Lyme', *Brit. J of Sociol.*, vol. 13, no. 3, pp. 273–83.

BOOTH, D. A. (1963), *Metropolitics: The Nashville Consolidation*, Michigan State University.

CARVER, H. (1962), *Cities in the Suburbs*, University of Toronto Press.

COLEMAN, J. S. (1957), *Community Conflict*, Free Press.

COWAN, L. G. (1958), *Local Government in West Africa*, Columbia University Press.

DAHL, R. (1961), *Who Governs?*, Yale University Press.

DUNCAN, O. D. (1951), 'The optimum size of cities', in P. K. Hall and A. J. Reiss (eds.) *Cities and Society*, Free Press.

DYE, T. R. (1962), 'Metropolitan integration by bargaining among sub-areas', *Amer. Behav. Scientist*, vol. 5, p. 11.

FESLER, J. (1949), *Area and Administration*, University of Alabama Press.

GREER, S. (1962), 'The emerging city: Myth and reality', in *Governing the Metropolis*, Wiley.

GREER, S. (1963), *Metropolitics*, Wiley.

GULICK, L. (1962), *The Metropolitan Problem*, Knopf.

HICKS, U. K. (1961), *Development and American Ideas from Below*, Clarendon Press.

JEGER, L. (1962), 'The human awful wonder of God', *New Statesman*.

LASSWELL, H. (1958), *Politics: Who Gets What, When, How*, Meridian Books.

MAASS, A. (1959), *Area and Power*, Free Press.

MARTIN, R. (1957), *Grass Roots*, University of Alabama Press.

MARTIN, R. (1963), *Metropolis in Transition*, HHFA.

MARTIN, R. C., and MUNGER, F. J. (eds.) (1961), *Decisions in Syracuse*, Indiana University Press.

NORTON, J. A. (1963), *The Metro Experience*, The Press of Western Reserve University.

OSTROM, V., TIEBOUT, C. M., and WARREN, R. (1961), 'The organization of government in metropolitan areas: a theoretical enquiry', *Amer. Pol. Sci. Rev.*, vol. 55, pp. 831–42.

PARKINSON, M. (1962), 'Rutland's last stand', *Sunday Times Magazine*, 9 October, pp. 14–15.

POLSBY, N. (1963), *Community Power and Political Theory*, Yale University Press.

ROBSON, W. A. (1957), *Great Cities of the World*, Allen & Unwin.

SALISBURY, R. H. (1961), 'The dynamics of reform: charter politics in St. Louis', *Midwest J. of Pol. Sci.*, vol. 5, no. 3, August, pp. 260–75.

SAYRE, W. S., and KAUFMAN, H. (1960), *Governing New York City*, Russell Sage Foundation.

SCHATTSCHNEIDER, E. E. (1960), *The Semi-Sovereign People*, Holt, Rinehart & Winston.

SHARPE, L. J. (1962), *A Metropolis Votes*, London School of Economics.

SMALLWOOD, F. (1963), *Metro Toronto: A Decade Later*, Bureau of Municipal Research.

SMALLWOOD, F. (1964), 'Labourites sweep London elections', *Nat. Civic. Rev.*, July.

SOFEN, E. (1963), *The Miami Metropolitan Experiment*, Indiana University Press.

WALLAS, G. (1962), *Human Nature in Politics*, Constable.

WATSON, R. A., and ROMANI, J. (1961), 'Metropolitan government for metropolitan Cleveland: an analysis of the voting record', *Midwest J. of Pol. Sci.*, vol. 5, no. 4, November, pp. 365–90.

WHALEN, H. (1960), 'Democracy and local government', *Canad. Pub. Admin.*, vol. 3, pp. 1–13.

WOLFINGER, R. (1960), 'Reputation and reality in the study of community Power', *Amer. Sociol. Rev.*, October, pp. 636–44.

WOOD, R. C. (1959), *Suburbia*, Houghton Mifflin.

YLVISAKER, P. (1959), 'Criteria for the "proper" areal division of powers', in A. Maass (ed.), *Area and Power*, Free Press.

18 H. J. Gans

Planning for People, not Buildings

H. J. Gans, 'Planning for people, not buildings', *Environment and Planning*, vol. 1, 1969, pp. 33–46.

The title of this paper is an oversimplifying catchphrase. Even so, it is probably fair to say that city planning has concerned itself primarily with buildings and the physical environment, and only secondarily with the people who use that environment. As the title suggests, I believe these priorities ought to be reversed; the aim of planning is to help people solve their problems and realize their goals. It should be noted at the outset, that this paper concerns only American city planning, and British planners must judge how relevant are the observations and proposals to their own experience.

The planner's physical bias

If the proverbial 'Man from Mars' came face to face with city planners, he would surely be amazed. Here is a profession which sees itself as planning for the community, but deals with only a portion of that community. In planning land uses, the location and design of buildings, streets, other transportation facilities, utility lines and open spaces, the profession sees mainly the natural and man-made physical artifacts of the city. It aims to arrange and rearrange these artifacts to create an orderly – often even static – efficient and attractive community. Even more strangely, it tries to arrange these artifacts according to a theory of urban form which, sometimes borrowing from the shapes of geometry, attempts to squeeze the city into a star pattern or a series of fingers, as if the major purpose of a city was to present a symmetrical and pleasing spectacle when seen from an airplane.

By including only a limited portion of the community in his professional concerns, the planner ignores almost entirely the people who live in that community, and without whom there would be no buildings or land uses. He does not plan for them either as individuals or as members of groups. He pays no attention to the social structures, institutions, culture and sub-cultures, socio-economic classes, age-groups and political blocs which are the fabric of society. He does not see that most people live most of their lives around the family, the job, their friends, the church and a couple of clubs; he does not recognize that they have goals or aspirations, problems or worries; he sees them only as occupants of dwellings, offices, factories and moving vehicles. Indeed, he does not even pay much attention to how they use these facilities. For the planner, people are little more than artifacts. They are expected to function within the housing, land uses and other community arrangements which he provides, and are supposed to subordinate their personal and familial interests to the needs of the neighbourhood, the community and the community plan, and to share the planner's goals of order, efficiency and beauty for their community.

The historical and political sources of physical planning

Why has city planning taken this direction? Why has it not concerned itself with planning for the groups in which people live, and for the way in which they want to live? In America, the answer can be found in events in the nineteenth century and in more recent political alignments.

American city planning developed as a reform movement in the late nineteenth century, and grew out of earlier reform movements which had begun shortly after the middle of the century, particularly the model tenement, park and playground movements. These were organized by Protestant upper middle class reformers and philanthropists who were disturbed by what was happening to the cities, which they and their class had once dominated politically and culturally, by the transformation from small predominantly middle class towns to rapidly growing urban centres, and by the large numbers of non-Protestant poor European immigrants, who streamed into the cities and were forced to live in slums.

The reformers wanted to improve the terrible living conditions of these people. However, they also wanted to make the immigrants into middle class Protestant Americans like themselves; people who would uphold the old socio-political order. Presumably the reformers could have developed anti-poverty programmes, reorganizing the industrial economy so that unemployment and poorly-paid employment would be eliminated. They failed to do so, not because such programmes had not yet been invented, but primarily because the reformers were politically quite conservative. They had no desire to change the economy or the social order, and were in fact fighting against the socialist movements which began to develop in the slums.

Partly because they were of a conservative nature, the reformers held what one might call *a facility-centred theory of social change*. They believed that if poor people were provided with a set of properly designed facilities, ranging from model tenements to better work places and parks and playgrounds, they would not only give up their slum abodes but also change themselves in the process. Thus, Frederick Olmsted, the great American park builder, thought that man could be truly healthy only in rural surroundings, and he proposed that large parks be built in the city as a substitute for these surroundings. The founders of the playground movement believed that if the poor could be provided with playgrounds and community centres, they would stop frequenting the taverns, cafes, brothels and later the movie houses in which they spent their leisure time, and would desert the street corner gangs and clubs which they had created for social life.

This theory of social change was not entirely facility-centred. In fact, some of the reformers argued that the crucial ingredient was not the facility but the men and women who staffed it, and that if the poor came into contact with these well-intentioned middle class people, they would soon give up their lower class ways.

Today, we know that this theory was absurd. The immigrants were desperately poor people living in a strange land in which they were often discriminated against. Because they were poor, they suffered not only from economic problems but also from the social and individual pathologies which come with being poor; alcoholism, family breakdown, vice and violence, for example. These pathologies were not deliberate as the reformers thought; they were by-products of a lower class culture which enabled people to adapt to poverty, but which was (and still is) anathema to middle class people because of its emphasis on sensual and material pleasures. What the immigrant poor needed was economic aid. To assume that they could be transformed into middle class people simply by their joining settlement houses and other facilities was ludicrous. It was also wrong to assume that they would even come to such facilities, for the immigrants had their own social groups and had no reason to desert these for strange new facilities, staffed by strange and often condescending Yankees.

The reformers were not social scientists, however, and they had so little contact with the immigrant that they could not understand why he behaved as he did. Moreover, they were missionaries, and had the missionary's faith in their approach. To them it seemed that their theory worked; the few facilities which they were able to build were used by the immigrants, though rarely in the numbers that the reformers expected. What the reformers did not know was that the new amenities attracted an atypical minority – the upwardly mobile who were able and willing to become middle class Americans.

By the early twentieth century, the reform movement had coalesced with business groups who were fighting the urban political machines, and the philanthropists were replaced by business leaders and their economic and political associates. The businessmen were mainly downtown retailers, large property owners, real estate agents and builders. These groups were interested in creating an attractive downtown retail area that would bring in shoppers and office workers, in building middle class residential areas to house them, and transportation facilities to move them around. They were particularly interested in making sure that the slums, usually located right next to the central business district, did not 'infect' this district. They therefore wanted them contained or removed. As businessmen and property owners, they were, of course, concerned primarily with buildings and facilities, and they made common cause with the earlier reformers. However, seeing that the facility-by-facility approach did not achieve their aim of an orderly, efficient and attractive downtown environment, they turned to zoning and then to comprehensive planning.

After the First World War, the business interests, supported by middle class voters, had developed enough political strength to make planning and zoning into a municipal function, usually in the form of planning commissions – on whose boards they sat – which sometimes worked with, sometimes opposed, the political machines. Because the activities of the commission required a staff, a new profession was created, and because the work dealt with the improvement of buildings, neighbourhoods and facilities, it naturally attracted people trained in the manipulation of physical artifacts, that is, architects and engineers.

From about 1920 on, the new planners planned and zoned. They developed master plans which segregated land uses by a variety of criteria, most of them class-based, so that upper and middle class residences were separated from working and lower class residences, affluent shopping districts from poor ones, and industry, which employed mainly working and lower class people, from everything else. They planned for new transportation systems which would bring people into the central retail district, and in all areas, for all classes, they planned the parks, playgrounds, community centres, schools and other facilities which the nineteenth century reformers had advocated. They also laid out new areas of the city for future growth, although, true to their reformer ancestors who wanted to stop the influx of immigrants, they were basically against growth itself and wanted to limit the size of the city. The new areas consisted of single family houses in middle class neighbourhoods, having schools in the centre, but including no housing or institutions for the poor. The planners assumed that if they planned for middle class housing, poor people would somehow become middle class and so no new low cost housing was envisaged. If the planners provided only middle class facilities, people would use nothing else. Consequently, in an era when most Americans went to the movies at least once a week, the planners planned for cultural centres and museums, but did not bother to locate movie theatres.

For a long time, the formulators of comprehensive planning had no means to implement their proposals other than zoning or subdivision ordinances, the political power of their business and reform patrons, and moral appeals for good planning. In the late 1930s, however, the federal government created public housing projects, which, by clearing slums and replacing them with new housing, would enable the poor to live in good buildings and thus to stop behaving like poor people. A decade later, this escalated into slum clearance and urban renewal. It never occurred to the formulators of urban renewal that private enterprise could only rebuild for the affluent. The planners and housers were so convinced that slums 'bred' the pathologies associated with poverty that they were sure that the behaviour of the poor could be altered simply by tearing down homes, doing away with slum areas, and scattering the inhabitants all over the city.

When it became apparent that urban renewal did nothing but move slum dwellers into other slums, the planning profession embraced human renewal. It was hoped that through education, social casework and community organization, the poor could be helped and changed into middle class people, while their homes were being renewed. With the coming of the Kennedy administration and the War on Poverty, some attempt was made to provide more low-income housing. In 1965 Congress approved the Model Cities legislation: a broad form of urban renewal which included provision for low-income housing, rent supplements, human renewal, and programmes to deal with poverty, unemployment and under-employment among the poor. Some of these innovations came from planners, and others from social scientists who entered planning after the Second World War. In a very real sense, however, the innovations came from the poor themselves. Slum dwellers had been saying for decades that they needed more jobs, higher incomes and more low-cost housing, but it was not until they began to oppose urban renewal, and then to rebel and riot, that anyone began to listen to them. Even today, however, most planners continue to work on master plans, and to plan for the City orderly, efficient and beautiful.

The affluent beneficiaries of physical planning

Although city planning has been concerned principally with improving the physical environment, it has also been planning for certain people, although only indirectly and implicitly. These people were the planner himself, his political supporters and the upper middle class citizen in general. Insofar as the planner was seeking to create the kind of city he himself liked, he was planning for himself and his professional peers. He formulated his plans so that they would gain the respect of his peers, just as architects often seem to design buildings so that they will be published in the architectural journals.

The planner was also working on behalf of his political supporters, the businessmen and civic leaders who sat on planning commissions. The master plans emphasized a growing downtown retail area and many neighbourhood shopping areas, and they often over-zoned for future business districts. The planner's ideal city was good for business and for property ownership.

Finally, the planner planned for people of his own class-culture, for other middle and upper middle class professionals who wanted solid single family house neighbourhoods, and who used theatres, museums, civic centres and other cultural facilities that cater to the upper middle class. This came out most clearly during urban renewal, when the planners justified slum clearance in order to bring the middle class back to the city. They favoured this return because otherwise the poor might begin to dominate the city politically and culturally, and the cultural facilities which the planners liked would have to close down for lack of customers.

The planner did not realize he was planning for himself, his supporters and people of his class, however; he thought that by focusing on what he felt were desirable types of housing, business and industry, he was planning for everybody. As a professional he thought he knew what was best for the community and for people. He thought he had the expertise that gave him the right to change the community, and to change people's lives according to the traditional dictates of the old reform movements. Because he was a descendant of a missionary reform cause, he never questioned his aims or his activities.

Of course, the master planners were not really experts; their judgments were not based on expert knowledge or even on any kind of empirical analysis. Although they applied planning standards for housing, schools, libraries and recreation facilities, for example, these standards were made up by housers, educators, librarians and recreation officials who had the same missionary zeal – and a vested interest in building more of their own facilities. Thus the standards themselves were not based on expert knowledge or empirical analysis. Usually they measured the 'best' facility in the country and translated these measurements into general planning standards for all communities. The planners did not notice that the best facilities were usually found in the most affluent communities, and that poorer communities could not afford them. Nor did they notice that all the standards together called for such large allocations of land and public expenditure that, if they were implemented, there would be little room or money left for anything else in the city.

In short, the standards and other tools used by planners in various community facilities often reflected the vested interests and cultural values and biases of the planner himself and of his allies. Sometimes the plans were even based on the fads and fashions of the era. For example, until about the Second World War, most planners shared the common middle-class belief that multi-family dwellings were undesirable. They thought that since poor people lived in them, and poor people exhibited high rates of individual and social pathology, apartments must be pathological. Consequently, planners wanted to put as many people as possible into single-family housing.

Today, planners generally favour just the reverse. With the development of post Second World War suburbia, and the exodus of the lower middle class from the city, suburbs were no longer the ideal community they had been when they were exclusively upper middle class. Planners therefore decided that suburban single family housing was undesirable, that it bred conformity, matriarchy, divorce and a number of other pathologies which in England are described as the 'New Town Blues'. Now, the professional judgment was to build apartment housing, for apartments were identified with urbanity, and only by building on an urban scale could the city and the upper middle class life style described as urbanity be brought to the new suburbs.

This brief history of planning is not intended to expose the city planner as a conspirator who intentionally allied himself with conservative political reformers, and then with businessmen and property owners, in order to enrich himself and his profession. Indeed, until recently, most planners were not aware of the political implications of their theory and their practice, and whatever they did, they usually did with the best intentions – which is, of course, part of the problem. Moreover, their plans have been by no means entirely undesirable. Even if they are often irrelevant to the city's problems, they have helped to create more orderly, efficient and attractive communities, at least for the affluent. Their ideas and site plans for low density neighbourhoods were borrowed by post Second World War builders, resulting in better-designed suburbs for the newly affluent. Planners have also fought against the corruption of urban political machines, using planning principles to argue for facility, land use and location decisions closer to the public interest than those made by politicians, whose first priority was often to enrich the political machine and its leaders. Even so, planning could have contributed more to the solution of urban problems and the achievement of urban goals had it not been saddled with the history from which only now is it freeing itself.

The lack of effects of physical planning

There is considerable evidence that the physical environment does not play as significant a role in people's lives as the planner believes. Although people reside, work and play in buildings, their behaviour is not determined by the buildings, but by the economic, cultural and social relationships within them. Bad design can interfere with what goes on inside a building, of course, and good design can aid it, but design *per se* does not significantly shape human behaviour.

A number of studies have now been carried out on the effects of what is, for people, the most important part of the physical environment – their house. Wilner's study of slum dwellers (Wilner *et al.*, 1962) who were moved to a new public housing project, Berger's study of factory workers (Berger, 1960) who were moved out to suburbia, my own study (Gans, 1967) of working and lower middle class people who moved out to Levittown, and Willmott's study of the London slum dwellers (Willmott, 1963) who moved to Dagenham all indicate that lives are affected little by the change of community or by the change of housing. Wilner found no change in health, mental health, social life, or community participation. Berger and Willmott both found that the working class people they studied continued working class styles of life in their new surroundings, and I found that people's lives were not changed drastically either by the move from city to suburb, or even by the move from apartment to house.

As reported in *The Levittowners* (Gans, 1967), research into changes in health, morale, boredom, loneliness, family life, social life, community participation and the like showed that generally about half the people reported no change, and those who reported change were changed in different ways. For example, among my sample of ex-city dwellers, 69 per cent reported no change in the state of their marriage after coming to Levittown, 20 per cent said it had improved and 11 per cent said it had deteriorated. When changes were greater, for example in visiting neighbours and friends, which increased considerably, the cause of the change was not the community but people's goals; they had moved out to Levittown with the hope of improving their social life. The presence of young people with similar interests made the improvement possible, of course, but residents who did not want to do more socializing generally did not do so. Perhaps the most drastic change came for people who moved from apartments to houses, but here, too, the change was intended. People wanted to own a new house, and they believed, rightly so, that raising children was easier in a house than in an apartment. The greatest amount of *unintended* change, that is change other than that which people intended to make or which brought them to suburbia in the first place, was caused by the population mix, in other words, the kinds of people whom they met once they had arrived in the community. The primary effect on people is not created by the physical environment of the community, but by the social environment.

This conclusion is supported by the fact that the site-plan and the provision of facilities had little impact on the Levittowners. This can be illustrated by an event which also tested the popularity of the classic neighbourhood scheme. When the Levittown school board polled parents of a crowded neighbourhood school on whether they wanted larger classes or preferred that their children be given transport to a less crowded school in another neighbourhood, the data showed that the significant factor was neither the neighbourhood nor even class size but the parents' attitude toward their child's teacher. Parents who liked the teacher opposed any change; those who disliked the teacher favoured change, so that the child would get another teacher.

Moreover, for most people community facilities are relatively unimportant. The number of people who use such public facilities as playgrounds and libraries is always small. Although a few may be so attracted to the facility that their life is changed by it, the majority of people use a facility only rarely, and it becomes important to them only when it becomes part of their social environment. For example, teenagers may shun a community centre as individuals, but a gang or informal club may come in as a group and make it its headquarters. In fact, and ironically, unless a facility becomes part of the social environment it will be used on the whole only by the people excluded from that social environment, by marginal and socially isolated individuals. This is a worthy use, but it questions the planner's assumption about the importance of facilities in everybody's life.

Although research on the effects of the physical environment is still sparse, the data indicate so far that these effects are not as great as the planner believes. Unless neighbours are homogeneous, they do not choose their friends on the basis of physical closeness, and one site plan is about as good as another in its impact on social life. A site plan in which houses are bunched together so that people are forced to have visual contact will, of course, create more social contact than an open plan; it will create some friends, some enemies, and frenzied efforts to protect individual privacy. Similarly, overcrowding within a dwelling may have deleterious effects on the occupants, although one mental health study in New York found no correlation between mental illness and overcrowding (Langner, private communication). Here, too, social and cultural variables play a major role. Middle class individuals seem to need more privacy than working class people, and I suspect that if the former had to live at the internal (or dwelling unit) density endured by many of New York's Negroes and Puerto Ricans, they would probably go crazy.

The lack of data on the effects of the physical environment on human beings has encouraged some planners to cite the ethological studies of rats and other animals, which show that they suffered intensely from overcrowding. These data cannot be applied to human beings in the city, however, because human beings do not live in as close and direct a relationship to land and space as do animals. It is possible, however, that if farmers were crowded in the same way as were the experimental rats, they might suffer in the same way, or else move off the land and go to the city.

What affects people, then, is not the raw physical environment, but the social and economic environment in which that physical environment is used. People's lives are not significantly affected by whether they live in cities or suburbs, in detached or multifamily dwellings, or with or without a certain amount of public open space. Webber (1963, p. 52) puts it very well when he writes:

I contend that we have been searching for the wrong grail, that the values associated with the desired urban structure do not reside in the spatial structure *per se*. One pattern of settlement and its associated land use form is superior to another only as it better serves to accommodate ongoing social processes and to further the non-spatial ends of the political community.

These social processes and non-spatial ends, people's lives and their life-styles, are determined by their income, occupation, and education, by their age and sex, and to a lesser extent by their ethnic, religious and political allegiances. These characteristics and allegiances are expressed in their behaviour, their goals and their problems, and in the social, economic and political environments in which they live. If the planner wants to affect people's lives, it is these environments for which he must plan.

How to plan for people

How then, does one go about planning for people? The first step, I would suggest, is to give up all traditional planning concepts related to the physical environment, and to begin at the beginning: to ask how people live, what they want, and what problems they have that need to be solved. Such questions would show quickly that people are not all the same; different age-groups and classes have different life styles, goals and problems. Once these groupings are identified, one can then develop plans that achieve their goals and solve their problems.

If one wanted to plan for lower middle class Levittowners, for example, and began with their problems, it would emerge that the most urgent of these are financial and familial. Money shortages, husband–wife conflicts, parent–child conflicts and illness are the greatest sources of worry. Planning to resolve financial problems would require intervention in the economy to give greater productivity and equality of income, so that income could be raised. Planning to resolve familial conflict would involve a variety of programmes. Some types of family conflict would be eliminated if the men could earn more; other types would be tackled by creating jobs for women, both to provide more money for the household and to give women an additional source of social usefulness. Parent–child conflict could be relieved to some extent by enabling women to get away from young children for part of the day, and to be with other adults. This would require day-care centres, and some counselling to relieve the guilt that many lower middle class women feel about being away from their children. The generational conflict between parents and adolescents can be ameliorated by deliberate planning to increase the social and physical distance between the two age groups. By giving adolescents their own institutions where they can spend much of their after-school and after-work time, and where they can feel that their own culture is as valid as adult culture, many of the present conflicts could be minimized. Planning to reduce illness would, of course, require considerably more and cheaper medical care.

If one wanted to plan for the elimination of poverty, on the other hand, one would have to begin by identifying the different types of people who suffer from poverty. Older people, the majority of America's poor, simply need more social security and pension payments. Among young people, the primary need is for the elimination of unemployment, a higher minimum wage for the underpaid worker, job training programmes and general income redistribution. The most rapidly growing group of poor people in America, unmarried mothers, need income grants which are higher and less punitive than present social welfare payments, so that they can devote themselves to making sure that their children will grow up in a relatively stable home environment, can go to school, and can obtain the skills they need to get jobs and thus to escape from poverty (Gans, 1968, ch. 5).

These examples are too few and too brief to serve even as outlines of plans, and are suggested only to show what planning for people means. This kind of planning would require the planner either to become a sociologist and psychologist or to work closely with behavioural scientists to observe what problems people are trying to solve and what goals they are seeking. This is not easy, for people cannot always identify their problems, and do not always know what they want. Interviews, observation and planning *with* people rather than just *for* them can provide many of the answers. When these fail, the planner has two options. He can make inferences about problems and goals from people's behaviour. In addition, the planner can provide for choice by offering people a *variety* of solutions and programmes.

Planners have, of course, traditionally argued that if people only had more choice, they would choose what the planner thinks is best. In America, at least, planners often explain that people live in speculative builder suburbs like Levittown because they have not had enough choice; they have not been given a chance to live in a community designed on planning principles. Sometimes this is true, but equally often it is not. For example, one reason for the failure of the much-publicized planned new town of Reston is that people did not want what the planner thought they should want; they did not like the community-focus of the plan, in which public open space replaced private open space, and in which more attention was paid to community facilities than to the house. As a result, the houses were too small, and since most people buy a house, not a community, the development sold poorly.

Planning to solve people's problems and to help them achieve their goals does not, of course, rule out physical planning, but seeks to put such planning in its proper place. The social and economic environments to which planners ought to address themselves are located in houses, offices, community facilities and communities, and in some, although not all, instances, plans for a social environment will require physical expression. However, the physical plan ought to express the goals of social environment planning; housing and other aspects of the physical environment ought to be planned in terms of what people want. Moreover, in the overall plan, it should be given the importance and priority that people assign to physical goals.

On giving people what they want

The argument that the planner should give people what they want, not what he thinks himself is best for them, requires further discussion. I suggest that the planner gives people what they want on two grounds.

The first ground is practical; it is very difficult to change people unless they want to be changed; they are not likely to give up their habits, customs or goals just because the planner asks them to do so. People can, of course, be forced to change, but this is neither democratic nor politically wise, for unless the change is in the public interest, and people agree that it is in the public interest, they will react politically and defeat the plan. The history of American planning is full of such defeats.

When people reject a planner's idea, it is rarely because they are stupid or evil but because they have different life-styles and goals. For example, most Americans prefer private to public open space, not because they are anti-planning, but because they want to spend their spare time with family members and friends and do not want to have to share outdoor space with people they do not know or do not like.

Similarly, most Americans reject the planner's goal of urbanity because they do not practise or want the life-style associated with urbanity. Whether they live in the city or the suburbs, people are intensely home-centred; they rarely go out even to the movies, and they do not often go to the theatre, the museum or other typically urban facilities. Most Americans do not enjoy walking, they do not like the city's congestion, and they do not much care for the heterogeneity of population they find in the city. They may want the excitement and vitality of the city when they go on vacation, but for their daily life they want the smallness of scale, the compatible neighbours, and what they call 'the peaceful outdoor life' that they find in the single-family house areas of the outer city, and in suburbia.

Nor do most people accept the planner's ideal of the balanced community, in which people from diverse incomes and backgrounds are thrown together in order mutually to enrich their lives by their diversity. This ideal, which stems from the nineteenth century, when the reformers thought that if the poor were brought into close contact with middle class people they would learn from 'their betters', conflicts with the very basis of group formation, for most people want to have neighbours who are sufficiently like them in class and age to share the same interests; this is what creates much of the vital and positive social life of the suburbs. Nor do poor people particularly want to live next door to more affluent people, especially if they have young children. Poorer people do not want to be improved by 'their betters', and they cannot afford to have their youngsters come home demanding toys they have seen in affluent homes. The ideal also ignores the fact that people do not want to lose prestige by living near neighbours whom they consider to be of lower status. Indeed, the only thing that can be said in favour of balance is that it provides a principle by which to oppose the exclusion from a community of low income and non-white people. Although no one should be excluded from any community on the basis of race, class or age, the planner's ideal of balance requires more tolerance of heterogeneity than even he can practise when he chooses a place to live.

In almost all instances, the differences in goals between the planner and the people for whom he plans are a function of class. Most planners are upper middle class; most of the people they plan for are not. Although there are a number of differences between working and lower middle class life-styles, the two classes are united in their opposition to the urbane upper middle class style of involvement in 'culture' and civic activity, and they will reject plans which force them to live by that style.

Probably the biggest difference between the planner and the people he plans for is in the priority given to aesthetics. Planners are trained in aesthetics, and see the city from a perspective in which aesthetic goals rank high; indeed, they often plan the city as if it were a work of art, not a place in which people live. Most people give lower priority to beauty than do the planners, and they pay little attention to the visual environment in their every-day life; this, too, is reserved for vacations. The planner may complain that people are uncultured, but here again a basic difference in life-style is at work. The planner, true to upper middle class culture, is highly aware of objects; people who are not upper middle class are most aware of other people; for them, the social environment is more important than the aesthetic. Consequently, the planner is upset because he sees the mass-produced houses of suburbia as objects, and as such they are all alike. The suburbanites, however, see each house in terms of the people who live in it, and, because every person or family is unique, it is as unimportant that the house is mass-produced and much like the next, as it is that the car is mass-produced and just like all the others.

Moreover, there are vast differences in standards of beauty between the planner and the people he plans for. These differences again reflect cultural distinctions between the upper middle class and the other classes (Gans, 1966). Although not all planners feel that Le Corbusier's buildings are attractive, they tend to agree on aesthetic standards; many prefer simplicity to ornateness, and functional design to design that seeks to hide a building's function. Most of the people planned for, however, have quite different standards of beauty. Simplicity, sparseness and functionalism strike them as cold and inhuman, and so many American home buyers prefer the pseudo-Colonial elevations for their house, just as many English home buyers seem to prefer pseudo-cottages.

The second reason for believing that the planner should give people what they want is philosophical. I do not think the planner has the right, except in special circumstances to be described, to force people to change their behaviour so that he can achieve his vision of the well planned community. As I have tried to indicate, I believe that this vision is not based on expert knowledge but on the planner's own class-culture, and I see no reason why people should be asked to give up their own culture for his.

I make this judgment for two reasons.

First, I do not believe that the planner has a monopoly of wisdom on goals and values, and I do not believe that his upper middle class culture is the only desirable life style. There are many diverse ways of living in a heterogeneous urban-industrial society, and unless these can be proven to be harmful to those who practise them, or to other people, they should be treated as equally valid, at least within the present socio-economic system.

Second, life-styles and their underlying goals and values do not develop in a vacuum; they are functions of the existential situations with which people must cope, and they are closely related to people's class position, particularly their educational level and income. Asking people to give up their life-style for that of the planner is actually demanding that they change their behaviour to that of a 'higher' class without obtaining the socio-economic prerequisites which that class enjoys. One could argue that, in the abstract, upper middle class life-styles are more desirable than lower middle or working class life-styles, and I am willing to defend that position (Gans, 1966). However, if planners want people to behave in upper middle class ways, they must provide the funds and the education that will make them upper middle class people. Until this is done people should be allowed to live in the way that accords with their level of income and education.

Only one exception might be made to this general rule. This is that the planner has the right to ask people to change if he can prove that a present behaviour pattern or a community arrangement is dangerous either to the people concerned or to others. For example, if he can prove that parents who are unwilling to pay the taxes required for a good school system will make it impossible for their children to get a good job ten years hence, he has the right to ask them to change their behaviour. Similarly, if he can prove that people living alongside a much travelled highway may get lung cancer from automobile exhaust fumes, the planner is entitled to ask them to move. He must, however, be able to present reasonable proof of the consequences he predicts, and he must demonstrate that these consequences will violate people's own values and interfere with the achievement of their own goals.

On the other hand, he cannot force people to accept changes because he thinks they are good by his own professional or personal values, or to give up a life-style because he thinks it is bad. For example, he cannot demand that people stop moving to suburbia simply because the exodus conflicts with his goal of the urbane city. Nor can he argue that they stop moving to suburbia because he thinks it has pathological results for them, for he cannot prove that these results exist. Indeed, I think it is irresponsible to use pathology as an argument when there is no evidence. This is then merely a device for frightening people into changing their behaviour.

It should be emphasized that in arguing to let people live as they choose, I am not proposing that the planner necessarily encourages them to live as they do now. As I noted before, he ought to provide them with choices, one of which is the present way of doing things. He should give them other choices as well, including even his own, but there must be a choice. If people are satisfied with the *status quo*, however, and resources are too scarce to provide many alternatives, the planner ought to limit himself to recommending experimental projects. He should then determine how people like them, and the results of these experiments could help him decide which choices ought to be offered on a wider basis.

Planning for the allocation of benefits among competing populations

My argument for a client-oriented or user-oriented approach is most relevant to planning for a relatively homogeneous population. It is only one consideration in planning for heterogeneous groups or communities. When the planner's client is the city, he must plan for a heterogeneous population, and in this process he is inevitably allocating scarce resources among sectors of the population, providing benefits to some and costs to others. For example, if he proposes a new set of highways, he is primarily benefiting the middle class suburbanites who will be the main users of such a highway. If he proposes a low income housing project in a middle class neighbourhood, he is benefiting the poor population and exacting status costs from the affluent.

Consequently, the planner must decide how to allocate resources among competing groups, and for which people to plan. This is probably the most difficult and perplexing question in planning, and only now is it beginning to be asked. In the past, the planner avoided the question altogether, for by focusing on buildings and land uses, he did not have to think about who would use them and benefit from them. Moreover, he saw himself as planning in the public interest and had few doubts about what that constituted; it was whatever he said it was, and coincided with his well-planned city.

Today, he can no longer feel so certain about the nature of this interest. The widespread political opposition to urban renewal, the ghetto rebellions and the planner's rising influence in city government, which has brought him much closer to urban politics, are beginning to make him aware of the fact that his plans have benefit–cost consequences, that competing groups have different demands for what benefits and costs planning ought to award, and that there is no simple way of determining the public interest.

For example, urban renewal may do away with slums, but if it reduces the amount of low cost housing and forces the poor to pay higher rents, where is the public interest? Advocates of urban renewal have suggested that, despite these costs to the poor, such programmes are desirable because they bring the middle class back into the city, preserve the cultural facilities and increase the tax rolls of the city. However, when there is no evidence that urban renewal does bring back the middle class, and when there is some evidence that the cultural facilities are only used by the affluent, and that many of these are suburbanites, and when developers of cleared areas can only be attracted by tax write-offs, where, then, is the public interest?

Similarly, the suburban exodus has made life considerably more pleasant for many middle and working class whites, but it has also increased residential racial segregation, and as industry has also moved to the suburbs, it has prevented Negroes from going where the jobs are. To what extent, then, is the suburban exodus in the public interest?

Moreover, it is often doubtful that there is a unique public interest, for in a heterogeneous community, there are few goals on which the entire community can agree, and still fewer goals which the community must pursue even if there is no consensus. Most residents in the community favour plans which will raise incomes for everybody, and economic plans to attract more industry are probably in the community interest – although attracting industry to already affluent cities may not be in the national public interest. Similarly, community survival is a goal which must be pursued, even if not all residents desire it, and although, here too, the national public interest might demand the depopulation of communities no longer having a viable economic or social role.

How is this dilemma resolved? Once again, it is necessary to begin with goals, and by determining and understanding the goals of all the groups in the community, to identify those shared by all and those intrinsic to the community as a whole. But when the slim stock of such goals is exhausted, the planner must decide for which people to plan, and how resources are to be allocated between competing interests. These decisions are difficult to make, and there are no technical criteria for guidance. A partial solution to the dilemma is to look for allocations that will benefit as many groups as possible. For example, if the planner can demonstrate that a new highway will not only make commuting easier but will also attract industry, and create jobs for the unemployed, he can satisfy simultaneously the goals of two quite different sectors of the population. Similarly, if he can demonstrate that a system of family allowances, or another form of income grant to the poor, will not only help them escape from poverty but will also reduce the amount of pathology and antisocial behaviour so as to improve the quality of city living and reduce the taxpayers' costs of fighting crime, he will in one programme be satisfying the goals both of the poor and of the affluent taxpayer.

However, when benefit–cost studies indicate that a plan will aid one group more than another – and this is probably true of most plans – the planner must make a political decision and take a political stand. With respect to allocations for socio-economic groups, for example, he can align himself with the poor and say that they need benefits more than the affluent; he can align himself with the working class – or the lower middle class – and say that they are most crucial to the community's economy, or he can align himself with the upper middle class because it pursues the goals and life-styles which he himself favours. In the real world, only rarely can he choose between one or another group, however; usually he must decide who ought to get more of the economic pie and who ought to get less. He must also make other choices, for example between different age-groups and ethnic or racial groups.

My own position is as follows. I believe that in America, private enterprise allocates resources primarily to the affluent, and that the government policies with which the planner is concerned ought to be *compensatory*; they ought to allocate as much as possible to the poor and deprived to reduce inequities in American society. This choice is partly a political position, for I believe strongly in an egalitarian society, but it is also partly a public interest position. I think that many if not most of the problems of American cities are caused, directly or indirectly, by the problems of the poor and non-white populations of the city, and that if poverty and segregation can be eliminated, even the so-called physical problems of the city will be ameliorated. Slums, after all, are primarily created by the inability of poor people to afford better housing and by the inability of Negroes to gain access to white neighbourhoods, so that they become a captive market for slum landlords who can earn high profits without maintaining their buildings. The low quality of urban facilities, the city's tax problems, and many other urban problems are actually the result of urban poverty and segregation, and if the cities are to be saved, for the poor and the affluent alike, it is in the public interest to eliminate poverty and segregation. And once the presently poor can be incorporated into the affluent society, they will want the physically more orderly, efficient and attractive city for which city planners have been striving for all these years (Gans, 1968, chapter 5).

The role of the planner

In summary, I view the planner not as a reformer, nor as a professional who is free to impose his expertise and his values on the people for whom he plans. As a public official he ought rather to be their servant, helping them solve their problems and achieve their goals, except when these goals have antisocial and self-destructive consequences. In this process, the planner ought to propose a variety of programmes to solve problems and achieve goals so that people have maximum choice; and in this variety, he ought to be free to include some programmes that are based on his own goals. When it comes to planning for heterogeneous populations, however, and the public interest is difficult to determine, he has to take a political stand, and propose the allocation of resources so that the maximal benefits accrue to those people, interest groups and communities he feels are in greatest need of public benefits.

The prime function of the planner, however, is not to determine goals, for that is the duty of the elected official and of the electorate. The planner ought to concern himself principally with determining the best programmes for achieving goals, and since most goals pertain to the improvement of the social and economic environments, he ought to devote himself to programmes which will realize these goals. In this process he must also plan for the physical environment, but he ought to devote himself first to people, and only secondarily to buildings.

[Note. The author recommends that for a more detailed statement of the argument given in the sections 'The Planner's Physical Bias' and 'The Historical and Political Sources of Physical Planning', the reader should consult Gans (1968, ch. 5). In addition, a thoughtful analysis of the studies mentioned under the section 'The Lack of Effects of Physical Planning' is to be found in a paper by P. Hall 'The Urban Culture and the Suburban Culture' presented at the Lions International Symposium, University of Puerto Rico, October 1967].

References

BERGER, B. (1960), *Working Class Suburb*, University of California Press.
GANS, H. J. (1966), 'Popular culture in America', in H. S. Becker (ed.), *Social Problems. A Modern Approach*, Wiley, pp. 549–620.
GANS, H. J. (1967), *The Levittowners*, Allen Lane, The Penguin Press.
GANS, H. J. (1968), *People and Plans: Essays on Urban Problems and Solutions*, Basic Books, Penguin edn, 1972.

LANGNER, T. (unpublished), private communication of unpublished findings of the Manhattan Midtown Mental Health Study.

WEBBER, M. M. (1963), 'Order in diversity: community without propinquity', in *Cities and Space, The Future Uses of Urban Form*, L. Wingo, Jr (ed.), Johns Hopkins University Press.

WILLMOTT, P. (1963), *The Evolution of a Community*, Routledge & Kegan Paul.

WILNER, D., WALKLEY, R., PINKERTON, T., and TAYBACK, M. (1962), *Housing Environment and Family Life*, Johns Hopkins University Press.

Part Five
Power and Legitimacy

Previous sections have been concerned with the nature of the
urban process and with the points at which planners can
intervene to adjust the working of the urban system. This final
section raises key questions such as who exercises power in cities,
and on whose behalf; what are the objectives and rationale of
planning; and how can one legitimize political, social and
economic action. Such questions are central to the main theme of
this reader, and have already been raised in one form or another
in the majority of the earlier readings. They are important since
not only does the planner need to be able to analyse and
understand the factors involved in the exercise of power or the
allocation of resources, but also it is necessary for the social
scientist (or planner) concerned with the solution of urban
problems to understand the role his own values, training, and
approach may play in determining the nature of the solution
which he may put forward. Salisbury's analysis of the power
structure in American cities (Reading 19) follows neither the
traditional reputational or pluralist approaches to power
studies, but suggests rather a 'new convergence of power'
between businessman, mayor and the technical expert. Eddison,
in an article specially written for this reader (Reading 20), takes
further the role of the technical planner through a discussion of
the nature of rational planning in the UK and the possibilities of
a comprehensive approach via PPBS and corporate planning,
and points the way to another convergence – between rational
analysis, political values and community participation. Many of
the same issues are raised by Rein (Reading 21) who asks where
the reform-oriented planner gets his authority. He suggests that
the planner and the social science based reformer employ different
and mutually exclusive bases of authority and that this can limit
the effectiveness of the planning mechanism. If planning does not
become legitimate in the eyes of the consumer, if inequalities in

welfare are maintained or even increased, if political power or professional expertise is misused, and if minorities remain repressed, then the urban system can break down. Urban violence is usually attributed to racial tensions in American cities, but Lupsha argues that there is a broader context for civil disorder than this, and that violence is a political activity stemming from the failure of the social and economic planning processes of the city (Reading 22).

19 R. H. Salisbury

Urban Politics: The New Convergence of Power

R. H. Salisbury, 'Urban politics: the new convergence of power', *Journal of Politics*, vol. 26, 1964, pp. 775–97.

Economically, culturally, and in many ways even politically, the United States has become a thoroughly urban nation.[1] One aspect of this urbanization is that scholars have increasingly paid attention to phenomena occurring in cities. Sociologists, political scientists, economists, geographers and historians have all developed urban sub-fields of specialization; and in recent years the sub-fields have been infused with the great enthusiasm of virtual armies of researchers. When these efforts are combined with those of architects, planners, social workers, administrative managers and all the other urbanists asking questions about life in the city, the resulting stack of data, reports, proposals, admonitions and manifestos is truly staggering. Inevitably, perhaps, concern for the substance of city life gets mixed with concern for the methods of inquiry. Both, of course, are legitimate and important areas of concern. Each helps illuminate and is illuminated by the other. Specifically, the study of power structure – a basic issue for all political inquiry – has come to focus very largely on the city. In the process, both the substantive and methodological issues surrounding this generic political question – the question, as Dahl puts it, of Who Governs? – have been involved in virtually every discussion of urban affairs in recent years.[2]

Yet despite, or perhaps because of, this special ferment some

1. For a most comprehensive and thoughtful history of urban growth in America see McKelvey (1963).

2. Robert A. Dahl's study of New Haven was a classic of political science almost before it was published. See *Who Governs?* (1961). Dahl chose not to integrate his findings with those available concerning other communities, and in a number of respects one may argue that his conclusions are limited to the New Haven context. One cannot deny, however, that the larger question of how to approach the study of power has been given theoretically sophisticated stimulus from the work of Dahl and his associates. See Polsby (1963). For a convenient summary of many of the items in the large monographic literature on community power structure, see Press (1962).

important gaps on this question – who governs the city? – have remained. Many of these relate to the basic criticism to be made of almost all urban studies, the absence of comparative dimensions. Serious, theoretically sophisticated social and political analysis of urban data is relatively new on the scholarly scene, however. It is perhaps not so surprising therefore that so little genuine comparative work has been undertaken. One may be encouraged by the very recent emergence of a number of comparative studies.[3] Most of these, however, deal with relatively small communities. One who is interested in general patterns of big city politics must deal with a series of case studies, each study dealing with a single community. Each study then serves its author as the empirical foundation for a series of generalizations about politics (or society – the sociologists have been firmly in the tradition since the days of the Lynds). Some of these are brilliant. At best, however, they are sophisticated insights and theoretical conjectures built upon descriptions of a single case which, one hopes intuitively, may fit a larger number of cases.

The limitations of the data are compounded by variations in conceptual apparatus and/or data-gathering technique. One wishes that there were a clear basis for determining that Atlanta was or was not a pyramid-shaped monolith; that Springdale was 'really' controlled by a caucus, and that New Haven actually conforms to Dahl's analysis.[4] None of these three was studied in a manner which permits accurate comparisons with the other two (or twenty more which might be named), and hence no generalizations about either of two central points is possible. First, what is (are) the structure(s) of power in American cities? Second, what are the principal independent variables affecting the shape, scope and operation of these putative structures? It may turn out that each city is unique and no useful generalizations can be made using the city as the unit of analysis. Or the city may really be the most useful microcosm of the political system in which all essential processes, structures and relationships can be found. The professional conclusion probably lies somewhere between. We will not know without systematic comparative study.

One major effort at synthesis of exciting materials about city, principally big city, politics is that of Edward C. Banfield and

3. Recent attempts to engage in genuinely comparative analysis include Williams and Adrian (1963); Hawley (1963, pp. 422–31); Schnore and Alford (1963, pp. 1–17).

4. See the categorization suggested by Rossi (1960, p. 398).

James Q. Wilson (1963). To a large extent they draw upon the same materials as this essay, and there are many areas of agreement. There are important differences, too, however, both in conclusions and approach. Thus Banfield and Wilson give only passing attention to the historical dimension of urban politics. I propose to examine the question of the structure of power and do so over time. By viewing the city historically a number of critical elements, particularly those which have changed, can be seen more clearly than if a more strictly contemporaneous study were made. My discussion focuses upon the big cities in the United States that experienced major growth prior to the First World War. The pattern I shall describe may apply to other communities as well, but my model city in what follows is heterogeneous in ethnic and racial terms, contains considerable industry and a suburban ring, is experiencing core city decay, and is, in short, what those who write about urban problems generally have in mind when they refer to 'the city'.

Anyone who talks about urban structures of power must take a stand on two related questions: what is meant by power and how does one go about trying to establish its empirical dimensions. By 'structure of power' I mean the set of relationships among community roles, durable over time, through which scarce resources are allocated in a community. I am primarily concerned with those allocations which involve decisions by governmental agencies. We should recognize, however, the shifting importance over time of public allocations to the total of allocations made in the community, and remember, too, that public and private actions are always mixed together, nowhere more than in the city. I shall not give attention to the allocation of all those resources that might be deemed scarce, but only those that are of substantial volume or scope. I recognize the difficulty of drawing clear distinctions between 'important' and 'unimportant' decisions, but there *is* a difference, and it is recognized by decision-makers in a city. Thus the structure of power affecting a primary fight over the nomination for recorder of deeds may bear no relationship to the structure within which the city's urban renewal program is determined. In such a case it is only the latter that is of much interest; the decisions involve much more substantial resource allocations and the structure of power involved is therefore a more important one.

In short, we shall examine the most crucial structures of policy-relevant power in the large American city and attempt partly to identify and partly to postulate a pattern of development that seems warranted by the histories and present circumstances of several such cities. In doing so we must necessarily make comparisons among fragments of data drawn from sources that are widely diverse in concept and method. The result must obviously fall short of definitive status, but hopefully it may at least provide some stimulus to systematic comparative research in urban data.

II

Two systematic historical studies of urban power structure are those of New Haven by Dahl and Cibola by Schulze (1961). Both identify patterns of change that, despite considerable differences between the communities, are roughly similar. Much of the other published material on American urban history can be read as confirming this general pattern.[5]

Dahl finds that political office in New Haven was dominated first by the 'patricians', then by the 'entrepreneurs', and finally by the 'ex-plebes'. Patrician dominance rested upon oligarchic control of all of the major resources from which influence could be fashioned. '[S]ocial status, education, wealth and political influence were united in the same hands' (1961, p. 24). The entrepreneur's prominence emerged as wealth and social standing were separated, and the new men of business displaced the patricians in controlling economic resources. The entrepreneurs, moreover, were popular as the crabbed patricians were not. But the increasing immigrant labor force led to changing standards of popularity, and by about 1900 '[P]opularity had been split off from both wealth and social standing. Popularity meant votes; votes meant office; office meant influence' (Dahl, p. 51). The resulting pattern Dahl refers to as one of 'dispersed inequalities'. Many actors possess politically relevant resources but none possesses enough to dominate a broad range of actions. Particular actors exercise influence over particular policy decisions depending on the resources relevant to that decision, and several types of coalitions may aggregate the influentials concerned with specific problems, but no continuous structure of influence is operative for the broad range of public decision.

Robert Schulze describes a similar historical pattern in Cibola

5. The volume of historical work dealing with American cities is immense in weight but often disappointing when it comes to the questions of greatest interest to political scientists. McKelvey's work is masterful both as a summary and as an introduction to the literature.

except that Cibola, a much younger community, had no patrician era. Instead it experienced two stages, local capitalism and non-local or absentee capitalism. In the former stage, until 1900, the economic dominants were also the political dominants. They held public office as well as controlling local economic resources and their pre-eminent social standing reinforced their hegemony. After 1900 Cibola increasingly became an economic satellite and local economic resources came increasingly under the control of national firms. Local officials of these firms did not involve themselves in the active influence structure of the community, much less hold office. Rather, there developed a separate category of influentials, the public leaders, whose influence rested primarily upon such factors as popularity and commitment to the locality. Schulze describes this as a bifurcation of power, but it may not be amiss to suggest that Schulze's data permit the inference that Cibola is more polylithic – influence is widely dispersed and discontinuous – than the bifurcation image implies.

Both Dahl and Schulze give support to the general view that roughly from the end of the Civil War until 1900 American cities were dominated by the merchantry. Where the community had long existed as a substantial population center, notably in the East, the entrepreneurs were likely, as Dahl describes, to have displaced the patricians. Where there hardly had been a city in the ante-bellum years, there were no patricians to displace, and the commercial elite, relatively open to talents and money, but an elite nonetheless, dominated all the major institutions of the community. Political offices were typically held for short terms with each important merchant expected to contribute some time to the marginal activity of public office-holding.

Although the economic elite of the mercantile city dominated political institutions as well, it is unlikely that much additional influence accrued to them as a result. Public authority did relatively little in this stage of urban development. Only gradually were such elemental functions as water supply and sewage disposal, street construction and maintenance, police and fire protection undertaken (McKelvey, 1963, pp. 12–13). In many cases, too, the initial phases of service were provided by a mixture of public and private effort that mirrored the mixture of public and private position held by influentials. Public improvements were undertaken not only to make life possible in the increasingly crowded and extended city, but also as 'booster activities'. 'Let's put good old —— on the map!' was an oft-repeated watchword of civic promotion. As McKelvey notes, chambers of commerce were formed to promote economic development in a number of post-Civil War cities (p. 43), and the promotion of canals, railroads, exhibition halls, and – the classic booster gimmick – the World's Fair, all were part of the merchantry's effort to sell their particular community to the nation. Boosterism, even for the one-shot, short-run promotion, almost invariably involved a complex intermixture of public and private efforts and rested, therefore, on an elite which dominated both public and private office.

The gradual expansion of public services, however, had a significance for the structure of influence that booster gimmicks did not. Water and sewer systems, schools, streets, parks, police and fire were functions that required continuous operation by larger and larger corps of public employees. With the industrial growth of the city, the object for which boosterism strove, more and more people, requiring near-geometric increases in services, came to the city. Further, the new immigrants came to work in the new industries. Whereas the mercantile city had been as nearly classless as the frontier itself, the industrial city was the site of a differentiated class structure; differentiated by income and life chances, by ethnic origins, by religion, and by political potential.

At the same time, the industrial economic giant viewed the city very differently from the merchant. He was far less dependent on local sales or real estate values and thus less concerned with growth itself. His was a contingent investment in the community – gradually in the several communities housing his several branches – and his civil liability was therefore limited just as the corporate form limited his legal liability. His participation in the allocation of community resources, while potentially great, was infrequent and discontinuous. He was concerned only to protect his relatively narrowly defined corporate interests, not a generalized pattern of influence.

The merchantry had been deeply committed to the city in an economic and emotional way that was missing from the industrial manager. In the industrial city the modes by which civic obligations were discharged became more diverse and more specialized. Service on special boards or committees for libraries or schools, or parks, or slum dwellers was increasingly the way that the local notables – and their wives! – made their community contributions. These were likely to be structurally separated from the main body of governmental institutions and something of a preserve for 'the best people', insulated from 'politics'. In addition, the slowly growing concern for planning the City Beautiful and reforming inefficient or corrupt government provided larger and larger amounts of 'program material' for the luncheon clubs and merchants' association.[6] That occasionally reform campaigns would actually elect a mayor or effect a change in governmental operation did not cancel the fact that economic and social influence had been separated from political influence, and that each now (c. 1900) rested on a different social base.

An autonomous political elite was, of course, a function of expanded governmental activity and a growing working class population that altered the numerical balance of the city. As Dahl points out, not only were the political entrepreneurs now more popular than the economic entrepreneurs but the criteria of political popularity changed. Effective representation of the Booster spirit and promotion of industrial growth gave way to effective representation of the needs of the poor for elemental services and the promotion of the political organization itself. The boss and his machine we now recognize to have been functional for the newly industrial city; a growing army of public job-holders were recruited, a vast immigration was socialized and provided means of advancement in the urban society, welfare needs were at least minimally provided for, further extensions of public improvement programs were constructed, albeit expensively, and specific services were rendered to the economic elites as well. Railroad spurs, street car franchises, assessment adjustments, police protection of imported labor and a variety of other benefits could be conferred upon business by governmental agencies, even though the latter were no longer controlled by the businessmen themselves. Although businessmen were often appalled and sometimes intimidated by the 'new men' of city politics, they rarely intervened or even protested against the system in any continuous way.

Surely a portion of the reason that the boss remained in power was that although government was far more formidable in this period than formerly, the major decisions allocating resources in the city were still made by private interests. Governmental functions were no doubt of crucial importance to the machine itself and to its followers, but, for the most part, they were of marginal importance to the private sector of the economy. It therefore made relatively little difference whether they were done well or

6. The suggestion that civic reform issues provide 'program material' and sometimes little else is developed in Banfield (1961, pp. 298 ff.).

not. This is the obverse of the point that economic notables tended to withdraw from civic involvement after about 1900. Not only did the changing city pretty well force them out of office; it was quite rational for them to tend their private gardens and only enter the political arena on behalf of specific policy questions with an immediate payoff to their specialized economic concerns.

What Schulze describes as the bifurcation of power between economic and political elites was thus a function of a changing industrial and social order in the city supported by the enlarged opportunities for political entrepreneurs in the growth of governmental activity. At the same time, the economic and social notables were fragmented by the split between absentee and local capital, the diffusion of energies in a myriad of specialized civic but largely non-political enterprises, and finally by the exodus from the city's corporate limits of the middle class. The efforts of the Progressive WASPs to reform local government, to cleanse the stables of municipal corruption, were in the main doomed by the inexorable movements of people. The middle class moved to suburbia and put political popularity – the ability to get elected – permanently on a working class basis.

The final seal on the bifurcation was effected by the shift of the voting habits of the urban working class to overwhelming Democracy. From the beginning of the New Deal more and more of the large cities became safely Democratic. The metropolitan middle class maintained its Republican loyalties with respect to the national scene, but in local matters a *modus vivendi* on a business-like basis with the Democratic leadership – a matter of necessity for those with local interests at stake – was often achieved.

Yet the Democratic partisan hegemony provided a kind of cover by which middle class values could reappear in the public decisions of a working class city. By the end of the 1940s the machines were fading. The disciplined delivery of votes was rarely possible, at least on a city-wide basis, and the professionalization of the city bureaucracy was well along. Political office still went to those who mustered majorities from a predominantly working class city electorate but the circular pattern that characterized the era of 'Politics for Profit' – votes gave power, power provided favors, favors provided votes – was increasingly broken. It is significant that a move toward 'Good Government' – meaning rational policy-making – came from within the political stratum itself in these years in Chicago, St Louis, Pittsburgh, and New

Orleans. This move coincided with a change in the agenda of urban resource allocation, and this change in turn has led to a change in the structure of influence.

III

I propose to designate the contemporary structure of urban power as the 'new convergence'. It is similar in many ways to what Dahl calls the executive-centered coalition. It is headed, and sometimes led, by the elected chief executive of the city, the mayor. Included in the coalition are two principal active groupings, locally-oriented economic interests and the professional workers in technical city-related programs. Both these groupings are sources of initiative for programs that involve major allocations of resources, both public and private. Associated with the coalition, also, are whatever groups constitute the popular vote-base of the mayor's electoral success. Their association is more distant and permissive, however. Their power to direct specific policy choices is severely limited. In the following pages I shall examine each element in the coalition as well as some of the groups in the city that largely lack power. In all cases I am concerned with power that is relevant to key resource allocation decisions.

In the period roughly centered on the turn of the century business leadership was transformed from local to absentee capital, from merchantry to corporate managers. Accompanying this shift in economic organization was a shift in community political commitment and orientations, and this shift, in the direction of reduced interest, coincided with and reinforced the burgeoning autonomous political organization. Now, however, I am saying that business plays an important role in the structure of city affairs. The apparent contradiction points to some complexities in the notion of 'business'.

First, some kinds of business never experienced the nationalizing effects of industrial reorganization. These often remained intimately associated with politics throughout the era of the bosses. Real estate dealers, building supply firms, insurance agents and corner confectioneries were always likely to have an iron or two in the political fire. They still do, but these interests are not part of the coalition we are examining. Their interests are small with respect to resource allocations, and they deal in channels that are peripheral to the main body of decisions. Their politics is a kind of eternal process which goes on in many different kinds of worlds without affecting them. Petty business and petty politics are thus hand-maidens but irrelevant to the larger issues of power.

The large international corporation continues to regard the local scene with the same investment calculus described earlier. In general, the branch plant will do only as much about the community as is required to develop and maintain an image of good corporate citizenship, and this is far less than is necessary for power or even concern about community resource allocation.[7] Occasionally, the needs of the firm may require it to intrude into the community political system, but such intrusions would be very much on an *ad hoc* basis. The same is likely to be true of large, nationally oriented unions (Banfield and Wilson, pp. 277–80). The exception occurs when the union or the firm has a large home office or plant in the city or has grown large from a base in a particular community. Then 'good citizenship' may require more than charitable work and involve the company or union leadership in larger urban policy issues.

The most active business firms in the new convergence, however, are those with major investments in the community, which are dependent on the growth of a particular community, and which have come to recognize that all the major issues and decisions of the city affect their interests (Banfield and Wilson, ch. 18). Furthermore, they all share a growing concern with that congeries of problems labeled 'core city decay'. They include the major banks, utilities, railroads, department stores, large real estate firms, and metropolitan newspapers. Functionally, the list is remarkably similar from city to city. Also similar is the fact that active concern with community affairs is relatively recent, largely post-Second World War, and coincides with the perception of threat to tangible 'downtown' economic values. Finally, the re-entry of these groups into the active quest for power coincides with the weakening of the party-political dominance of the governmental arena. This permitted the numerically inferior business groups to assert their claims on a more continuous basis than formerly had been the case. In Chicago, where the machine did not weaken so much, the loop businessmen continued to operate a largely *ad hoc* basis.[8] Elsewhere, however,

7. See the provocative essay by Long (1962, pp. 122–36).

8. See Banfield (1961, pp. 291 ff). Banfield himself emphasizes the tangible conflicts of interest which divide Chicago business interests. Even so, however, one may suspect that without the Daley machine Loop business interests would have developed more commonality of interests.

the downtown business interests articulated their concerns more forcefully and organized their community-centered energies more efficiently than ever before. Instead of boosterism, business-centered groups helped to trigger a variety of problem-solving programs such as redevelopment and traffic revision and provided continuing support for efforts at solving other problems such as delinquency and crime. Much of the lay leadership of public campaigns for bonds, for example; much of the stimulus to action itself; and much of the private portion of new investment necessary to redevelopment came from this newly organized group. It is important to recognize, however, that, although the support and stimulus of downtown business was and is an essential element in the coalition that dominates decisions in the city, downtown business does not constitute a power elite. It does not run the city, or call the shots for its puppets.

The second element in the coalition – one would be tempted to call it the Civic Establishment except that the term may connote more tradition-based power than this coalition possesses – is composed of the technician, the professional, the expert. As Barry Karl (1963) has pointed out, the innovative function of the Progressive reform groups has largely been taken over by the professional (ch. 1). The social worker has replaced Jane Addams. The social scientist in a Charles Merriam has replaced the amateur politician/reformer. Police administration, comprehensive budgeting and capital programming, systematic traffic control, land-use planning, and renewal and rehabilitation have all become, in one degree or another, the domains of the expert. Technical criteria play a far greater role than before in determining choices, and the specification of alternatives is likewise largely a function of the technician who, often alone, knows what is possible.[9]

Perhaps the policy area most obviously dominated by the expert is that of public education. Teachers and school administrators not only set the agenda for action. They provide most of the arguments and evidence relevant to the choices that can be

9. Banfield and Wilson note that the city manager often acquires power by virtue of 'his virtual monopoly of technical and other detailed information' (p. 175). They pay little attention to the possibility that other technicians in the city bureaucracy may acquire power over limited segments of policy in the same manner. Banfield and Wilson do note that in many cities it is the bureaucracy which can initiate and implement change but do not concede increasing significance to this group. See pp. 218–23.

made and constitute the most active and powerful interests participating in the decision-making process. If non-professionals protest against certain policies – Negroes denouncing *de facto* segregation, for example – the professional educators cite technical criteria as a sufficient justification for their decisions and frequently carry the day.

The existence of professional skills relevant to city problems is, of course, a relatively new feature on the urban scene. Even now we are a long way from a technocracy, for the skills fall far short of the problems. Nevertheless, the growth of what broadly may be called applied social science has added a significant number of new people in new roles to the urban system, and these people help formulate and specify the problems and alternative courses of action for the other interests in the coalition. In this way the technician analyses power over resource allocation that is every bit as real as that of the economic interests or authority-wielders.

Let us turn to the peak of the loose coalition of interests that dominate today's urban scene, the mayor. He presides over the 'new emergence', and, if the coalition is to succeed, he must lead it. More than anyone else he determines the direction of urban development; yet his sanctions are few, his base of support insecure. The mayor is both the most visible person in the community and, on questions of public policy, probably the most influential. Yet his is the classic example of the separation of influence and power.[10] Few city mayors have significant patronage resources. Even fewer use their appointments to give themselves direct leverage over policy. Though the mayor in a partisan city is necessarily elected through canvasses that involve the ward organizations, no big-city mayor, not even Daley, can be regarded as the creature of the machine. Moreover the mayor is an individual who has 1) sufficient mass appeal or organizational support to win election, 2) enough awareness of the complexity of urban problems to rely heavily on a professional staff for advice and

10. Banfield and Wilson suggest that as the mayor's machine-based power declined his formal authority has increased, by virtue of reformers' efforts to achieve greater centralization. They recognize, of course, that the increased authority does not compensate for the loss of power. Moreover, in the contemporary city the scope of the perceived problems and needs is often so broad that the strongest political machine could have done little about it with its own resources. Providing investment capital to rebuild downtown opening employment opportunities for Negroes must be negotiated in the wider community. The mayor is likely to be the chief negotiator and neither formal authority nor political clout is as effective as bargaining skills.

counsel, and 3) the ability to negotiate successfully with the economic notables in the city to mobilize both public and private resources in efforts to solve core city economic and social problems.

Successful electioneering in the city requires that the candidate be palatable to a lower income constituency, especially to Negroes. Where there remain vestiges of party organization with vote-delivering capabilities the successful candidate must have some appeal for them, too. An ethnic background or family association that evokes support from the delivery wards is often helpful. At the same time, however, the successful mayoral candidate is likely to appeal to that portion of the urban electorate which historically has been reformist or mugwumpish in orientation.[11] He personifies good government by his espousal of professionalism in local administration. Frequently his personal style, despite his name or political forbears, is thoroughly white-collar and middle class. He is relatively articulate on local television, and his campaigns are likely to stress his competence at communal problem-solving rather than the particular group benefits that may accrue following his election. Nor is this mere campaign talk. His administration concentrates on solving or alleviating particular problems rather than building memorials or dramatizing the city's commercial prospects. Again, this posture requires collaboration with those possessing the relevant resources, the experts and the businessmen.

Obviously, there are variations in the way the mayoral role is played. From city to city and mayor to mayor many differences may appear. The main lines of demarcation may be twofold, however. Some mayors, possessing the gifts of self-dramatization, may more fully personify the programs of the city than others. This has little effect on the content of the decisions but may have consequences in terms of support. Mayors may also differ in the degree to which they actively seek out problems and solutions. Banfield describes Daley waiting for things to come to a head; other mayors more actively seek to forestall the problem entirely or to structure the whole process through which the issue develops. The latter distinction may be related to the structure of the city; the larger and more diverse the city, the less effectively can the mayor actively shape the problem-solving process.

Of what is mayoral influence composed? Much of it is con-

11. Lorin Peterson greatly overstates the case for connecting contemporary urban influentials with the mugwump tradition, but there is something in his argument. See Peterson (1961).

tained in the office itself. Of all the roles in the community none is so well situated with respect to the flow of information concerning the city's problems. This alone gives the occupant of the office a great advantage over other influentials. He knows more about more things than anyone else. Although his patronage power may be relatively slight, his budgetary authority is typically substantial. Insofar as he, by himself or in a board or commission, presents the budget to the council, he is determining much of the agenda for the discussion of public affairs, and no one else in the city can compete with him. Third, his ability to co-opt persons into *ad hoc* committees is unmatched in the city. As the only official with formal authority to speak for the entire city, he can confer legitimacy on co-opted leaders as no one else can. Thus, if he chooses to, a shrewd mayor may have a good deal to say about who shall be regarded as leaders and who shall not. Negotiations on civil rights issues in a number of cities illustrate the point well. Finally, as noted earlier, the mayor is, or soon becomes, far better-known in the community than anyone else, and is far better able to command and structure public attention.[12]

A considerable factor in the mayor's ability to structure public debate is his superior access to and influence over the press. City hall reporters not only cover his office closely but their view of city problems is very largely gained through their daily contacts with the official city fathers. The latter, in turn, are cordial and by being helpful can be reasonably assured that most of the news stories out of city hall will reflect mayoral interpretation. The newspapers as major businesses with their economic future tied to the local community and its elites are likely to favor editorially a mayor whose style embraces their interests. Thus even though the editors may differ with some specific recommendation of the mayor, they give him general support, while through them the mayor communicates his conceptions of city problems and program. One result, of course, is to make it difficult for others to challenge successfully the incumbent mayor for re-election.[13]

12. Scott Greer found that Mayor Tucker was the only person in the St Louis community, city or suburbs, with any substantial visibility with respect to community-wide issues (1963, pp. 106–7).

13. Banfield and Wilson note that the city hall reporter 'is likely to be in a symbiotic relationship with the politicians and bureaucrats whose activities he reports' (p. 316). They do not conclude, however, that this relationship strengthens the elected leadership. Indeed, they imply the opposite. See, e.g., p. 325. This difference in judgment calls for more systematic empirical analysis than is presently available.

Thus despite the unstable character of the coalition's base – predominantly low income voters and downtown businessmen – the mayor, once elected, may serve a good many terms. No outsider can find a sufficiently sharp wedge of controversy to drive between the disparate elements, or sufficient visibility to exploit whatever gaps develop.

Nevertheless, the mayor is influential only relative to other groups in the city. He is not powerful relative to the problems he tries to solve. The mayor cannot determine by fiat or, apparently, any other way that the economic resources of the city shall increase, that crime and poverty shall decline, that traffic shall move efficiently. He only has rather more directly to say about how the problems shall be approached than anyone else.

This discussion omits those cities which have adopted the council-manager form of government. In Kansas City or Cincinnati, for example, the aggregative and legitimating functions are less likely to be performed by the mayor who is seldom more than the ceremonial head of the city. The manager can rarely perform these functions either, since they are largely incompatible with his professional role. The result may be that the functions are not performed at all. On the other hand, the manager does possess some of the elements of leadership, especially information. As Banfield and Wilson note, the manager 'sits at the center of things, where all communication lines converge. In the nature of the case, then, the councilman must depend on him for their information. Whether he likes it or not, this gives him a large measure of control over them' (1963, p. 175).

IV

The 'new convergence' we have described actively seeks out solutions to certain problems it regards as critical to the city's growth. This activist posture may be viewed as somewhat at variance with the approaches to decision-making described by Dahl and by Banfield. Dahl suggests that in New Haven the coalition led by Mayor Lee has actively sought to resolve certain major issues with Lee serving as the principal negotiator among the contending forces. But, says Dahl, Lee selected issues with a view towards their effect upon his chances for re-election. Permanently conditioning the mayor's strategy was the fact that 'the mayor and his political opponents were constantly engaged in a battle for votes at the next election, which was always just around the corner' (Banfield, p. 214). So far as most large cities are concerned, this may greatly overstate the impact of the necessity for re-election on the specific choices made by the mayor and his allies. We shall try to suggest both the role of the electorate and some of the more immediate restraints upon mayoral choice-making in a moment.

Banfield's analysis of Chicago leads to the conclusion that issues are raised primarily by large formal organizations, some of which are governmental and some of which are not (1961, p. 263ff). As the maintenance or enhancement needs of the organization require governmental decisions they enter the political arena and usually seek the support of Mayor Daley. Daley himself, however, operates in primarily a reflexive fashion. Although he desires to 'do big things', he must move slowly and cautiously, fearful of generating further controversies, and aware that the ponderous and intricate structure of power he heads can be disrupted and his influence capital used up if he moves too soon or too often. But Banfield selects issues that illustrate this argument. His cases fall far short of representing the range of major resource allocation decisions for Chicago. It may still be true, therefore, that Daley initiates or actively participates in the process involved in making other decisions. Certainly it seems that other big-city mayors do.[14]

I focused originally on the processes of allocating scarce resources. These processes may sometimes involve bitter conflict among rival interests. They may sometimes be resolved, however, in a highly consensual way. Particularly is this likely to be the case when the technical experts play a large role in shaping the decision. Much of the time such major areas of public policy as expressway planning, zoning and budget-making are determined in ways that evoke little complaint or dispute. The fact that no one in the city effectively objects to the decision makes the decision no less important in terms of resource allocation.

A closely related aspect of urban decision-making is that a great many decisions are made in a fashion that may best be described as habitual. The pressures on the time and attention of decision-makers are such that many decisions must continue to

14. In addition to Dahl's discussion of Mayor Lee's active role, one may cite as particularly pertinent the discussions of Philadelphia, Detroit, Nashville and Seattle reported in the appropriate volumes of Edward Banfield (ed.), *City Politics Reports*, Cambridge: Joint Center for Urban Studies, mimeo. My own research in St Louis, the initial foundation for much of the argument in this essay, certainly leads to this conclusion.

be made (or avoided) as they have been in the past. No continuing calculation can be made of the costs and benefits for each area of possible choice. Much is done routinely. Much is left undone in the same way. Control of the routine is largely in the hands of the technicians with the mayor in the best position to alter it at the margins.

Some issues are forced 'from the outside', of course. Things which city leaders would prefer not to have to deal with may be pressed in the fashion Banfield describes. Race relations issues generally come under this category. Almost every large city mayor has been compelled to take action, not because he or his coalition particularly wanted to, but because they were forced to by external pressure.

The recent demands of militant Negro groups have often been concentrated on city hall, however, even when the substance of the demands dealt with jobs in private employment. Negro leaders have correctly identified the mayor as the appropriate figure to convene local elites in order to negotiate agreements that will open job opportunities to Negroes. Militant Negroes have often greatly over-estimated the power of the mayor to effect a satisfactory solution, however. For while he is in a stronger position than any other person or group or functioning organization, his resources and those of his allies may fall far short of the requirements.

Pressure from the constituency would not be the usual way for policy to be initiated, however. The bulk of the city's working agenda is made up of proposals drawn up by the city's own technicians to meet problems identified by them or by their allies in the problem-oriented sectors of the community. The need for new revenue sources, for example, is perceived by the mayor and his staff long before public pressure is exerted, and it is the mayoral coalition which seeks a viable solution to the problem.

Not all mayors, not all corps of technicians, and not all downtown business groups are equal in ability to perceive problems, devise solutions, or negotiate settlements. One of the significant variables that distinguishes one city's political system from another is the energy and imagination of its newly convergent elites. In some cities solutions may be found that escape the leaders of another. It is probably true, however, that these differences have been narrowed somewhat by the collaboration among urban elites throughout the nation. The American Municipal Association and the US Conference of Mayors provide organized communication networks that link the political executives. So does HHFA in its field. So do the various associations of urban technicians in their respective specialities. The metropolitan press facilitates a certain amount of interchange with respect to both problems and solutions in urban areas. Thus there has developed some degree of consensus as to what should be done and some uniformity in the structure of power by which action may be accomplished.

Cities vary with respect not only to energy and skill of leadership but in tangible resources, public and private that, may be mobilized for reallocation. In Pittsburgh, for example, there was probably no available substitute for the Mellon cash. In St Louis the scarcity or stodginess or both of local private capital has made the redevelopment task more difficult. These are variables involved in the power structure of a community. That there are also variations in the range and severity of the problems cities face is obvious and complicates further the task of comparative analysis.

V

I have suggested that a large portion of the content of urban public policy is provided directly by one or more of the three main elements of the governing coalition; the mayor, the technical experts and the downtown business community. They identify the problems, they articulate the alternative actions that might be taken, and they themselves take most of the relevant actions. This structure of decision-making provides no immediate role for the community-at-large, the voters; and, although Dahl may overstate the significance of their role in limiting New Haven's executive-centered coalition, they do play a role in resource allocations, and so do the organized groups that represent segments of the electorate that are outside the dominant coalition.

Dahl's attribution of 'weight' to the electorate seems to be based on the relatively intense partisan competition in New Haven, and it may be reinforced by the need to run every two years. But in many cities the direct competition for office is neither so sharp nor so frequent. The tenure in office of prominent mayors such as Tucker, Daley or Wagner suggests that survival in office may not always require the close attention to voter desires that Dahl suggests. Particularly is this likely in a city where elections are partisan, for the safety of the Democratic ticket is not often in question in many of these cities. The primary may occasionally present peril to the incumbent, and in both partisan and non-partisan cities incumbents sometimes lose. But there is little evidence to show that mayors, or other elected executives for that matter, have any reliable way of perceiving voter needs very accurately or consciously building support for himself among them. The new mayor may say, with Richard Daley, that 'good government is good politics', in part because he doesn't have the option to engage in any other kind.

Nevertheless, generalized constituency sentiment remains a factor that affects policy-making, albeit in a secondary, boundary-setting way. It works primarily in three ways. First, the technician as social scientist often takes into account the interests and needs of the public he hopes to serve when making his plans and recommendations. If he proposes an enlarged staff of case workers for the Welfare Department, he does so partly because in some sense he expects the public to benefit. It is rarely, however, because any public demand for the larger staff is expressed. Rather, the technician believed the proposal would be 'good' for the constituents. Secondly, the electorate must make certain broad choices directly. Bond issues and tax rates must often be voted upon; other types of referenda must be approved; key policy-making officials must be elected. Very often this involves 'selling the public' on the desirability of the proposal. They have not demanded it. They often have no strong predispositions one way or another except perhaps for a class-related bias on public expenditures in general. But this approval is required, and in anticipation of the limits of tolerance the key decision-makers must tailor their proposals. This is influence, of course, but of a general and largely negative kind. Thirdly, there is the active demand stemming directly from the constituents to which policy-makers respond, but which response would not have been made in the absence of the public demand. Some of these demands go counter to the policies espoused by the coalition; spot zoning, for example, or construction unions' demands on the building code. In some instances the coalition may have the power to change the demands; in other cases, not. Some demands, however, are more difficult to deal with because, if they arise, they cannot be altered by the exercise of power, but at the same time they are so controversial that almost any solution is likely to damage the overall position of the leaders. As we have noted, many of the issues of race relations are in this category. The city fathers have not agitated upon issues, but once raised they must be met.

As we assign 'the public' to a largely secondary role, we must thus relegate those officials most closely associated with immediate constituency relationships to a similarly secondary position. Councilmen or aldermen, ward leaders and other local party leaders are likely to play only supportive or obstructive roles in the community's decision-making process. The demands for action do not come from or through them, they are not privy to the councils either of the notables or the experts. They may well play out their traditional role of precinct or ward politician, but, unlike the machine leader before, these roles are separated quite completely from those of policy-making. Even in Chicago, where the mayor's position in part depends on his vote-getting strength through the party organization, such little participation in policy-making filters down to the ward workers. Similarly, William Green's rise to power in the party organization in Philadelphia had little effect on the content of public policy. It is essential to see that the difference between the policymaking leadership and the 'politicians' is more than rhetorical. It implies a substantial impact on the content of policy.[15]

Even though neither the party professionals nor the electorate generally are active participants in the process of resource allocation, is not the top political leadership, specifically the mayor, constrained by his desire for re-election? In part, of course, the answer is yes. In partisan cities the mayor must be nominated and elected on the party ticket, and, particularly in the primary, this may involve getting party organization support. In a non-partisan community too, the mayor must get enough votes to win. It does not follow, however, that there is much connection between what is needed to gain votes and the specific decisions made once in office. Dahl emphasizes the vote-getting popularity of Richard Lee's program in New Haven, especially of urban renewal. Yet that popularity was not really evident in advance of the decisions and was largely dissipated within a very few years. Doubtless Mayor Collins has increased his popularity in Boston by rationalizing and reducing the fiscal burden, but, if Levin is at all correct, his election was not a mandate for *any* particular decisions he has made (Levin, 1960). The same, I think, could be argued for Dilworth, Tucker, and others of the 'new mayors'. Certainly the limits of public understanding and acceptance constitute restraints

15. For an illustration, see Salisbury (1960, pp. 498–507).

upon the decision-making system, but these are broad restraints, rarely specific in directing choices, and operating largely as almost subconscious limits to the kinds of choices that may be made.[16]

VI

It may not be amiss to conclude this discussion by juxtaposing three quite different strands of thought concerning the urban scene. On the one hand, Dahl and his associates have generally denied the existence of a single structure of power in the city. We have argued, not contradicting Dahl but changing the emphasis, that on a substantial set of key issues such a structure may be discerned. Hunter, *et al.*, have stressed an essentially monolithic structure heavily weighted in behalf of the economic elites. We have stressed the central role of elected political leadership. Finally, such writers as Lewis Mumford and Jane Jacobs, less interested in the problems of power, have doubted the capacity of the urban community to serve man's essential needs at all. In a sense, we are suggesting that each may be partly correct, partly wrong. The coalition of interests headed by the mayor may indeed lack the resources, public and private, separately or combined to solve the communal problems now dominating the civic agenda. This is the irony that lies behind the convergence of power elements in the modern city. Where once there seemed to be ample resources to keep what were regarded as the major problems of urban life within quite tolerable limits, now, with a more self-conscious collaboration of governmental and private economic power than ever before, and with those structures of power themselves larger and more extensive than ever, the capacity to cope with the recognized problems of the environment seems almost pathetically inadequate. Partly, this may be because the problems have changed in magnitude, and, partly, that we perceive their magnitude in more sophisticated fashion. In any case, it makes the notion of an elite with ample power to deal with the urban community if ever

16. Banfield and Wilson also discuss a shift in the contemporary city, at least in political style, from working class to middle class. They conclude that the new style politician, reflecting middle class values in a working class city, will be compelled to offer broad inducements to the electorate in the form of major civic accomplishments if he wishes re-election (p. 329 ff.). This argument, like Dahl's, seems to me to assume that the urban electorate 'shops' more actively than I think it does. It also assumes that political leaders in the urban community are more acutely conscious of their re-election problems than I think they are.

it chooses to, seem a romance, a utopian dream. Like other municipal utopias – Progressive-era reform or today's metropolitan reorganization – it may be yearned for but largely unrealized.

References

BANFIELD, E. (1961), *Political Influence*, Free Press.

BANFIELD, E. C., and WILSON, J. Q. (1963), *City Politics*, Harvard University Press.

DAHL, R. A. (1961), *Who Governs?*, Yale University Press.

GREER, S. (1963), *Metropolitics*, Wiley.

HAWLEY, A. H. (1963), 'Community power and urban renewal success', *Amer. J. of Sociol.*, vol. 8, pp. 422–31.

KARL, B. (1963), *Executive Reorganization and Reform in the New Deal*, Harvard University Press.

LEVIN, M. B. (1960), *The Alienated Voter*, Holt, Rinehart & Winston.

LONG, N. (1962), 'The corporation and the local community', in C. Press (ed.), *The Polity*, Rand McNally.

McKELVEY, B. (1963), *The Urbanization of America*, Rutgers University Press.

PETERSON, L. (1961), *The Day of the Mugwump*, Random House.

POLSBY, N. W. (1963), *Community Power and Political Theory*, Yale University Press.

PRESS, C. (1962), *Main Street Politics*, Michigan State University for Community Development.

ROSSI, P. (1960), 'Power and community structure', *Midwest J. of Pol. Sci.*, vol. 4, pp. 390–401.

SALISBURY, R. H. (1960), 'Relationships, interests, parties and governmental structure', *Western Pol. Q.*, vol. 13, pp. 498–507.

SCHNORE, L. F., and ALFORD, R. R. (1963), 'Forms of government and socio-economic characteristics of suburbs', *Admin. Sci. Q.*, vol. 8, pp. 1–17.

SCHULZE, R. (1961), 'The bifurcation of power in a satellite city', in M. Janowitz (ed.), *Community Political Systems*, pp. 19–81, Free Press.

WILLIAMS, O. P., and ADRIAN, C. (1963), *Four Cities*, University of Pennsylvania Press.

20 P. A. Eddison

Comprehensive Planning for Local Government

P. A. Eddison, 'Comprehensive planning for local government', specially commissioned, 1972.

Any picture of the state of urban planning in British local government presented at this moment in time is very much a 'still' from a moving situation – more so than would normally be the case, simply because it happens that change is occurring more rapidly now. Some change was planned, some has been unexpected and a lot is confused but not yet confounded. There have been at least two distinct paths along which these changes have taken, and continue to take, place. The first was a desire to remedy the inadequacies of the management systems in local government. The second was a move to improve the processes of development plan-making, which had fallen sadly into disrepute. Both these movements arose roughly at the same time, i.e. in the mid 1960s and have since been slowly converging until the current situation, where a variety of relationships between the two are at once being advanced, analyzed, discounted or enthusiastically welcomed.

In as much as one is concerned to use planning in a broad sense to improve our cities rather than simply to improve planning itself, it is important to trace out these two strands of change.

Management awareness

Any committee of inquiry derives from a general concern about the subject of inquiry before the committee is set up. The Maud Committee on Management of Local Government was no exception. An awareness of shortcomings in the way local authorities were fulfilling their obligations, in the methods and procedures they had adopted over the years had been growing since the late fifties and early sixties. The effect of the publication of the Committee's Report was greatly to increase the active interest in improving the management operations of local government. In practice the greatest interest centred on the committee structures of local authorities. Indeed, there are very few large authorities which since the Report was produced have not at least reviewed their internal organization (Greenwood *et al.*, 1971). The Report has given rise to other developments, which are not quite so well documented but which in many ways are more significant. The emphasis, if anything, was on the need for administrative efficiency through internal reorganization of departments and committees. Many of the changes which have taken place since have been aimed in this direction but more recently there has been a more searching questioning not of efficiency but of effectiveness, deriving from a redefinition of the role of local government, or at least from the emergence of a new perspective of local government's responsibility in its area, perhaps best summed up by Derek Senior in his Memorandum of Dissent in volume 2 of the Report of the Royal Commission:

Local government has a general responsibility for the well-being of the communities it represents: its concern is not confined to the discharge of the duties imposed on it by Parliament. It must seek to promote community well-being in all its aspects – economic as well as social, cultural as well as physical – whether or not it has a statutory duty in relation to any particular aspect. And in discharging its statutory duties it must put the general well-being of the local community before the sectional interest of the central government department that is nationally responsible for the function concerned (Redcliffe-Maud, 1969).

What has been exposed is the need to look not so much at the organizational structures for management in local government but the processes of management and policy formulation which those structures are designed to sustain. This in turn has exposed a related weakness, the tradition of seeing the services as separately managed, separately administered. What has happened in the development of local government is that a whole series of arbitrary compartments, called professions, departments, committees or units of government have been created. The effect of the creation of all these has been twofold. Either problems in society are totally ignored because they neither fall in one compartment nor another or those problems are distorted to fit the arbitrary compartments. One only has to scan a list of current problems for which local government has varying degrees of concern to realize how true this is – poverty, leisure, labour shortages, unemployment, vandalism, racial conflict, gypsies, problem families, educational deprivation. Clearly the links *between* the objectives of services are too significant to be isolated in one compartment, whether it be a profession, department, committee or tier of government. The policies of one affect the climate for change, the scope for action in another. Problems are mercurial in their origins and the movement towards their remedies are equally complex and elusive.

A series of reports – Redcliffe-Maud (1969), Plowden (1967), Seebohm (1968), Buchanan (1963), Sharp (1970) – have in their own ways highlighted the weakness inherent in the separatist tradition. Perhaps more important than the organizational implications are the effects that such an approach has on attitudes and thinking of both professional and political personnel.

Increasing interest is being shown, therefore, in ways of developing the idea of general management, that is to say, to give expression in some form or other to the need to plan the affairs of a local authority as a whole. The desire in turn is to relate moves in this direction to a greater awareness of the environment in which the local authority operates, to relate policies and action to the needs of the community. The developments along these lines are taking a variety of forms. Corporate planning, local authority policy planning, community planning and PPBS are all being introduced to different degrees in many authorities.[1] They are all manifestations of the management changes taking place in local government.

Development plans

Almost entirely separate from the management revolution has been the planning revolution – the considerable changes in the system of land-use planning which are now being implemented and which are still developing. The Town and Country Planning Act 1947 established in this country the most sophisticated land-use planning and control system in the world. Its originators and the town planning profession sincerely believed that the future shape of cities, at least in a physical sense, would emerge from this system. To some extent this was true but the development plans produced under it are open to criticism.

(a) they are deficient in policies, particularly those not directly related to land use, and they are inadequate as guides to developers and as bases for development control;

(b) they concentrate on detail and on what are often misleadingly precise boundaries;

1. See Lambeth Community Plan (1971).

(c) they try to illustrate in standard forms different kinds of information, much of which is not relevant to positive promotion or control of development;

(d) they are ill-equipped to influence the quality of development as distinct from its location;

(e) finally, their inflexible form and content are not adaptable to new techniques and concepts, and the centralized procedures required for amendment impose long delays on attempts to deal with rapidly changing circumstances (James, 1965).

To meet these and other criticisms a new system was advanced and enshrined in the Town and Country Planning Act 1968 (now the 1971 Act). Other supporting documents have been and are about to be produced.[2] Very briefly, the new system has three major characteristics. Firstly, it establishes a split between (a) major policy issues which are of interest to central government for its specific control purposes, issues such as employment and population distribution, major communications networks and major public capital investments, which will find expression in 'structure' plans and (b) local issues to be determined within a framework laid down by the structure plan but approved and adapted locally. It also recognizes the need for a physical development plan to be underpinned by a deeper understanding of the relationships between the physical, economic and social systems of an area. The town planning world has been much influenced by systems thinking. The recognition of the dynamic in city systems has had a major impact. It is under this influence that the ideal of comprehensiveness has received an added impetus. The third characteristic of the new system relates to resource allocation. In the past development plans have tended to reflect pious hopes and aspirations. Very few of them were ever subject to any financial appraisal. Structure plans will have to be realistic in terms of resources likely to be available.

Convergence

These movements towards more effective local authority management and improved urban planning are converging. Common elements are being identified and new forms of planning are coming to the fore combining these elements. The concept of urban management might be a good description – it is very much

2. See Development Plans Manual (MHLG, 1970).

a planning style given to local authority management. The process itself has attracted the label, corporate planning. It is the process by which a local authority draws on its wide variety of professional and political skills to formulate, carry out and review its overall policies. The corporate planning process is seen as being freed from a particular department or profession. It derives from a common basis of information, of understanding and analysis and represents a central process within the local authority on which are based a wide range of plans and policies for implementation in specialist areas. The urban town planner's plan thus ceases to be seen in isolation from other plans. It in no way represents, as it has tended to do in the past, a starting point for other plans or a framework within which other plans must fit but, much more realistically, is only one of a series of plans emerging from this central process, but giving expression to policies in the physical development field.

Underlying the movement towards corporate planning is the desire for more rational decision-making processes. In some places PPBS is being seen as the most appropriate framework for rational decision-making, e.g. Coventry, Islington, Gloucestershire, Liverpool, Greater London and others. It is not the only approach being adopted. But the trend is towards developing systems of corporate planning which present to decision-makers information derived from a more rational approach to the analysis of urban issues. The institutional and political framework in the United Kingdom offers more scope for the introduction of these approaches than exists, say, in the United States. Although the ardent opponents of PPBS in America like Wildavsky (1966) make exaggerated statements about the extent of its failure, in fact there are some successes (Carlson, 1971). The important point, however, is that the local government system in the United Kingdom, with its much stronger professional and simpler political bases, is adopting and adapting PPBS more flexibly, more slowly and with more encouraging results. The point is taken up later.

Rationality and corporate planning

The literature of public administration and political science is full of models of decision-making. Controversy has centred for a long time on the limits of rationality. The pure-rationality model has been described thus:

1. Establishing a complete set of operational goals, with relative weights allocated to the different degrees to which each may be achieved.

2. Establishing a complete inventory of other values and of resources with relative weights.

3. Preparing a complete set of the alternative policies open to the policymaker.

4. Preparing a complete set of valid predictions of the costs and benefits of each alternative, including the extent to which each will achieve the various operational goals, consume resources and realize or impair other values.

5. Calculating the net expectation for each alternative by multiplying the probability of each benefit and cost for each alternative by the utility of each, and calculating the net benefit (or cost) in utility units.

6. Comparing the net expectations and identifying the alternative (or alternatives, if two or more are equally good) with the highest net expectation (Dror, 1968).

Writers like Lindblom seem to dismiss the rational approach simply because it does not happen in practice. What happens, they say when they observe decision-making processes, is 'disjointed-incrementalism'. Braybrooke and Lindblom (1963) hold that decision-making is

1. Incremental or tending towards relatively small changes

2. Remedial, in that decisions are made to move away from ills rather than toward goals

3. Serial, in that problems are not solved at one stroke but rather successively attacked

4. Exploratory, in that goals are continually being redefined or newly discovered

5. Fragmented or limited, in that problems are attacked by considering a limited number of alternatives rather than all possible alternatives; and

6. Disjointed, in that there are many dispersed 'decision-points'.

The implications of all this are that planners should not attempt comprehensiveness but should work on problems as they arise. It means abandoning considering ripple-effects – forgetting goals and objectives and concentrating on solving current ills. Because it happens this way they end up in the position of recommending it as *the* way. It is easy to attack the purely rational model on these telling grounds:

1. That we do not operate in a state of certainty either in the present or even less as far as the future is concerned. Our diagnosis of what is, is often wrong, our predictions of what will be are virtually always wrong.

2. The process of building up plans or policies is an unconscious process of cutting off options on the way. Even at the start of the planning process, the assembly of data, vast numbers of alternative solutions are excluded by the decisions as to what data is relevant.

Attacking rationality does not, however, demolish its attraction as a basis for other approaches and certainly the other extreme is positively harmful to advance in policy-making. It is the easiest thing in the world for complacency to set in. Writers in public administration and political science who describe what actually happens in decision-making and whose interest stops there are perhaps knowingly or unwittingly buttressing complacency and we know that the world is full of people expending vast energies to stay the same – the dynamic conservatives described by Donald Schon (1971). Because it does not happen does not mean that it cannot.

Limits and constraints on rationality

The only safe conclusion one can draw from the evidence of actual practice is that there are limits to rationality, whether it is expressed in a PPB or some other system.

The setting of objectives is one area where difficulties have arisen. Some local authorities have spent quite some time drawing up sets of objectives and sub-objectives in an attempt to arrive at an 'ideal' programme structure for their PPB system. This has proved a quite demoralizing experience for some and contrasts sharply with the authorities, e.g. Coventry and Islington, which have gone through this process fairly quickly, recognizing that their initial efforts will be far from perfect but that putting them to the true test of actually using them in the policy-making processes will be the best way to secure improvements. Of course, no scheme of objectives will be free from overlaps. Undoubtedly difficulties have been experienced in making objectives operational. But in the places where new processes have been put into operation, the process of working through the objectives, of arguing what objectives are, has opened vast areas to challenge and to questioning, has opened up new alternative courses of action *between* traditional departments. The resulting schemes of objectives are open to challenge, perhaps, but the benefit derived from the lead-up process is claimed to have been well worth the effort.

Evaluation and the establishment of satisfactory output measures are frequently advanced as great weaknesses in the rational approach. The point here is that even when judgments between alternative courses of action are entirely subjective, the fact that (a) alternatives have been considered at all and (b) they have been considered in the light of an objective represents an improvement over current policy-making approaches. The fundamental assumption behind PPBS is that decisions are likely to be better if the decision-maker is conscious of what it is he is trying to achieve. Many policies are established, many plans are carried out against an entirely different background. There are many swimming pools now built for no other reason than it seemed like a good idea. Roads are improved, schools built, areas rehabilitated, standards applied with no clear idea of what they were designed to achieve. Any system which asks the question 'Why?' is an improved system. This does not solve the problem of evaluation, it simply and starkly exposes it, but therein lies the road to improvement.

With a fairly complex and often tense relationship politically between central and local government, any system of decision-making is inevitably likely to suffer a loss of rationality. Central government uses a variety of control devices on local government, which often generates frustration, if not annoyance. There are countless examples of loan sanctions being granted from one central government department for half a project and withheld for the other half by another department. Frequently an argument against introducing more rational systems of decision-making in local government is that the exercise would be fruitless without a parallel change in central government. What this argument lacks is a realization that improved decision-making approaches at the local government level represent a strong negotiating base for confronting central government. Too often (and there is plenty of evidence to support it) local government readily submits to constraints imposed by central government, frequently in the form of standards or to general policies which could be challenged effectively. Indeed, both levels of government could greatly benefit from more challenge.

These and other constraints are perhaps better looked at against developments in practice and further organizational possibilities.

Organizational implications
Internal to the authority

One of the major constraints of any move towards corporate planning arises from the effects of departmentalism and professionalism and one of the first requirements is for heads of departments in local government to see their role increasingly less as running a separate service and more as joining with other chief officers in helping to shape a much more integrated, but wider basis for choice for elected members. This means more than the traditional chief officers' group. This group, therefore, would require servicing – it would require a group of people to provide information, to carry out problem analysis, to ensure that needs in the community were being identified, to ensure that members knew how current policies were working. There will never be a clean start. Policy will have to be formulated very quickly sometimes in response to a variety of pressures requiring new or reshaped policies. This will require a group within the authority manned by all the disciplines to collect information but, more important, to analyze it to give insights, new approaches, new possibilities for action, a wider choice. This group would be regarded by the chief officers and the elected members as a key point in the policy formulation process. It would be drawn on regularly to service both the chief officers' group and the major political party group.

This has implications for the role of the traditional department. There has been a tendency in the last few years to recast departmental boundaries to embrace a wider range of activities. This has varied from the Liverpool approach, which has grouped activities together according to the objectives which they are designed to achieve, to the approach whereby different departments are grouped together with one chief officer to represent two or three departments. This has perhaps been most common in the idea of a director of technical services. This approach does little to meet the needs of the situation and indeed, probably makes things worse. No one profession can adequately represent the views, approaches and perspectives of another. Thus it is unsatisfactory for an engineer to represent a planning officer's views or *vice versa*. Both have different backgrounds, different skills, different insights, which are equally valid in the policy formulation process. The notion that a directorate of technical services improves co-ordination is a naïve one. The problem is one of boundaries – in this case, departmental boundaries. Wherever they are put, there will be problems. This is inherent in boundaries always. Local government problems will always transcend these boundaries. What is needed is an approach which overcomes the difficulties of departmentalism. It probably means an extension of the growing practice of establishing inter-disciplinary working groups. These are quite common in local government but tend to be *ad hoc* and mostly operate on a part-time basis. It would perhaps be more helpful to regard departments as pools of professional skills. Set against these skills would be a changing pattern of tasks which would draw on different combinations of these skills from time to time to form new, temporary but full-time units to tackle problems as they arose. This would be a flexible arrangement outside the framework of traditional departmental structure. Problems and solutions do not lie within one field and organizational design should therefore reflect this reality. This does not mean the abandonment of professional departments, which would remain to administer services. For planning purposes, however, these pools of skills need to be used in an entirely different way.

In practice authorities are attempting a variety of approaches to the problem of overcoming departmentalism. In Liverpool, as a result of extensive reorganization, the whole of the local authority's activities have been recast into programme areas along PPB lines and a new departmental structure has been created around these. Examples of the departments are Education, Transportation and Basic Services, Housing, Recreation and Open Spaces, Personal Health and Social Services, and Environmental Health and Protection. The great criticism of this system is that old boundary problems have been replaced by new ones and that there is little possibility within the system for these boundary problems to be overcome. PPBS is best seen as an aid to policy formulation and review. To base organizational structure change on programme areas probably defeats the object of PPBS. The PPB system needs to be a changing, a learning system and as such cannot be too closely identified with rigid organizational structures. In Coventry most of the traditional departments have been retained.[3] A chief officers group with policy formulation responsibilities has been created and this is supported by nine programme area teams, drawing expertise from the whole range of professional skills in the Corporation. Each programme area team is chaired by a chief officer. This seems on the whole to be a better system than the Liverpool one, in that the programme area teams are flexible, additional teams may be created, existing ones may be reformulated to meet the needs of the changing situation. In addition, there is much more chief officer commitment to the process of corporate planning.

Between tiers of government

A more than one-tier system of local government or a multi-agency system of public authorities presents major problems of implementing corporate planning. The difficulties of departmentalism are increased greatly when different agencies are involved. Ways are required of securing co-operation between levels of government and between different agencies. The starting point should perhaps be for local government as a whole to accept that, wherever a function is being administered, it is but one part of a combined effort to ensure that certain community objectives are met. Devices are required to give a basis for co-operation and it is possible that this basis might be derived from an agreement about the aims and objectives of local government in a particular area. This will generate conflict and dispute but at least the arguments will be explicit and will focus more on the different ways in which objectives might be met. Too often in local government at present, controversy rages almost for its own sake, because there are two tiers of government. The argument is best centred on whether or not a particular objective is better achieved in one way rather than another, whether it is better achieved through one authority's powers rather than another's. Again, the programme budgeting system offers this kind of framework for co-operation, not just between tiers of local government activities, but also between local government and the health services, between local government and other agencies. This raises the possibility of joint teams being set up, similar to the working group idea, within a single local authority. These will not be easy to mount and will depend to a very large extent on the political will of the agencies concerned. They may represent a pious hope.

3. See reports on progress in Coventry (Coventry Corporation, 1971).

The future role of rational analysis

The problems the policymaking machine chooses to focus on, those it ignores or those it remains ignorant of altogether, are a reflection of its values and preferences. So too are the solutions and priorities it chooses to adopt relative to those problems. It is not possible to devise a value-free approach to policy-making. All groups in the community cannot be satisfied. Public policy-making is essentially a conflict situation and the conflict centres on values. It is often argued that democracy is the carrying out of the will of the people and our interest in values etc. should stop there if we are ever to get anything done. Would it were so simple.

The unfortunate feature of democracy is that it is too coarsely grained – that an awful lot of harm can be done to a whole range of interests before 'popular disapproval' takes a hand. In fact, of course, there are many things which one might regard as un-desirable but which would never give rise to 'popular dis-approval' sufficient to change a government, local or national. In this respect politicians are not blameless – they too often steer just within the safe political limits and care little about those lost on the way. It is impossible at an election to vote on separate issues – one opts for a package of policies (or non-policies, as the case may be). Elections represent a sieving out of values and preferences. They form part of the policy-making process but it is crude and there is a need for other devices to secure more useful and relevant inputs into the process. It concerns communications and it will have to be dealt with briefly. There is no need to mention Skeffington participation efforts except to say that we seem to be appallingly unaware of their paternalistic nature. Instead, there are two points which need attention from both professionals and politicians. The first concerns public relations. It is rightly argued that public relations and public participation are different – the former is no substitute for the latter. That much can be agreed. What is not seen is that the two are very closely related, that a base of much better public relations than now exists needs to be laid before any form of participation has even a chance of success. Local government fails or succeeds at its points of contact with its clients, whether this is at an enquiry desk, in the classroom, in the press, the receipt of a letter or of a planning refusal notice or the cheerfulness of a refuse collector. Accessibility, ease of communication in information terms, is vital. For this reason, there is a great need in reformed local government for completely new devices, e.g. local authority bureaux to be set up, equipped with sophisticated communications systems, where clients can go and have the majority of their problems dealt with, or at least where the relevant contacts can be made.

The second point concerns an understanding of the value systems with which local government policy-making activities interact. A missing link in our communications system seems to be a flow of information into the planning process about a wider range of values and aspirations. A relatively simple analysis of our current policy-making processes reveals a successive narrowing down of options. How to generate input about different sets of values is no easy matter but there are encouraging signs that something can be achieved. Some of the Community Development Projects recently established as a joint venture between the Home Office and selected local authorities demonstrate that constructive community involvement can work and moreover with a substantial initiative coming from the community itself. It is true that the experience so far is with 'local' issues but interest is spreading to a concern for the wider policy implications and could easily develop further. One significant lesson from the Coventry example is that new alternatives for action are thrown up which would otherwise not have occurred.

Rationality in the practical political arena has limitations. What is required is the development of a system which harnesses:

1. The advance in analytical and other skills of the professional and other expertise,

2. The growing desire of politicians to debate and exercise more influence on policy-making, and

3. The aspirations and values of a much wider section of the community.

That the planning process is best regarded as cyclic has become a truism. What is not often realized, however, is that the process has a variety of 'break-in' points. Clean-slate operations are rarely possible, we break in to the cycle at many points, there is no right one. For descriptive purposes one has to start somewhere and here it is proposed to break in at the stage which is almost invariably placed as the last stage – that is at the monitoring and feedback stage. In a sense the most important stage in the planning process is where feedback and the identification of needs meet. The point is that the planning process depends on data –

admittedly data of many sorts but perhaps the richest vein of data lies in the information about how good or how bad, how effective or ineffective *present* policies are, or even old policies or someone else's similar policies. This is best regarded as the *learning* process whether by feedback on our own activities or from comparative sources. In many instances the asking of the question, 'How effective are our current policies?' will be a source of embarrassment because more often than not policies are or have been no more than cherished ideas, pet schemes or simply fashionable notions and adopted with little grasp of what they were intended to achieve. This reflects badly on the politicians but the fault is not entirely theirs. Feedback does not mean just the systems designs which may or may not be required to give expression to the feedback flows – it means simply the development of the habit of recognizing in the political arenas that policies are always wrong – less effective, unexpectedly effective or completely ineffective and in order to advance, not the art of policy-making but the state of the world, this simple fact needs to be given high recognition in the political processes. Feedback and learning is one of the sparks of planning – maybe the most tangible. It is a spark which gives the momentum to another cycle of the process. But there are other sparks to the process which may be related to existing policies or not. They are perhaps best described as problems, issues of concern or specific requirements of certain groups. They are not static and do not fit readily into the compartments or framework of any planning process and less still into any pattern of organization structures set up to carry out the planning process. They may be of continuing concern or may occur suddenly.

All these 'sparks' of the process are crucial and point to certain lessons. Feedback is one, the other is that our public policy-making institutions need to be sensitive to the other sparks, the requirements of groups, new or recurring problems, issues of concern. The important point is that *behind* formal organizational structures a common policy planning framework needs to be developed, orientated to what the organization is fundamentally trying to do. It will not be static, it will hardly ever be right but it will be an *enabling* framework – enabling challenge, questioning, innovation, change and advancement towards the identification and solution of urban problems. Creating it is not easy but neither is it impossible as the emerging developments in some progressive local authorities are showing.

Local government in the United Kingdom is slowly developing an improved model of public policy-making. It is a model which is orientated towards goals and objectives. The point here is that the model is goal-orientated, it is not dominated or constricted by pure rationality. It is an increasingly *learning* model. The PPBS framework is being used and adapted as a way of improving public policy-making – it is not being allowed to determine it. It is being used to highlight areas where knowledge is weak, where information is lacking, and it is exposing the need to learn more about output–input. Local government is learning about learning, too. A final example which possibly typifies the approach comes from the town of Stockport, Cheshire. Here the organizational structure has been changed and new approaches are being adopted to the policy-making process, the first stage of which is the most interesting and significant. All areas of the corporation's activities have drawn up a compendium, a position statement of current policies, specifying what the policies are, what they are designed to achieve, for whom, by when, how successful they have been and what output measures can be used. All this has been completed quickly and crudely. What is important is that it had never been done before. No one previously had any overall notion of what the policies were or how successful they were. For the first time, there is a basis for learning, a basis for challenge, a basis for building wider choices and scope for rational analysis. It would not fit a model of rationality in any sense but this and the other developments in the United Kingdom represent the beginnings of a more rational approach to urban policy-making within the political system.

References

BRAYBROOKE, D., and LINDBLOM, C. E. (1963), *Strategy of Decision*, Free Press.

BUCHANAN, C. (1963), *Traffic in Towns*, HMSO, Penguin edition, 1964.

CARLSON, J. W. (1971), 'The status and next steps for PPBS', ch. 15 in R. Haveman and J. M. Margolis (eds.), *Public Expenditures and Policy Analysis*, Markham Publishing Co.

CENTRAL ADVISORY COMMITTEE FOR EDUCATION (1967), *Children and their Primary Schools*, 2 vols, HMSO, (The Plowden Report).

COVENTRY CORPORATION (1971), *Structure Plan Progress Report*.

DROR, Y. (1968), *Public Policy-Making Re-Examined*, Chandler.

GREENWOOD, R., SMITH, A. D., and STEWART, J. D. (1971), 'New patterns of local government organization', Occasional Paper, no. 5, series A, INLOGOV, University of Birmingham.

JAMES, J. R. (1965), *The future of development plans*, Town and Country Planning School.

LAMBETH BOROUGH COUNCIL (1971), *Lambeth Community Plan*.

MINISTRY OF TRANSPORT (1970), *Transport Planning. The Men for the Job*, HMSO, (The Sharp Report).

REDCLIFFE-MAUD (1969), *The Royal Commission on Local Government in England and Wales*, cmnd no. 4040, HMSO.

REPORT OF THE COMMITTEE ON LOCAL AUTHORITY AND ALLIED PERSONAL SERVICES (1968), '*The Seebohm Report*', cmnd no. 3703, HMSO.

SCHON, D. (1971). *Beyond the Stable State*, Temple-Smith.

WILDAVSKY, A. (1966), 'The political economy of efficiency', *Pub. Admin. Rev.*, vol. 26, pp. 292–310.

21 M. Rein

Social Planning: The Search for Legitimacy

M. Rein, 'Social planning: the search for legitimacy', *Journal of the American Institute of Planners*, vol. 35, 1969, pp. 233–44.

All planning must in some fashion resolve the problem of legitimacy – what authority justifies its intervention. This is particularly true for those types of social reform and city planning that share a common ideological commitment to introduce *social innovation* – new programs and new ideas that will reduce or eliminate social problems.

What makes the intervention of the reformer and planner meaningful and desirable? How is the need for innovative intervention justified and support for it secured? The problem of legitimacy is especially acute in American democratic society because the reformer-planner has only limited power to implement his objectives. Lacking power, 'the ability to control external and internal environments and/or to counteract the consequences of imperfect control' (Armstrong, 1964, p. 8), he needs, therefore, to win co-operation to achieve his aims. He must collect and harness fragmented power in order to bring about planned change.

Some planning organizations hope to bypass this dilemma by repudiating the mandate to innovate or to promote planned change. They define their mission as providing only a forum to help others reach agreement through the intervention of 'enablers' rather than 'planners'.[1] In contrast, organizations promoting planned change must seek the authority to impose limits on the freedom of other organizations. They attempt to subordinate interests or change functions and purposes of some organizations in order to promote that elusive ideal we call the public interest. Yet, as soon as such organizations are powerful enough to be effective, they are also strong enough to abuse their power. Efforts must then be developed to contain their power. In

1. For an analysis of the dilemma that such organizations confront when they seek to promote change or when they fail to embrace all relevant community interests in their forum, see Rein and Morris (1962).

a democratic society, great restraints are placed on the centralization of power, while greater freedom is given to individual units. Still, when injustices exist, some centralized power is needed to correct them. How to reconcile the clashing demands between the resources needed to check social abuse and the power needed to reduce human suffering, with their reduction in the freedom of action of others which such action requires, is a great challenge to democratic societies. The search for legitimacy is an effort to resolve this dilemma.

City planning sources of authority

A review of the experience of city planners in the United States suggests that they have relied on four different sources of authority to justify and legitimate their intervention. These might be called the authorities of *expertise, bureaucratic position, consumer preferences* and *professional values*.

The authority of expertise

This approach is based on the assumption that planners have command of a technical-scientific body of knowledge that enables them to challenge irrationality in the political process of city government, which has produced decisions based on 'opportunistic bargaining among vested political economic interests of great strength' (Sayre and Kaufman, 1960, p. 372). The early planning movement was based on a doctrine which said that what planners needed was great formal powers, independent of the political process, which would enable them to act as an autonomous 'fourth power' in city government.[2] In 1934, the first City Planning Commission of New York City was comprised of a majority of members who 'were committed to the premise that the Commission should be an institution of experts with an authoritative voice in the decisions of city government, yet be itself aloof and protected, without the necessity of bargaining with and making concessions to the "politicians" and special interests' (Sayre and Kaufman, p. 372). Experience soon suggested that political autonomy leads to isolation and independence leads to impotence. Authority that is depoliticized, that is independent from the political process and based on technical-scientific rationality, offers only the authority to propose, rather

2. This argument was again set forth when a group of planners was asked to advise on the development of planning in Puerto Rico. See Trigwell (1954).

than the power to achieve (Fried, 1969). Not surprisingly, the need for new sources of authority was soon recognized.

The authority of bureaucracy

During the 1940s, public administrators debated the possibility of separating politics and administration.[3] This debate centered around the issue of whether every administrative act also entailed a political consequence that obviated the purely technological solution. If politics cannot be separated from administration, then the planner secures his authority from politicians rather than technology. However, the more incomplete the control over the administrative process, the wider the influence of the professional, thus the planner's role in developing policy is ambiguous. According to this interpretation, the difficulty with the concept of planning as a 'fourth power' was that the claims of the planners conflicted with those of the politicians.

In a recent analysis of this debate, Beckman took the position that this conflict of identity between the planner and the politician 'can best be resolved . . . if he (the planner) is willing to accept the vital but more limited role that our system assigned to the public employee'.[4] Beckman urges the planner to assist and serve the policy-maker since the planner's

influence on public policy is achieved within the bureaucracy through competence. Planners and other staff advisers have influence only as they can persuade their political superiors . . . it must be remembered that in our system of government politics subordinates the public employee, grants responsibility and power to the politician, invests open authority in the voter[5] (Altshuler, 1965, p. 326–7).

The planner who repudiates a decision of his superiors can try to persuade them to accept his opinion or he can resign in indignation. But in his role as an employee, the planner secures his authority from the director of a planning organization whose head is appointed by elected representatives who in turn secure their authority from voting citizens.

3. For opposing arguments see Friedrich (1946); and Finer (1949, pp. 871–85). For a useful summary of the debate, see Schubert (1960, pp. 120–21).

4. See Beckman (1964, p. 324). See also Altshuler (1965).

5. Altshuler argues that since 'political officials seldom give planners any clear instructions to guide the value-choice aspects of their work, much discretion remains with the experts'. He thus appears to reject Beckman's formulation of the planner's role as bureaucrat. Mr Altshuler's comments apply to any bureaucrat in the strict Weberian sense of the term.

The theory about the relationship between the planner as a bureaucrat and the politician as the representative of the electorate often disintegrates in practice. The scope and complexity of public bureaucracies make them increasingly independent of review by elected officials. They control the information by which their competence can be challenged, and they outlast the politicians whose policies they execute. Moreover, elected officials serve the interests of certain groups better than the interests of others or of some hypothesized overall public interest. In theory an aggrieved citizen can protest directly to his representative against any intrusion of his rights or neglect of his needs. In practice, in a democracy, the needs and preferences of unpopular, unwanted and powerless groups are neglected. Politicians are committed to political survival. They respond to the preferences of the constituencies that elect them rather than the needs of the inarticulate and hence unrepresented groups.

The authority of consumers

In the 1950s, the critique against the planner as a bureaucrat began to emerge in Herbert Gans', John Dyckman's, and Martin Meyerson's studies of recreation, education and health care facilities. They came to recognize that planning which was responsive to professional discretion and to political leadership might in the process forsake the preferences, needs and desires of the consuming population. What they seemed to be calling for was a new technology which could develop new standards by feeding new information into the planning process – namely data derived from social scientific inquiries about the preferences of present and potential service users. Gans, Dyckman, and Meyerson wrote that planning must be responsive to the consumer market. Explicit criteria as to how to establish procedures to resolve differences among the clashing preferences of different income or age groupings or to resolve conflicts that might arise when consumer preferences clashed with the policies of planners, the established bureaucracy, or elected officials were not developed.[6]

Rapkin, Winnick, and Blank (1952) in their monograph on Housing Market Analysis developed a similar position, holding that the criteria for developing public policy should rest on the choices of users as these are identified through the mechanism

6. Though they taught together and wrote a great deal on this theme, these scholars have not yet written up their work in a single report.

of the market. Turning to the ultimate consumer as the source of legitimacy for planning opened important ideological questions concerning the limits and possibilities of exploiting the market as a mechanism for assessing consumer choices. Davidoff and Reiner (1962) extended the general argument – 'It is not for the planner to make the final decision transforming values into policy commitments. His role is to identify distribution of values among people, and how values are weighed against each other' (1962, p. 108).

By 1960, new forces emerged in the political process which gave currency and acceptability to the idea of consumer advocacy. A new body of literature and experience developed which sought to derive the legitimacy of the planner from the preferences of consumers, especially those who are politically inarticulate. Some planners were urging that a new source of legitimacy be found with the planner acting as a more direct advocate of the values, preferences and needs of consumer groups – planning should derive its legitimacy from the needs of the people to be serviced. The planner could then offer his skills to a user-bureaucracy as contrasted with the supplier-bureaucracy to which planners presently offer their services.

These ideas found expression in the theory of advocacy planning which asserts that planners can derive their legitimacy from the clients to be served. Advocacy implies argument and contention on behalf of a point of view or of a specific proposal. Paul Davidoff in his influential article, 'Advocacy and Pluralism in Planning', makes this position explicit when he urges that 'the advocate planner would be responsible to his client and would seek to express his clients' views' (1965, pp. 331-8).

All of these writers accepted the position that planners derive their legitimacy from the preferences, choices and needs of the users, consumers, and clients who are affected by planning decisions. But they differ on this position's implications for action. A point of view oriented to clients can lead to social surveys of consumer choices, or to faith in the market as the ultimate mechanism for the expressions of choice, or to the defense of consumer rights within an adversary rather than a market framework. Each position has its difficulties. The preferences of all individuals as revealed from survey rankings of values cannot be aggregated into collective preferences without violating the choices of some individuals (following the famous Arrow paradox). Planning originated as an effort to supplement or supersede the market when it failed to meet individual needs or solve the problem of externalities. Faith in market freedom and choice for users did not contribute substantially to resolving these issues of public policy, and as we have begun to experiment with advocacy, intractable problems have emerged.

One account of an advocate planner's experience suggests some of these formidable difficulties. First it proved very difficult to identify the client or community to be serviced. A community is heterogenous, and efforts to locate a single-client-organization to represent it, as well as speak for the unrepresented elements of the community, proved exceedingly difficult. But even if such a group could be organized, it was difficult to identify the interests of a heterogenous community client. However, when these interests were articulated, the planner discovered that local decision units can be parochial and even punishing to the poor with special problems, such as welfare mothers, skid row, gypsies and so on. Peattie offers the following grim observation: '. . . a consequence of giving every neighborhood in a city its advocate planner might be a general closing up of the city against the poor' (1968, p. 84). But even if the problems of locating the client and identifying and accepting his interests can be overcome, the advocate planner confronts a disturbing dilemma when he discovers that 'the citizen client group seems . . . to serve a kind of legitimizing function which permits the planners to represent themselves as something more than merely proponents of another opinion' (Peattie, p. 86).

The authority of professional values

Another source of legitimacy rests on the professional values to which the planner is committed as well as the technical competence he claims. According to this formulation, city planning is a value-laden profession, and these values offer a course of authority – a sanction to plan. There is surely an uneasy nestling together of expertise and ideology, and a general reluctance to act on the authority of the latter is evident. Nevertheless, as the impossibility of separating values and technology is accepted, action based on values is taken. One form is the creation of a competing professional association committed to implementing different values. 'It appears that the profession is being split into progressive and conservative wings: the former calling for social planning to reduce racial and economic inequalities, and the latter defending traditional physical planning and the legitimacy of the middle-class values' (Gans, 1968, p. 131).

Increasingly planners are enjoined to act as insurgents within the bureaucracies where they are employed and to seek change in the policies and purposes of the bureaucracy according to the declared value assumptions. These values are procedural as well as substantive. Decision rules, such as involvement of those affected by decisions, illustrate the former, and goals, such as racially and economically integrated communities or reduction of inequalities illustrate the latter.

Public opinion and official policies of the bureaucracy may be hostile to these values. The planner who acts as a rebel within his bureaucracy challenges its established procedures and policies. A declaration of open warfare forces the bureaucrat to resign on principle. As an outsider he may elect to infiltrate in his role as consultant or researcher. Many private consultant firms and individual planners are committed to promoting their professional values as well as their technology. The bureaucrat may elect to stay and wage guerilla warfare, choosing points where the system is internally vulnerable, or he may develop coalitions with external groups to create internal change. He may lie dormant for years when levers for change are absent. Yet, every bureaucracy has insurgents who are ready to act as guerilla-reformers to shake up the bureaucracy.[7]

An unusual example of this procedure is the action of a group of young professional insurgent staff members of the New York City Planning Commission who call themselves the 'urban underground'. They attended a public hearing held by the Commission and 'charged that the agency had disregarded its own planners' findings and had yielded to powerful real estate speculators in proposing to rezone a section of Manhattan for luxury housing' (Arnold, 1969, p. 34). What makes this experience so unusual is the concerted and open actions of these insurgents. The more typical pattern of bureaucratic insurgency of professionals is to try to promote change within the bureaucracy, that is to say, through closed door politics rather than open door politics.

This source of legitimacy poses awkward issues concerning the boundaries between professional and personal values, ethics of

7. In the planning field, there has been at least one effort to create a loose coalition of insurgents who are seeking to change the policies of their own and other programs. Leonard Duhl calls this coalition a 'floating crap game'. The analogy is misleading though because the players are not in competition with each other, but rather seek to support each other in their common mission. Professional associations, such as Planners for Equal Opportunity (PEO), may also serve as reference groups.

means and ends to be adopted, and procedures of professional accountability to judge when ethics have surrendered to expediency. But despite these and other difficulties, planners who repudiate the position that values and technology are separable are experimenting with this source of legitimacy.

Strategies of legitimacy

Even this condensed review of the history of physical planning makes it evident that city planners have sought different sources of legitimacy: as scientific experts, independent of the political process; as agents of elected political representatives and the bureaucracies which are accountable to them; as translators and advocates of the preferences of user-groups; and finally, as implementors of professional values. Each source of legitimacy has its characteristic difficulties, as this brief review of the experience of physical planners as expert, bureaucrat, advocate and insurgent has suggested.

But why must planners be forced to choose among these alternative sources of legitimacy? The position of planning could be substantially strengthened if it could simultaneously call upon professional technology, values and standards, established political power and the needs and wishes of client groups as sources of legitimacy. However, if these sources of legitimacy conflict when pursued together – and they nearly always do – then the planner must choose among them.

A review of the experience of what Reston called the 'new breed of anti-poverty planners' helps to illuminate the problems which arise in adapting each source of legitimacy and in pursuing multiple sources of legitimacy which are in conflict. Federal legislation, such as the Juvenile Delinquency and Youth Offences Control Act of 1961 and the Economic Opportunity Act of 1964, provided the resources which made this form of social planning possible. More recently, through legislation made possible by the Demonstration Cities and Metropolitan Act of 1966, the style of planning has been extended to cope with problems of deterioration in the urban environment. The search conducted by these social planners and reformers for a relevant form of legitimacy is strikingly parallel to the search for legitimacy among city planners.

The city planner and this type of social planner share much in common. They both spend a great deal of their energies writing proposals in an effort to secure federal and state funds; they are both concerned with developing specific programs to implement ambiguous and ill-defined social objectives; they are both committed to drawing up both long-range and short-range plans; both are in principle committed to introduction of new ideas and to generation of social innovations that can lay the foundation for further experimentation; and finally, both hope to have the plans they developed implemented administratively. But, in the context of this paper, the important common ground they share is the search for legitimacy. How can their intervention be justified?

In the remainder of this paper three strategies are examined from the perspective of how they contribute to resolving the problem of legitimation of reform.[8] They are *elite consensus*, *rational analysis* and *citizen participation*. Each strategy is crucial. None is sufficient by itself, for each has inherent limitations, but the efforts to pursue more than one strategy at a time often lead to conflict and contradiction. Thus in the effort to resolve one dilemma another is created.

The consensus of elites

One way of justifying intervention is to have it endorsed and supported by the leadership of the major institutions in the community. This strategy acknowledges the power of established institutions. One version seeks to influence power by boring from within, by co-opting the institutions to serve its purposes. The endorsement by established power legitimates the efforts of reform and change.

At one time in the social services this power of change was vested in the coalition of *voluntary* institutions that represented the elite of the community.

Welfare services and planning became recognizably controlled by an essentially elite leadership in each community. . . . Associated with the socially elite were an economic elite. . . . These economic sinews became the foundation for the support of much of social welfare. It was only later recognized that this elite leadership was primarily white and Protestant, representing the early stratification of American society (Morris and Rein, 1963, p. 156).

8. The claim to a source legitimacy must be only illusory. Hence we need to pay attention to inauthentic claims to legitimacy. Under special circumstances, myths can be very important in convincing others that the claim should be heeded. This article does not systematically explore this important issue.

These early economic and social elites often rejected the role of government in welfare, substituting voluntary health and welfare councils. They held an elitist view of democracy, assuming that they were best able to comprehend, to represent and to protect the interests of the 'total community'.

Today, because of the changing role of government and the development of new centers of power, such voluntary bodies can no longer provide an adequate base for legitimate change. Consequently, planners have had to seek the participation of city government by forming a coalition of departments such as welfare, recreation, police and the like, or a coalition of units of government such as the city, the county, the school boards and the state. Legitimacy depends on bringing together a broad range of groups representing old and new sources of power – influential leaders, established organizational interests and government.

A new factor is national influence on local action. In a penetrating analysis of the relationship between sociology and the welfare state, Gouldner (1968) calls attention to the manner in which social reform in the United States has changed in character. What is new is not the 'plight of the cities', however increasing their deterioration, but rather . . . the locus of reform initiatives and resources is increasingly found on the level of national politics and foundations, rather than in the political vitality, the economic resources or the zealous initiatives of elites with local roots (Gouldner, p. 109).

A broad based representative organizational structure that serves to legitimate reform may likely conflict with its very purpose – the search for innovation and change.[9] The greater the diversity of institutional interest that is embraced within such a

9. The use of the terms innovation and change may require some explanation. I find useful the distinction developed by Lake in his review of theories and research about social change. He states, 'there is no clear distinction in the literature reviewed between a *strategy* of innovation and a theory of change. . . . When concepts are tied in with tactics of inducing those concepts (about change) and when time phasing activities are suggested, then the theories become strategies of innovation . . . a theory of change . . . is not accompanied by a program for inducing change' Lake (1968, pp. 4–5). Kahn and his colleagues treat innovation as the procedures, roles, and activities that enable an organization to depart from fixed rules in the face of changing circumstances. For their discussion of innovative roles within an organization, see Kahn *et al.* (1964, ch. 7).

This paper is concerned with the efforts of some organizations to induce innovation in other organizations. This process I define as planned change or social reform.

planning structure, the greater can be the claim for legitimacy, since it can be claimed that most of the total community is represented. But as legitimacy is strengthened, innovation will probably be forsaken in favor of maintaining a consensus on which these divergent interests can agree. These new planning structures are continually beset with internal insurrection. In practice the commitment to shared goals seems less compelling than the preservation of organizational autonomy. Involvement of community leaders does little to resolve the problems of jurisdictional conflict; indeed, it may only aggravate the task. Voluntary planning bodies and the elite community leaders who represent them want more influence than they receive as only members (rather than convenors) of the coalition. Whereas they once enjoyed pre-eminence in the area of planning, they have now been cast aside and relegated to a secondary role by this new, more widely representative structure. Consequently, much of the energy of the planning organization is directed away from promoting innovation and change and toward solving the more intractable problems of sheer survival – maintenance of the coalition.[10]

The national reformers who made available the funds for these local planning organizations recognized this dilemma, but hoped that it could be solved. Essentially, their strategy rested on two related assumptions: that a marginal increase in funds can stimulate change, and that the involvement of voluntary and public bureaucracies is a necessary precondition for change. They hoped the power of federal money – small outlays with the anticipation of larger amounts of funds – and the process of participation would lead to change. They assumed that financially starved institutions would be willing to make changes in their operation in order to secure available and needed funds. Local reformers operating from these local planning organizations would play a central role in this process, for they could serve as interpreters of the institutional changes that would be required if funds were to be forthcoming. The professional reformer, enjoying a monopoly of knowledge and special access to non-local funders, could assert a substantial amount of influence on the

10. For further evidence on the conflict between innovation and broad-based organizations in voluntary social welfare organizations and in health and welfare councils, see Rein (1964, pp. 32–41; and Rein and Morris (1962, pp. 32–41). For a review of the literature of international organizations that reaches a similar conclusion, see Walton (1965, pp. 167–79).

direction in which the local coalition of elites would develop in order to obtain the wanted funds. *The fundamental premise in these negotiations was that because funds were so desperately needed by local institutions, they would be willing to participate in self-reform in order to secure them.* That the institutions might both obtain the funds from established and new sources and resist change was a contingency to which local and national planners seemed to have given little attention.

This second assumption rested on the faith that the process of involvement and participation might lead to self-education and the acceptance of the need to change. The implicit theory of bureaucracy on which this belief rests is that the sources of organizational rigidity are largely ignorance and faulty communication. If a context were provided in which institutional representatives could more freely communicate with one another, the validity of the need for change would more readily be recognized and accepted. Such a theory is, however, incomplete, for it ignores the existence of the more fundamental conflict of values and interests among institutions that more open communication might serve to exacerbate rather than to alleviate. The insistence upon participation of power in self-reform appeals to common sense yet it rests on inadequate assumptions about how institutions perform. In practice, organizations often agreed or participated to protect their interests rather than to promote the more illusive common goals on which the concept of the public interest rests. Thus agreement on a new form that committed organizations to involvement in a process did not equally commit them to accept changes in their policy and programs. The latent conflict was only postponed. When it emerged, the coalition of autonomous participants was in danger of falling apart. As a result of these challenges, compromises were made to assure survival, and in the process innovation was sacrificed to achieve consensus.

Much as a representative structure may reduce innovation, participation by institutions in their own reform may lead to continuity of established policy. The funds made available by planners were simply not large enough to finance major reforms in these institutions. But even if sufficient funds were available, it is hard to see how planners could conceivably hope to initiate major structural changes unless the changes were in conformity with the institutions' prevailing interpretation of their functions and reflected directions the institutions were already prepared to take. Under these conditions it is the planners who have been co-opted by the institutions. *Involvement, although it facilitates legitimation, impedes innovation.*

An alternative to the theory that institutions change with self-education is derived from the assumption that institutions must be challenged, for they will not change of their own accord. The public health movement, which was promoted largely by lay groups, arose (with the support of some professionals) above the vigorous opposition of physicians; similarly, the Charity Organization Society (the mainstay and bulwark behind social casework before the depression) was opposed to pensions for widows and the aged in the early part of the century; and the Charity School opposed public education. According to this view, reform cannot depend solely upon the willing co-operation of the institutions to be reformed.

While it is useless to ignore the realities of established institutional power, a program of planned change runs the dire risk of losing its sense of purpose if it relies only on established leadership. Increasingly, planners find that the more they work with established institutions, the more compromises they have to make, the more difficult it becomes to ensure that funds are spent for innovation rather than for expansion of the *status quo*. This frustration has led to a tendency to bypass major service institutions. For example, we find in education the development of preschool programs, afterschool programs, summer school programs, tutorial programs which consistently circumvent the heart of the school's mission – everyday teaching – and create instead a whole series of special remedial programs. Remediation becomes a kind of index of the failure to achieve more basic structural change. It represents response to the more frustrating task of directly influencing the essential functions of the institution itself. Institutional resistance leads to program proliferation.

Many manpower training programs have ignored the state vocational training system and have worked through other agencies or set up their own agencies to provide special programs for work training. Here duplication and remediation do not represent a retreat but a strategy of confrontation. But to challenge institutions so frontally, a different source of legitimacy is necessary.

The power of knowledge

Another way of legitimizing planned change is to offer reforms as rational, coherent, intellectual solutions to the problems that are being dealt with. This tends to be the approach favored by academia and professional consultants. Knowledge in the rationalistic-scientific tradition in general and knowledge derived from empirical research in particular can provide a basis for legitimacy because, presumably, it can yield valid solutions. These, in turn, depend on a value-free social science capable of objectively probing the etiology of social problems and presenting programs for action based upon fact rather than upon institutional or other value biases. The analysis of social problems and the remedies proposed for reducing or eliminating them are viewed as technical rather than ideological issues. For example, the President's Committee on Juvenile Delinquency was especially committed to the importance of rational analysis as the basis for planning and program development. As a condition for receiving funds, national reformers required that communities attempt to conceptualize the problems of delinquency, poverty, or physical and social decay in the light of relevant data and social theory.

Reform stakes out a claim for legitimacy when it is based, not upon political consensus or ideological bias, but primarily upon the hard dispassionate facts provided by a rigorous social science analysis. Proponents of this position believe that science can and should 'supersede moral and ideological speculation'. Earlier, this position was expressed by those committed to the idea of policy sciences (1940s) and the end of ideology thesis (1950s).[11] Consistent with this philosophy, the President's Committee promoted the ideals that not only are social plans to be based on a thorough, objective appraisal of the social problem, but the efforts at solution themselves are to be rigorously evaluated. With ruthless disregard for bureaucratic interests, those programs judged to be successful would be continued, whereas those falling short of the objective standards would be rejected and discontinued. Change is to be based not upon fads and vested interests but upon the evidence provided by evaluative research of program outputs. Science, rather than elitism, justifies intervention.

This strategy of reform has its own inherent contradictions. Perhaps not in the long run since researchers can always justify their activities as ultimately contributing to truth and knowledge; but in the short run, it does indeed involve conflict, for gathering information is not without its costs. Consider the difficulty that

11. For a thoughtful review of these issues see Simey (1968, p. 138).

many planning organizations have encountered in their efforts to study the conditions and problems of the Negro urban ghetto. Research, as one angry account has put it, can serve as 'transparent dodges for the postponement of action, that those involved in the charade of research into the problems of disadvantaged youth are willing or inadvertent accessories to those who seem to perpetuate the clear and present injustices' (Harlem Youth Opportunities, 1964). A disillusioned Negro community wants authentic action, not rhetoric, promises, or studies.

Although these resentments may not be altogether rational, they are surely understandable, particularly when we recognize that the preliminary research and analysis of so many of the community action programs became extremely esoteric, and in many cases never really issued any pragmatic proposals. Indeed, it is often difficult to find coherence among the social theory, the facts presented, and the programs that are developed to reduce the problem. This widespread disjunction between programs of reform and research and theoretical insights represents an important limitation of the contribution of research and theory to the reduction of social problems. Much of the research growing out of these planning efforts has not yielded new knowledge about the poor, nor has it yielded especially new insights into our understanding of delinquency, nor has it led to the kinds of new programs that need to be developed to tackle these problems. From these experiences it would appear that the contribution of value-free social science information to the development of social policy has been greatly oversold.

The rigorous testing of experimental action programs has also encountered fundamental obstacles. The most difficult problem the researcher found was explication of the social objectives for which the intervention was introduced. This was especially true for programs with broad, multiple and partially conflicting goals directed at expanding opportunity or promoting organizational change. There were administrative as well as conceptual problems. It is difficult to include in most experimental social action programs the rigid controls that are necessary to provide the kind of clear-cut findings upon which it is possible to accept or reject particular techniques of intervention.

When this rationale of reform calls for comprehensive action involving many interrelated programs, committed to broad and diffuse goals, a difficult research task becomes even more discouragingly complex. The demands of action are such that planners need to be somewhat opportunistic, flexibly adapting to shifting political coalitions that substantially alter the content on which their comprehensive program rests. But when the input variables are subject to significant change, the research task becomes even more tangled. As the limitations of the research design grow more apparent, it becomes hard to know what caused the measured outcomes. As a result, the interpretation to be drawn from the findings is open to serious question. Staunch supporters of particular programs are more likely to reject the research methodology and repudiate the criteria of evaluation, rather than accept the implications of negative findings that most evaluative research tends to yield.[12]

A strategy that relies upon the power of knowledge has other inherent limitations as well, for it can also conflict with other strategies of change. Research requires a degree of autonomy if it is to follow a problem, not yielding to political expediency and feasibility. But the ruthless pursuit of a problem, without regard to the question of implementation, may lead to a solution that, while it is rational, is not politically relevant. This, of course, is the fundamental dilemma of all rational planning, the attempt to reconcile the conflicting requirements of rationality and feasibility. Planning that disregards the question of implementation languishes as an academic irrelevancy; it may be right but not relevant, correct but not useful. While planning and research require close integration, they make competing claims for resources. Enterprising researchers have been able to secure a very substantial portion of total budgets available to planning agencies, while unwary planners are left with reduced resources to carry out their tasks. Irrelevancy can arise not only in the competition for resources, but in the conflicting value biases of the researcher and reformer – the different emphases they give to knowledge and action. Research can become preoccupied with a spurious rigor, leading to a kind of dustbowl empiricism that provides data overload. Without theory to guide in sorting the findings we have a situation where answers (data) are in search of questions. Bewildered planners are left with a maze of tables and data that yield no immediately coherent themes and that provide little information from which implications can be drawn. Reformers often hope that researchers will guide the development of planning policy by conducting studies that will help confirm or reject the basic underlying rationale of the organizations. Yet to

12. See Herman (1965); US Congress (1968).

develop new programs requires social inventiveness, rarely a product of formal research.

Even more than being a costly irrelevance, research can subvert the reformers' goals. The experience of the delinquency prevention programs offers an interesting example. The national reformers sought programs that would test the assumption that social institutions throw up barriers and block access to achievement – a process that contributes to increased disengagement and deviancy on the part of the rejected populations. Yet the methodological bias of researchers led the reformers away from their original commitment to institutional change and toward a redefinition of the problem in terms of individual rehabilitation. Thus, social scientists sometimes act to reinforce those pressures on planning organizations that prevent focus on community institutions as prime targets of change. Researchers usually favor the more rigorous, traditional and tested approaches of their disciplines, such as surveys of individual attitudes, self-perceptions and role models. The indices they have developed to measure the impact of demonstration programs have occasionally been behavioral but more often attitudinal. They have, by and large, avoided indices that would measure institutional change in favor of a more individualistic approach.

Research may conflict not only with the purposes of reform, but also with the search for elite consensus. Organizational studies that lead to the documentation of bureaucratic rigidities and social injustice may conflict with efforts to promote co-operation and secure consensus among institutions that are being researched. If research relentlessly pursues data on the operation of the bureaucracy, it will uncover findings that could become a source of embarrassment to co-operating institutions. Indeed, where such information is available, it is extremely awkward to know exactly what to do with it. If the information becomes public knowledge, it would only antagonize the institutions whose co-operation is so desperately sought. Yet, maintaining secrets is always hazardous. This may account, in part, for the fact that planners have rarely insisted that researchers study institutional performance.

Finally, research may not be able to answer the problems posed by the reformer. Consider briefly one such question that local, gradual and comprehensive programs must confront. The hub of a comprehensive social welfare program can be developed around many institutions – the outreach school, the welfare department, the health department, the mental hygiene clinic and employment centers. Some of the traditional voluntary services – settlement houses and welfare councils – are no longer regarded as adequate focal institutions for the co-ordination of local service programs. But do we have any factual data that can guide us in the selection of one or another of these institutions as the appropriate focus for a comprehensive community program? Should social programs center around health, housing, employment, education, reducing dependency? If all of these are legitimate, must we then abandon the search for a truly comprehensive program and settle for the present muddle of co-ordination, saturation and concerted services?

Just as a broadly representative planning structure can subvert innovation in order to preserve the frail coalition of conflicting interests, so too can researchers subvert the reformers' mission if they become preoccupied with methodology and use their studies to promote their professional identities rather than the interests of the action program. The concern for rigor and professional identity may lead to neglect of relevant action problems. The concern for knowledge without explicit, carefully developed social purposes contributes to narrow technicism.

The power of the people

Reformers can also claim legitimacy if their programs are endorsed, supported and created by the recipients of the service. Such an approach has the advantage of avoiding the arrogant assumption that the technical expert or the elitist best knows the needs of the poor. It avoids the onerous charge of welfare colonialism or paternalism, wherein one group in society provides services on behalf of another. Recipients of the service are defined as politically articulate consumers, as citizens rather than as clients in need of therapy and care. Democracy is, after all, not only the search for elite consensus but also the mobilization of interest groups, each striving to pursue its own aims in the context of a pluralistic society. The American democratic system, according to this view, depends on rectifying 'the basic imbalance between elites and non-elites by modifying the power differential between them' (Bachrach, 1962). It attempts to carry out this strategy by providing disadvantaged groups with more powerful instruments for articulating their demands and preferences. It helps them to organize protests in which their moral claim to justice and equal treatment can find expression. In addition to collective action it places before the poor the machinery of law through which they can act as plaintiffs against institutions that have bypassed their rights.

Strategies of planned change, which derive their legitimacy from the direct participation of local citizens and service users, have had a stormy history since they were launched by the President's Committee on Juvenile Delinquency and Youth Crime in 1962. These developments must be seen in the context of the civil rights revolution and the emergence of militant demands for black power. In response to pressures, representative communitywide structures were broadened to include individuals and groups that were the targets of change. The principle of 'maximum feasible participation' articulated in the Economic Opportunity Act was administratively interpreted in many ways including direct participation of the poor on policy-making boards of Community Action Agencies.[13] In some cities, such as San Francisco (and later Oakland under the Model Cities Program), participation was interpreted as control, and the poor dominated the board with the mayor retreating to a subordinate role.[14] As organizational resistance to social change was encountered, participation turned from planning to social protest and social action, taking the form of rent strikes, boycotts, picketing and other strategies of confrontation to promote change.[15] More recently, citizen participation has come to mean community control of social services, such as multi-service centers, health programs, and a decentralized public school system (Spiegel, 1968, pp. 271–91). The Model Cities Program encouraged experimentation with advocacy planning, where local groups (Boston, for example) were able to win resources to hire their own planners to develop plans incorporating social and physical resources for the reduction of urban blight. Under the Nixon Administration, the Community Self-Determination Act of 1968, now before Congress, may usher in yet a new phase of user control for it is designed to create community-controlled business enterprises that would permit the people of the community 'to utilize a share of the profits of (these) enterprises to

13. For a discussion of the critique of participation as policy-making, see Donovan (1967, pp. 41–8).

14. Cunningham (1967). See pp. 57–69 for an account of community action in the city of San Francisco.

15. For a thoughtful appraisal of the limits and strengths of protest, see Lipsky (1967). Mimeographed.

provide needed social services' (US Congressional Record, July 24, 1968).

The acceptance of this argument leads to an anomalous position for it inadvertently supports a different interpretation of democracy for the poor than for other segments of society (Rein and Miller, 1968, pp. 221–43). In the middle-income style of democratic involvement, citizens work through their representatives, whereas in low-income communities, democracy tends to be interpreted as a form of direct participation at the grassroots level. Community competence through self-help becomes defined as a therapeutic process for promoting social integration. Competent communities produce competent men, as each man is his own politician. Organizations are expected to develop spontaneously out of the mutual interests of residents working side by side on common problems. The rewards of participation are defined as civic pride, personal growth and the reduction of community deviancy. The groups are not forged out of the more pragmatic interests in personal favors and economic advantages which more typically characterize the motives of those who join local political parties. The task might better be defined not as increasing the competence of low-income communities to manage their own affairs, but rather as creating more representative structures which will be more responsive to the special needs and interests of low-income groups. Paid politicians rather than paid community enablers may be necessary if representative rather than direct democracy is to be achieved. Direct democracy may thus be seen as a stage in the process of developing new political coalitions and new political leadership rather than as an ideal in the 'good' community.

Richard Cloward and Francis Piven (1965) argue that a fundamental conflict between elite and low-income collective protests arises because they are based upon 'quite divergent beliefs about the nature of social, economic and political institutions and what it takes to change them'. The elitist approach assumes that institutions change by persuasion and education and that issues are largely technical and capable of analysis in terms analogous to a cost-benefit evaluation. Low-income collective protests, by contrast, view institutions as responsive to naked power and pressure; issues are defined in personalized terms; opponents are seen as culprits; and exploitation of the poor is rejected, whatever the benefits.

Efforts to organize low-income communities encounter difficulties in sustaining a high level of interest and participation, especially when programs have only marginal meaning for the residents and offer little opportunity for changes in jobs, housing, or other amenities. There is also the danger that issues are selected more for their capacity to rally interest than for their intrinsic merit. Protests can become ends in themselves instead of platforms for bargaining and negotiating. But without an issue for protest, organizations are likely to succumb to the meaningless ritual of organization for its own sake. Saul Alinsky's work is a prototype of one approach that attempts to sustain commitment by polarizing a community around an issue and then ruthlessly attacking the villain who is alleged to have created the problem.

While it has been exceedingly difficult to organize the poor on the basis of their poverty or social class in the occupational hierarchy, there is at least precedent for politicalization along ethnic and religious lines. Citizen participation reflects this aspect of American political life and extends it by inadvertently becoming a program for organizing the Negro community – the growing militancy of black urban action programs reflects the militants' discovery of the difficulties of change. The heightened sense of relative deprivation converted the process from reform (defined either as therapy and self-help to achieve a competent community or as provision of opportunities through organizational change to promote mobility) to revolution, which found expression in riots and the repudiation of integration as a realizable social ideal. How established power will respond to violence and assault on its citadels is unclear. There is evidence of both backlash and increased liberalization as the desire for social stability and social justice is joined and divided.

Lipsky has pointed out that 'protest groups are uniquely capable of raising the saliency of issues, but are unequipped – by virtue of their lack of organizational resources – to participate in the formulation or adoption of solutions to problems they dramatize' (Lipsky, 1967). When protest groups are sponsored by social welfare organizations, they rapidly lose their authenticity as grassroots movements. They drift into labor-saving self-help projects and clean-up and fix-up programs. It is rather startling to note how many bureaucracies attempt to organize low-income residents to promote bureaucratic goals. Sanitation departments create block groups; settlements organize neighborhood councils; the schools promote PTAs; and urban renewal in a similar fashion attempts to mobilize a community as a device for co-opting and reducing opposition to renewal plans. The professional comes to plan the agenda, and when the professional leaves, the organization collapses.

The process of involving the poor as a form of therapy and self-help on the one hand and legitimation of the activities of the planners on the other hand does not take adequate account of the potential role that citizen participation may have in politicalizing the poor. It can serve as well to create a new center of power by revitalizing the urban political machinery in low-income areas, replacing the atrophied structures that once helped generations of immigrants to adjust to American society. It is paradoxical that the targets of reform in one generation should become the ideals of the next generation: ethnic politics and the political machine were once seen as major impediments to good local government. However, many of the groups that do participate in these 'establishment' sponsored programs are suspiciously regarded as having 'sold out' their allegiance to the community from which they came. But this harsh assessment of betrayal fails to recognize that involvement, when seen from the point of view of its consumers, is a way of 'buying in' to a system they aspire to be part of.

Dilemmas in the search for legitimacy

We have described, then, the three strategies that reformers and planners rely on to legitimate their actions. Each appeals to a different aspect of the democratic process: the need for consensus among elite institutional interests; the reverence for science and fact; and the validation of pluralism, diversity and conflict on which democracy depends for its vitality. The dilemma seems to be the reform that works with the establishment, searching for a consensus, tends to lose its soul and its purpose. It abandons its real feeling and commitment for the poor as it sacrifices innovation and reform for survival and growth. Yet, any program that is based solely on a fight for the rights of the poor and that fails to work with established institutions not only is likely to create conflict, but also may fail to generate any constructive accommodation that can lead to real reform. Organizing the poor on a neighborhood basis cannot achieve very much fundamental change. Vision is limited to issues around which local initiative can be mobilized; most typically there is failure to give attention to broad social and economic policy. Research can interfere with both functions, for it can be used, in Gouldner's graphic term, as a 'hamletic strategy' of delay and procrastination, responsive to political realities, while avoiding action that will provide authentic services for the poor. Research can compete with reform for resources, and it may pursue competing aims. The documentation of social injustice, which seeks action by confrontation, may embarrass the bureaucracies and make co-operation with the reformers more difficult. But without research, without some kind of objective analysis of the consequences of action, social policy moves from fashion to fashion without ever learning anything. It is, after all, useless to continue to create innovations and to spread new ideas if one never checks to see whether the new ideas and innovations are mere fads or whether they do indeed produce any kind of demonstrable change.

How then can these dilemmas be resolved? The answer, I believe, is that they cannot, for the contradictions are inherent in the nature of American social life.[16] It is futile to search for paradigms and prescriptions that will clear the whole problem out of the way and ultimately demonstrate that the strategies are indeed consistent and mutually reinforcing, not fundamentally in conflict. The search for a welfare monism that rejects pluralism and conflict only fosters utopian illusions. When all three strategies are pursued simultaneously in the same organization, internal conflict develops over time.

Eugene Litwak has suggested that we typically resolve such conflicts by having the conflicting functions carried out by separate organizations.

A society might stress both freedom and physical safety. These two values may conflict . . . yet the society seeks to maximize each. One way of assuring that each will be retained, despite the conflict, is to put them under separate organizational structures; i.e., have the police force guard physical safety and the newspapers guard freedom of the press (Litwak and Hylton, 1962, p. 396).

Fragmentation of function does not, however, resolve the dilemma; it serves only to exacerbate the problem of inter-organizational relationships as lack of co-ordination becomes a perpetual crisis.

The government's delinquency prevention program stressed rational planning and the power of knowledge, the anti-poverty

16. For a further discussion of each of these strategies and how they conflict, see Marris and Rein (1967).

program sought to implement the ideals of 'maximum feasible involvement of the poor', while the Model Cities Program seems to direct its energies, at least initially, to establish power, and it was guided by the principle of 'widespread' rather than 'maximum' participation. This does not imply that each of the programs neglects the other strategies, but they do indeed seem to emphasize one at cost to the others. Typically, then, we pursue all the strategies in the same and in different organizations, but also at different points in history we stress one or another of them. We move to research when we become particularly conscious of a lack of knowledge, a lack of clear ideas. We move toward advocacy and direct action to help the poor when we are aware of the extent to which programs seem to be ensnarled in or captured by established power. We move toward established power when we feel that organized programs, whatever their merit, fail to keep pace with the changing conditions of society, yet direct democracy seems to threaten our commitment to representative government.

Conclusions

Physical and social planners have proceeded under the assumption that the consensus of values which binds society together offers the most compelling frame of reference for a 'community regarding' planning process. However, when the divisions separating society become evident and the chasms dividing its groups become deep, planning at all levels comes to reflect these conditions. And although the need for disinterested planning becomes more urgent when the disharmonies in the society become more evident, it also becomes more difficult to perform as harmonizers and integrators. Rational planning is a myth when the value consensus on which it must depend is illusory and technology for eliminating arbitrary decisions is not available. But as the conditions of society become more complex and as each decision is a response to short range expediencies and accommodations of conflicting vested interests, the need to protect society's long-term interests becomes more insistent and the demands for rational solutions grow more urgent.

The crucial dilemma of planning cannot be altogether avoided: society's social problems require disinterested, rational and politically independent solutions. However, we have no technology which lends itself to objective assessment, nor have we or can we ever devise a way to detach planning from political pressure, without at the same time converting the detachment into irrelevance. Nor is advocacy planning a solution, for one planner as advocate implies yet another (not necessarily a planner) as judge. A judge is not simply a mediator among conflicting interests; what makes his decisions just is that they conform to some normative standard, some moral value judgment (Gouldner, 1968, p. 113). But the society has created neither mechanisms of adjudication nor a body of law and tradition to provide us with norms and standards to judge conflicting social policies. This situation arises because the effect of social policies tends to be distributional in that they leave some groups better off and others worse off. Social planning impels us to go beyond Pareto Optimality as a criterion for public decision-making. Even the choices of means are never neutral insofar as ends are concerned. Because the tools for intervention embody values, no simple calculus for distinguishing means and ends is at hand. As a result, social science alone cannot help us choose among conflicting goals, nor can it offer criteria when public policy requires interpersonal comparison of utilities, nor can it offer criteria other than efficiency and effectiveness in empirical studies that try to bring together means and ends.

Since resolution of these fundamental dilemmas is not at hand, each source of authority that legitimates planning offers an alternative interpretation of its role. Thus one role can be seen as disinterested planning, which seeks to exploit whatever available consensus is at hand and to plan in terms of these areas of common agreement. Planning is then interpreted as a rational scientific process by which the relative efficiency of various means can be assessed when goals are known. Alternatively, as Reiner has suggested, the planner can be a rational goal technician, explicating the muffled goals among choices already made on other grounds (Reiner, 1967, pp. 232–47). Or, when agreement is lacking, planning can offer a forum through which the planner tries to forge harmony among conflicting interests. Or the planner may be seen as a bureaucrat acquiring his goals from elected officials' interpretation of his mission. When established political patterns are rigid, the planner may act as an advocate for rejected and excluded groups, organizing them to enter the political process. Or he may serve as a guerilla attempting to initiate change in bureaucracy by enhancing internal competence and responsiveness, having no explicit agenda of reform other than the wish to be relevant to current social problems.

From this review of the problems of legitimacy in social planning, two general conclusions can be reached:

1. The source of legitimacy in planning is neither self-evident nor narrowly restrictive. Indeed, there are multiple sources of legitimacy. However, they cannot all be pursued under the auspices of one planning organization and hence choice is required.

2. Each source of authority has its characteristic weaknesses and strengths which present to the planner a set of intractable problems that are moral in character from which there can be no retreat into technology. These issues become explicit when one understands the implications and consequences of choosing among various sources of authority to legitimate planning.

Schools of city and social planning should not organize their planning curricula around a single source of legitimacy – physical planning around technology and social planning around advocacy. We must prepare students to understand that there are far wider choices to legitimate their work and roles. Meanwhile we need to probe more deeply the various dilemmas of planning, where each source of legitimacy is accepted, in order to extend our understanding of the moral problems posed for planners in a pluralistic society.

But since we have no final answers to the moral dilemmas presented by the conflicting values we seek to realize, teachers of social policy must accept the awkward conclusion that they cannot offer to their students a methodology and technology for doing policy analyses and reaching policy conclusions. We characteristically offer questions without answers, for rules and principles for choosing among alternative social objectives and competing sources of legitimacy are not at hand. Moreover, the search for decision rules ensnarls us in a pre-occupation with technology which leads us to retreat from the fundamental moral and value problems that lie at the center of the study of social policy. If these generalizations seem valid, then we may need to reluctantly conclude that if our students, at the finish of their training, end up with no special competences to undertake policy analysis it is because there are none available to master – other than the skills derived from the student's own intellectual resources or the special knowledge he has already acquired from the professional and academic discipline in which he has been trained. Social policy planning as a field of inquiry cannot serve as a substitute for professional and/or academic training but only as a supplement to it. But in building on this base of knowledge, we must not succumb to the temptation to take up the solveable problems and forsake the intractable dilemmas on the assumption that this is the orderly route to knowledge. Social policy is all about social objectives and the values that embody the choice of social programs. These are precisely the problems that touch the limits of social science and raise the spectre of that ancient but still inadequately explored terrain where facts and values merge. How and in what sense can science contribute to 'the clarification and the formulation of values . . . and whether this requires the widening of the concept of social science to incorporate some of the attributes of philosophical criticism'? (Simey, 1968).

References

ALTSHULER, A. (1965), *The City Planning Process: A Political Analysis*, Cornell University Press.

ARMSTRONG, D. A. (1964), 'Some notes on the concept of planning', mimeograph, Tavistock Institute of Human Relations.

ARNOLD, M. (1969), 'Young insurgents in planning commission charge it operates in secrecy', *New York Times*, March 30, p. 34.

BACHRACH, P. (1962), 'Elite consensus and democracy', *J. of Pol. Sci.*, vol. 24, pp. 439–42.

BECKMAN, N. (1964), 'The planner as a bureaucrat', *J. of the Amer. Inst. of Planners*, vol. 30, p. 324.

CLOWARD, R., and PIVEN, F. (1965), *Low-Income People and Political Process*, A paper presented at the Training Institute program on Urban Community Development Projects, New York.

CUNNINGHAM, J. (1967), 'The struggle of the American for freedom and power', Ford Foundation.

DAVIDOFF, P. (1965), 'Advocacy and pluralism in planning', *J. of the Amer. Inst. of Planners*, vol. 31, pp. 331–8.

DAVIDOFF, P., and REINER, T. A. (1962), 'A choice theory of planning', *J. of the Amer. Inst. of Planners*, vol. 28, p. 108.

DONOVAN, J. C. (1967), *The Politics of Poverty*, Pegasus.

FINER, H. (1949), *Theory and Practice of Modern Government*, revised edn, Holt.

FRIED, R. C. (1969), 'Professionalism and politics in Roman planning', *J. of the Amer. Inst. of Planners*, vol. 35, pp. 150–59.

FRIEDRICH, C. (1946), *Constitutional Government and Democracy*, Ginn & Company.

GANS, H. (1968), 'Social planning: regional and urban planning', in *International Encyclopedia of the Social Sciences*, Free Press and Macmillan.

GOULDNER, A. W. (1968), 'The sociologist as partisan: sociology and the welfare state', *The American Sociologist*, vol. 3, p. 109.

HARLEM YOUTH OPPORTUNITIES UNLIMITED (1964), *Youth in the Ghetto: A Study of the Consequences of Powerlessness and a Blueprint for Change*, Har YOU.

HERMAN, M. (1965), 'Problems of evaluation', *The American Child*, vol. 47, pp. 5–10.

KAHN, R. *et al.* (1964), *Organizational Stress: Studies in Role Conflict and Ambiguity*, Wiley.

LAKE, D. G. (1968), 'Concepts of change and innovation in 1966', *J. of Appl. Behav. Sci.*, vol. 4, pp. 4–5.

LIPSKY, M. (1967), 'Protest as a political resource', Institute for Research on Poverty, University of Wisconsin, mimeograph.

LITWAK, E., and HYLTON, L. F. (1962), 'Interorganizational analysis: a hypothesis on co-ordinating agencies', *Admin. Sci. Q.*, vol. 6, pp. 395–420.

MARRIS, P., and REIN, M. (1967), *Dilemmas of Social Reform: Poverty and Community Action in the United States*, Atherton Press.

MORRIS, R., and REIN, M. (1963), 'Emerging patterns in community planning', in *Social Work Practice 1963*, Columbia University Press.

PEATTIE, L. R. (1968), 'Reflections on advocacy planning', *J. of the Amer. Inst. of Planners*, vol. 34, pp. 80–88.

RAPKIN, C., WINNICK, L., and BLANK, D. (1952), *Housing Market Analyses: A Study of Theory and Method*, Institute for Urban Land Use.

REIN, M. (1964), 'Organization for change', *Social Work*, vol. 9, no. 2. pp. 32–41.

REIN, M., and MORRIS, R. (1962), 'Goals, structures and strategies of planned change', in *Social Work Practice*, Columbia University Press.

REIN, M. and MILLER, S. M. (1968), 'Citizen participation and poverty', *Univ. of Connecticut Law Rev.*, vol. 1, pp. 221–43.

REINER, T. A. (1967), 'The planner as value technician: two classes of utopian constructs and their impacts on planning', in H. Wentworth Eldredge (ed.), *Taming Megalapolis*, vol. 1, Doubleday.

SAYRE, W. S., and KAUFMAN, H. (1960), *Governing New York City: Politics in the Metropolis*, Russell Sage Foundation.

SCHUBERT, G. (1960), *The Public Interest*, Free Press.

SIMEY, T. S. (1968), *Social Science and Social Purpose*, Constable.

SPIEGEL, H. (1968), 'How much neighborhood control?', in *Citizen Participation in Urban Development*, Institute of Applied Behavioral Science.

TRIGWELL, R. G. (1954), 'The place of planning in society', Technical paper no. 7, Puerto Rico Planning Board.

US CONGRESS (1968), *Hearings on section 1545, Part 10*, Subcommittee on Employment, Manpower and Poverty of the Committee on Labor and Public Welfare.

WALTON, R. E. (1965), 'Two strategies of social change and their dilemmas', *J. of Appl. Behav. Sci.*, vol. 1, pp. 167–9.

22 P. Lupsha

On Theories of Urban Violence

P. Lupsha, 'On theories of urban violence', *Urban Affairs Quarterly*,
vol. 4, 1969, pp. 273–96.

Before one can discuss the theories of urban violence, it is necessary to clarify what is meant by this term. For the purposes of this
paper, urban violence refers to the city riots that are becoming a
common part of life in urban America. These riots can be defined
as more or less spontaneous outbursts of group hostility, characterized by excitement, rage and acts of destruction directed
against generalized perpetrators of injustice or violators of the
community norms and mores.[1] All other acts of urban violence,
be they individual or collective, are thus excluded from the
analysis.

Unfortunately, in the literature on urban violence many kinds
and types of riots are lumped together. But all riots are not alike,
and it is important, therefore, to separate and classify the various
types of riots so that one can have a clearer understanding of the
theories of urban violence. While theories of urban violence often
strive for explanation at the most general level, they can have
more theoretical usefulness if one understands them as applicable
to different species of riots. In order to move in this direction a
typology of riots was created. This typology is by no means a final
product, but it does, I believe, help to sort and classify various
types of riots. It is a starting point from which more sophisticated
and developed schemes for understanding urban violence will
hopefully emerge.

This typology attempts to classify riots at a level of abstraction
that allows for cross-cultural comparisons and which is not tied
to idiosyncratic riot differences. It is formed by using two generalized variable continua to separate and place a variety of civil
disorders in conceptual space. The first continuum is the degree
of leadership definition in the riot situation. It runs from the
extremes of well-defined leadership to vague, amorphous and

1. This definition is a synthesis of several found in the literature. A similar
definition is found in Conant (1968).

sporadic leadership. By well-defined leadership I do not mean that one can necessarily isolate and identify individual riot leaders or instigators; rather, that one can define a participant cadre group which could act as a group spokesman in some less violent form of adversary relationship. Similarly, where leadership is vague and poorly defined it is virtually impossible to identify a core cadre that could serve as an accepted spokesman for the contesting parties.

The second variable consists of the continuum of targets and the degree of target definition in the riot situation. This continuum ranges from the extreme of highly specific, unidimensional, target objects to diffuse and generalized, multidimensional, target objects. A particular industrial employer, or class of employers, a particular racial, ethnic, or religious group, would be classified as highly specific target objects. The authority structure, the government and its representatives, the economic system, and economic conditions in general are multidimensional target objects which are considered to be more diffuse and general in their definition. It is important that target objects not be confused with goal objects even though the catharsis of target contact may satisfy or substitute for goal attainment, for the two are not the same.

The citation and placement of various riots in the matrix of the typology is, of course, open to argument and debate.[2] Some statement of clarification is, therefore, in order. First, it must be kept in mind that the typology represents a continuum, with individual riots falling on points within a conceptual space, and not dichotomous variables divided into four extreme cell ideal types.

The placement of these riots rests, therefore, on the belief that they would generally fall at some point within the quadrant space they are listed in, although they may vary greatly in the degree of leadership and target definition within that space. Secondly the listing of riots is in no sense complete, for it is meant to suggest and illustrate the variety of riots, in widely dispersed cultural and temporal settings, that might be fitted within this frame.

The purpose of this exercise is to clarify different kinds and types of riots, and this the table succeeds in doing. Into the first

2. Information on these riots comes from a variety of sources: Library of Congress (1967), Rude (1964), and Headley (1966).

quadrant (I) fall the worker–management riots of both the industrial and pre-industrial eras. Hobsbawm (1963, pp. 111–24) has referred to the earlier period as 'collective bargaining by riot', but the phrase is equally applicable to the latter period as well. In these riots the adversaries and the target object of the violence are clearly and narrowly defined. They only indirectly focus on the political structure, although they often result in a confrontation with the government and its forces. They also have a rather clearly defined instrumental orientation, although it is often difficult to separate the instrumental from the expressive aspects of a rioting collectivity.

Table 1 **A typology of riots in terms of leadership and target definition**

| | **Target Definition** | |
	Specific well defined	*Diffuse ill defined*
Well defined	(I)	(II)
	Homestead Steel, 1892	Roman Republic Riots, 149–133 B.C.
	Pullman Riots, 1894	Stamp Act Riots, 1765
	Captain Swing-Rebecca Riots	Wilkite Riots, 1768
	Luddite Riots, 1811–1816	Paris Riots, 1789
	Plug Plot Riots, 1842	Shay's Rebellion
		Selma
		Birmingham
Leadership Continuum	(IV)	(III)
	Anti-Catholic Riots, 1840s	
	Gordon Riots, 1780	NYC Draft Riots, 1863
	Church and King Riots, 1790s	Watts, 1965
	Astor Place Riot, 1849	Detroit, 1967
	Doctor's Riot, 1788	Newark, 1967
	Anti-Chinese Riots, 1870s	
	Race Riots: Chicago, 1919	
	East St Louis, 1917	
	Detroit, 1943	
	Durban, 1949	
	Kashmir, East Pakistan, 1963–1964	
Vague, ill defined		

The riots that fall into the second quadrant (II) have certain common elements, while varying considerably in their individual scope and intensity. All of these riots possess a leadership stratum, engaged in a confrontation with authority structures, or quasi-legal corporate entities (political factions or parties) linked with the authority structure, and contain normative or value-oriented goals. While all of the participants in these riots could not specify either targets or goals – and these riots often contained a good deal of 'spillover' to tangential targets – a leadership or core cadre possessing a specifiable set of goals can be identified. Thus, these riots were lead or manipulated value-oriented confrontations with authority structures and their representatives for the redress of grievances. These riots were often the prelude to revolution.

Smelser (1965), in his work on collective behavior, separates norm-oriented and value-oriented movements from each other, and from his discussion of hostile outbursts. His work is one of the few efforts to recognize not only these distinctions, but the transitions between them. Even so, he does not fully exploit and develop these transitional zones between types of riots.

Into the third quadrant (III) fall those confrontations with diffuse authority structures, which lack a leadership, or cadre structure. Thus, these riots tend to be diffuse in their target definition, lashing out at the authority structure, the economic structure and a variety of groups and individuals. While this pattern of target definition is ill-defined, the pattern is not totally random, for there is usually a value-orientation to these riots. And, although this goal-orientation is not articulated by some core cadre, the general pattern of these riots is to seek redress of some generalized grievances against the authority structure.

Quadrant four (IV) contains those riots which tend to lack an identifiable core cadre or leadership structure, but which are directed at specific, rather than generalized, targets. Into this quadrant fall the race, ethnic and religious riots that have occurred in every time and region. These riots are usually aided and abetted by the political, or authority structure, and are usually directed at the elimination or repression of a sub-group in the population. While certain of these riots have an ill-defined, but identifiable, core leadership that may have certain long-range instrumental orientations, the function of leadership in these riots is generally more expressive than instrumental. The leadership does not attempt to direct and establish goals for the collectivity, as much as to simply express and implement the generalized feelings of the group.

In terms of goals, and goal attainment, the instrumental and expressive orientations exhibited in these riots help to clarify the different types of disorder. The table can, in a sense, be divided in half with the more instrumental orientations tending to be found in the upper half, while expressive orientations tend to predominate in the lower half. The instrumental orientation is reflected in the existence of a leadership cadre which is hopeful of achieving its goals, and which possesses a conceptualization of desired ends. The more expressive orientation tends to find its goal in the expression of hostility and the catharsis of destruction.

The various kinds of riots illustrated in the typology can be clarified further by dividing the table down the middle. The riots on the left side of the typology tend to be structurally oriented riots, indicative of the cleavages that divide and separate groups in society. On the right side of the typology are the more value-oriented confrontations with the political structure. Here are the more ideological and slogan-filled forms of riot that are basically political phenomena.

Rude (1964, pp. 214–34) has attempted a somewhat similar separation of riots into either 'backward-looking' attempts at preserving traditions, of 'forward-looking' attempts to change the *status quo* and provide for a more equitable distribution of rights and benefits. His conceptualization, however, is unwieldy and difficult to apply.

The purpose of this typology was to suggest and illustrate the fact that there are many types of riots, and that a clarification of these types can be useful in increasing our understanding of urban violence. Political scientists have long ignored the phenomenon of riots, viewing them as aberrant behavior or anomic events which were more the concern of the sociologist than the student of politics. If I have accomplished my purpose, it can now be seen that the study of certain kinds of riots may be of interest to both political scientists examining social change and revolution, and those seeking understanding of system stability and the mechanisms of non-violent adjustment and adaptation.

Theories of urban violence have generally not taken account of the implications of such a typology, or any notion of differentiation. For they, like our notions of riots, have tended (with minor exceptions) to operate at the grossest levels of conceptualization. In fact, to use the word 'theory' in discussing many of these conceptualizations is to endow them with a rigor that is usually not present. Many of these theories – 'pseudo- or folk theories' might be a better term – are no more than popular hypotheses about the causes and explanations of urban violence. Few of them meet the criteria normally used by social scientists in discussing theory or theory construction. Nevertheless, it is necessary to discuss even briefly some of these folk theories simply in hope of finally laying to rest some of the more blatant of these notions. In the following pages, therefore, the folk theories of urban violence will be discussed, followed by an examination of those approaches to the study of urban violence which are often called middle-range. Finally, those general conceptualizations which fit the usually accepted definition of theory will be examined.

Some of these theories are basically attempts to uncover and explain the causes of urban violence, others are directed more at explaining and understanding the phenomenon of urban violence, its structure and conditioning elements. Few theories are directed at the explanation of a specific kind or type of urban violence, but by examining this broad theoretical landscape, perhaps we can move a little further in developing a better understanding of this phenomena.

Folk theories

Folk theories are the ever popular and common ways of explaining urban violence. These theories, or pseudo-theories, consist of those hypotheses, notions and beliefs about the causes of events which – while, they may bear only a limited relation to the reality of the situation – are generally accepted as prime explanatory variables underlying the event. Folk theories cannot be denied out of hand, for they often contain a grain of truth. They cannot be summarily dismissed, for their acceptance is so widespread. Some of them are essentially 'buck-passing' hypotheses, transferring responsibility outside of the community. Other folk theories resemble more the devil theories common to primitive tribes and cultures in seeking almost mystical force causation. Most importantly, almost all these theories are neither limited by time nor culture, but appear as the perennial buds of explanation blooming in a variety of civil disorders. In the following section some of the more popular folk theories will be examined, especially as they are related to recent urban violence in the United States.

Conspiracy theories

One of the most popular and commonly held explanations of urban violence is the conspiracy theory. Since riots can be one stage of unrest – especially quadrants III and II of the typology given earlier – on the path to insurrection, civil war and revolution, the conspiracy theory often contains a seed of truth. But this truth often lies more in the self-fulfilling aspects of such theories, than in an explanation of the urban violence that has occurred. The conspiracy view holds that riots result from the premeditated actions of a small number of individuals who promote civil disorder in order to gain their own ends. This theory is usually extremely popular among elites, and local authority figures most closely linked to the confrontation, but it has wide general popularity as well.

As thoughtful a commentator as Voltaire saw the French Corn Riots of 1775 as a conspiracy to starve the French capital (see Rude, 1964, p. 26), while a survey of the United States Congress after the 1967 riots found that 62 per cent of the Southern Democrats and 59 per cent of the Republican members of the House believed 'outside agitators' were a prime cause of the disturbances (Congressional Quarterly, 1967). A national survey found that 45 per cent of the whites interviewed concurred in this conspiracy belief, while not surprisingly, only 10 per cent of the blacks interviewed did (*Newsweek*, August 21, 1967, p. 19). Before the Kerner report, much of the popular press and media reporting tended to reinforce this conspiracy view, just as, in 1863, Horace Greeley's *Tribune* reinforced the view that the New York Draft riots resulted from a copperhead conspiracy (McCague, 1968).

The investigating commissions – Kerner, McCone, New Jersey, Chicago, etc. – of course found no evidence of organized conspiracy.[3] And, the historians sifting the evidence of the Corn riots, New York Draft riots, or the French Grocery riots of 1793 – in which the recently installed revolutionary Jacobins saw the specter of a royalist conspiracy – found little documentation to reinforce the conspiratorial perspectives of some of the most informed men of the period (see Rude, 1964, p. 119).

3. A typical example, the Kerner Commission (1968, p. 202), stated 'that the urban disorders were not caused by, nor were they a consequence of, any organized plan or conspiracy. Specifically the Commission has found no evidence that all or any of the disorders or incidents that lead to them were planned or directed by any organization or group, international or local'.

The conspiracy theories of urban violence have rarely been substantiated; yet, they are common to every period and culture.[4] From what is known about urban violence there are at least three situations in which one can expect a conspiracy theory to appear: first, a situation involving minority or subgroups in the population who differ from the majority culture and have only a low, or superficial, level of information exchange with that culture; second, highly complex multi-variable situations which require long-range, interdependent analysis and solutions; and third, sudden and unexpected traumatic crisis situations. Even if one is tempted to accept a conspiracy theory in these situations, one still has difficulty explaining the obvious mass support given riots without admitting that some more fundamental basis of unrest exists. For if the people were content, the best organized conspiracy should fail for lack of support.

The recent migrant theory

Another perennial theory of urban violence is the recent migrant notion. This theory contends that riots are basically the products of 'culture shock'. The riots, according to this view, are rooted in the inability of recent migrants to adjust to the stress and complexity of urban ghetto living. It is argued that the failure to adapt, to acculturate to the norms and mores of the city, results in alienation from, and hostility towards, the economic and political system. This theory has been with us for a long time. Plutarch and Livy, writing of the mob violence and riots in Rome during the close of the Republic, noted that the source of trouble rests with the recent migrants – the rural population that was leaving the land and flocking to the city (see Heaton, 1938). More recently, a Los Angeles paper noted during the Watts riot that

Half of the Negro residents of the city are new. They come here from the South and East where violence is not new and where hatred of white people is deeply ingrained (*Valley News and Green Sheet*; Aug. 15, 1965, p. 8).

Not only have the press and other commentators opted for this explanation of urban violence, but one of the more prominent research centers studying violence has also accepted this view. Examining six cities, three which had riots in 1966 and three matching cities which did not, these social scientists found that

4. For an interesting analysis of conspiracy theories in American history see Hofstadter (1965).

75 per cent of the black respondents in the riot cities were born in the South, while only 55 per cent of the black respondents in the non-riot cities were Southern born. They conclude that the migration hypothesis 'has definite relation to the occurrence of violence' (Lemberg Center, 1967, p. 10).

The recent migrant theory is one of the popular perennials in the American culture. It has been used as an explanation of the east St Louis riots of 1917, the Chicago riots of 1919, and the Detroit riots of 1943, as well as the recent outbreaks of violence. Unfortunately for this theory, recent, as well as historical, analysis suggests that it is wrong. It appears that this 'buck-passing' notion is not only incorrect, but that a counter-hypothesis – that recent migrants act as a dampener to riots – may have some merit.

Aggregate analysis of seventy-six pairs of riot cities and similar non-riot cities for the period 1919–1963 found, for example, that the recent migrant thesis (defined as rapid expansion of the black population) did not hold (Lieberson and Silverman, 1965). These researchers found that black in-migration tended to be greater in the non-riot control city. Similarly, Williams' *et al.* (1964) study of racial conflict in a national sample of cities found that tensions were no higher in cities with rapid black population growth, than in cities with stable black populations. Data from the UCLA riot study (see Murphy and Watson, 1967, pp. 6–8), which closely examined the socialization and residence patterns, found that 60 per cent of their sample lived in Watts for more than ten years, while a Detroit study (*Detroit Free Press*, Aug. 20, 1967, pp. 1–8) found that 46 per cent of the 1967 rioters were Detroit natives. Finally, the data of the Kerner Commission (1968, p. 130) reinforces this evidence with socialization information from Detroit and Newark showing that 74·4 per cent and 74 per cent of the rioters in these cities, respectively, were raised there. Thus it would appear that the recent migrant theory has little usefulness in explaining urban violence.

The criminality (riff-raff) theory

This notion holds that urban violence is caused by the 'street people' of our cities, the petty thieves, hustlers and the action of oriented riff-raff that make up two to three per cent of the urban ghetto population. Fogelson and Hall (1968), in their recent work for the riot commission, have laid this theory to rest so there is no need to spend time on it here. Suffice to say, that this notion is without foundation, for while the riff-raff certainly take part in urban violence, all evidence indicates that the bulk of the rioters are the mature, employed, better educated and more aware members of the riot community (Kerner Commission, 1968, pp. 128–33). Interestingly, the riff-raff theory was a popular explanation of the seventeenth- and eighteenth-century French and English riots, but historical evidence also casts doubt on its validity (Rude, 1964, pp. 195–209).

The teenage rebellion (youth) theory

This notion holds that the riots are the result of the overflow of pent-up frustration and youthful exuberance of teenagers in the densely populated ghettoes. Juvenility, it is argued, pervades the ghetto – indeed the median age of most inner-city ghettoes is under twenty-one years – and these immature elements make up the hard core of the activities of the riots (see *New Haven Register*, Aug. 20, 1967, p. 1, Feb. 11, 1968, p. 34; *Detroit Free Press*, Aug. 21, 1967).

While youth may make up the most active element – or 'gladiators', as Sears and McConahay (1967, p. 13) call them – of the riots, the data indicate that every age group is represented in these outbursts. Fifty-eight per cent of the Watts arrests, for example, were over twenty-three years of age (Oberschall, 1969), while 74 per cent of the New Haven arrestees (where Fogelson and Hall tell us 35 per cent of the ghetto community participated in the riot) were over twenty years of age (*New York Times*, July 28, 1968, p. 58). Considering that the median male age in the New Haven riot area is approximately seventeen years, this data suggests that the rioters were, in the main, the older and mature elements in the community. Thus, the teenage rebellion theory seems of little value as a major explanatory aid for understanding urban violence.

The underclass theory

This theory – which has wider acceptance among academics than some of the folk theories stated above – contends that the riots are basically a class phenomenon, a welling up of the grievances of the dispossessed and hard-core poor. In this view the riots are rooted in that class of persons who have been left out of the system: the dropouts, the unemployables, and the hard-core poor.

Unfortunately, analysis of the data from the recent riots does not support this theory. In both Watts and Detroit, for example, there was no difference in education between rioters and non-rioters (Murphy and Watson, 1967, pp. 8–9; *Detroit Free Press*, Aug. 20th, 1967). And, education, or the lack of it, should be one indicator of underclass status. On employment, another under-class indicator, the data from these cities indicates that there is little difference between rioters and non-rioters (Murphy and Watson, 1967, pp. 10–11). In fact, Fogelson and Hall (1968, p. 58) state that about 75 per cent of the persons participating in riots in Cincinnati, Dayton, Detroit, Grand Rapids, Newark, New Haven, Boston, Plainfield and Phoenix were employed. Thus, these indicators of underclass status, or lack of it, suggest that rather than the riots being underclass phenomena, they cut across all classes, and every education, income and occupation group in the ghetto.

The police brutality (gestapo) theory

This notion holds that police brutality and police malpractice are one of the tap roots of hostility fueling and fermenting the out-breaks of urban violence. This theme has been played up by editorial writers and a number of white and black activist leaders (Kerner Commission, 1968, chs. 1, 2, 11; Hayden, 1967). While one cannot deny that this thesis contains the seeds of truth, it has been so overplayed that it has distorted the reality of the situation.

In general, most ghetto residents do not hate the police. They are more often victims than perpetrators of crimes, and thus tend to want more and better police protection (Kraft Survey, 1967, p. 1395). What the ghetto residents hate is the inadequate, capricious and impersonal handling of problems by the police. They dislike double standards, hypocrisy and stereotyping that seem a part of urban law enforcement (Kraft Survey, 1966, pp. 1420–1423). Murphy and Watson (1967, pp. 23–24), in their study of the structure of discontent in Watts, found that living conditions, not the police, were the chief grievances of residents. A New York survey arrived at similar conclusions, finding that police brutality was not of as much concern as that the police were inadequate in handling their jobs (Kraft Survey, 1967, pp. 1383–1423). What inner-city residents want is better, fairer, more rational law enforcement. The role of police brutality has been overdone; the problem is more the reality of inadequacy, not the shibboleth of brutality.

While one could continue questioning and explicating these folk theories of urban violence for many pages, there are more relevant levels of conceptualization that deserve some attention. Let us, therefore, move on to some of the middle-range approaches to urban violence.

Middle-range approaches

Middle-range theory is somewhere between the everyday working hypotheses used in research and general speculations having some grand conceptual scheme. Unfortunately, there is little in the way of middle-range theory in the study of urban violence. The theory that exists consists either of stringing together various folk theories, or a somewhat haphazard borrowing from more general notions and assumptions. Rather than discussing theories, therefore, this section will examine three middle-range approaches to the study of urban violence and some of the theoretical propositions that have been developed from this work. These three approaches are: social-psychological, historical-economic and structural-situational.

Social-psychological

This approach places emphasis on the individual's attitudes and perceptions. The individual operating in groups and collectives is emphasized and survey tools are frequently used to test hypotheses. Often at the root of these approaches is some notion of deprivation or frustration, but, rather than focusing on this as the general theories do, this approach focuses on some of the social indicators of these more basic elements.

'Relative deprivation' and 'rising expectation' theories are common to this approach. These theories are based on the notion that there is a gap between a person's perception of the values, goods and status he is entitled to, and his perception of his actual condition. When a person is aware of this gap he feels deprived and can become hostile, angry and aggressive. A theory of rising expectations differs only slightly from this, by giving greater emphasis to the mechanisms that make for awareness of this gap. Thus in this latter view, population mobility, mass media and advertising are seen as agents of changing expectations. This relative deprivation-rising expectation gap of course should affect every group in society. Lower middle-class whites should feel as deprived as lower middle-class blacks. Suburban middle-class whites should be engaged in this value consumption scramble just as are middle-class blacks. Furthermore, when members of these groups do not achieve their goals they all should feel frustrated, angry and aggressive. Unfortunately for this theory, suburban and working-class whites have not been rioting, but working-class and middle-class blacks have. Why? The theory doesn't tell us. But there is obviously something here other than simple relative deprivation or rising expectation theories. Another problem with these two theories has been raised by James Q. Wilson (1968, p. 23) who points out that when one looks at historical periods in which, by all indicators, expectations were most rapidly rising among the black population (First World War, Second World War, and the Korean War) one finds no black-instigated riots.

A sophisticated approach has been taken by Murphy and Watson in their analysis of the structure of discontent in Watts. They combine attitudinal and structural variables in an attempt to get at the value structure of rioters. They take as given that there is a high level of discontent in all riot situations, and search for the relationships between types of discontent and types of riot support. While their work is not conceptualized into a theory of urban violence, several of their basic findings have theoretical implications for future work. First, they found that every social strata of the ghetto participated, and supported the riot. Second, they found that lower-class support was more related to the material problems and conditions, while middle-class support was more related to social and status relationships. Perhaps most interestingly, they found that the level of discontent among middle-class blacks increases with their contact with whites. Integration, in terms of lessening social distance appears, then, to increase discontent. The theoretical implications of this finding for relative deprivation theories is obvious. More than one form of deprivation is occurring in the ghettoes. For one strata the problem is to establish and maintain an adequate standard of living. For another it is the problem of maintaining pride and identity in oneself. These different types of deprivations need to be taken into account in any social-psychological explanation of urban violence. This will be developed further in later sections of this paper.

Historical-economic

These conceptualizations operate on the macro-level of the polity. Rude's work (1964), which emphasizes the historical and economic aspects of urban violence, is one example of this approach. Rostow's work (1949), showing the relationship of riots to economic upheavals, is another. The focus of this approach is to examine the long-range trends and the systematic aspects of the violence, rather than individual attitudes and motivations. According to this view, people tend to riot because their political and economic alternatives have been cut off, often by conditions beyond their control. Changes in the structure of the law, changes in the relationship between the citizen and the polity, changes in technology, changes in monetary structure, are all looked to in this approach as explanations of urban violence. Riots occur because the social system is undergoing rapid and dynamic changes.

The notion of relative deprivation is also a part of this approach. But, deprivation is seen here as based on systematic changes and adjustments rather than individual ones. Davies in his theory of revolutions provides a good example of this view. He states that revolutions (one can read riots)

are most likely to occur when a prolonged period of economic and social development is followed by a short period of sharp reversal. People then subjectively feel that ground gained with great effort will be quite lost; their mood becomes revolutionary (Davies, 1962, p. 5).

The sharp relative or absolute deprivation following a period of gain and struggle, it is argued, results in tension and violence. This is a very useful theorem, for it provides insight into many occurrences of urban violence, but not all. As Davies himself points out, the American depression of the 1930s possesses all of the elements that the theorem postulates, and while the mood may have been revolutionary, non-violent change took place (1962, p. 19).

A third aspect of this historical approach is the search for 'tentative uniformity' in situations of riot and revolution. While Rude's studies contain examples of this, Crane Briton's work (1960) on revolutions is perhaps the best known. Briton found that class conflict, desertion of the intellectuals, an advancing economic system, inefficient government, ineffective or un-responsive political elites, and poor methods of social control, were common underlying themes in revolutionary situations. Unfortunately they are also present in many non-revolutionary ones; the theoretical catalyst for violence is missing.

While macro-themes have been laid bare by this approach, little effort appears to have been made, beyond Davies' theorem and Briton's underlying themes, to develop theories of urban violence using this approach.

Structural-situational approach

This approach is based on the notion that there is an interaction, and interactional effects, between persons and the structure of a given situation. It is, perhaps, the most common research approach to the investigation of urban violence. The work of Grimshaw (1960) and Dahlke (1952), using the sociological model to discuss the ecology of race riots, are typical examples of this view. So, too, are works (see Lieberson and Silverman, 1965) which concentrate on examination of aggregate data, population growth, density, unemployment, etc., to make statements about the situational concomitants to violent behaviors. While this work often provides a detailed portrait of a particular instance of violence, it rarely provides generalizations, or even propositions that are more generally applicable. In the middle fifties, when Merton (1957) made his plea for middle-range theories, it was because he saw a gap in sociological research. That gap still exists in the study of urban violence.

General theories

The most general theoretical conceptualizations involve the specification of a set of interrelated variables, the development of definitions and propositions, and the presentation of a systematic view of the phenomenon of urban violence. Such a conceptualization meets what we normally consider to be the requirements of theory construction in the social sciences, and should provide us with a good foundation for conducting further empirical investigations.

The two most popular current general conceptualizations of urban violence arise from the two basic sister disciplines of the social sciences – psychology and sociology.[5] It is not surprising, therefore, that these theories start from rather different basic assumptions and premises. While there is, perhaps, a greater degree of overlap between these approaches than is commonly acknowledged, it is necessary to examine them separately if we are to gain a basic understanding of them.

The psychology of urban violence

While there are several major psychological theories of aggression and violence [(a) that it is an innate, instinctual behavior and (b) that it is a learned behavior[6]], the most popular by far in dis-

5. See Freud (1962), Lorenz (1966), and Storr (1968).
6. See Hilgard (1956), Mowrer (1960), and Bandura and Walters (1963).

cussing urban violence is the theory that aggression is a response to frustration. This frustration-aggression hypothesis of Dollard *et al*. (1939), as it has been developed and modified by the research of Berkowitz (1965, 1968), Yates (1962), and others, simply states that aggression is a response to the blocking or interference with some goal-oriented behavior (frustration). Anger is seen as an intervening drive variable.

Frustration ———→ Anger ———→ Aggression

As this hypothesis has been developed into a theory of urban violence, one starts with the behavioral expression of anger, or aggression, and works backwards to an assumption of frustration. The most developed and sophisticated psychological model of urban violence puts it this way:

If anger implies the presence of frustration, there is compelling evidence that frustration is all but universally a characteristic of participants in civil strife: discontent, anger, rage, hate and their synonyms are repeatedly mentioned in studies of strife (Gurr, 1968b, p. 350).

While this is put as an 'if' statement, the question of whether or not anger can only be generated by conditions of frustration is essentially assumed away. It is, of course, a question which, when answered, could significantly alter this model.

The introduction of anger as a drive is merely one modification of the original hypothesis; others have been made to fit it to situations of urban violence. Perhaps the most basic of these changes is the transference of this hypothesis, which focuses on individual behavior, to the collective actions of the group. The fundamental psychological unit of analysis, the frustrated organism, becomes the group with its collective frustration, i.e., '. . . events and patterns of conditions that are likely to be widely seen as unjust deprivation' (Gurr, 1968a, p. 254). Related to this shift to a macro-level of analysis is the redefinition of frustration as relative deprivation, i.e., 'the actors perceptions of the discrepancy between their value expectations and their environments' value capabilities' (Gurr, 1968a, p. 253). This shift is accomplished by viewing the environmental discrepancy as a basically frustrating situation, and the actor as aware of the discrepancy as the frustrated organism, i.e., 'The awareness of interference is equivalent to the concept of relative deprivation' (Gurr, 1968a, p. 253). A third modification in the concept of frustration is the shift from viewing frustration as the actual 'blocking of ongoing goal-directed activity', to relative deprivation, a notion of anticipated frustration, 'the belief that one will encounter frustration in the near future' (Gurr, 1968a, p. 257).

The theory of urban violence developed out of this recast frustration-aggression model provides a sophisticated and elegant model of the phenomenon. Gurr (1966, 1967, 1968b), in several articles and monographs, is perhaps the most brilliant exponent of this view. Rather than explicate in detail here all of his propositions on the instigation and mediation of civil violence, let me simply recommend the reader to his work.

One finds the frustration-aggression model satisfying, for the existence of a 'reservoir of frustration' has been pointed to by many students of the recent riots. In spite of this, I would argue that the frustration-aggression approach is a too facile, easy and inaccurate explanation of urban violence. Anger is certainly present in riot situations, but to leap from this fact to an assumption of frustration and/or deprivation is, I believe, in error.

Anger can occur without one's being frustrated or deprived. One can learn that certain events, or violations of one's rights and values, should be responded to with hostility. One can be angry and aggressive because one's values or sense of justice (a learned phenomenon) have been affronted, without any blocking of the individual's goal-directed activity, or awareness of any personal 'want–get ratio' deprivation, or any personal feelings of 'anticipated frustration'. One can be angry and aggressive simply because one believes the behaviors of the situation are wrong or illegitimate. The so-called just anger of Christ whipping the money changers from the temple, or the rock throwing of the black youth in Watts who believes he has just seen a pregnant woman dragged screaming into a police car, is not the anger of frustration, but simply the immediate reaction to a situation which violates learned standards of justice and right. The anger of black Vietnam veterans at a system that has failed to keep its promise, contains elements of frustration, but it also contains many learned beliefs about the values of the system and the ways these values *ought* to work. The typology cited at the beginning of this paper suggests that recent riots differ from many of the other kinds of riots, and that one way in which they differ is that they involve a questioning of the general values, the legitimacy of the system, and especially its authority structure. While race riots may, perhaps, contain many elements of the frustration-aggression hypothesis, the recent riots are a more *learned questioning* of the legitimacy of the system.

Another aspect of the frustration-aggression hypothesis which is troublesome in explaining urban violence is the leap this theory makes to a notion of relative deprivation. Relative deprivation does not necessarily lead to anger. In fact, psychologists (see Berkowitz, 1968) now argue that relative deprivation by itself means nothing, and is inadequate to account for most motivated behavior. It is the nearness to the desired goal that now seems more important than the extent of deprivation: a finding which might explain why the better educated, more conscious, dynamic and aware elements of the ghetto population tended to be over-represented among the rioters (Kerner Commission, 1968, pp. 129–133). It is a finding which should be fitted into any psychological theory of urban violence.[7]

The sociological approach to urban violence

While the psychological approach to urban violence moves from certain assumptions about the individual organism, or micro-system, the sociological approach moves from certain assumptions and propositions about the societal or macro-system.

The basic assumption of the sociology of urban violence is the notion of societal strain. This strain has been defined (Smelser, 1965, p. 47) as 'an impairment of the relations among, and consequently inadequate functioning of, the components of action'. A general definition, it permits many kinds of strain to be subsumed under the concept. Perhaps the most obvious of these are the cleavages (ethnic, religious, class, political) which can create conditions of conflict by separating different groups and components of society. A less obvious form of strain is relative deprivation.

The sociologists' view of deprivation differs somewhat from those mentioned previously. The sociological approach defines relative deprivation as the gap between the responsible performance in roles by individuals, groups, or organizations in society and the rewards which accrue to these roles. This deprivation gap, according to Smelser (1965, pp. 54–9) who has explicated the most developed sociological model of riots, can be either real, threatened, absolute, or relative. Real events such as economic depressions, natural disasters or political purges – 'all

7. Ted Gurr's work on violence is the only one I know of which attempts to incorporate this type of proposition.

of which sever the individual's membership ties or reduce the rewards of membership' – are sources of strain. Threatened events may also cause individuals to perceive deprivation. In speaking of the rioting that preceeded the French Revolution, Smelser (1965, p. 261) argues that the citizens felt threatened role-deprivation and feared that they would lose their position in society if their views were not adequately represented in the États Générales. In this view, deprivation relates to role and position strain at the individual and group levels, and thus 'plugs in' to the general concept of relative deprivation at a somewhat different level.

Strain is but one element in the sociological model. It is the basic proposition out of which the rest of the model flows, and, in a sense, is the underlying explanatory factor in the model. The other elements in the model focus more on the ways in which the structural elements of society promote the occurrence of violence.

The concept of structural conduciveness, for example, focuses directly on those elements in the ecological setting which promote violence. These basic elements in the promotion of a hostile outburst are: (a) the availability of communication conditions which can promote crowd mobilization; (b) the failure of responsible authorities to deal forcefully and equitably with all the conflicting parties; and (c) the inadequacy of grievance procedures and mechanism (Smelser, 1965, pp. 227–41). Writers taking this approach in the examination of the recent riots have more fully elaborated the conditions of structural conduciveness. One study notes that explanations of the origins of the recent disturbances must take into account (see Lang and Lang, 1968, p. 13):

1. Ghetto subculture which sanctions illegitimate means.
2. Limited opportunity structure for achieving status.
3. Remoteness and impersonality of the power structure.
4. Low level of political skill and organization.
5. Highly visible frictions (police, white store owners) at the inter-personal level.
6. Apparent effectiveness of disturbances in forcing recognition of conditions.
7. Tacit legitimation of extralegal forms of civil rights protests.
8. Reluctance of authorities to use force.
9. Presence of core agitating groups.

While one may not agree with either the impact or relevance of these various conditions, they are typical of the use of the structural conduciveness notion in trying to understand and explain urban violence.

A third major element in the sociological approach – as it focuses in from the abstraction of strain to the actual occurrence of the event – is the notion of precipitating factors. The precipitating incident, Smelser tells us, is more important in its context than in its content, for the precipitating incident channels the generalized beliefs into specific fears and antagonisms; it confirms the existence, sharpens the definition, or exaggerates the effect, of conditions (Smelser, 1965, p. 249). The precipitating incident is often thought of as a single event – the arrest of a drunk driver, the shooting of a ghetto youth – which explodes into a riot. Recent evidence suggests, however, that there is no such thing as *a* precipitating incident. Rather there is a long chain of escalating incidents and rumors which finally peak in the outbreak of hostility (Kerner Commission, 1968, pp. 117–21). The peaking or 'triggering incident' may involve neither some extraordinary escalation of hostilities, nor a traumatic event. It is simply the breaking point in a long chain of precipitating incidents. Interestingly, in 1968 there have been many riots but few precipitating incidents. It appears that hostilities have reached a point where simply the appearance of authority figures can trigger violence.

One of the difficulties in examining the sociological approach to urban violence is that it is more useful in providing a set of propositions for understanding the factors present in an outbreak of urban violence, than as an explanatory tool for understanding why urban violence occurred. In stressing strains, cleavages and threats of deprivations as the explanatory propositions, this approach tends to accept as given, elements that other theories are devoted to explaining. The sociological approach does, however, provide one of the best theoretical conceptualizations we have of the structure of urban violence. The need to link these propositions with those of other theories is necessary.[8]

Conclusion

These various theoretical conceptualizations of urban violence help to increase our understanding of the phenomena. There are, however, vast gaps in our understanding that need to be filled.

8. Again the work of Gurr must be cited as the only attempt that has tried to reach across disciplinary boundaries and link the sociological and the psychological approaches.

There is a need for middle-range theorizing. There is need to bridge some of the disciplinary differences and approaches. There is need to highlight some of the neglected areas.

One area that has been neglected, although it is often spoken around, is the political side of urban violence. Politics, political values, and the political system are intimately linked in the recent riots, as the typology offered at the beginning of this paper attempted to point out. The recent riots (quadrant III) and those in quadrant II are political in nature, involving a questioning of the legitimacy of public authority. This political fact has been overlooked in much of the research and theorizing about these riots.

If one begins with certain assumptions taken from learning theory, one can begin to construct a political theory of legitimacy and these occurrences of urban violence. The work of Richard Merelman (1966) on learning theory and legitimacy offers a suggestive base for beginning such a political theory. This approach would also avoid many of the difficulties present in the frustration-aggression formulation.

That the recent riots are basically political in nature has been illustrated time and again in recent research. Tomlinson (1968) has noted the development of a riot ideology among urban blacks, noting that most ghetto residents see riots as a form of protest. This fits the historical evidence that Rude (1964, pp. 232–234) and Hobsbawm (1963, pp. 10–12) have uncovered about pre-industrial riots. These riots were viewed as a legitimate way of making demands upon a rather distant and aloof authority structure. Rude (1964, pp. 93–133) also notes that in the beginning, the French food riots lacked political or ideological content, but in time political slogans and ideology were absorbed by the masses and the riots became focused on the authority structure and the acquisition of arms for a confrontation with it. Similarities to these events can be seen in recent urban riots: not only have political slogans and ideology blossomed, but the confrontation has escalated from an indirect pattern in 1967 – in which there were few verified cases of sniping at police – to a 1968 pattern in which in almost every outbreak of violence there have been direct armed attacks or counter-attacks on police agents. There is still a minor part of urban violence in America, carried out by a small minority of ghetto residents; yet, the signs of escalation and questioning of the legitimacy of government are present.

Campbell and Schuman (1968), interviewing in fifteen cities, found that six per cent, or approximately 200,000, blacks 'feel so little part of American society that they are withdrawing allegiance from the United States'. A recent *New York Times* (July 29, 1968, p. 1) survey of black Vietnam veterans reports that most of these 40,000 yearly returnees are more bitter and angry than when they left. Other studies have found that more than one third of the black respondents feel that there has been no real change for blacks in America since *Brown* vs *Board of Education*, 1954. This is a sorry commentary on the state of black life in the United States, but it only reveals an aspect of the political questioning of authority structures that is occurring.

David Sears (1967), in his study of political attitudes of Watts residents, found that the local political structure (mayor and police) was viewed negatively by most respondents, while the federal structure was viewed favorably. Federal programs, in part, were seen as a reason for this trend, yet considering the vulnerability of OEO and anti-poverty programs to budget-cutting, this is a weak structure to base even a small part of federal legitimacy. One day, perhaps, we will realize the error committed by shunting our black, our poor, citizens out of partisan politics and into the agency and administrative politics of welfare and OEO. The legitimacy of the local system would probably not be questioned if black citizens had been given a share of partisan political power. Instead of power politics, they have become skilled in administrative politics and grantsman-ship: short-term and inadequate skills. It has served to enhance the legitimacy of the federal sector, but this is a temporary, and transient condition: the world of OEO is fast ending, and black separation and 'autonomy' through community development corporations is still over the horizon.

Legitimacy must rest on more than largesse. It must rest, as Merelman (1966, p. 554) points out, on symbolic values and beliefs. Yet as he notes, these symbols must be positively re-inforced by concrete behavior if they are to be believed. Unfortu-nately, it appears that more negative than positive reinforcement is occurring in the ghettoes. Furthermore, it appears that insti-tutions which were once viewed positively are now given negative evaluations. Schools, for example, were not targets attacked in the 1967 riots. However, the Lemberg Center (1968) reports that schools have now become a major target of disorders. The political undertones and the questioning of legitimacy of authority structures and institutions are too evident in the recent riots to ignore, and the political consequences too important to speak around.

The problem with most theoretical conceptualizations of urban violence is that they ignore the essential point that the riots are not just products of frustration and deprivation, they are products of the political system. The anger of our black citizens is not the irrational rage of frustration, it is an anger arising from a rational evaluation of the situation. It is an anger directed at the inability and inadequacy of the political system and its institutions to live up to their promise. It is an anger directed at the inadequacy of the political system to process demands, and to make allocations in a responsive and responsible manner. It is the gap between the theory and the practice of government in the United States that is one of the root causes of urban violence.

References

BANDURA, A., and WALTERS, R. (1963), *Social Learning and Personality Development*, Holt, Rinehart & Winston.

BERKOWITZ, L. (1965), 'The concept of aggressive drive', in L. Berkowitz (ed.), *Advances in Experimental Social Psychology*, Academic Press, pp. 307–22.

BERKOWITZ, L. (ed.) (1968), *The Roots of Aggression: A Re-Examination of the Frustration–Aggression Hypothesis*, Atherton Press.

BRITON, C. (1960), *The Anatomy of Revolution*, Vintage Books.

CAMPBELL, A., and SCHUMAN, H. (1968), 'Racial attitudes in fifteen American cities', in Supplemental Studies for the National Advisory Commission on Civil Disorder, Government Printing Office, pp. 1–69.

CONANT, R. (1968), 'Rioting, insurrection and civil disobedience', *Amer. Scholar*, vol. 35, pp. 420–33.

CONGRESSIONAL QUARTERLY (1967), 'Urban problems and civil disorders', vol. 36, pp. 1738–40.

DAHLKE, O. (1952), 'Race and minority riots – a study of the typology of violence', *Social Forces*, vol. 30, pp. 419–25.

DAVIES, J. C. (1962), 'Toward a theory of revolution', *Amer. Sociol. Rev.*, vol. 27, pp. 5–9.

DOLLARD, J. *et al.* (1939), *Frustration and Aggression*, Yale University Press.

FOGELSON, R. M., and HALL, R. B. (1968), 'A study of participation in the 1967 riots', *New York Times*, July 28, p. 58.

FREUD, S. (1962), *Civilization and Its Discontents*, W. W. Norton.

GRIMSHAW, A. (1960), 'Urban racial violence in the United States: changing ecological consideration', *Amer. J. of Sociol.*, vol. 46, pp. 109–19.

GURR, T. (1966), *New Error-Compensated Measures for Comparing Nations*, Princeton University, Center of International Studies.

GURR, T. (1967), *The Conditions of Civil Violence*, Princeton University, Center of International Studies.

GURR, T. (1968a), 'Psychological factors in civil violence', *World Politics*, vol. 20, pp. 245–78.

GURR, T. (1968b), 'Urban disorder: perspectives from the comparative study of civil strife', *Amer. Behavior Scientist*, vol. 11, pp. 50–56.

HAYDEN, T. (1967), *Rebellion in Newark*, Vintage Press.

HEADLEY, J. T. (1966), *The Great Riots*, Seabury Press.

HEATON, J. W. (1938), 'Mob violence in the late Roman Republic', *Studies in the Social Sciences 23*, University of Illinois Press.

HILGARD, E. (1956), *Theories of Learning*, Appleton-Century-Crofts.

HOBSBAWM, E. J. (1963), *Primitive Rebels*, W. W. Norton.

HOFSTADTER, R. (1965), *The Paranoid Style in American Politics*, Alfred A. Knopf.

KERNER COMMISSION (1968), *Report of the National Advisory Commission on Civil Disorders*, Bantam Books.

KRAFT SURVEY (1967), 'Federal role in urban affairs', Hearings Before the Subcommittee on Executive Reorganization, Committee on Government Operations, in vol. 6, pp. 1383–1423, Government Printing Office.

LANG, K., and LANG, G. E. (1968), 'Racial disturbance as collective protest', *Amer. Behavioral Scientist*, vol. 11, pp. 11–13.

LEMBERG CENTER FOR THE STUDY OF VIOLENCE (1968), *Riot Data Review* 1, Brandeis University.

LEMBERG CENTER FOR THE STUDY OF VIOLENCE (1967), *Six City Study*, Brandeis University.

LIBRARY OF CONGRESS (1967), 'Civil disorder', L. C. Legislative Reference Service, E 185E, GGR 135.

LIEBERSON, S., and SILVERMAN, A. (1965), 'The precipitants and underlying conditions of race riots', *Amer. Sociol. Rev.*, vol. 30, pp. 887–98.

LORENZ, K. (1966), *On Aggression*, Harcourt, Brace & World.

MCCAGUE, J. (1968), *The Second Rebellion: The New York City Draft Riots July, 1863*, Dial Press.

MERELMAN, R. (1966), 'Learning and Legitimacy', *Amer. Pol. Sci. Rev.*, vol. 60, pp. 548–61.

MERTON, R. (1957), *Social Theory and Social Structure*, Free Press.

MOWRER, O. H. (1960), *Learning Theory and Symbolic Process*, John Wiley.

MURPHY, R. J., and WATSON, J. M. (1967), *The Structure of Discontent*, UCLA Institute of Government and Public Affairs.

OBERSCHALL, A. (1969), 'The Los Angeles riot of August, 1965', *Social Problems*, vol. 17.

ROSTOW, W. W. (1949), *British Economy in the Nineteenth Century*, Clarendon Press.

RUDE, G. (1964), *The Crowd in History*, John Wiley.

SEARS, D. O. (1967), *Los Angeles Riot Study: Political Attitudes of Los Angeles Negroes*, UCLA Institute of Government and Public Affairs.

SEARS, D. O., and MCCONAHAY, J. (1967), *Los Angeles Riot Study: Riot Participation*, UCLA Institute of Government and Public Affairs.

SMELSER, N. J. (1965), *Theory of Collective Behavior*, Free Press.

STORR, A. (1968), *Human Aggression*, Atherton Press.

TOMLINSON, T. M. (1968), 'The development of a riot ideology among urban Negroes', *Amer. Behav. Scientist*, vol. 11, pp. 27–31.

WILLIAMS, R. *et al.* (1964), *Strangers Next Door*, Prentice-Hall.

WILSON, J. Q. (1968), 'Why we are having a wave of violence', *New York Times Magazine*, May 19, p. 23.

YATES, A. (1962), *Frustration and Conflict*, John Wiley.

Further Reading

The function of the Further Reading list is normally to indicate a literature which amplifies and complements the material actually presented in the volume of readings. In the context of an interdisciplinary study of the problems of urban planning this presents a number of difficulties. In the first place the topic in question – the city – is so large that any reading list must inevitably be highly selective and must omit considerable important material. Secondly, the essence of interdisciplinary study is not so much to identify areas of interest and then suggest that some books and articles are relevant whilst others, by implication, are less so. Rather it is to be prepared to draw relevant material from the widest possible range of sources, to interpret selectively, and to emphasize the interrelationships between a variety of disciplines as well as acknowledge their respective contributions. Finally the volume already contains numerous references, both in the general introduction and in the individual readings, which indicate areas for further reading. For convenience, however, a number of books representing useful background literature are listed below.

Essential historical background is provided by
A. Briggs, *Victorian Cities*, Penguin, 1968.
E. Jones, *Towns and Cities*, Oxford University Press, 1969.
B. McKelvey, *The City in American History*, Allen & Unwin, 1969.

The historic perspective is more explicitly linked to contemporary urban problems and analysis by
H. Blumenfeld, *The Modern Metropolis: Its Origin, Growth, Characteristics, Planning*, MIT Press, 1967.
H. J. Dyos (ed.), *The Study of Urban History*, Arnold, 1968.
J. Burchard, and O. Handlin (ed.), *The Historian and the City*, MIT Press, 1963.

Many of the gloomy prognostications about our urban future do not bear close attention but no reading list could sensibly omit
Jane Jacobs, *The Death and Life of Great American Cities*, Random House, 1961, or alternatively, and perhaps less pessimistically
J. Q. Wilson (ed.), *The Metropolitan Enigma*, Harvard University Press, 1968.
L. Wingo (ed.), *Cities and Space*, Johns Hopkins, 1963.

As suggested in the Introduction there are relatively few books which seek to link traditional social science with urban problems. Amongst those most relevant to the themes of this volume are, however,

E. C. Banfield (ed.), *Urban Government*, Free Press, 1969.
R. Netzer, and H. S. Perloff, *Economics and Urban Problems*, Basic Books, 1970.
R. E. Pahl, *Patterns of Urban Life*, Longman, 1970.
H. S. Perloff and L. Wingo (eds.) *Issues in Urban Economics*, Johns Hopkins Press, 1968.
L. Reissman, *The Urban Process*, Free Press, 1964.
H. W. Richardson, *Urban Economics*, Penguin, 1971.

The spatial aspects of urban structure are conveniently (and fairly comprehensively) dealt with in

B. J. Berry, and F. E. Horton, *Geographic Perspectives on Urban Systems*, Prentice-Hall, 1970.
L. S. Bourne, *Internal Structure of the City*, Oxford University Press, 1971.
F. S. Chapin, *Urban Land Use Planning*, University of Illinois Press, 1965.

Alternatively there are numerous studies which approach the question of city structure more specifically from a sociological or economic viewpoint. A few examples are

J. M. Beshers, *Urban Social Structure*, Free Press, 1962.
R. F. Muth, *Cities and Housing*, Chicago University Press, 1969.
J. Rex and R. Moore, *Race, Community and Conflict*, Oxford University Press, 1967.
B. Robson, *Urban Analysis*, Cambridge University Press, 1969.

The central theme of community can be looked at in a variety of ways. Three contrasting approaches are those of

C. Bell and H. Newby, *Community Studies*.
A. Maass, *Area and Power*, Free Press, 1959.
B. Chinitz (ed.) *City and Suburb*, Prentice-Hall, 1964.

The interrelationship of the urban fiscal system with local government reorganization is examined in

J. Margolis (ed.), *The Public Economy of Urban Communities*, Resources for the Future, 1965, and Redcliffe-Maud Report on the Reform of Local Government, cmnd 4040, HMSO, 1969.

Useful introductory books on the planning process are

W. Ashworth *The Genesis of Modern British Town Planning*, Routledge & Kegan Paul, J. B. Cullingworth, *Town and Country Planning in England and Wales*, Allen & Unwin, 1967.

J. B. McLoughlin, *Urban and Regional Planning. A Systems Approach*, Faber, 1969.

M. Scott, *American City Planning*, University of California, 1969.

The scope and relevance of urban social planning can be further seen by a reading of

B. J. Frieden, and R. Morris, *Urban Planning and Social Policy*, Basic Books, 1968.

H. J. Gans, *People and Plans*, Penguin, 1972.

R. E. Pahl, *Whose City?*, Longman, 1970

or more specifically

Judy Hillman (ed.), *Planning for London*, Penguin, 1971.

There are few, if any, texts which satisfactorily link economic analysis and urban planning, although Jerome Rothenberg's *Economic Evaluation of Urban Renewal* Brookings Institute, 1967, is an exception in its specific context (of urban renewal).

Finally on the questions of power and legitimacy, there are numerous studies relating to the questions of power in cities, and to the rationale and legitimacy of planning. For example,

W. D. Hawley, and F. M. Wirt, *The Search for Community Power*, Prentice-Hall, 1968.

A. Altshuler, *The City Planning Process*, Cornell University Press, 1965.

J. G. Davies, *The Evangelistic Bureaucrat*, Tavistock, 1972.

N. Dennis, *People and Planning*, Faber and Faber, 1970.

P. Maorris, and M. Rein, *Dilemmas of Social Reform*, Atherton, 1967.

Acknowledgements

Permission to reproduce the following Readings in this volume is acknowledged to the following sources:

1 Mrs Ruth Glass
2 The MIT Press
3 *New Society*
4 The Johns Hopkins University Press, for Resources for the Future Inc.
5 Regional Science Association
6 University of Chicago Press
7 The Brookings Institution
8 University of Chicago Press
9 Macmillan Co Inc.: Free Press of Glencoe Inc.
10 *Town Planning Review*
11 The Johns Hopkins University Press, for Resources for the Future Inc.
12 Macmillan Co Inc.: Free Press of Glencoe Inc.
13 University of North Carolina Press
14 *Land Use Controls Quarterly*
15 Harvard University Press
16 Colston Research Society
17 The Bobbs-Merrill Co Inc.
18 Pion Limited
19 *Journal of Politics*
21 *Journal of the American Institute of Planners*
22 Sage Publications Inc.

Author Index

Subject Index